TAKING SIDES

Clashing Views on Controversial

Psychological Issues

TWELFTH EDITION

TAKING SIDES

Clashing Views on Controversial

Psychological Issues

TWELFTH EDITION

Selected, Edited, and with Introductions by

Brent Slife
Brigham Young University

McGraw-Hill/Dushkin
A Division of The McGraw-Hill Companies

To my three garrulous sons, Conor, Nathan, and Jacob

Photo Acknowledgment
Cover image: © 2002 by PhotoDisc, Inc.

Cover Art Acknowledgment
Charles Vitelli

Library of Congress Cataloging-in-Publication Data
Main entry under title:
Taking sides: clashing views on controversial psychological issues/selected, edited, and with introductions by Brent Slife.—12th ed.
Includes bibliographical references and index.
1. Psychology. 2. Human behavior. I. Slife, Brent, *comp.*
150
0-07-248064-5
ISSN: 1098-5409

Printed on Recycled Paper

Preface

Critical thinking skills are a significant component of a meaningful education, and this book is specifically designed to stimulate critical thinking and initiate lively and informed dialogue on psychological issues. In this book I present 36 selections, arranged in pro and con pairs, that address a total of 18 different controversial issues in psychology. The opposing views demonstrate that even experts can derive conflicting conclusions and opinions from the same body of information.

A dialogue approach to learning is certainly not new. The ancient Greek philosopher Socrates engaged in it with his students some 2,400 years ago. His point-counterpoint procedure was termed a *dialectic*. Although Socrates and his companions hoped eventually to know the "truth" by this method, they did not see the dialectic as having a predetermined end. There were no right answers to know or facts to memorize. The emphasis in this learning method is on how to evaluate information—on developing reasoning skills.

It is in this dialectical spirit that *Taking Sides: Clashing Views on Controversial Psychological Issues* was originally compiled, and it has guided me through this 12th edition as well. To encourage and stimulate discussion and to focus the debates in this volume, each issue is expressed in terms of a single question and answered with two points of view. But certainly the reader should not feel confined to adopt only one or the other of the positions presented. There are positions that fall between the views expressed or totally outside them, and I encourage you to fashion your own conclusions.

Some of the questions raised in this volume go to the very heart of what psychology as a discipline is all about and the methods and manner in which psychologists work. Others address newly emerging concerns. In choosing readings I was guided by the following criteria: the readings had to be understandable to newcomers to psychology; they had to have academic substance; and they had to express markedly different points of view.

Plan of the book Each issue in this volume has an issue *introduction*, which defines each author's position and sets the stage for debate. Also provided is a set of point-counterpoint statements that pertain to the issue and that should help to get the dialogue off the ground. Each issue concludes with *challenge questions* to provoke further examination of the issue. The introduction and challenge questions are designed to assist the reader in achieving a critical and informed view on important psychological issues. Also, at the beginning of each part is a list of Internet site addresses (URLs) that should prove useful as starting points for further research. At the back of the book is a listing of all the *contributors to this volume,* which gives information on the psychologists, psychiatrists, philosophers, professors, and social critics whose views are debated here.

In the interest of space, the reference lists of many of the original articles have been omitted or severely curtailed. Although I welcome further scholarly investigations on these issues, I assume that readers who engage in such investigation will want to look up the original articles (with the original reference lists) anyway. Furthermore, many of the articles have been heavily edited.

Changes to this edition This edition represents a considerable revision. There are eight completely new issues: *Are Genetic Explanations of Attention Deficit Hyperactivity Disorder Faulty?* (Issue 4); *Should Psychology Adopt a Theory of Multiple Intelligences?* (Issue 8); *Do Rewards Facilitate Learning?* (Issue 10); *Do Multiple Personalities Exist?* (Issue 12); *Is Treating Homosexuality Ethical and Effective?* (Issue 13); *Does Electroshock Therapy Cure Depression?* (Issue 14); *Are Medications for Treating Depression Harmful?* (Issue 15); and *Is Pornography Harmful?* (Issue 18). Also, for Issue 6 on spanking, the NO selection was replaced to bring a fresh perspective to the debate. In all, there are 16 new selections. The issues that were dropped from the previous edition were done so on the recommendation of professors who let me know what worked and what could be improved.

A word to the instructor An *Instructor's Manual With Test Questions* (multiple-choice and essay) is available through the publisher for the instructor using *Taking Sides* in the classroom. A general guidebook, *Using Taking Sides in the Classroom,* which discusses methods and techniques for integrating the pro-con approach into any classroom setting, is also available. An online version of *Using Taking Sides in the Classroom* and a correspondence service for *Taking Sides* adopters can be found at http://www.dushkin.com/usingts/.

Taking Sides: Clashing Views on Controversial Psychological Issues is only one title in the Taking Sides series. If you are interested in seeing the table of contents for any of the other titles, please visit the Taking Sides Web site at http://www.dushkin.com/takingsides/.

Acknowledgments In working on this revision I received useful suggestions from many of the users of the previous edition, and I was able to incorporate many of their recommendations for new issues and new readings.

In addition, special thanks go to Theodore Knight, list manager for the Taking Sides series at McGraw-Hill/Dushkin, for his support and perspective.

Brent Slife
Brigham Young University

Contents In Brief

Contents

Psychologist Diana Baumrind argues that Stanley Milgram's study of obedience did not meet ethical standards for research, because participants were subjected to a research design that caused undue psychological stress that was not resolved after the study. Social psychologist Stanley Milgram, in response to Baumrind's accusations, asserts that the study was well designed, the stress caused to participants could not have been anticipated, and the participants' anguish dissipated after a thorough debriefing.

Elizabeth Baldwin, a research ethics officer for the American Psychological Association's Science Directorate, maintains that the benefits of behavioral research with animals are substantial and that the animals are being treated humanely. Professor of educational psychology Alan D. Bowd and Kenneth J. Shapiro, executive director of Psychologists for the Ethical Treatment of Animals, argue that the harm done to animals in this research is not widely known and that the "benefits" are not sufficient to balance this cruelty.

Psychotherapy researcher Martin E. P. Seligman defends the conclusion of *Consumer Reports* that psychotherapy is effective by pointing to the importance of client satisfaction in the actual settings in which the clients are treated. Psychotherapy researchers Neil S. Jacobson and Andrew Christensen contend that the *Consumer Reports* study is essentially the same as 40-year-old studies that have long been rejected as inadequate.

PART 2 BIOLOGICAL ISSUES   53

After reviewing the literature on the genetic causes of ADHD, professor of psychology Jay Joseph concludes that such claims are unsupported and that psychosocial causes need further exploration. Clinical psychologists Stephen V. Faraone and Joseph Biederman reject Joseph's conclusions on the grounds that he makes errors in scientific logic and ignores much of the relevant research.

Anthropologist Helen Fisher contends that love is a chemical mechanism through which natural selection initiates and sustains human pair-bonds. Furthermore, she maintains that serial monogamy has adaptive advantages and is visible in worldwide patterns of divorce. Freelance writers Jeffrey S. Reber and Marissa S. Beyers contend that love is not merely biological but also fundamentally relational, social, and psychological. Additionally, they argue that Fisher's commitment to an evolutionary perspective leads to a biased interpretation of the evidence.

PART 3 HUMAN DEVELOPMENT   103

Professor of sociology Murray A. Straus argues that several studies show a link between childhood spanking and aggressive behavior in later life because spanking teaches a child violence. Pediatricians Den A. Trumbull and S. DuBose Ravenel, of the Family Research Council, argue that the current research on spanking fails to distinguish between spanking and physical abuse and, thus, leads to inaccurate results about parents who appropriately spank their children.

Brandon S. Centerwall, an epidemiologist, argues that children act out the violence they see on television and carry the violent behaviors into adulthood. Brian Siano, a writer and researcher, contends that children with nonnurturing parents, regardless of the children's television viewing habits, tend to be more aggressive than children who closely identify with either parent.

PART 4   COGNITIVE PROCESSES   149

Psychologist Howard Gardner argues that humans are better understood as having eight or nine different kinds of intelligence rather than as having one general intelligence. Psychologist Linda S. Gottfredson contends that despite some popular assertions, a single factor for intelligence can be measured with IQ tests and is predictive of success in life.

May Benatar, a clinical social worker and lecturer, asserts that repressed memories are a common response to child sexual abuse and that they can be recovered in adulthood. Susan P. Robbins, an associate professor of graduate social work, contends that there is little support for the idea of repressed or dissociated memories of child sexual abuse in scientific studies.

Issue 10.   Do Rewards Facilitate Learning?   196

YES: **Paul Chance,** from "The Rewards of Learning," *Phi Delta Kappan* (November 1992)   *198*

NO: **Alfie Kohn,** from "Rewards Versus Learning: A Response to Paul Chance," *Phi Delta Kappan* (June 1993)   *209*

Paul Chance, a teacher at James H. Groves Adult High School in George-town, Delaware, asserts that using reinforcement is the most effective way to help people learn. Alfie Kohn, a writer and lecturer on psychological and educational issues, argues that using external reinforcers actually decreases an individual's interest in learning.

PART 5 MENTAL HEALTH   219

Issue 11.   Classic Dialogue: Do Diagnostic Labels Hinder Treatment?   220

YES: **D. L. Rosenhan,** from "On Being Sane in Insane Places," *Science* (January 19, 1973)   *222*

NO: **Robert L. Spitzer,** from "On Pseudoscience in Science, Logic in Remission and Psychiatric Diagnosis: A Critique of 'On Being Sane in Insane Places,' " *Journal of Abnormal Psychology* (vol. 84, 1975)   *238*

Psychologist D. L. Rosenhan describes an experiment that he contends demonstrates that once a patient is labeled "schizophrenic," his behavior is seen as such by mental health workers regardless of the true state of the patient's mental health. Psychiatrist Robert L. Spitzer argues that diagnostic labels are necessary and valuable and that Rosenhan's experiment has many flaws.

Issue 12.   Do Multiple Personalities Exist?   254

YES: **Frank W. Putnam,** from "Response to Article by Paul R. McHugh," *Journal of the American Academy of Child and Adolescent Psychiatry* (July 1995)   *256*

NO: **Paul R. McHugh,** from "Resolved: Multiple Personality Disorder Is an Individually and Socially Created Artifact," *Journal of the American Academy of Child and Adolescent Psychiatry* (July 1995)   *260*

Psychiatrist Frank W. Putnam defends the diagnosis of multiple personalities on the basis of research that demonstrates agreed-upon criteria of validity. Psychiatrist Paul R. McHugh rejects the notion of a multiple personality disorder and proposes that its appearance is a product of therapist suggestion.

Warren Throckmorton, director of college counseling and an associate professor of psychology at Grove City College, maintains that efforts to assist homosexually oriented individuals to modify their patterns of sexual arousal have been effective and can be conducted in an ethical manner. Barry A. Schreier, coordinator of training and a psychologist at the Counseling and Psychological Services of Purdue University, counters that homosexuality is not an illness, so there is no need to treat it.

Physician Max Fink argues that electroconvulsive therapy (ECT) is a safe procedure that will reduce the cost of patient care in the long term. Leonard R. Frank, editor and cofounder of the Network Against Psychiatric Assault, protests that ECT is a dangerous, brainwashing practice no matter what modifications have been made to make it safer.

Psychiatrist Peter R. Breggin argues that psychotherapeutic interventions are preferred over medications for treating depression because psychotropic medications damage the brain and hurt the morale of both clients and therapists. Psychiatrist Peter D. Kramer contends that antidepressant drugs such as Prozac can alleviate depression and transform clients' personalities from withdrawn and timid to outgoing and fun loving, with almost no side effects.

Research scientist James E. Katz and Philip Aspden, executive director of the Center for Research on the Information Society, contend that the Internet has positive effects on the lives of its users. They also maintain that the Internet creates more opportunities for people to foster relationships with people, regardless of their location. Robert Kraut, a professor of social psychology and human computer interaction, and his colleagues at Carnegie Mellon University question how beneficial Internet use really is. They argue that Internet use reduces the number and quality of interpersonal relationships that one has.

David B. Larson, president of the National Institute for Healthcare, maintains that religious commitment improves mental health and that spirituality can be a medical treatment. Albert Ellis, president of the Institute for Rational-Emotive Therapy, challenges Larson's studies and questions particularly whether a religious commitment of "fanatic" proportions is truly mentally healthy.

Sociology professor Diana E. H. Russell argues that pornography is profoundly harmful because it predisposes men to want to rape women and undermines social inhibitions against acting out rape fantasies. Michael C. Seto, Alexandra Maric, and Howard E. Barbaree, of the Centre for Addiction and Mental Health, contend that evidence for a causal link between pornography use and sexual offense remains equivocal.

Introduction

Unresolved Issues in Psychology

Brent Slife

Stephen C. Yanchar

Eminent psychologist Edward Bradford Titchener (1867–1927) once stated that although psychology has a short history, it has a long past. He meant that even though the science of psychology is of relatively recent origin, the subject matter of psychology extends back to ancient history. Unfortunately, this dual history—the short and the long—is rarely treated in psychology texts; most texts focus almost exclusively on the shorter history. This shorter history is thought to be guided by the scientific method, so texts are generally filled with the scientific facts of the discipline. However, we cannot fully understand psychology without also understanding its longer intellectual history, a history of age-old questions that have recently been addressed by science but rarely been completely answered. Some history texts portray this longer intellectual history, but they do not deal with its contemporary implications. *Taking Sides: Clashing Views on Controversial Psychological Issues* is dedicated to the unresolved issues that still plague psychologists from this longer history.

Why Are There Unresolved Issues?

The subject matter of psychology is somewhat different from the subject matter of the natural sciences. In fact, psychology has been termed a "soft" science because it deals with neither the "hard" world of observable entities and physical elements—like zoology, biology, physiology, and chemistry—nor the rigorous computational analyses of mathematics, physics, and astronomy. These hard sciences are disciplines in which the crucial questions can usually be answered through scientific observation and experimentation.

Psychologists, on the other hand, deal with the warm, "soft" world of human beings—the thoughts, attitudes, emotions, and behaviors of people interacting with other people. Psychologists are therefore concerned with many of the philosophical questions that seem so central and unique to humanity. These questions have no quick and simple answers. Indeed, these questions have occupied thinkers—scientists and philosophers alike—since at least the time of the ancient Greeks.

For example, psychologists regularly deal with the topic of mind and matter, or what is sometimes referred to as the mind-body problem. The mind-body problem essentially asks, Does the mind (which is often viewed as *not* being entirely composed of matter) control the body (which *is* entirely composed of matter), or does the brain control the mind? Yet the essence of what we mean by the mind-body problem has been a topic of debate since at least the time of the Greek philosopher Aristotle (Robinson, 1989). Aristotle (384–322 B.C.) believed that the human mind had to be distinct from the crude matter of the human body. While the human body would eventually die and decay, the human mind (or soul) was imperishable. Aristotle accounted for much of human psychology on biological grounds (i.e., in terms of matter), but he still considered the higher rational activities of a human to be aspects of a mind that are independent of the body (Robinson, 1986). However, what is left out of his and other accounts is a precise explanation of how mind and body are connected. That is, if we assume that the mind is *not* composed of matter and is thus intangible, then how can it connect or interact with something material and tangible like the body? If, on the other hand, we decide that the mind *is* tangible and material, then we inherit a host of other problems associated with reductionism (see Slife & Williams, 1995, for details).

The point is that these and other such questions may not be resolved merely through scientific observation and experimentation. Scientific method is helpful for answering certain empirical questions, but its benefits are limited for many philosophical questions. And, for better or worse, psychology is infused with philosophical questions as well as empirical questions. There are basically two reasons for this infusion: the complexity of psychology's subject matter and the methods that psychologists use to study their subject matter.

Human beings—the primary subject matter of psychology—appear to operate with wills of their own within a hopelessly complex network of situations and relationships. This, it would seem, hinders the ability of scientists to attain the kind of certainty with people that they can attain with inanimate objects. Perhaps more important, it is difficult to know *why* people act in a particular manner because we cannot directly observe their intentions, thoughts, and desires. Thus, there are some aspects of human beings that elude the traditional methods of natural science.

The scientific method itself provides no irrefutable verification of an explanation. This is because data alone do not provide answers. Scientists sometimes talk as if the data from their experiments "tell" them what to believe or "give" them results, but this is somewhat misleading. Data are meaningless until they have been interpreted by the scientist (Slife & Williams, 1995). That is, scientists have a lot to do with their findings. Because there are a number of possible interpreters, there are, in principle, a number of possible interpretations. As some of the issues in this volume show, results that seem to supply indubitable proof for one interpreter might appear quite dubious to another. The reason for this is that the scientific method is set up in a manner that requires interpretation. As many who have studied this method have noted (e.g., Popper, 1959; Rychlak, 1988), the scientific method basically takes the form of a logical if-then statement: *If* my theory is correct, *then* my data will come out as I predict. However, problems can occur when we use this logic inappropriately. What if we know, for example, that we have the "then" portion of our statement, that the data did come out as I predicted? Do we then know that my theory is correct? Of course we cannot know this, because there can be an alternative theory (or many alternatives) that could explain the same data.

Unfortunately, however, this is the way in which science is conducted. We do not know the "if" portion of our logical statement—that my theory is correct; we can only know the "then" portion—that my data came out as I predicted. And our knowledge of our data cannot tell us that our theory is correct. All we can ever do is *interpret* what our data mean because our data can always mean something else.[1]

So, as a little logic has shown, data from human subjects can always be interpreted in different ways. In fact, because of these possible interpretations, there can never be a final and definitive experiment to determine what is really true about human beings (Slife & Williams, 1995). This is what scientists mean when they say that they cannot *prove* a theory but can only *support* it. Unfortunately, this simple distinction leaves many important questions unresolved, such as the mind-body problem. Still, this lack of resolution does not mean that scientists can ignore these issues. Just because certain issues are not amenable to scientific methods does not mean they go away. The issue of whether or not the mind controls matter, for example, is vital to cancer patients who wonder whether or not positive mental attitudes will alter the course of their disease. Such issues require exploration and debate regardless of the state of scientific knowledge. Whatever scientific information is available is important, and the lack of a complete scientific answer cannot prevent us from debating what information we do have, particularly when we may never get a complete scientific answer.

A Dialectical Approach

This volume introduces some of the most important contemporary debates in psychology as well as some classical issues that remain unresolved. As mentioned, this volume is different from texts that focus exclusively on what is known scientifically. Most texts with an exclusive scientific focus adopt a "banking conception" of education.

The banking conception of education assumes that students are essentially "banks" in which scientific facts are "deposited." Because psychology is considered a science, there are presumably many scientific psychological facts, derived from experiments, that need to be deposited in students' minds. The banking conception makes teachers and textbooks fact distributors or information transmitters. Lectures are monologues through which the facts of experiments or the findings of method are distributed and transmitted into the mental "banks" of students. At test time, then, teachers make information "withdrawals" to discern how well students have maintained the deposits of educational currency referred to as knowledge.

Since the time of the Greek philosopher Socrates (470–399 B.C.), the banking conception of education has not been considered effective for learning about unresolved conceptual issues. One reason for this is that nestled within the banking conception lies the assumption that knowledge is above reasonable criticism and that the facts of a scholarly discipline are approximations of truth—distilled and ready for distribution to students. This is the notion of education that considers knowledge to be strictly objective. Students are thought to acquire a clear and objective picture of reality—the way things really are. As we have observed, however, it is questionable whether teachers of the "soft" sciences have access to clear and objective facts only. In many cases, the "facts" are not so clear and objective but rather puzzling and debatable. Indeed, interpretations of data are always debatable, in principle.

An alternative to the banking tradition of education is the *dialectical* tradition of education. In this tradition, there can be no meaning (and thus no knowledge) without opposition. For example, there is no way to understand what "beauty" or "upness" means without implicitly understanding what "ugliness" or "downness" is, respectively. To judge the beauty of a work of art, one must have some notion of the contrast to beauty. In other words, opposing notions only make sense when considered at the same time, one complementing the other and together forming a complete concept. In this Greek conception of the dialectic, there are no quick and easy answers to difficult questions, and there are few incontestable facts to present. Instead, there are at least two sides to every issue.

Socrates taught his students that we may begin in error or falsity, but we will eventually arrive at truth if we continue our dialectical conversation. This is because truth, for Socrates, involves uncovering what is already there. Because all conceptions—true or false—supposedly have their dialectical complements implicit within them, truth is itself already implicit and waiting to be revealed. Truth, then, according to Socrates, is uncovered by a rational analysis of the relevant (and perhaps even false) ideas and arguments already under discussion.

The discipline of psychology is often considered to be dialectical, at least in part. Any student who has studied the many different theories of human behavior (e.g., humanism, behaviorism, psychoanalysis) can attest to this. Psychology frequently consists of two or more voices on the same psychological issue. Consequently, many of the ideas of psychology develop through conversation that takes place among psychologists or among the students of psychology. Although this is understandable when we consider the complexity of psychology's subject matter, it can create problems for the banking approach to education. What can be deposited in a mental bank when two or more voices are possible and the conversation among the voices is ongoing? Some information distribution is certainly important. However, information distribution alone cannot capture this type of knowledge in the discipline, because that knowledge is dialectical in nature.

Benefits of a Dialectical Approach

The dialectical approach is the focus of this volume: Psychological issues are presented in true dialectical fashion, with two distinct sides. Students are asked to familiarize themselves with both sides of an issue, look at the supporting evidence on both sides, and engage in constructive conversation about possible resolutions. This approach to education requires students to take an active role in making sense of the issues. In so doing, students benefit in several ways.

First, students come to a richer understanding of the subject matter of psychologists. It is important to understand that there is a dialectical, or humanities, side of psychology as well as an informational, or scientific, side of psychology. As necessary as data may be, there will always be a human interpreter of the data that will never permit psychology to dispense with humanities entirely.

Second, students develop a healthy respect for both sides of a debate. There is a natural tendency to underestimate reasonable arguments on one side or the other of a debate. Often, of course, the side one favors is the "most reasonable." Without exception, the issues in this book have reasonable people and reasonable arguments *on both sides*. That is, these issues are issues in psychology precisely because they have reasonable arguments and evidence on either side. This is not to say that both sides are correct (although this too is possible). It is to say, rather, that a proper appreciation of both sides is necessary to understanding what is at issue and thus to begin to find a resolution.

A third benefit of this dialectical approach is that students better understand the nature of psychological knowledge in general. Although contemporary psychologists have taken up the scientific challenge of exploring behavior and mind, many questions are still far from being answered. Psychology's parent, like all sciences, is philosophy. Hence, philosophical (or theoretical) issues always lurk behind the activities of psychologists. Issues such as mind versus body, free will versus determinism, nature versus nurture, and the philosophy of science are both philosophical and psychological questions. Students will necessarily have to entertain and explicate these types of issues as they learn about and advance the discipline.

Fourth, students become more aware of alternative views on controversial psychological issues. People often do not even realize that there is another point of view to an issue or evidence to the contrary. This realization, however, can help students to be more cautious in their knowledge. As the dialectician Socrates once noted, this caution is sometimes the first step toward true wisdom —knowing what it is that you don't know.

Finally, the dialectical approach promotes critical thinking skills. As authorities on critical thinking have noted (e.g., Brookfield, 1987), thinking skills require an awareness of what one *does* believe and a knowledge of alternatives regarding what one *could* believe. *Taking Sides: Clashing Views on Controversial Psychological Issues* provides both elements. Finely honed critical skills give students a better position from which to examine the psychological literature critically and to select or develop their own positions on important psychological issues.

Note

1. Unfortunately, falsifying the consequent—the "then" portion of our logical statement—does not prevent us from needing to interpret either, as Slife and Williams (1995) have shown.

References

Brookfield, S. (1987). *Developing critical thinkers: Challenging adults to explore alternative ways of thinking.* San Francisco: Jossey-Bass.

Popper, K. (1959). *The logic of scientific discovery.* New York: Basic Books.

Robinson, D. (1986). *An intellectual history of psychology.* Madison, WI: University of Wisconsin Press.

Robinson, D. (1989). *Aristotle's psychology.* New York: Columbia University Press.

Rychlak, J. F. (1988). *The psychology of rigorous humanism* (2d ed.). New York: New York University Press.

Slife, B. D., & Williams, R. N. (1995). *What's behind the research: Discovering hidden assumptions in the behavioral sciences.* Thousand Oaks, CA: Sage Publications.

On the Internet ...

Psychnet

Information on psychology may be obtained at this Web site through the site map or by using the search engine. You can access the American Psychological Association's newspaper, the *APA Monitor*; APA books on a wide range of topics; PsychINFO, an electronic database of abstracts on over 1,350 scholarly journals; and the Help Center for information on dealing with modern life problems.

http://www.apa.org/psychnet/

Research Methods & Statistics Links

This site of the Social Psychology Network features links related to research methodology, human and animal research ethics, statistics, data analysis, and more.

http://www.socialpsychology.org/methods.htm

National Health and Medical Research Council: Ethical Issues

This site discusses the role of the National Health and Medical Research Council's Animal Welfare Committee and offers several links to further information about animal ethical issues.

http://www.health.gov.au/nhmrc/issues/
animalethics.htm

PsychotherapistResources.com

PsychotherapistResources.com provides interviews with leading contemporary therapists, high-quality therapy videos, book reviews, humor, and other resources for therapists. It also offers a selection of articles from leading and obscure practitioners, within and on the fringes of traditional psychotherapy, as well as reviews of books with topics that are relevant to psychotherapy.

http://www.psychotherapistresources.com/current/
index.html

PART 1

Research Issues

*R*esearch methods allow psychologists to investigate their ideas and subject matter. How psychologists perform their research is often a subject of controversy. For example, sometimes animals are used to test experimental procedures before they are applied to humans. Is this right? Should animals be experimented upon—and sometimes sacrificed—in the service of humans? Similarly, what limits, if any, should be set on psychological research that is conducted on humans? Are there some experiments that are so potentially psychologically harmful to people that they should not be performed?

- Classic Dialogue: Was Stanley Milgram's Study of Obedience Unethical?

- Should Animals Be Used in Psychological Research?

- Is the *Consumer Reports* Conclusion That "Psychotherapy Helps" Valid?

ISSUE 1

Classic Dialogue: Was Stanley Milgram's Study of Obedience Unethical?

YES: Diana Baumrind, from "Some Thoughts on Ethics of Research: After Reading Milgram's 'Behavioral Study of Obedience,' " *American Psychologist* (vol. 19, 1964)

NO: Stanley Milgram, from "Issues in the Study of Obedience: A Reply to Baumrind," *American Psychologist* (vol. 19, 1964)

ISSUE SUMMARY

YES: Psychologist Diana Baumrind argues that Stanley Milgram's study of obedience did not meet ethical standards for research, because participants were subjected to a research design that caused undue psychological stress that was not resolved after the study.

NO: Social psychologist Stanley Milgram, in response to Baumrind's accusations, asserts that the study was well designed, the stress caused to participants could not have been anticipated, and the participants' anguish dissipated after a thorough debriefing.

Are there psychological experiments that should not be conducted? Is the psychological distress that participants experience in some studies too extreme to justify the experimental outcomes and knowledge gained? Or is it sometimes necessary to allow participants to experience some anguish so that a researcher can better understand important psychological phenomena? These questions lie at the heart of ethical considerations in psychological research. They have traditionally been answered by the researcher, who attempts to weigh the costs and benefits of conducting a given study.

The problem is that a researcher's ability to accurately anticipate the costs and benefits of a study is severely limited. Researchers are likely to have an investment in their studies, which may lead them to overestimate the benefits and underestimate the costs. For these and other reasons, in 1974 the U.S. Department of Health, Education, and Welfare established regulations for the protection of human subjects. These regulations include the creation of institutional review boards, which are responsible for reviewing research proposals and ensuring that researchers adequately protect research participants.

The establishment of these regulations can be traced to past ethical controversies, such as the one raised in the following selection by Diana Baumrind regarding Stanley Milgram's famous 1963 study of obedience. Baumrind's primary concern is that the psychological welfare of the study's participants was compromised not only through the course of the study but also through the course of their lives. She contends that participants were prone to obey the experimenter because of the atmosphere of the study and the participants' trust in the experimenter. As a result, participants behaved in ways that disturbed them considerably. Baumrind maintains that these disturbances could not be resolved through an after-study debriefing but rather remained with the participants.

In response to these accusations, Milgram argues that the atmosphere of a laboratory generalizes to other contexts in which obedience is prevalent and is thus appropriate to a study of obedience. Furthermore, he and a number of other professionals never anticipated the results of the study; they were genuinely surprised by its outcome. Milgram also asserts that the psychological distress experienced by some participants was temporary, not dangerous, and that it dissipated after the true nature of the study was revealed.

POINT

- Milgram's indifference toward distressed participants reveals his lack of concern for their well-being.
- A study of obedience should not be conducted in the laboratory because subjects are particularly prone to behave obediently and to put trust in the researcher.
- The psychological distress experienced by participants exceeded appropriate limits.
- Participants experienced long-term, negative psychological consequences as a result of their participation in Milgram's experiment.
- In planning and designing the study, Milgram ignored issues regarding the extreme psychological distress that was experienced by some participants.

COUNTERPOINT

- Milgram made special efforts to assure participants that their behavior was normal.
- The laboratory setting is well suited to a study of obedience because it is similar to other contexts in which obedience is prevalent.
- The psychological distress was brief and not injurious.
- Participants spoke positively about the experiment, indicating that it was psychologically beneficial.
- The extreme psychological tension experienced by some participants was unanticipated by Milgram and many other professionals.

Diana Baumrind  **YES**

Some Thoughts on Ethics of Research

Certain problems in psychological research require the experimenter to balance his career and scientific interests against the interests of his prospective subjects. When such occasions arise the experimenter's stated objective frequently is to do the best possible job with the least possible harm to his subjects. The experimenter seldom perceives in more positive terms an indebtedness to the subject for his services, perhaps because the detachment which his functions require prevents appreciation of the subject as an individual.

Yet a debt does exist, even when the subject's reason for volunteering includes course credit or monetary gain. Often a subject participates unwillingly in order to satisfy a course requirement. These requirements are of questionable merit ethically, and do not alter the experimenter's responsibility to the subject.

Most experimental conditions do not cause the subjects pain or indignity, and are sufficiently interesting or challenging to present no problem of an ethical nature to the experimenter. But where the experimental conditions expose the subject to loss of dignity, or offer him nothing of value, then the experimenter is obliged to consider the reasons why the subject volunteered and to reward him accordingly.

The subject's public motives for volunteering include having an enjoyable or stimulating experience, acquiring knowledge, doing the experimenter a favor which may some day be reciprocated, and making a contribution to science. These motives can be taken into account rather easily by the experimenter who is willing to spend a few minutes with the subject afterwards to thank him for his participation, answer his questions, reassure him that he did well, and chat with him a bit. Most volunteers also have less manifest, but equally legitimate, motives. A subject may be seeking an opportunity to have contact with, be noticed by, and perhaps confide in a person with psychological training. The dependent attitude of most subjects toward the experimenter is an artifact of the experimental situation as well as an expression of some subjects' personal need systems at the time they volunteer.

The dependent, obedient attitude assumed by most subjects in the experimental setting is appropriate to that situation. The "game" is defined by the experimenter and he makes the rules. By volunteering, the subject agrees

From Diana Baumrind, "Some Thoughts on Ethics of Research: After Reading Milgram's 'Behavioral Study of Obedience,'" *American Psychologist,* vol. 19 (1964). Copyright © 1964 by The American Psychological Association. Reprinted by permission.

implicitly to assume a posture of trust and obedience. While the experimental conditions leave him exposed, the subject has the right to assume that his security and self-esteem will be protected.

There are other professional situations in which one member—the patient or client—expects help and protection from the other—the physician or psychologist. But the interpersonal relationship between experimenter and subject additionally has unique features which are likely to provoke initial anxiety in the subject. The laboratory is unfamiliar as a setting and the rules of behavior ambiguous compared to a clinician's office. Because of the anxiety and passivity generated by the setting, the subject is more prone to behave in an obedient, suggestible manner in the laboratory than elsewhere. Therefore, the laboratory is not the place to study degree of obedience or suggestibility, as a function of a particular experimental condition, since the base line for these phenomena as found in the laboratory is probably much higher than in most other settings. Thus experiments in which the relationship to the experimenter as an authority is used as an independent condition are imperfectly designed for the same reason that they are prone to injure the subjects involved. They disregard the special quality of trust and obedience with which the subject appropriately regards the experimenter.

Other phenomena which present ethical decisions, unlike those mentioned above, *can* be reproduced successfully in the laboratory. Failure experience, conformity to peer judgment, and isolation are among such phenomena. In these cases we can expect the experimenter to take whatever measures are necessary to prevent the subject from leaving the laboratory more humiliated, insecure, alienated, or hostile than when he arrived. To guarantee that an especially sensitive subject leaves a stressful experimental experience in the proper state sometimes requires special clinical training. But usually an attitude of compassion, respect, gratitude, and common sense will suffice, and no amount of clinical training will substitute. The subject has the right to expect that the psychologist with whom he is interacting has some concern for his welfare, and the personal attributes and professional skill to express his good will effectively.

Unfortunately, the subject is not always treated with the respect he deserves. It has become more commonplace in sociopsychological laboratory studies to manipulate, embarrass, and discomfort subjects. At times the insult to the subject's sensibilities extends to the journal reader when the results are reported. Milgram's (1963) study is a case in point. The following is Milgram's abstract of his experiment:

> This article describes a procedure for the study of destructive obedience in the laboratory. It consists of ordering a naive S to administer increasingly more severe punishment to a victim in the context of a learning experiment. Punishment is administered by means of a shock generator with 30 graded switches ranging from Slight Shock to Danger: Severe Shock. The victim is a confederate of E. The primary dependent variable is the maximum shock the S is willing to administer before he refuses to continue further. 26 Ss obeyed the experimental commands fully, and administered the highest shock on the generator. 14 Ss broke off the experiment at some point after the victim protested and refused to provide further answers. The procedure created ex-

treme levels of nervous tension in some Ss. Profuse sweating, trembling, and stuttering were typical expressions of this emotional disturbance. One unexpected sign of tension—yet to be explained—was the regular occurrence of nervous laughter, which in some Ss developed into uncontrollable seizures. The variety of interesting behavioral dynamics observed in the experiment, the reality of the situation for the S, and the possibility of parametric variation within the framework of the procedure, point to the fruitfulness of further study [p. 371].

The detached, objective manner in which Milgram reports the emotional disturbance suffered by his subject contrasts sharply with his graphic account of that disturbance. Following are two other quotes describing the effects on his subjects of the experimental conditions:

I observed a mature and initially poised businessman enter the laboratory smiling and confident. Within 20 minutes he was reduced to a twitching, stuttering wreck, who was rapidly approaching a point of nervous collapse. He constantly pulled on his earlobe, and twisted his hands. At one point he pushed his fist into his forehead and muttered: "Oh, God, let's stop it." And yet he continued to respond to every word of the experimenter, and obeyed to the end [p. 377].

In a large number of cases the degree of tension reached extremes that are rarely seen in sociopsychological laboratory studies. Subjects were observed to sweat, tremble, stutter, bite their lips, groan, and dig their fingernails into their flesh. These were characteristic rather than exceptional responses to the experiment.

One sign of tension was the regular occurrence of nervous laughing fits. Fourteen of the 40 subjects showed definite signs of nervous laughter and smiling. The laughter seemed entirely out of place, even bizarre. Full-blown, uncontrollable seizures were observed for 3 subjects. On one occasion we observed a seizure so violently convulsive that it was necessary to call a halt to the experiment... [p. 375].

Milgram does state that,

After the interview, procedures were undertaken to assure that the subject would leave the laboratory in a state of well being. A friendly reconciliation was arranged between the subject and the victim, and an effort was made to reduce any tensions that arose as a result of the experiment [p. 374].

It would be interesting to know what sort of procedures could dissipate the type of emotional disturbance just described. In view of the effects on subjects, traumatic to a degree which Milgram himself considers nearly unprecedented in sociopsychological experiments, his casual assurance that these tensions were dissipated before the subject left the laboratory is unconvincing.

What could be the rational basis for such a posture of indifference? Perhaps Milgram supplies the answer himself when he partially explains the subject's destructive obedience as follows, "Thus they assume that the discomfort caused the victim is momentary, while the scientific gains resulting from the experiment are enduring [p. 378]." Indeed such a rationale might suffice to justify the means used to achieve his end if that end were of inestimable value to humanity or were not itself transformed by the means by which it was attained.

The behavioral psychologist is not in as good a position to objectify his faith in the significance of his work as medical colleagues at points of breakthrough. His experimental situations are not sufficiently accurate models of real-life experience; his sampling techniques are seldom of a scope which would justify the meaning with which he would like to endow his results; and these results are hard to reproduce by colleagues with opposing theoretical views.... [T]he concrete benefit to humanity of his particular piece of work, no matter how competently handled, cannot justify the risk that real harm will be done to the subject. I am not speaking of physical discomfort, inconvenience, or experimental deception per se, but of permanent harm, however slight. I do regard the emotional disturbance described by Milgram as potentially harmful because it could easily effect an alteration in the subject's self-image or ability to trust adult authorities in the future. It is potentially harmful to a subject to commit, in the course of an experiment, acts which he himself considers unworthy, particularly when he has been entrapped into committing such acts by an individual he has reason to trust. The subject's personal responsibility for his actions is not erased because the experimenter reveals to him the means which he used to stimulate these actions. The subject realizes that he would have hurt the victim if the current were on. The realization that he also made a fool of himself by accepting the experimental set results in additional loss of self-esteem. Moreover, the subject finds it difficult to express his anger outwardly after the experimenter in a self-acceptant but friendly manner reveals the hoax.

A fairly intense corrective interpersonal experience is indicated wherein the subject admits and accepts his responsibility for his own actions, and at the same time gives vent to his hurt and anger at being fooled. Perhaps an experience as distressing as the one described by Milgram can be integrated by the subject, provided that careful thought is given to the matter. The propriety of such experimentation is still in question even if such a reparational experience were forthcoming. Without it I would expect a naive, sensitive subject to remain deeply hurt and anxious for some time, and a sophisticated, cynical subject to become even more alienated and distrustful.

In addition the experimental procedure used by Milgram does not appear suited to the objectives of the study because it does not take into account the special quality of the set which the subject has in the experimental situation. Milgram is concerned with a very important problem, namely, the social consequences of destructive obedience. He says,

> Gas chambers were built, death camps were guarded, daily quotas of corpses were produced with the same efficiency as a manufacture of appliances. These inhumane policies may have originated in the mind of a single person, but they could only be carried out on a massive scale if a very large number of persons obeyed orders [p. 371].

But the parallel between authority-subordinate relationships in Hitler's Germany and in Milgram's laboratory is unclear. In the former situation the SS man or member of the German Officer Corps, when obeying orders to slaughter, had no reason to think of his superior officer as benignly disposed towards himself or their victims. The victims were perceived as subhuman and not worthy of consideration. The subordinate officer was an agent in a great cause. He did not need to feel guilt or conflict because within his frame of reference he was acting rightly.

It is obvious from Milgram's own descriptions that most of his subjects were concerned about their victims and did trust the experimenter, and that their stressful conflict was generated in part by the consequences of these two disparate but appropriate attitudes. Their distress may have resulted from shock at what the experimenter was doing to them as well as from what they thought they were doing to their victims. In any case there is not a convincing parallel between the phenomena studied by Milgram and destructive obedience as that concept would apply to the subordinate-authority relationship demonstrated in Hitler Germany. If the experiments were conducted "outside of New Haven [Connecticut] and without any visible ties to [Yale University]," I would still question their validity on similar although not identical grounds. In addition, I would question the representativeness of a sample of subjects who would voluntarily participate within a noninstitutional setting.

In summary, the experimental objectives of the psychologist are seldom incompatible with the subject's ongoing state of well being, provided that the experimenter is willing to take the subject's motives and interests into consideration when planning his methods and correctives. Section 4b in *Ethical Standards of Psychologists* (APA, undated) reads in part:

> Only when a problem is significant and can be investigated in no other way, is the psychologist justified in exposing human subjects to emotional stress or other possible harm. In conducting such research, the psychologist must seriously consider the possibility of harmful aftereffects, and should be prepared to remove them as soon as permitted by the design of the experiment. Where the danger of serious aftereffects exists, research should be conducted only when the subjects or their responsible agents are fully informed of this possibility and volunteer nevertheless [p. 12].

From the subject's point of view procedures which involve loss of dignity, self-esteem, and trust in rational authority are probably most harmful in the long run and require the most thoughtfully planned reparations, if engaged in at all. The public image of psychology as a profession is highly related to our own actions, and some of these actions are changeworthy. It is important that as research psychologists we protect our ethical sensibilities rather than adapt our personal standards to include as appropriate the kind of indignities to which Milgram's subjects were exposed. I would not like to see experiments such as Milgram's proceed unless the subjects were fully informed of the dangers of serious aftereffects and his correctives were clearly shown to be effective in restoring their state of well being.

References

AMERICAN PSYCHOLOGICAL ASSOCIATION. Ethical Standards of Psychologists: A summary of ethical principles. Washington, D.C.: APA, undated.
MILGRAM, S. Behavioral study of obedience. *J. abnorm. soc. Psychol.*, 1963, 67, 371–378.

NO

Stanley Milgram

Issues in the Study of Obedience:
A Reply to Baumrind

Obedience serves numerous productive functions in society. It may be en-nobling and educative and entail acts of charity and kindness. Yet the problem of destructive obedience, because it is the most disturbing expression of obe-dience in our time, and because it is the most perplexing, merits intensive study.

In its most general terms, the problem of destructive obedience may be defined thus: If X tells Y to hurt Z, under what conditions will Y carry out the command of X, and under what conditions will he refuse? In the concrete setting of a laboratory, the question may assume this form: If an experimenter tells a subject to act against another person, under what conditions will the subject go along with the instruction, and under what conditions will he refuse to obey?

A simple procedure was devised for studying obedience (Milgram, 1963). A person comes to the laboratory, and in the context of a learning experiment, he is told to give increasingly severe electric shocks to another person. (The other person is an actor, who does not really receive any shocks.) The exper-imenter tells the subject to continue stepping up the shock level, even to the point of reaching the level marked "Danger: Severe Shock." The purpose of the experiment is to see how far the naive subject will proceed before he refuses to comply with the experimenter's instructions. Behavior prior to this rupture is considered "obedience" in that the subject does what the experimenter tells him to do. The point of rupture is the act of disobedience. Once the basic pro-cedure is established, it becomes possible to vary conditions of the experiment, to learn under what circumstances obedience to authority is most probable, and under what conditions defiance is brought to the fore (Milgram, in press).

The results of the experiment (Milgram, 1963) showed, first, that it is more difficult for many people to defy the experimenter's authority than was gener-ally supposed. A substantial number of subjects go through to the end of the shock board. The second finding is that the situation often places a person in considerable conflict. In the course of the experiment, subjects fidget, sweat,

From Stanley Milgram, "Issues in the Study of Obedience: A Reply to Baumrind," *American Psychol-ogist,* vol. 19 (1964). Copyright © 1964 by Stanley Milgram. Reprinted by permission of Alexandra Milgram.

and sometimes break out into nervous fits of laughter. On the one hand, subjects want to aid the experimenter; and on the other hand, they do not want to shock the learner. The conflict is expressed in nervous reactions.

In a recent issue of *American Psychologist,* Diana Baumrind (1964) raised a number of questions concerning the obedience report. Baumrind expressed concern for the welfare of subjects who served in the experiment, and wondered whether adequate measures were taken to protect the participants. She also questioned the adequacy of the experimental design.

Patently, "Behavioral Study of Obedience" did not contain all the information needed for an assessment of the experiment. But... this was only one of a series of reports on the experimental program, and Baumrind's article was deficient in information that could have been obtained easily....

At the outset, Baumrind confuses the unanticipated outcome of an experiment with its basic procedure. She writes, for example, as if the production of stress in our subjects was an intended and deliberate effect of the experimental manipulation. There are many laboratory procedures specifically designed to create stress (Lazarus, 1964), but the obedience paradigm was not one of them. The extreme tension induced in some subjects was unexpected. Before conducting the experiment, the procedures were discussed with many colleagues, and none anticipated the reactions that subsequently took place. Foreknowledge of results can never be the invariable accompaniment of an experimental probe. Understanding grows because we examine situations in which the end is unknown. An investigator unwilling to accept this degree of risk must give up the idea of scientific inquiry.

Moreover, there was every reason to expect, prior to actual experimentation, that subjects would refuse to follow the experimenter's instructions beyond the point where the victim protested; many colleagues and psychiatrists were questioned on this point, and they virtually all felt this would be the case. Indeed, to initiate an experiment in which the critical measure hangs on disobedience, one must start with a belief in certain spontaneous resources in men that enable them to overcome pressure from authority.

It is true that after a reasonable number of subjects had been exposed to the procedures, it became evident that some would go to the end of the shock board, and some would experience stress. That point, it seems to me, is the first legitimate juncture at which one could even start to wonder whether or not to abandon the study. But momentary excitement is not the same as harm. As the experiment progressed there was no indication of injurious effects in the subjects; and as the subjects themselves strongly endorsed the experiment, the judgment I made was to continue the investigation.

Is not Baumrind's criticism based as much on the unanticipated findings as on the method? The findings were that some subjects performed in what appeared to be a shockingly immoral way. If, instead, every one of the subjects had broken off at "slight shock," or at the first sign of the learner's discomfort, the results would have been pleasant, and reassuring, and who would protest?

Table 1

Excerpt From Questionnaire Used in a Follow-up Study of the Obedience Research

Now that I have read the report and all things considered . . .	Defiant	Obedient	All
1. I am very glad to have been in the experiment	40.0%	47.8%	43.5%
2. I am glad to have been in the experiment	43.8%	35.7%	40.2%
3. I am neither sorry nor glad to have been in the experiment	15.3%	14.8%	15.1%
4. I am sorry to have been in the experiment	0.8%	0.7%	0.8%
5. I am very sorry to have been in the experiment	0.0%	1.0%	0.5%

Note—Ninety-two percent of the subjects returned the questionnaire. The characteristics of the nonrespondents were checked against the respondents. They differed from the respondents only with regard to age; younger people were overrepresented in the nonresponding group.

Procedures and Benefits

A most important aspect of the procedure occurred at the end of the experimental session. A careful post-experimental treatment was administered to all subjects. The exact content of the dehoax varied from condition to condition and with increasing experience on our part. At the very least all subjects were told that the victim had not received dangerous electric shocks. Each subject had a friendly reconciliation with the unharmed victim, and an extended discussion with the experimenter. The experiment was explained to the defiant subjects in a way that supported their decision to disobey the experimenter. Obedient subjects were assured of the fact that their behavior was entirely normal and that their feelings of conflict or tension were shared by other participants. Subjects were told that they would receive a comprehensive report at the conclusion of the experimental series. In some instances, additional detailed and lengthy discussions of the experiments were also carried out with individual subjects.

When the experimental series was complete, subjects received a written report which presented details of the experimental procedure and results. Again their own part in the experiments was treated in a dignified way and their behavior in the experiment respected. All subjects received a follow-up questionnaire regarding their participation in the research, which again allowed expression of thoughts and feelings about their behavior.

The replies to the questionnaire confirmed my impression that participants felt positively toward the experiment. In its quantitative aspect (see Table 1), 84% of the subjects stated they were glad to have been in the experiment; 15% indicated neutral feelings, and 1.3% indicated negative feelings. To be sure, such findings are to be interpreted cautiously, but they cannot be disregarded.

Further, four-fifths of the subjects felt that more experiments of this sort should be carried out, and 74% indicated that they had learned something of personal importance as a result of being in the study. . . .

The debriefing and assessment procedures were carried out as a matter of course, and were not stimulated by any observation of special risk in the experimental procedure. In my judgment, at no point were subjects exposed to danger and at no point did they run the risk of injurious effects resulting from participation. If it had been otherwise, the experiment would have been terminated at once.

Baumrind states that, after he has performed in the experiment, the subject cannot justify his behavior and must bear the full brunt of his actions. By and large it does not work this way. The same mechanisms that allow the subject to perform the act, to obey rather than to defy the experimenter, transcend the moment of performance and continue to justify his behavior for him. The same viewpoint the subject takes while performing the actions is the viewpoint from which he later sees his behavior, that is, the perspective of "carrying out the task assigned by the person in authority."

Because the idea of shocking the victim is repugnant, there is a tendency among those who hear of the design to say "people will not do it." When the results are made known, this attitude is expressed as "if they do it they will not be able to live with themselves afterward." These two forms of denying the experimental findings are equally inappropriate misreadings of the facts of human social behavior. Many subjects do, indeed, obey to the end, and there is no indication of injurious effects.

The absence of injury is a minimal condition of experimentation; there can be, however, an important positive side to participation. Baumrind suggests that subjects derived no benefit from being in the obedience study, but this is false. By their statements and actions, subjects indicated that they had learned a good deal, and many felt gratified to have taken part in scientific research they considered to be of significance. A year after his participation one subject wrote:

> This experiment has strengthened my belief that man should avoid harm to his fellow man even at the risk of violating authority.

Another stated:

> To me, the experiment pointed up ... the extent to which each individual should have or discover firm ground on which to base his decisions, no matter how trivial they appear to be. I think people should think more deeply about themselves and their relation to their world and to other people. If this experiment serves to jar people out of complacency, it will have served its end.

These statements are illustrative of a broad array of appreciative and insightful comments by those who participated.

The 5-page report sent to each subject on the completion of the experimental series was specifically designed to enhance the value of his experience. It laid out the broad conception of the experimental program as well as the logic of its design. It described the results of a dozen of the experiments, discussed the causes of tension, and attempted to indicate the possible significance of the experiment. Subjects responded enthusiastically; many indicated a desire to be in further experimental research. This report was sent to all subjects several years ago. The care with which it was prepared does not support Baumrind's assertion that the experimenter was indifferent to the value subjects derived from their participation.

Baumrind's fear is that participants will be alienated from psychological experiments because of the intensity of experience associated with laboratory procedures. My own observation is that subjects more commonly respond with distaste to the "empty" laboratory hour, in which cardboard procedures are employed, and the only possible feeling upon emerging from the laboratory is that one has wasted time in a patently trivial and useless exercise.

The subjects in the obedience experiment, on the whole, felt quite differently about their participation. They viewed the experience as an opportunity to learn something of importance about themselves, and more generally, about the conditions of human action.

A year after the experimental program was completed, I initiated an additional follow-up study. In this connection an impartial medical examiner, experienced in outpatient treatment, interviewed 40 experimental subjects. The examining psychiatrist focused on those subjects he felt would be most likely to have suffered consequences from participation. His aim was to identify possible injurious effects resulting from the experiment. He concluded that, although extreme stress had been experienced by several subjects,

> none was found by this interviewer to show signs of having been harmed by his experience.... Each subject seemed to handle his task [in the experiment] in a manner consistent with well established patterns of behavior. No evidence was found of any traumatic reactions.

Such evidence ought to be weighed before judging the experiment.

Other Issues

Baumrind's discussion is not limited to the treatment of subjects, but diffuses to a generalized rejection of the work.

Baumrind feels that obedience cannot be meaningfully studied in a laboratory setting: The reason she offers is that "The dependent, obedient attitude assumed by most subjects in the experimental setting is appropriate to that situation [p. 421]." Here, Baumrind has cited the very best reason for examining obedience in this setting, namely that it possesses "ecological validity." Here is one social context in which compliance occurs regularly. Military and job situations are also particularly meaningful settings for the study of obedience precisely because obedience is natural and appropriate to these contexts. I reject Baumrind's argument that the observed obedience does not count because it occurred where it is appropriate. That is precisely why it *does* count. A soldier's obedience is no less meaningful because it occurs in a pertinent military context. A subject's obedience is no less problematical because it occurs within a social institution called the psychological experiment.

Baumrind writes: "The game is defined by the experimenter and he makes the rules [p. 421]." It is true that for disobedience to occur the framework of the experiment must be shattered. That, indeed, is the point of the design. That is why obedience and disobedience are genuine issues for the subject. *He must really assert himself as a person against a legitimate authority.*

Further, Baumrind wants us to believe that outside the laboratory we could not find a comparably high expression of obedience. Yet, the fact that ordinary citizens are recruited to military service and, on command, perform far harsher acts against people is beyond dispute. Few of them know or are concerned with the complex policy issues underlying martial action; fewer still become conscientious objectors. Good soldiers do as they are told, and on both sides of the battle line. However, a debate on whether a higher level of obedience is represented by *(a)* killing men in the service of one's country, or *(b)* merely shocking them in the service of Yale science, is largely unprofitable. The real question is: What are the forces underlying obedient action?

Another question raised by Baumrind concerns the degree of parallel between obedience in the laboratory and in Nazi Germany. Obviously, there are enormous differences: Consider the disparity in time scale. The laboratory experiment takes an hour; the Nazi calamity unfolded in the space of a decade. There is a great deal that needs to be said on this issue, and only a few points can be touched on here.

1. In arguing this matter, Baumrind mistakes the background metaphor for the precise subject matter of investigation. The German event was cited to point up a serious problem in the human situation: the potentially destructive effect of obedience. But the best way to tackle the problem of obedience, from a scientific standpoint, is in no way restricted by "what happened exactly" in Germany. What happened exactly can *never* be duplicated in the laboratory or anywhere else. The real task is to learn more about the general problem of destructive obedience using a workable approach. Hopefully, such inquiry will stimulate insights and yield general propositions that can be applied to a wide variety of situations.

2. One may ask in a general way: How does a man behave when he is told by a legitimate authority to act against a third individual? In trying to find an answer to this question, the laboratory situation is one useful starting point —and for the very reason stated by Baumrind—namely, the experimenter does constitute a genuine authority for the subject. The fact that trust and dependence on the experimenter are maintained, despite the extraordinary harshness he displays toward the victim, is itself a remarkable phenomenon.

3. In the laboratory, through a set of rather simple manipulations, ordinary persons no longer perceived themselves as a responsible part of the causal chain leading to action against a person. The means through which responsibility is cast off, and individuals become thoughtless agents of action, is of general import. Other processes were revealed that indicate that the experiments will help us to understand why men obey. That understanding will come, of course, by examining the full account of experimental work and not alone the brief report in which the procedure and demonstrational results were exposed.

At root, Baumrind senses that it is not proper to test obedience in this situation, because she construes it as one in which there is no reasonable alternative to obedience. In adopting this view, she has lost sight of this fact: A substantial proportion of subjects do disobey. By their example, disobedience is shown to be a genuine possibility, one that is in no sense ruled out by the general structure of the experimental situation.

Baumrind is uncomfortable with the high level of obedience obtained in the first experiment. In the condition she focused on, 65% of the subjects obeyed to the end. However, her sentiment does not take into account that within the general framework of the psychological experiment obedience varied enormously from one condition to the next. In some variations, 90% of the subjects *dis*obeyed. It seems to be *not* only the fact of an experiment, but the particular structure of elements within the experimental situation that accounts for rates of obedience and disobedience. And these elements were varied systematically in the program of research.

A concern with human dignity is based on a respect for a man's potential to act morally. Baumrind feels that the experimenter *made* the subject shock the victim. This conception is alien to my view. The experimenter tells the subject to do something. But between the command and the outcome there is a paramount force, the acting person who may obey or disobey. I started with the belief that every person who came to the laboratory was free to accept or to reject the dictates of authority. This view sustains a conception of human dignity insofar as it sees in each man a capacity for *choosing* his own behavior. And as it turned out, many subjects did, indeed, choose to reject the experimenter's commands, providing a powerful affirmation of human ideals.

Baumrind also criticizes the experiment on the grounds that "it could easily effect an alteration in the subject's... ability to trust adult authorities in the future [p. 422]." But I do not think she can have it both ways. On the one hand, she argues the experimental situation is so special that it has no generality; on the other hand, she states it has such generalizing potential that it will cause subjects to distrust all authority. But the experimenter is not just any authority: He is an authority who tells the subject to act harshly and inhumanely against another man. I would consider it of the highest value if participation in the experiment could, indeed, inculcate a skepticism of this kind of authority. Here, perhaps, a difference in philosophy emerges most clearly. Baumrind sees the subject as a passive creature, completely controlled by the experimenter. I started from a different viewpoint. A person who comes to the laboratory is an active, choosing adult, capable of accepting or rejecting the prescriptions for action addressed to him. Baumrind sees the effect of the experiment as undermining the subject's trust of authority. I see it as a potentially valuable experience insofar as it makes people aware of the problem of indiscriminate submission to authority.

Conclusion

My feeling is that viewed in the total context of values served by the experiment, approximately the right course was followed. In review, the facts are these: *(a)* At the outset, there was the problem of studying obedience by means of a simple experimental procedure. The results could not be foreseen before the experiment was carried out. *(b)* Although the experiment generated momentary stress in some subjects, this stress dissipated quickly and was not injurious. *(c)* Dehoax and follow-up procedures were carried out to insure the subjects' well-being. *(d)* These procedures were assessed through questionnaire and psychiatric studies and were found to be effective. *(e)* Additional steps were taken to enhance the value of the laboratory experience for participants, for example, submitting to each subject a careful report on the experimental program. *(f)* The subjects themselves strongly endorse the experiment, and indicate satisfaction at having participated.

If there is a moral to be learned from the obedience study, it is that every man must be responsible for his own actions. This author accepts full responsibility for the design and execution of the study. Some people may feel it should not have been done. I disagree and accept the burden of their judgment.

Baumrind's judgment, someone has said, not only represents a personal conviction, but also reflects a cleavage in American psychology between those whose primary concern is with *helping* people and those who are interested mainly in *learning* about people. I see little value in perpetuating divisive forces in psychology when there is so much to learn from every side. A schism may exist, but it does not correspond to the true ideals of the discipline. The psychologist intent on healing knows that his power to help rests on knowledge; he is aware that a scientific grasp of all aspects of life is essential for his work, and is in itself a worthy human aspiration. At the same time, the laboratory psychologist senses his work will lead to human betterment, not only because enlightenment is more dignified than ignorance, but because new knowledge is pregnant with humane consequences.

References

BAUMRIND, D. Some thoughts on ethics of research: After reading Milgram's "Behavioral study of obedience." *Amer. Psychologist,* 1964, **19**, 421–423.

LAZARUS, R. A laboratory approach to the dynamics of psychological stress. *Amer. Psychologist,* 1964, **19**, 400–411.

MILGRAM, S. Behavioral study of obedience. *J. abnorm. soc. Psychol.,* 1963, **67**, 371–378.

MILGRAM, S. Some conditions of obedience and disobedience to authority. *Hum. Relat.,* in press.

CHALLENGE QUESTIONS

Classic Dialogue: Was Stanley Milgram's Study of Obedience Unethical?

1. Investigate the role that your college's institutional review board (see the introduction to this issue) plays in protecting subjects from undue harm.
2. Sometimes people make the wrong decisions and end up hurting other people. Apart from utilizing institutional review boards, what can researchers do to avoid making wrong decisions regarding potentially harmful studies?
3. Imagine that you have just participated in Milgram's study. How would you feel about the deception that occurred? Is it ever appropriate to deceive participants in research studies? If so, when? If not, why not?
4. Both Baumrind and Milgram might agree that there are cases in which some low-level tension for research participants is allowable. Under what conditions might it be acceptable to allow participants to experience some distress? Under what conditions is it inappropriate to subject participants to any distress?
5. Baumrind raises the issue of trust. Do you think the participants in the Milgram study lost trust in psychological researchers or authority figures in general? Why, or why not?
6. If you were on an ethics review board and the Milgram study was brought before you, would you allow Milgram to run the study? Support your answer.

ISSUE 2

Should Animals Be Used in Psychological Research?

YES: Elizabeth Baldwin, from "The Case for Animal Research in Psychology," *Journal of Social Issues* (vol. 49, no. 1, 1993)

NO: Alan D. Bowd and Kenneth J. Shapiro, from "The Case Against Laboratory Animal Research in Psychology," *Journal of Social Issues* (vol. 49, no. 1, 1993)

ISSUE SUMMARY

YES: Elizabeth Baldwin, a research ethics officer for the American Psychological Association's Science Directorate, maintains that the benefits of behavioral research with animals are substantial and that the animals are being treated humanely.

NO: Professor of educational psychology Alan D. Bowd and Kenneth J. Shapiro, executive director of Psychologists for the Ethical Treatment of Animals, argue that the harm done to animals in this research is not widely known and that the "benefits" are not sufficient to balance this cruelty.

Until relatively recently, humans were thought to be distinctly different from lower animals. Only humans were considered to have self-consciousness, rationality, and language. Today, however, these distinctions appear to have been blurred by modern research. Many scientists, for example, believe that chimpanzees use language symbols and that many animals have some type of consciousness.

This apparent lack of hard and fast distinctions between humans and other animals has many implications. One of these concerns the use of animals in experimental research. For hundreds of years animals have been considered tools of research. In fact, research ethics has demanded that most experimental treatments be tested on animals before they are tested on humans. Another view, however, has come to the fore. Because there is no clear distinction between lower and higher animals, this view asserts, the lower animals should be accorded the same basic rights as humans. Animal experimentation, from this perspective, cannot be taken for granted; it must be justified on the same moral and ethical grounds as research on humans. This perspective has recently gained considerable momentum as supporters have become politically organized.

Elizabeth Baldwin disagrees with this perspective. In the following selection, she argues that animals should be used in psychological research and that although people should be held responsible for the humane treatment of animals, animals do not have the same rights as humans. Baldwin describes the important role that animals have played in improving the human condition through research and how animal research benefits the health and welfare of other animals. Baldwin argues that many people are not aware of the many federal regulations and laws that protect animals from inhumane treatment. Ultimately, she contends, humans and animals cannot be viewed as essentially the same, with the same ethics and rights.

In the second selection, Alan D. Bowd and Kenneth J. Shapiro do not concur with this view. Their case against the use of animals for psychological research hinges on the idea that these animals are denied basic rights. Bowd and Shapiro have developed what they call a "scale of invasiveness," which is an index of the suffering and harm done to animals before, during, and after an experimental procedure. Unlike Baldwin, they argue that federal laws and regulations are not sufficient because they do not consider the animals. Bowd and Shapiro also maintain that the research revealing the harm done to animals is not being published and, in turn, is not being sufficiently recognized. Consequently, they suggest that alternatives to the use of animals in laboratory research be found.

POINT

- Animals do not have the same rights as humans, but people have a responsibility to ensure the humane treatment of animals.
- There are elaborate federal regulations protecting animals in research, as well as state laws and professional guidelines on the care of animals.
- Society has made a collective judgment that the benefits derived from animal research far outweigh the costs.
- Animals have played a pivotal role in improving the human condition and, in return, society should strive to treat them well.

COUNTERPOINT

- Those who accord rights to human beings and deny them to other species must show a morally relevant difference between these species.
- Many species are not covered by the Animal Welfare Act and are therefore not reported as part of federally mandated inspections.
- In contrast to the uncertain benefits of laboratory animal research, the cost to animals is clear and real.
- The benefits of animal research are indeterminate because they depend on unknowns, such as human welfare.

Elizabeth Baldwin  **YES**

The Case for Animal Research
in Psychology

Animal liberationists do not separate out the human animal. A rat is a pig is a dog is a boy.

—Ingrid Newkirk, Director, People for the
Ethical Treatment of Animals.

The shock value of this quote has made it a favorite of those defending the use of animals in research. It succinctly states the core belief of many animal rights activists who oppose the use of animals in research. Although some activists work for improved laboratory conditions for research animals, recent surveys suggest that most activists would like to eliminate animal research entirely (Plous, 1991). These activists believe animals have rights equal to humans and therefore should not be used as subjects in laboratory research.

The debate over animal research can be confusing unless one understands the very different goals of animal welfare organizations and animal rights groups. People concerned with animal welfare seek to improve laboratory conditions for research animals and to reduce the number of animals needed. These mainstream goals encompass traditional concerns for the humane treatment of animals, and most researchers share these goals. In contrast, the views of animal rights activists are *not* mainstream, since there are few people who would agree with the above quote from Ingrid Newkirk. Indeed, in a national poll conducted by the National Science Foundation, half the respondents answered the following question affirmatively: "Should scientists be allowed to do research that causes pain and injury to animals like dogs and chimpanzees if it produces new information about human health problems?" (National Science Board, 1991). These findings are particularly impressive given the explicit mention of "pain and injury" to popular animals such as dogs and chimpanzees. My own position is that animals do not have rights in the same sense that humans do, but that people have a responsibility to ensure the humane treatment of animals under their care. Animals have played a pivotal role in improving the human condition, and in return, society should strive to treat them well.

From Elizabeth Baldwin, "The Case for Animal Research in Psychology," *Journal of Social Issues,* vol. 49, no. 1 (1993), pp. 121–129. Copyright © 1993 by The Society for the Psychological Study of Social Issues. Reprinted by permission of Blackwell Publishers Ltd. References omitted.

Background

The modern animal rights movement is intellectual and spiritual heir to the Victorian antivivisection movement in Britain (Sperling, 1988). This 19th-century movement was a powerful force in Britain and arose in part from accelerating changes brought about by science and technology (and the resulting challenges to the prevailing view of humanity's relationship to nature).

The British movement peaked in 1876 with the passage of the Cruelty to Animals Act. This compromise legislation required licenses for conducting animal research, but recognized the societal value of continuing to use animals in research. It was about this time that the scientific community began to organize a defense of animal research. Several challenges to animal research were made in the ensuing 20 years, but in the end, the medical and scientific community were able to successfully protect their interests. The Victorian antivivisection movement, however, did bring about the regulation of research and helped prevent outright abuse (Sperling, 1988).

The beginning of the modern animal rights movement is generally dated to the 1975 publication of *Animal Liberation* by philosopher Peter Singer. Although Singer himself is not an advocate of animal "rights," he provided the groundwork for later arguments that animals have rights—including the right not to be used in research. Most animal rights activists believe animals have a right not to be used for research, food, entertainment, and a variety of other purposes. An inordinate amount of attention is devoted to animal research, however, even though far fewer animals are used for research than for other purposes (Nicoll & Russell, 1990).

There has been a phenomenal growth in the animal rights movement since the publication of Singer's book. People for the Ethical Treatment of Animals (PETA), the leading animal rights organization in the United States, has grown from 18 members in 1981 to more than 250,000 members in 1990. (McCabe, 1990). By any standard, the animal rights movement is a force to be reckoned with.

Philosophical Issues

There are two basic philosophies that support the animal rights movement, although activists are often unable to articulate them (Sperling, 1988). These two positions are summarized by Herzog (1990) as the *utilitarian* argument and the *rights* argument.

The utilitarian position is that the greatest good is achieved by maximizing pleasure and happiness, and by minimizing suffering and pain. Although traditionally applied only to humans, Singer argues that animals should be included when considering the greatest good. He states, "No matter what the nature of the being, the principle of equality requires that its suffering be counted equally with the like suffering—insofar as rough comparisons can be made—of any other being" (Singer, 1990, p. 8). Utilitarians would thus argue that animals have an interest equal to that of humans in avoiding pain and suffering, and should therefore not be used in experiments that could cause them harm. Two problems with this philosophy are that (1) it is hard to draw a line between creatures that suffer and creatures that do not, and (2) the argument does not address *qualitative* differences in pain and pleasure across species (Herzog, 1990).

The rights position states that animals possess certain rights based on their inherent value. This philosophy, first developed by Tom Regan (1983), argues that animals have a right not to be used by humans in research (and for many other purposes). Major problems with this position arise in deciding just what rights are and in determining who is entitled to hold them (Herzog, 1990).

While the above positions have been developed relatively recently, the alternative view of animals as qualitatively different from humans has a long history in Judeo-Christian thought. Traditionally, humans were believed to have been created in the image of God and to have dominion over animals. Robb (1988) uses this perspective in arguing that humans are unique by virtue of their capacity for moral choice. Because of this capacity, humans can be held responsible for their choices, and can therefore enter into contractual agreements with binding rights and responsibilities for *both* parties. Robb acknowledges that some animals have human capacities in certain areas, but he argues that this does not make them morally equal to humans or give them rights that take precedence over human needs.

The most persuasive argument for using animals in behavioral research, however, is the untold benefit that accrues to both humans and animals. The benefits of behavioral research with animals have been enumerated by such authors as Miller (1985) and King and Yarbrough (1985), and for most people, these benefits are the reason that they support the continued use of animals in research. This argument—which is basically utilitarian—is the one most often cited by the research community in defense of animal research. In contrast to Singer's utilitarianism, however, animals are not given the same degree of consideration as people.

In conclusion, both sides in the animal rights debate have philosophical underpinnings to support their position, but what often emerges in the rhetoric is not reasoned debate but emotion-laden charges and personal attacks. This is not surprising, given the strong passions aroused in the discussion.

Framing the Debate

In the 1980s, activists targeted certain researchers or areas of research that they viewed as vulnerable to attack, and researchers were forced to assume a defensive posture. Unfortunately, activists were right about the vulnerability of individual scientists; little or no institutional defense was mounted against these early attacks. The prevailing attitude was to ignore the activists in hopes that they would go away, and thus attract less attention from the public and the press. This passivity left the early targets of animal rights activists in the position of a man asked, "Why do you beat your wife?" No matter how researchers responded, they sounded defensive and self-serving. It took several years for the research community to realize that animal rights activists were not going away, and that the activists' charges needed to be answered in a systematic and serious manner.

This early failure on the part of the research community to communicate its position effectively left the public with little information beyond what was provided by the animal rights activists. Framing the debate is half the battle, and the research community was left playing catch-up and answering the question, "Why do you abuse your research animals?"

The research community also faced the daunting task of explaining the use of animals in research to a public whose understanding of the scientific method was almost nil. The most difficult misconception to correct was the belief that every research project with animals should produce "useful" results (Orem, 1990). Social scientists who have received Senator William Proxmire's "Golden Fleece Award" are well aware of this line of thinking—a line of thinking that displays a complete misunderstanding of how science works, and ignores the vast amount of basic research that typically precedes each "useful" discovery.

It is difficult for scientific rationales to compete with shocking posters, catchy slogans, and soundbites from the animal rights movement. The most effective response from the scientific community has been to point out innumerable health advances made possible by the use of animals as research models. This approach is something that most people can relate to, since everyone has benefited from these advances.

The early defensive posture of scientists also failed to allay public concerns about the ability of researchers to self-regulate their care and use of research animals. Unlike the participation of humans in research (who are usually able to speak in their own defense and give consent), there seemed to be no one in the system able to "speak" for the animals. Or so people were encouraged to believe by animal rights activists. As discussed below, there are elaborate federal regulations on the use of animals in research, as well as state laws and professional guidelines on the care and use of animals in research.

Restoring Trust

Scientists, research institutions, and federal research agencies finally came to realize that the charges being leveled by animal rights activists needed to be publicly—and forcefully—rebutted. Dr. Frederick Goodwin, former Administrator of the Alcohol, Drug Abuse, and Mental Health Administration (ADAMHA), was one of the first federal officials to defend animal research publicly, and point out the difference between animal welfare and animal rights (Booth, 1989). Recently, many more federal officials and respected researchers have publicly spoken on the importance of animal research (Mervis, 1990).

Countering Misinformation

Animal rights literature often uses misleading images to depict animal research —images such as animals grimacing as they are shocked with electricity. These descriptions lead readers to believe animals are routinely subjected to high voltage shocks capable of producing convulsions (e.g., Singer, 1990, pp. 42–45). Such propaganda is far from the truth. In most cases, electric shock (when used at all) is relatively mild—similar to what one might feel from the discharge of static electricity on a cold, dry day. Even this relatively mild use of shock is carefully reviewed by Institutional Animal Care and Use Committees before being approved, and researchers must demonstrate that alternate techniques are not feasible. Stronger shock *is* used in animal research, but it is used to study medical problems such as epilepsy (a convulsive disorder). It is also used to test the effectiveness and side effects of drugs developed to control such disorders. It is not within the scope of this article to refute the myriad charges issued against animal research in general, specific projects, and individual researchers. Suffice it to say that such allegations have been persuasively refuted (Coile & Miller, 1984; Feeney, 1987; Johnson, 1990; McCabe, 1986).

Benefits to Animals

Animal rights activists often fail to appreciate the many benefits to animals that have resulted from animal research. Behavioral research has contributed to improvements in the environments of captive animals, including those used in research (Novak & Petto, 1991). The list of benefits also includes a host of veterinary procedures and the development of vaccines for deadly diseases such as rabies, Lyme disease, and feline leukemia. Research in reproductive biology and captive breeding programs are also the only hope for some animals on the brink of extinction (King et al., 1988).

Regulations and Guidelines

It is clear that many people concerned about the use of animals in research are not aware of the elaborate structure that exists to regulate the care and use of animals in research. This system includes federal regulations under the Animal Welfare Act (U.S. Department of Agriculture, 1989, 1990, 1991), Public Health Service (PHS) policy (Office for Protection from Research Risks, 1986), and state laws that govern the availability of pound animals for research.

The Animal Welfare Act, most recently amended in 1985, is enforced by the USDA's Animal and Plant Health Inspection Service (APHIS). The regulations connected with this law include 127 pages of guidelines governing the use of animals in research. It also includes unannounced inspections of animal research facilities by APHIS inspectors who do nothing but inspect research facilities. Their inspections are conducted to ensure compliance with regulations that include everything from cage size, feeding schedules, and lighting to exercise requirements for dogs and the promotion of psychological well-being among nonhuman primates.

In addition to APHIS inspectors who make unannounced inspections of animal research facilities, there are local Institutional Animal Care and Use Committees (IACUCs) that review each proposed research project using animals. Research proposals must include a justification for the species used and the number of animals required, an assurance that a thorough literature review has been conducted (to prevent unnecessary replication of research), and a consideration of alternatives if available. IACUCs are also responsible for inspecting local animal research facilities to check for continued compliance with state protocols.

Each grant proposal received by a PHS agency (National Institutes of Health, and the Centers for Disease Control) that proposes using animals must contain an assurance that it has been reviewed by an IACUC and been approved. IACUCs must have no less than five members and contain at least one veterinarian, one practicing scientist experienced in research involving animals, one member who is primarily concerned in nonscientific matters (e.g., a lawyer or ethicist), and one member who is not affiliated with the institution in any way and is not an immediate family member of anyone affiliated with the institution (Office for Protection from Research Risks, 1986; USDA, 1989).

Beyond federal animal welfare regulations, PHS policy, and the PHS Guidelines (National Research Council, 1985), there are professional guidelines for the care and use of research animals. Examples include the American Psychological Association's (APA) *Ethical Principles of Psychologists* (1990) and *Guidelines for Ethical Conduct in the Care and Use of Animals* (1993), and the Society for Neuroscience's Handbook (Society for Neuroscience, 1991).

The APA also has a Committee on Animal Research and Ethics (CARE) whose charge includes the responsibility to "review the ethics of animal experimentation and recommend guidelines for the ethical conduct of research, and appropriate care of animals in research." CARE wrote the APA's *Guidelines for Ethical Conduct in the Care and Use of Animals,* and periodically reviews it and makes revisions. These guidelines are widely used by psychologists and other scientists, and have been used in teaching research ethics at the undergraduate and graduate level. The APA's Science Directorate provided support for a conference on psychological well-being of nonhuman primates used in research, and published a volume of proceedings from that conference (Novak & Petto, 1991). The APA also helps promote research on animal welfare by membership in and support for such organizations as the American Association for the Accreditation of Laboratory Animal Care (AAALAC).

AAALAC is the only accrediting body recognized by the PHS, and sets the "gold standard" for animal research facilities. To receive AAALAC accreditation, an institution must go beyond what is required by federal animal welfare regulations and PHS policy. AAALAC accreditation is highly regarded, and those institutions that receive it serve as models for the rest of the research community.

Even with all these safeguards in place, some critics question the ability of the research community to self-regulate its use of animals in research. The system can only be considered self-regulating, however, if one assumes that researchers, institutional officials, members of IACUCs (which must include a member not affiliated with the institution), USDA inspectors, animal care and lab technicians, and veterinarians have identical interests. These are the individuals with the most direct access to the animals used in research, and these are the specialists most knowledgeable about the conditions under which animals are used in research.

In several states, animal rights activists have succeeded in gaining access to IACUC meetings where animal research proposals are discussed. On the whole, however, research institutions have fought—and are still fighting —to keep these meetings closed to the general public. There is a very real fear among researchers that information gleaned from such meetings will be used to harass and target individual researchers. Given the escalating nature of illegal break-ins by such organizations as the Animal Liberation Front, this is a legitimate concern. Indeed, on some campuses "reward posters" offer money to individuals who report the abuse of research animals.

Even though IACUC meetings are generally closed to the public, the elaborate system regulating animal research is by no means a closed one. The most recent animal welfare regulations were finalized after five years of proposals recorded in the *Federal Register;* comments from the public, research institutions, professional associations, animal welfare groups, and animal rights groups; the incorporation of these comments; republication of the revised rules; and so forth. Neither researchers nor animal rights groups were entirely pleased with the final document, but everyone had their say. Although certain elements of the regulatory system rely on researchers, it is hard to imagine a workable system that would fail to use their expertise. The unspoken assumption that researchers cannot be trusted to care for their research animals is not supported by the records of APHIS inspections. Good science demands good laboratory animal care, and it is in a researcher's best interest to ensure that laboratory animals are well cared for.

The Benefits of Behavioral Research With Animals

The use of animals in psychological and behavioral research was an early target of animal rights activists. This research was perceived as a more vulnerable target than biomedical research, which had more direct and easily explained links to specific human health benefits. Psychological and behavioral research also lacked the powerful backing of the medical establishment (Archer, 1986).

There is, of course, a long list of benefits derived from psychological research with animals. These include rehabilitation of persons suffering from stroke, head injury, spinal cord injury, and Alzheimer's disease; improved communication with severely retarded children; methods for the early detection of eye disorders in children (allowing preventive treatment to avoid permanent impairment); control of chronic anxiety without the use of drugs; and improved treatments for alcoholism, obesity, substance abuse, hypertension, chronic migraine headaches, lower back pain, and insomnia (Miller, 1985). Behavioral research with nonhuman primates also permits the investigation of complex behaviors such as social organization, aggression, learning and memory, communication, and growth and development (King et al., 1988).

The nature of psychological and behavioral research makes the development and use of alternatives difficult. It is the behavior of the whole organism, and the interaction among various body systems, that is examined. Computer models may be used, but "research with animals will still be needed to provide basic data for writing computer software, as well as to prove the validity and reliability of computer alternatives" (U.S. Congress, Office of Technology Assessment, 1986). The alternative of using nonliving systems may be possible with epidemiologic data bases for some behavioral research, but chemical and physical systems are not useful for modeling complex behaviors. Likewise, in vitro cultures of organs, tissues, and cells do not display the characteristics studied by psychologists.

Conclusion

Research psychologists have been asked to eschew emotionalism, and bring logic and reason to the debate over animal research (Bowd, 1990). This is certainly the style most researchers are comfortable with—yet they have also been advised to quit trying to "apply logic and reason in their responses [to animal rights activists]" (Culliton, 1991). Culliton warns that while "animal rights people go for the heart, the biologists go for the head" and are losing the public in the process.

Which path is best? A reasoned approach draws high marks for civility, but will it help scientists in their trench warfare with animal rights activists?

Do animals have rights that preclude their use in laboratory research? I, and the psychologists I help represent, would say no. But researchers do have responsibilities to the animals they use in their research. These responsibilities include ensuring the humane care of their research animals, using the minimum number of animals necessary, and seeing to it that all laboratory assistants are adequately trained and supervised. As stated in the APA's *Ethical Principles,* "Laws and regulations notwithstanding, an animal's immediate protection depends upon the scientist's own conscience" (APA, 1990).

Researchers and others concerned with animal welfare can engage in a useful dialogue as standards of care and use evolve. This dialogue has proven fruitless with animal rights activists, though, since they seem unwilling to compromise or consider other viewpoints. What is the middle ground for a discussion with someone whose goal is the elimination of all research on animals?

The collective decision society has made is that the benefits derived from animal research far outweigh the costs. As public opinion polls indicate, most people are willing to accept these costs but want assurances that animals are humanely cared for. Yes, I'm "speciesist" in the eyes of Ingrid Newkirk—I will never believe my son is a dog is a pig is a rat.

Alan D. Bowd and Kenneth J. Shapiro  **NO**

The Case Against Laboratory Animal Research in Psychology

In this article, we will (1) present empirical evidence documenting several serious problems with the use of animals in psychology, (2) consider philosophical objections to the use of animals in invasive research, (3) give an overview of how the research community has responded to these concerns, and (4) suggest directions for change.

The Problem

The number of nonhuman animals used in psychological research in the United States is difficult to estimate. Many species are not covered by the Animal Welfare Act and are therefore not reported as part of federally mandated inspections (Rowan & Andrutis, 1990). The Animal Legal Defense Fund (a nonprofit animal protection group) is currently challenging this loophole, but at present, rats, mice, and birds—which comprise roughly 90% of all nonhuman research subjects—are not considered "animals" under the Animal Welfare Act. Attempts to arrive at estimates from departmental surveys, analyses of *Psychological Abstracts,* and extrapolations from countries where better records are kept all have their limitations, but integrating these sources of information, we estimate that roughly 1–2 million animals are used in psychological research each year.

Although some laboratory animals are obtained from shelters—a practice that is illegal in 14 states and is abhorred by a majority of the public—most laboratory animals are "purpose bred" for research. This method of procuring subjects is not without problems, however. For example, the legal office of the United States Department of Agriculture is currently investigating a major producer of animals for alleged abuse (Holden, 1990). Other problems with producing animals for laboratory research arise from selective breeding and genetic engineering. Producing animals that are susceptible to audiogenic seizures or cancerous tumors, or that adapt well to confinement, raises significant ethical questions (President's Commission, 1982).

From Alan D. Bowd and Kenneth J. Shapiro, "The Case Against Laboratory Animal Research in Psychology," *Journal of Social Issues,* vol. 49, no. 1 (1993), pp. 133–142. Copyright © 1993 by The Society for the Psychological Study of Social Issues. Reprinted by permission of Blackwell Publishers Ltd. References omitted.

Invasiveness in Research

In reviewing laboratory practices, it is important to distinguish between the experimental procedure itself and pre- or postexperimental care (i.e., "husbandry"). It is also critical to separate individual cases of abuse from customary practices. The case of the Silver Spring monkeys, for example, is an instance of individual abuse that became a cause célèbre of the animal rights movement. Charges against psychologist Edward Taub centered on abusive husbandry practices—inadequate veterinary care, food, ventilation, and cage space. However, much of the public outcry reflected objections to the experimental procedure (deafferentation) itself (Shapiro, 1989).

An example of a routine experimental procedure under scrutiny is the use of chair restraints. Primates that are chair restrained as part of a study spend a mean time of 5.7 hours confined in the chair each day (Bayne, 1991). An example of a customary husbandry practice under scrutiny is the housing of primates in individual cages. In one survey, 84% of the investigators housed their adult primates singly (Bayne, 1991), despite the importance of social interaction to these animals. Thus, quite apart from any trauma induced by experimental procedures, the animals suffered from routine husbandry practices.

Contrary to what defenders of animal research often say, a good deal of psychological research is highly invasive. Many studies involve stress, pain, punishment, social and environmental deprivation, and induced emotional and intellectual deficits. In their "scale of invasiveness," Field and Shapiro (1988) operationalized the term to encompass suffering and harm before, during, or after an experimental procedure. By this definition, most investigators targeted by the animal rights movement have conducted highly invasive research (e.g., maternal deprivation and drug addiction in macaques, physiology of taste in rats, visual deprivation in kittens). Beyond their invasiveness, these studies have been criticized for their nongeneralizability, redundancy, purely theoretical focus, parametric tinkering, and diversion of funds from treatment programs.

Areas of highly invasive research have shifted over time. In 1947, electroconvulsive shock and audiogenic seizures were prevalent, while in 1967 punishment, brain lesioning, and the administration of curare were more common (Field, 1988). The most frequently cited invasive studies in popular college introductory psychology textbooks (1984–1988 editions) are infant maternal deprivation, perceptual restriction in newborns, brain studies of the eating/satiety center, and learned helplessness (Field, 1990).

As a popular college major, psychology influences thousands of students each year. Typically, psychology coursework includes direct exposure to animal research in laboratories and/or indirect exposure through texts and audiovisual materials that feature animal research. Yet descriptions of invasive research in popular psychology textbooks are often sanitized (Field, 1989). For example, most discussions of Harlow's work on maternal deprivation—the most frequently cited invasive experiment—minimize the suffering involved, present pictures of "cute" animals, and omit reference to the subjective experience of the animals.

Ethical Issues

The animal rights movement began to have an impact on psychology shortly after the publication of Singer's *Animal Liberation* and Ryder's *Victims of Science* (both in 1975). Both books targeted behavioral research in particular for its painful and unnecessary experiments. The ethical foundation of the animal rights movement has since been broadened to include several other discourses: Regan (1983) provided a theory of rights to complement Singer's utilitarianism, Adams (1990) developed a feminist discourse that linked the subjugation of animals with patriarchy, and several authors provided theological perspectives on the use of animals (Linzey, 1987; McDaniel, 1989; Regenstein, 1991).

Experimental psychologists have been forced to defend their ethical positions with rational arguments. Many psychologists consider ethics a matter of personal preference, a view that exempts individuals from public scrutiny and justifies individual self-regulation. Others have attempted to reduce ethics to science, arguing that ethics is a naturally evolved phenomenon and that regulation from outside the field is inappropriate (e.g., Gallup & Suarez, 1980). However, the burgeoning field of moral philosophy suggests that ethical positions—like any other human beliefs—are subject to logical examination, and may be found to be ambiguous or contradictory.

Following Ryder (1989) and Rollin (1981), here we propose an ethic that draws upon the work of both Singer and Regan. To wit:

Interests and rights are not the sole preserve of the human species, and should be evaluated consistently and with due consideration to an animal's capacity to suffer. Our ethical obligations extend to individuals who are intellectually unable to reciprocate them, within and beyond our own species. Those who would accord rights to human beings but deny them to all other species must make the case that there is a morally relevant difference separating *Homo sapiens* from other creatures. We do not believe such a difference exists.

All creatures capable of experiencing pain and other forms of suffering have an interest in being spared it, and the rights that flow from this interest vary from individual to individual and species to species. Although this point may seem obvious, animal protectionists are often ridiculed for believing all animals are identical or for advocating that farm animals be given the right to vote. Such caricatures (usually based on quotations taken out of context) make easy targets and avoid serious discussion.

Many proponents of invasive research argue that the work is justified by morally relevant differences that exist between the human species and all others. However, by focusing on attributes such as intelligence, empathy, and a sense of moral responsibility (e.g., Fox, 1986; King, 1986), they exclude young children and developmentally delayed adults from moral consideration. Because humans and nonhumans overlap on some of these dimensions (e.g., intelligence, self-awareness), and because young or impaired humans wholly lack other characteristics (e.g., empathy, sense of moral responsibility), there is simply no morally relevant attribute that separates humans from nonhumans. To base ethical decisions on species membership alone in the absence of such an attribute is as arbitrary as relying on skin color or gender in hiring decisions.

The most morally relevant factor in a decision to cause suffering to others is their ability to experience it. Cognitive competence and related abilities are relevant to certain human rights (such as the right to vote), but not to other rights (such as the freedom to move one's limbs or to interact with others). Research justified by consequent human benefit abridges these rights. We feel methods involving inescapable pain, deprivation, or fear are unacceptable because each sentient being, regardless of its other capabilities, has an interest in being spared suffering. Modern-day society rejects the notion of performing painful experiments on humans who are incapable of granting consent, regardless of the benefits which might accrue to others. In the absence of morally relevant distinctions between ourselves and other animals, painful research on sentient nonhumans should be rejected for the same reasons.

The Response From Psychologists

Social constructionists and others have recently noted the Western, ethnocentric, and male-dominated agenda of traditional psychological research (Gergen, 1985; Hare-Mustin & Marecek, 1990; Irvine & Berry, 1988). The broad cultural changes represented by the women's movement, environmentalism, and the animal rights movement have been instrumental in fomenting the current debate within psychology regarding animal research, and many analysts now view the practice of invasive laboratory-based research as symptomatic of anthropocentrism in psychology.

Within the psychological community, a growing number of individuals have expressed reservations about animal research on both scientific and ethical grounds (Bowd, 1980, 1990; Fox, 1982; Giannelli, 1985; Segal, 1982; Shapiro, 1991; Ulrich, 1991). Nonetheless, many psychologists have defended current practices. We will first examine organizational responses and then discuss responses within the professional literature. The focus will be on developments in the United States, though it should be noted that similar debates are taking place among psychologists in Canada, Great Britain, Australia, and other countries.

Organizational Responses

In 1981, the American Psychological Association (APA) amended its Ethics Code to include the treatment of animals (American Psychological Association [APA], 1981). However, the APA Ethics Committee considered only one animal welfare case from 1982 to 1990 (APA, 1991)—a period during which the animal rights movement charged several laboratories with specific animal welfare violations. The Ethics Committee considered the case of Edward Taub, a psychologist who studied deafferentation (the severing of sensory nerves) in macaque monkeys at the Institute for Behavioral Research in Maryland. This case came to light after Alex Pacheco, cofounder of People for the Ethical Treatment of Animals, documented several explicit violations of animal welfare regulations.

According to Principle 10 of the current Ethics Code, researchers must ensure that "The acquisition, care, use and disposal of all animals are in compliance of current Federal, state or provincial, and local laws and regulations" (APA, 1981). After reviewing Pacheco's evidence, the National Institutes of Health (NIH) suspended Taub's grant because of violations in NIH guidelines, and Taub was convicted of cruelty to animals under Maryland law (a verdict that he later appealed). Nevertheless, even though the suspension of funding and the conviction of animal cruelty were known by members of the APA Ethics Committee, the panel cleared Taub of any wrongdoing on a split vote.

A second APA body charged with overseeing animal welfare, the Committee on Animal Research and Ethics (CARE), was established in 1925 "to combat attempts to prevent or restrict [animal experimentation]" (Young, 1928). In fact, the two events that led to the formation of CARE were both legislative efforts, outside APA, to curtail animal research (Young, 1928; Young, 1930). For the first 50 years of its existence, CARE's stated purpose was to defend and protect animal *research*, not *animals*. It was not until the early 1980s that the task of protecting animals was added (CARE, 1980), and even then the meetings continued to focus on the protection of animal research and animal researchers (Bernstein, personal communication, 1990). Furthermore, Field, Shapiro, and Carr (1990) found that the animal research conducted by recent CARE chairs was more invasive than comparable research published in leading journals. Thus, the APA responded to ethical challenges by forming advocacy groups rather than impartial or balanced review panels.

Responses Within the Professional Literature

APA publications have discussed animal welfare with increasing frequency in recent years (Phillips & Sechzer, 1989). However, in its scientific and news publications, the APA often takes a one-sided position (Bowd, 1990). We examined issues of the *APA Monitor* from 1980 to 1986, and found 30 articles and 43 letters dealing with the ethics of animal research. By our estimate, roughly 60% supported animal research and only 10% opposed it explicitly. Similarly, the *American Psychologist* published 17 relevant articles or commentaries during the same period, 10 advocating animal research and 7 opposing it. Of the 5 full-length articles that appeared during this interval, 4 explicitly supported animal research.

A recent article in the *APA Monitor* typifies this slant in coverage. Moses (1991) described how psychology students were upset by a laboratory break-in, but failed to mention a much more widespread source of student concern about animal research—the refusal of faculty to provide alternatives to the laboratory study of animals. In a recent survey of 300 psychology departments, one of the authors (KJS) found that 50% of the departments used animals in education, and of these, only 40% had a policy to accommodate students who objected.

Indeed, not only do APA publications neglect to mention such problems —the APA actively discourages their discussion. For example, the APA refused to sell exhibit space at its 1991 convention to Psychologists for the Ethical Treatment of Animals for the purpose of displaying publications, although other organizations were provided with space to display animal research publications and catalogues of laboratory equipment (Shapiro, 1990).

Turning to the scientific literature, most accounts defend animal research with some version of the following arguments: (1) animal research leads to applications that improve human welfare; (2) the costs to animals are relatively small; (3) whatever harm the animals incur is necessary, because there are no viable alternatives to animal research (Gallup & Suarez, 1985; King, 1984; Miller, 1985).

The tenor of these articles tends to be indignant, adversarial, and defensive. In fact, in their survey of the scientific literature, Phillips and Sechzer (1989) found a marked increase in defensiveness between the 1960s and the 1980s. Gluck and Kubacki (1991) have also described a "strategic defensive posture" assumed by researchers, part of which is to trivialize the issue of animal protection. For example, some researchers trivialize the issue by pointing out that laboratory rats fare better than their uncaged city conspecifics (e.g., Gallup & Suarez, 1987). Typically, there is little empirical evidence offered to support such assertions, and in many cases, the arguments are specious (Shapiro, 1988). For example, Gallup and Suarez (1987) failed to provide evidence about the relative welfare of laboratory and feral rats, although data are available regarding invasiveness of procedures undergone by the former, and Hendrickson (1983) found that rats in urban nonlaboratory settings often proliferate and live quite well. Furthermore, the suffering of laboratory rats is additional; its cost must be added to whatever suffering other rats endure. The argument advanced by Gallup and Suarez (1987) is particularly ironic given their portrayal of scientists as rational and animal activists as illogical and emotional.

Assessment of Costs and Benefits

Miller (1985) and other authors have claimed that animal research generates applications that improve human welfare. However, Kelly (1986) found that in the 1984 volume of the *Journal of Consulting and Clinical Psychology* (a journal devoted to studies of the treatments Miller explicitly linked to animal research), only 0.3% of more than 3,000 citations were of laboratory animal studies. In addition, Giannelli (1985) found that only seven of the 118 citations selected by Miller to demonstrate the value of animal research were listed in the 1985 Association for Advanced Training in the Behavioral Sciences, a well-known and comprehensive course for national licensure in psychology. Even more problematically, the potential benefits of any animal research are indeterminate, for they depend on several unknowns: the applicability of the results to human welfare, the question of whether the study will get published (rejection rates for mainstream psychology journals are over 50%), and more subtly, the *missed benefits of studies not undertaken*. Any research program implies paths not taken.

In contrast to the uncertain benefits from laboratory animal research, the cost to animals is clear and real. Reliable measures of the cost to animals do exist (Field & Shapiro, 1988), yet virtually no published study—or study proposal—presents detailed analyses of the costs of husbandry conditions, experimental procedures, and disposition of the animals. In any case, any analysis of costs to animals presumes they are willing participants. In truth, in the current research enterprise they are commodities produced, confined, and harmed in a system in which they are only incidental beneficiaries. Yet in our Western tradition, individuals have rights that safeguard against their welfare being compromised for the benefit of others. Because of these operational and ethical problems, cost–benefit analyses are an unsatisfactory tool in the assessment of the use of animals in research.

Suggested Directions

As an interim strategy, we favor the following: (1) the development of alternatives to laboratory animal research; (2) the specification and prohibition of experimental procedures that are deemed "intrinsically objectionable" (Heim, 1978)—that is, procedures generally agreed to be so invasive that they are objectionable regardless of possible benefits; and (3) a reduced reliance on the search for animal models of complex, culturally generated human phenomena. These practices should replace the hollow, justificatory language of cost–benefit analyses. In the longer term, we favor a shift from laboratory-based invasive research to minimally manipulative research conducted in naturalistic and seminaturalistic settings.

We urge psychologists, individually and through professional societies such as the APA, to (1) establish advocacy committees charged solely with the protection of animals used in psychology-related settings, (2) develop alternatives for students who object to the use of laboratory animals, and (3) include balanced coverage of animal welfare issues and a discussion of ethical issues in professional and textbook publications. Such policies will not only contribute to animal welfare—they will contribute to *human* welfare by broadening the education of tomorrow's psychologists.

CHALLENGE QUESTIONS

Should Animals Be Used in Psychological Research?

1. How and where would you draw the line on the use of animals in research? Even if the use of animals is justified in research that saves human lives, is the use of animals justified in cosmetic or plastic surgery research? Why, or why not?
2. Assuming you were against all instances of animal research, would you turn down medical procedures for yourself or your children because they were developed at the expense of animals? Would there be exceptions, such as vaccinations for your children or a cure for a life-threatening illness?
3. Baldwin makes the case that experimentation with animals has produced many important medical and psychological findings. Are there other types of research that use animals? Is this other research justified? Why, or why not?
4. Baldwin argues that the use of animals in research has been beneficial to animals as well as to humans. Does this assertion change the debate?
5. Locate the federal and state regulations on the use and care of animals in psychological research, and evaluate both authors' arguments regarding the sufficiency of those regulations.

ISSUE 3

Is the *Consumer Reports* Conclusion That "Psychotherapy Helps" Valid?

YES: Martin E. P. Seligman, from "The Effectiveness of Psychotherapy: The *Consumer Reports* Study," *American Psychologist* (December 1995)

NO: Neil S. Jacobson and Andrew Christensen, from "Studying the Effectiveness of Psychotherapy: How Well Can Clinical Trials Do the Job?" *American Psychologist* (October 1996)

ISSUE SUMMARY

YES: Psychotherapy researcher Martin E. P. Seligman defends the conclusion of *Consumer Reports* that psychotherapy is effective by pointing to the importance of client satisfaction in the actual settings in which the clients are treated.

NO: Psychotherapy researchers Neil S. Jacobson and Andrew Christensen contend that the *Consumer Reports* study is essentially the same as 40-year-old studies that have long been rejected as inadequate.

In 1994 *Consumer Reports* (*CR*), the well-known evaluator of appliances and automobiles (among other things), decided to evaluate something it had never evaluated before—the effectiveness of psychotherapy. True to its own philosophy, *CR* surveyed the consumers of psychotherapy to determine how these consumers felt about their treatment. Twenty-six questions about people's experiences with mental health professionals were asked, including questions about presenting problems, therapist competence, type of therapy, and satisfaction with treatment.

In the November 1995 issue *CR* published its controversial but seemingly clear-cut findings. Perhaps the most noteworthy finding was that over 90 percent of the people who responded to the survey found psychotherapy to be beneficial. Although this specific percentage can be disputed, other research has supported the overall conclusion that psychotherapy is generally helpful. (See, for example, Allen E. Bergin and Sol L. Garfield, eds., *Handbook of Psychotherapy and Behavior Change*, John Wiley, 1994.) This general conclusion is not the root of the controversy. The root of the controversy is the methods that *CR* used to reach its conclusion. Most mainstream psychotherapy researchers favor experimental methods—with control groups and manipulated variables—to evaluate psychotherapy's effectiveness. *CR*'s conclusions were reached without such methods. Were *CR*'s methods valid? If they were not, then the conclusion that "psychotherapy helps" would itself be in question.

In the following selection, Martin E. P. Seligman defends *CR*'s methods by making a distinction between efficacy research and effectiveness research. Efficacy research pertains to the experimental type of design that most researchers favor. Although Seligman believes that these designs have some advantages, he contends that they also have many disadvantages, which he feels the *CR* type of study (effectiveness research) can complement. The types of studies that *CR* conducts have their own problems, Seligman admits, but they can reveal whether or not people feel that psychotherapy is effective. In this case, the answer is yes.

In the second selection, Neil S. Jacobson and Andrew Christensen, compare the *CR* survey to outmoded studies that therapy researchers rejected long ago. Jacobson and Christensen point to "two fundamental problems" with retrospective surveys, or surveys based on participants' recollections of previous experiences. They admit that "consumer satisfaction is far from trivial." However, such ratings of satisfaction are "uncorrelated with... general [client] functioning." These authors contend that psychotherapy researchers were initially correct in rejecting these types of studies long ago.

POINT

- There are two types of therapy research—efficacy and effectiveness—that complement one another.
- *CR*'s survey type of study has many advantages, such as greater realism and comprehensiveness.
- *CR*'s study is large in scale and cost-effective.
- The *CR* study has several clear-cut results.

- *CR* has pioneered a whole new type of therapy outcome study.

COUNTERPOINT

- The "effectiveness" type of research was found to be inadequate many years ago.
- Surveys have two fundamental problems that disallow their use as serious studies of effectiveness.
- If such a study is not valid, its scale and minimal cost mean little.
- Some of the results of the *CR* study are strikingly different from the results of more highly controlled studies.
- The *CR* study is essentially the same as studies that were performed and subsequently rejected many years ago.

Martin E. P. Seligman

The Effectiveness of Psychotherapy: The *Consumer Reports* Study

How do we find out whether psychotherapy works? To answer this, two methods have arisen: the *efficacy study* and the *effectiveness study*. An efficacy study is the more popular method. It contrasts some kind of therapy to a comparison group under well-controlled conditions....

The high praise "empirically validated" is now virtually synonymous with positive results in efficacy studies, and many investigators have come to think that an efficacy study is the "gold standard" for measuring whether a treatment works....

But my belief has changed about what counts as a "gold standard." And it was a study by *Consumer Reports* (1995, November) that singlehandedly shook my belief. I came to see that deciding whether one treatment, under highly controlled conditions, works better than another treatment or a control group is a different question from deciding what works in the field (Muñoz, Hollon, McGrath, Rehm, & VandenBos, 1994). I no longer believe that efficacy studies are the only, or even the best, way of finding out what treatments actually work in the field. I have come to believe that the "effectiveness" study of how patients fare under the actual conditions of treatment in the field, can yield useful and credible "empirical validation" of psychotherapy and medication. This is the method that *Consumer Reports* pioneered....

Consumer Reports Survey

Consumer Reports (CR) included a supplementary survey about psychotherapy and drugs in one version of its 1994 annual questionnaire, along with its customary inquiries about appliances and services. *CR*'s 180,000 readers received this version, which included approximately 100 questions about automobiles and about mental health. *CR* asked readers to fill out the mental health section "if at any time over the past three years you experienced stress or other emotional problems for which you sought help from any of the following: friends, relatives, or a member of the clergy; a mental health professional like a psychologist or a psychiatrist; your family doctor; or a support group." Twenty-two thousand readers responded. Of these, approximately 7,000 subscribers responded to the mental health questions. Of these 7,000 about 3,000 had just talked to friends, relatives, or clergy, and 4,100 went to some combination of mental health professionals, family doctors, and support groups. Of these 4,100, 2,900 saw a mental health professional: Psychologists (37%) were the most frequently seen mental health professional, followed by psychiatrists (22%), social workers (14%), and marriage counselors (9%). Other mental health professionals made up 18%. In addition, 1,300 joined self-help groups, and about 1,000 saw family physicians. The respondents as a whole were highly educated, predominantly middle class; about half were women, and the median age was 46. . . .

There were a number of clear-cut results, among them:

- Treatment by a mental health professional usually worked. Most respondents got a lot better. Averaged over all mental health professionals, of the 426 people who were feeling *very poor* when they began therapy, 87% were feeling *very good, good,* or at least *so-so* by the time of the survey. Of the 786 people who were feeling *fairly poor* at the outset, 92% were feeling *very good, good,* or at least *so-so* by the time of the survey. These findings converge with meta-analyses of efficacy (Lipsey & Wilson, 1993; Shapiro & Shapiro, 1982; Smith, Miller, & Glass, 1980).
- Long-term therapy produced more improvement than short-term therapy. This result was very robust, and held up over all statistical models. . . .
- There was no difference between psychotherapy alone and psychotherapy plus medication for any disorder (very few respondents reported that they had medication with no psychotherapy at all).
- While all mental health professionals appeared to help their patients, psychologists, psychiatrists, and social workers did equally well and better than marriage counselors. Their patients' overall improvement scores (0–300 scale) were 220, 226, 225 (not significantly different from each other), and 208 (significantly worse than the first three), respectively.
- Family doctors did just as well as mental health professionals in the short term, but worse in the long term. Some patients saw both family doctors and mental health professionals, and those who saw both had more severe problems. For patients who relied solely on family doctors, their overall improvement scores when treated for up to six months was 213, and it remained at that level (212) for those treated longer than six months. In contrast, the overall improvement scores for patients of mental health professionals was 211 up to six months, but climbed to 232 when treatment went on for more than six months. The advantages of long-term treatment by a mental health professional held not only for the specific problems that led to treatment, but for a variety of general functioning scores as well: ability to relate to others,

coping with everyday stress, enjoying life more, personal growth and understanding, self-esteem and confidence.

- Alcoholics Anonymous (AA) did especially well, with an average improvement score of 251, significantly bettering mental health professionals. People who went to non-AA groups had less severe problems and did not do as well as those who went to AA (average score = 215).
- Active shoppers and active clients did better in treatment than passive recipients (determined by responses to "Was it mostly your idea to seek therapy? When choosing this therapist, did you discuss qualifications, therapist's experience, discuss frequency, duration, and cost, speak to someone who was treated by this therapist, check out other therapists? During therapy, did you try to be as open as possible, ask for explanation of diagnosis and unclear terms, do homework, not cancel sessions often, discuss negative feelings toward therapist?").
- No specific modality of psychotherapy did any better than any other for any problem. These results confirm the "dodo bird" hypothesis, that all forms of psychotherapies do about equally well (Luborsky, Singer, & Luborsky, 1975). They come as a rude shock to efficacy researchers, since the main theme of efficacy studies has been the demonstration of the usefulness of specific techniques for specific disorders.
- Respondents whose choice of therapist or duration of care was limited by their insurance coverage did worse, . . . (determined by responses to "Did limitations on your insurance coverage affect any of the following choices you made? Type of therapist I chose; How often I met with my therapist; How long I stayed in therapy").

These findings are obviously important, and some of them could not be included in the original *CR* article because of space limitations. Some of these findings were quite contrary to what I expected, but it is not my intention to discuss their substance here. Rather, I want to explore the methodological adequacy of this survey. My underlying questions are "Should we believe the findings?" and "Can the method be improved to give more authoritative answers?"

Consumer Reports Survey: Methodological Virtues

Sampling   This survey is, as far as I have been able to determine, the most extensive study of psychotherapy effectiveness on record. The sample is not representative of the United States as a whole, but my guess is that it is roughly representative of the middle class and educated population who make up the bulk of psychotherapy patients. It is important that the sample represents people who choose to go to treatment for their problems, not people who do not "believe in" psychotherapy or drugs. The *CR* sample, moreover, is probably weighted toward "problem solvers," people who actively try to do something about what troubles them.

Treatment duration   CR sampled all treatment durations from one month or less through two years or more. Because the study was naturalistic, treatment, it can be supposed, continued until the patient (a) was better, (b) gave up unimproved, or (c) had his or her coverage run out. This, by definition, mirrors what actually happens in the field. In contrast to all efficacy studies, which are of fixed treatment duration regardless of how the patient is progressing, the CR study informs us about treatment effectiveness under the duration constraints of actual therapy.

Self-correction   Because the CR study was naturalistic, it informs us of how treatment works as it is actually performed—without manuals and with self-correction when a technique falters. This also contrasts favorably to efficacy studies, which are manualized and not self-correcting when a given technique or modality fails.

Multiple problems   The large majority of respondents in the CR study had more than one problem. We can also assume that a good-sized fraction were "subclinical" in their problems and would not meet DSM-IV [Diagnostic and Statistical Manual of Mental Disorders, 4th Ed.] criteria for any disorder. No patients were discarded because they failed exclusion criteria or because they fell one symptom short of a full-blown "disorder." Thus the sample more closely reflected people who actually seek treatment than the filtered and single-disordered patients of efficacy studies.

General functioning   The CR study measured self-reported changes in productivity at work, interpersonal relations, well-being, insight, and growth, in addition to improvement on the presenting problem.... Importantly, more improvement on the presenting problem occurred for treatments which lasted longer than six months. In addition, more improvement occurred in work, interpersonal relations, enjoyment of life, and personal growth domains in treatments which lasted longer than six months. Since improvements in general functioning, as well as symptom relief, is almost always a goal of actual treatment but rarely of efficacy studies, the CR study adds to our knowledge of how treatment does beyond the mere elimination of symptoms.

Clinical significance   There has been much debate about how to measure the "clinical significance" of a treatment. Efficacy studies are designed to detect statistically significant differences between a treatment and control groups, and an "effect size" can be computed. But what degree of statistical significance is clinical significance? How large an effect size is meaningful? The CR study leaves little doubt about the human significance of its findings, since respondents answered directly about how much therapy helped the problem that led them to treatment—from *made things a lot better* to *made things a lot worse*. Of those who started out feeling *very poor*, 54% answered treatment *made things a lot better*, and another one third answered it made things *somewhat better*.

Unbiased Finally, it cannot be ignored that *CR* is about as unbiased a scrutinizer of goods and services as exists in the public domain. They have no axe to grind for or against medications, psychotherapy, managed care, insurance companies, family doctors, AA, or long-term treatment. They do not care if psychologists do better or worse than psychiatrists, marriage and family counselors, or social workers. They are not pursuing government grants or drug company favors. They do not accept advertisements. They have a track record of loyalty only to consumers. So this study comes with higher credibility than studies that issue from drug houses, from either APA [American Psychiatric Association], from consensus conferences of the National Institute of Mental Health, or even from the halls of academe. . . .

The Ideal Study

The *CR* study, then, is to be taken seriously—not only for its results and its credible source, but for its method. It is large-scale; it samples treatment as it is actually delivered in the field; it samples without obvious bias those who seek out treatment; it measures multiple outcomes including specific improvement and more global gains such as growth, insight, productivity, mood, enjoyment of life, and interpersonal relations; it is statistically stringent and finds clinically meaningful results. Furthermore, it is highly cost-effective.

Its major advantage over the efficacy method for studying the effectiveness of psychotherapy and medications is that it captures how and to whom treatment is actually delivered and toward what end. At the very least, the *CR* study and its underlying survey method provides a powerful addition to what we know about the effectiveness of psychotherapy and a pioneering way of finding out more.

The study is not without flaws, the chief one being the limited meaning of its answer to the question "Can psychotherapy help?" This question has three possible kinds of answers. The first is that psychotherapy does better than something else, such as talking to friends, going to church, or doing nothing at all. Because it lacks comparison groups, the *CR* study only answers this question indirectly. The second possible answer is that psychotherapy returns people to normality or more liberally to within, say, two standard deviations of the average. The *CR* study, lacking an untroubled group and lacking measures of how people were before they became troubled, does not answer this question. The third answer is "Do people have fewer symptoms and a better life after therapy than they did before?" This is the question that the *CR* study answers with a clear "yes."

NO

Neil S. Jacobson and Andrew Christensen

Studying the Effectiveness of Psychotherapy

[T]here is considerable debate about the merits of a recent *Consumer Reports (CR)* survey (1995).... This survey has received a great deal of attention within psychology and has been publicized in the popular press. Seligman (1995) suggested that this is the best study ever conducted on the effectiveness of psychotherapy.

Much like Freud's case studies, the report by *CR* (1995) is very persuasive and will probably have a great deal of influence on the public perception of psychotherapy. However, the purpose of this article is to show that most of what the *CR* study says has already been proven to the satisfaction of both practitioners and psychotherapy researchers. Moreover, those findings from the *CR* study that have not been previously established are highly questionable because of the study's methodological shortcomings. Finally, controlled experiments that avoid the methodological pitfalls of the *CR* study can answer virtually all of the questions considered by Seligman (1995) to be beyond the scope of clinical trials. In fact, it would be unfortunate if the field of psychotherapy research abandoned the controlled experiment when attempting to answer questions regarding the effectiveness of psychotherapy. Although clinical trials have their limitations and may need to be supplemented by other types of methodologies, they are far superior to the type of design reflected in the *CR* study, a design that has already been debated and rejected by both practitioners and researchers....

A Critique of the New Findings From the *Consumer Reports* Survey

The methodological shortcomings of the *CR* (1995) survey greatly limit their evidentiary value. Seligman (1995) mentioned some of these shortcomings but not others; the ones he did mention tended to be minimized. Here are a sample of these shortcomings.

A Retrospective Survey Is Not an Ideal Prototype for Effectiveness Research

Seligman (1995) suggested that the *CR* (1995) study is a well-done effectiveness study and was careful to distinguish this study from an efficacy study—a randomized clinical trial. However, in fact, the *CR* survey is not necessarily a good model for an effectiveness study as that term is typically used. The main virtue of the *CR* survey, according to Seligman, is its "realism"; that is, it is a report about real therapy, conducted by real therapists, with real clients, in the real world. The retrospective biases that are impossible to rule out are not seen as fatal flaws but simply as aspects of the design that need to be refined.

There are two fundamental problems with retrospective surveys. The first is that, because they are retrospective, there is no opportunity to corroborate respondents' reports. When participants are reporting on their own previous experiences, whether in therapy or otherwise, there is no way of assessing their accuracy. Various biases may contaminate their responses, ranging from demand characteristics to memory distortion. With a prospective study, some of these biases can be minimized, whereas others can be evaluated, using corroborative measures coming from different modalities. For example, self-report data can be supplemented with observational data. With retrospective surveys, such validation is impossible, and thus the responses are hard to interpret.

The second problem with retrospective surveys is the possibility that an unrepresentative subsample of those surveyed returned their questionnaires. Although it cannot be proven that those who benefited from psychotherapy were more likely to complete the survey than were those who did not, neither can that possibility be disproven. With a prospective study, one doesn't have to guess. This additional problem makes the improvement rates reported in the *CR* (1995) survey hard to interpret.

The most striking example of this selectivity problem is in the findings pertaining to Alcoholics Anonymous (AA), which had the highest mean improvement rate of any treatment category reported by Seligman (1995). In fact, as a treatment, AA significantly outperformed other mental health professionals. This finding can be contrasted with the lack of evidence supporting the efficacy of AA in prospective studies (McCrady & Delaney, 1995). Seligman acknowledged the strong possibility of sampling bias in AA and offered some speculations on why one might expect AA to be particularly susceptible to such biases. However, he then inexplicably minimized the likelihood of similarly extensive biases operating in the sample as a whole, suggesting that

> a similar kind of sampling bias, *to a lesser degree,* [italics added] cannot be overlooked for other kinds of treatment failures. At any rate, it is quite possible that there was a *large* [italics added] oversampling of successful AA cases and a *smaller* [italics added] oversampling of successful treatment for problems other than alcoholism.(p. 971)

Is it not possible that the oversampling of successful cases was as large for other problems as it was for AA? Is there any evidence to the contrary?

In addition to contaminating the overall estimates of treatment gains, sampling bias could easily explain the apparent superiority of long-term therapy reported by the respondents in the *CR* (1995) study. Unlike Howard et al. (1986), who found a negatively accelerated dose–response relationship, the *CR* survey found a linear relationship: the more therapy, the better the outcome. This would indeed be an important finding if it were interpretable; unfortunately, it is not interpretable. Seligman (1995) argued against the possibility of sampling bias by focusing on one potential source. He suggested that, if early dropouts are treatment failures and those who remain in treatment are beneficiaries, then earlier dropouts should have lower rates of "problem resolution" than later dropouts. In fact, the rates are uniform: About two thirds of dropouts quit because the problem is resolved, whether they quit therapy one month or two years after they started.

The problem with Seligman's (1995) refutation is that it fails to rule out the primary source of interpretive ambiguity—spontaneous remission. The longer people stay in therapy, the greater the opportunity for factors other than therapy to produce improvement. There is no way of knowing whether the superiority of long-term therapy is due to the treatment itself or simply to increased opportunities for other factors to produce improvements.

Seligman (1995) argued that the main virtue of the *CR* (1995) study is its realism. If one thinks of realism using the metaphor of a snapshot, the implication is that the *CR* survey provides a snapshot of what psychotherapy is really like. But, because the study is retrospective, the snapshot may be out of focus. With a prospective study, one can take a snapshot of psychotherapy whose focus is indisputable. But, with a retrospective survey, the negatives are gone forever.

The Absence of Control Groups of Any Kind Constitutes an Additional Fatal Flaw

Seligman (1995) fully acknowledged the problems introduced by the uncontrolled nature of the study but suggested that there are "internal controls" that can be used as surrogates. Unfortunately, none of Seligman's internal controls can be considered adequate substitutes for control groups.

First, he suggested that the inferior performance of marriage counselors allowed them to serve as a reference group because they controlled for various nonspecific factors such as the presence of an attentive listener. However, because marriage counselors may have differed systematically from other professionals in the client population with whom they worked, their performance cannot be compared with that of other mental health professionals who may have treated more mental health problems that were not primarily related to marital distress. In other words, there may have been a systematic confounding between type of problem treated and profession, which rendered marriage counselors useless as an internal control.

Second, Seligman (1995) noted that long-term treatment worked better than short-term treatment, thus allowing the use of the first point in the dose–response curve as a control group. As we have already suggested, this internal control is useless because of the confound with greater opportunity for spontaneous remission in long-term therapy.

Third, according to Seligman (1995), because it is known that drugs outperform placebos, and because psychotherapy did as well as psychotherapy plus drugs in the *CR* (1995) study, one can infer that psychotherapy would have outperformed an adequate placebo if one had been included in the *CR* study. This argument is specious for a number of reasons: It is not known what drugs were used for which problems in the *CR* study; it is not known whether the pharmacotherapy performed was adequate (compliance, dosage, etc.); and most importantly, it is not known whether the sample of patients in the *CR* study was similar to those in which drugs typically outperform placebos.

Fourth, family doctors did not perform as well as mental health professionals when treatment continued beyond six months, thus suggesting family doctors as an internal control. However, family doctors saw clients for a fewer number of sessions than did mental health professionals, creating a confound that Seligman (1995) himself acknowledged.

Seligman (1995) concluded that spontaneous remission is an unlikely explanation for the high improvement rates reported by respondents in the *CR* (1995) study. We come to a different conclusion, because none of the proposed internal controls are adequate. We conclude that factors other than psychotherapy might very well have accounted for the improvement rates reported by the respondents. We come to this conclusion for several reasons. First, there is no adequate control to rule it out, thus no compelling reason to reject the null hypothesis. Second, because the 4,000 respondents in the *CR* study were, to use Seligman's (1995) terminology, "middle class and educated" (p. 969) and "a good-sized fraction were 'subclinical'... and would not meet *DSM-IV [Diagnostic and Statistical Manual of Mental Disorders*, 4th Edition; American Psychiatric Association, 1994] criteria for any disorder" (p. 970), we have the kind of sample that is most likely to spontaneously remit, or to benefit from any treatment, specific or nonspecific (Jacobson & Hollon, 1996). As Seligman noted, in most clinical trials, the single largest basis for exclusion is that the client is not sufficiently distressed or dysfunctional to be included.

For example, in research on depression, by far the most common basis for exclusion is that not enough symptoms are present for the patient to meet criteria for major depressive disorder; even if *DSM-IV* criteria are met, participants are often excluded because the major depressive disorder is not severe enough (Jacobson et al., 1996). In efficacy studies, there is a good reason to exclude these participants: They seem to get better no matter what they receive. Even the less severe patients who make it into these trials tend to respond as well to placebos as they do to active treatments (cf. Jacobson & Hollon, 1996). Thus, it is a fair assumption that many of the respondents to the *CR* (1995) survey who improved would have improved without therapy.

The Measures in the *Consumer Reports* Survey Were Not Only Unreliable but Unrevealing

The *CR* (1995) survey measured little more than consumer satisfaction. Consumer satisfaction is far from trivial. However, consumer satisfaction ratings are uncorrelated with symptomatic outcome and general functioning. In the *CR* survey, three questions were asked in the assessment of improvement, one pertaining to "satisfaction with therapist," a second pertaining to "improvement in the presenting problem," and a third pertaining to "improvement in overall functioning." The latter measure was a change score, derived by subtracting posttest scores from pretest scores (both obtained retrospectively); the other two measures were simply posttest scores. Seligman (1995) seized on these three questions to argue that three different constructs are being measured: consumer satisfaction, symptom relief, and general functioning. However, since all three questions are global and retrospective and have method variance in common, they cannot be considered independent assessments of functioning or to be measuring different constructs. Furthermore, the three questions were combined into a multivariate composite for the calculation of improvement rates, thus making it impossible to separate out consumer satisfaction from the other items.

The Specificity Question Revisited: The *Consumer Reports* Survey Did Not Assess Which Therapies Led to Improvement in Which Problems

Researchers are long past the stage of referring to psychotherapy as if it were uniform, without specifying the nature of the problem being treated or the treatment used. Yet, the *CR* (1995) study failed to inform the public about any particular treatment for any particular problem and thus provides little information that advances knowledge about psychotherapy. The data may be available to answer more specific questions. But even if they were available, and were released, they would be based on respondent reports: Respondents would be reporting what their presenting problem was and the kind of treatment they received (we have already seen some data on this latter question), and they would be defining both the profession and the theoretical orientation of the therapist. How reliable are survey respondents at describing the theoretical orientation of their therapist or at fitting their presenting problem into one of a series of choices on a survey, especially in retrospect? Both of us have small private practices, and a large proportion of our clients are couples. We have heard ourselves referred to as marriage counselors, psychologists, and even, on occasion, psychiatrists. We doubt whether the number of our clients who could correctly identify our theoretical orientation would much exceed chance.

Even Assuming Methodological Adequacy, the Results as Reported by *Consumer Reports* and by Seligman Are Misleading

Although the sound bite coming out of both the *CR* (1995) report and Seligman's (1995) article says that 90% of the respondents found psychotherapy beneficial, it is worth noting that this figure comes from combining those who were helped "a great deal," "a lot," and "somewhat." Only 54% reported that they were helped "a great deal." This is not a very impressive figure from the standpoint of clinical significance, especially when one takes into account the number of subclinical respondents in the sample and the possibility that the respondents may be overrepresented by those who found treatment to be helpful.

The Eysenck Evaluation Revisited

The *CR* (1995) survey bears remarkable resemblance to the controversial evaluation of psychotherapy reported by Eysenck (1952). In this report, Eysenck summarized the results of 24 reports of psychoanalytic and eclectic psychotherapy with more than 7,000 neurotic patients treated in naturalistic settings. Using therapist ratings of improvement, Eysenck reported a 44% improvement rate for psychoanalytic therapy and a 64% improvement rate for eclectic psychotherapy. Unlike the *CR* survey, however, these reports were prospective in that the therapist evaluations occurred at the time of termination. Also unlike the *CR* survey, Eysenck used control groups: One consisted of all improved patients who had been discharged from hospitals in New York between 1917 and 1934 for "neurotic" conditions, receiving nothing but custodial care; the other consisted of 500 disability claimants who were periodically evaluated by general practitioners without receiving psychotherapy, so it could be determined whether they were improved enough to go back to work. Improvement for this latter control group was defined as their ability to return to work, which was decided by the general practitioner. Eysenck reported, on the basis of these two control groups, that the spontaneous remission rate for these minimally treated patients was 72% and that psychotherapy was therefore ineffective.

The merits of these findings and the methodology supporting them were debated vigorously for 20 years. Initially, Luborsky (1954) criticized the study on the grounds that the measures of improvement were flawed, the control groups were inadequate, and the treatments were lacking on both uniformity and representativeness. Similar critiques were registered by Rosenzweig (1954) and De Charrus, Levy, and Wertheimer (1954). These and more recent critiques (e.g., Bergin, 1971) argued, with considerable merit, that Eysenck (1952) had underestimated the success of therapy and overestimated the spontaneous remission rate. As recently as the mid-1970s, Eysenck's study was subject to refutation by more optimistic appraisals and interpretations of psychotherapy's impact (Luborsky et al., 1975; Meltzoff & Kornreich, 1970). Now, the controversy has largely subsided, and Eysenck's study has been rejected by clinical scientists. In fact, in the most recent edition of Bergin and Garfield's (1994) *Handbook of Psychotherapy and Behavioral Change* the study is not even cited.

When it is referenced nowadays, it is primarily for its historical impact and its heuristic value.

What is interesting about examining Eysenck's (1952) study in light of the *CR* (1995) survey is that virtually all of the criticisms leveled at Eysenck's evaluation also apply to the *CR* survey, even though Eysenck's evaluation was more sophisticated from a methodological perspective. Eysenck had a sample that was almost twice as large as the sample reported in the *CR* survey; he did at least include control groups, however inadequate they might have been; the measures of improvement were concurrent rather than retrospective; and the measures were obtained from trained therapists rather than from the clients themselves. Given Seligman's (1995) assumptions that therapists are able to self-correct their therapeutic work and cannily select which clients need drugs and psychotherapy, therapists should also be better judges of when clients have made genuine improvement versus transitory symptom change. However, the field was correct in rejecting Eysenck's evaluation: The control groups and the measures of outcome were inadequate. We don't see any reason to revert to a methodology that was rejected for its methodological inadequacies 20 years ago.

CHALLENGE QUESTIONS

Is the *Consumer Reports* Conclusion That "Psychotherapy Helps" Valid?

1. You have probably learned about the difference between correlation and causation in research and methods. How does this difference pertain to the controversy over the *Consumer Reports* study?
2. Do you think that psychotherapy is effective? Assert your own conclusion and support it with scientific research.
3. Jacobson and Christensen discuss the parallels between Hans Eysenck's 1952 study of psychotherapy and *CR*'s study. Look up Eysenck's original study and describe how it is also different from the *CR* study.
4. Why are "experimental" designs favored by not only therapy researchers but also psychological researchers in general?
5. How important do you feel "consumer satisfaction" should be in the evaluation of psychotherapy? Support your answer.

On the Internet . . .

National Attention Deficit Disorder Association

The National Attention Deficit Disorder Association (ADDA) has been active since 1989. The ADDA's constantly growing and changing Web site is packed with articles, personal stories, interviews with ADD professionals, book reviews, and links to other ADD-related sites.

http://www.add.org

Attention-Deficit Hyperactivity Disorder

In addition to a *Scientific American* feature article on ADHD by Russell A. Barkley, director of psychology and professor of psychiatry and neurology at the University of Massachusetts Medical Center in Worcester, Massachusetts, this page offers related links and suggestions for further reading.

http://www.sciam.com/1998/0998issue/
0998barkley.html

About: The Psychology of Love

If you want to learn about love and you want to know how and what psychology has learned about love, you will find the resources here helpful.

http://psychology.about.com/cs/love

Love and Relationships

This page contains links to various sources of information on love and relationships. Categories include types of love, findings from the Love Test, processing information, and female courtship strategies.

http://world.topchoice.com/~psyche/love/

PART 2

Biological Issues

*N*o behavioral or mental activity can occur without one's body. Our bodies and our biological processes are usually viewed as fundamental to all human activities, including emotion, perception, attention, and mental health. However, does this fundamental role of the body mean that it causes our behavior and our minds? Do biological processes cause the problems of many young children to learn and behave in school? Is the development of our bodies, through evolution, involved in our most important emotions, such as love, hate, and envy?

- Are Genetic Explanations of Attention Deficit Hyperactivity Disorder Faulty?

- Is Love a Mechanism of Evolution?

ISSUE 4

Are Genetic Explanations of Attention Deficit Hyperactivity Disorder Faulty?

YES: Jay Joseph, from "Not in Their Genes: A Critical View of the Genetics of Attention-Deficit Hyperactivity Disorder," *Developmental Review* (December 2000)

NO: Stephen V. Faraone and Joseph Biederman, from "Nature, Nurture, and Attention Deficit Hyperactivity Disorder," *Developmental Review* (December 2000)

ISSUE SUMMARY

YES: After reviewing the literature on the genetic causes of ADHD, professor of psychology Jay Joseph concludes that such claims are unsupported and that psychosocial causes need further exploration.

NO: Clinical psychologists Stephen V. Faraone and Joseph Biederman reject Joseph's conclusions on the grounds that he makes errors in scientific logic and ignores much of the relevant research.

For many years, children who were hyper and who experienced learning problems were viewed as needing special education. According to this perspective, if they could just be educated differently, these children would probably be all right. Today, however, many psychologists are considering the possibility that these children—now called ADHD (for attention deficit hyperactivity disorder) children—have biological, or, more specifically, neurochemical, problems; that is, problems of "nature" rather than just problems of "nurture."

Many psychologists today believe not only that the mind and body are intricately connected but also that the body causes the problems of the mind. If medical illnesses such as Down's syndrome and cancer are biological in nature, then why not mental illness? If genes that cause cancer and other illnesses can be found, then why not try to find the genes that cause mental illness? If one's heart and other organs can become diseased and ill, perhaps mental illness is a sickness of the brain.

As plausible as this biological explanation of psychology might sound, a causal connection between the mind and the body has not been discovered.

Indeed, some critics suggest that there is such a desire for this connection that its existence is assumed without any proof or taken on faith. Consequently, many of these critics contend that psychologists should avoid pie-in-the-sky mind/body connections and search instead for nonbiological causes for mental illness, such as poverty, neglect, abuse, and socioeconomic injustice.

It is in this spirit that Jay Joseph, in the first of the following selections, examines the evidence supporting a genetic link between the mind and body for ADHD. Specifically, he examines the three main buttresses that supposedly support a genetic cause of ADHD: family studies, twin studies, and adoption studies. Joseph argues against these three kinds of studies and offers a twofold conclusion: that there is no substantive research to support a genetic cause for ADHD and that psychosocial causes need to be explored further.

Replying to Joseph in the second selection are Stephen V. Faraone and Joseph Biederman. They reject Joseph's conclusions on the grounds that he makes serious errors of scientific logic and ignores much of the relevant research. They admit that the environment plays a major role in ADHD. However, they argue that ADHD is ultimately caused by a complex interaction between genes and environment—both of which are equally important.

POINT	COUNTERPOINT
• Family studies cannot distinguish between genetic and environmental components.	• Family studies show that ADHD runs in families.
• The assumption in twin studies that both identical and fraternal twins share equal environments is false.	• Unequal environments does not mean that identical twins are exposed to more "trait-relevant" environmental factors than fraternal twins are.
• Adoption studies have major flaws and are inconclusive.	• Minor methodological flaws only limit the strength with which conclusions can be drawn.
• The role of genetic factors in ADHD is not supported, and future research should focus on psychosocial causes.	• Genetic theories are the most parsimonious explanations for ADHD.

Jay Joseph

Not in Their Genes: A Critical View of the Genetics of Attention-Deficit Hyperactivity Disorder

This article examines evidence cited in favor of the operation of genetic factors in attention-deficit hyperactivity disorder (ADHD). Like
other psychiatric conditions, a belief in the genetic basis of ADHD
is derived from the results of family, twin, and adoption studies. Because family studies are widely believed to be confounded by environmental factors, primary emphasis is placed on twin and adoption
studies. ADHD twin studies depend on the validity of the equal environment assumption (EEA), which holds that the environments of
identical (MZ) and fraternal (DZ) twins are the same. Here it is argued
that however the EEA is defined, it cannot be accepted. Therefore,
the greater similarity or concordance of MZ twins when compared
to DZ twins is plausibly explained by environmental factors. Adoption studies constitute a third method of investigating the role of
genetic factors in ADHD. It is argued that these studies are greatly
flawed by factors including non blinded diagnoses and the failure
to study the biological relatives of adoptees. After an examination
of the total weight of evidence in favor of a genetic basis or predisposition for ADHD, it is concluded that a role for genetic factors is
not supported and that future research should be directed toward
psychosocial causes

The current period is marked by the widespread acceptance of an important
genetic influence on most psychological traits. This view is based on three pil-
lars of support: (1) family studies, (2) twin studies, and (3) adoption studies. In
psychiatry, schizophrenia has served as the model for the use of these methods.
For the most part, the authors of over 2 dozen schizophrenia family studies,
14 schizophrenia twin studies, and 6 schizophrenia adoption studies concluded
that their findings supported the existence of a genetic predisposition for the
condition.

Here, we are interested in assessing the evidence in support of a genetic
component for "attention-deficit hyperactivity disorder" (ADHD) which, like

From Jay Joseph, "Not in Their Genes: A Critical View of the Genetics of Attention-Deficit Hyperactivity Disorder," *Developmental Review*, vol. 20, no. 4 (December 2000). Copyright © 2000 by
Academic Press. Reprinted by permission of the publisher and the author.

schizophrenia, is a psychiatric diagnosis made on the basis of a person's behavior and whose supposed genetic component is based on the evidence from family, twin, and adoption studies. For reasons of consistency, the term "ADHD" is used throughout this article in place of diagnoses which include "hyperactive child syndrome," "minimal brain dysfunction," "hyperactivity," "attention deficit disorder," and so on. As is shown, the way the condition has been defined is of secondary importance to an examination of the methods used to determine its possible genetic component.

According to Russell Barkley (1998a), ADHD is a "developmental failure in the brain circuitry that underlies inhibition and self-control" (p. 67). Barkley cites studies whose authors claimed to have found that a portion of ADHD children's brains are smaller than in normal children, which he links to genetic factors. Tannock (1998) also concluded that ADHD is caused by a brain dysfunction of probable genetic origin. Some have taken a more interactionist approach (e.g., Diller, 1998), while others have stressed environmental factors and have questioned the validity of the ADHD concept (e.g., Breggin, 1998; De-Grandpre, 1999). What follows is a review of the ADHD genetic study literature. In the concluding section, I will discuss possible future directions for research into the causes of the condition.

ADHD Family Studies

Background

The family (or consanguinity) method of study constitutes the first systematic attempt to determine whether a condition clusters in families, thereby laying the basis for the possibility of finding a genetic component. Family studies locate persons affected with a particular trait or condition and attempt to determine whether their biological relatives are similarly affected more often than members of the general population or a control group. If a condition is found to cluster or "run" in families, it is said to be familial. Note that "familial" is not the same as "genetic." Unfortunately, many people view these terms as being synonymous, when in fact they are not. As most genetic researchers now acknowledge, the aggregation of a particular condition in families is consistent with a genetic or an environmental etiology. Psychiatric geneticists Faraone and Tsuang (1995), for example, noted that a family study can provide "the initial hint that a disorder might have a genetic component," while cautioning that "Disorders can 'run in families' for nongenetic reasons such as shared environmental adversity, viral transmission, and social learning.... Although family studies are indispensable for establishing the familiality of disorders, they cannot, by themselves, establish what type of transmission" (pp. 88–89). However, this has not always been the prevailing view.

The first schizophrenia family study (Rüdin, 1916) was published over 80 years ago, and the most influential study of this type was performed by Kallmann (1938). Most of the early family studies were authored by strong proponents of the genetic position, and most did not perform blind diagnoses.

Kallmann believed that the familiality of schizophrenia *proved* that the condition was genetic in origin: "The principal aim of our investigations was to offer *conclusive proof* [italics added] of the inheritance of schizophrenia and to help, in this way, to establish a dependable basis for the clinical and eugenic activities of psychiatry" (Kallmann, 1938, p. xiv). Pam (1995) noted Kallmann's faulty logic and commented further on the family study method:

> The most serious breach in inductive logic committed by Kallmann was his use of kinship concordance rates to determine genetic transmission of psychopathology. We have already noted that no family inheritance study can control for environment in human research; such data, therefore, are nowhere near "suggestive"—they are at best inconclusive and at worst misleading.... This inferential limitation holds with respect to any consanguinity finding, even if the design and technique employed in the investigation were scientifically impeccable. (p. 19)

Today, most behavior genetic and psychiatric genetic researchers (e.g., Faraone & Tsuang, 1995; Gottesman, 1991; Plomin, DeFries, & McClearn, 1990; Rosenthal, 1970; Wender, 1995) acknowledge that family studies by themselves cannot establish the existence of genetic factors and have cited twin and adoption studies as the primary evidence in favor of the genetic basis of schizophrenia and other conditions.

The authors of the ADHD family studies (Biederman et al., 1986, 1995; Biederman, Faraone, Keenan, Knee, & Tsuang, 1990; Cantwell, 1972; Faraone, Biederman, Keenan, & Tsuang, 1991a; Morrison & Stewart, 1971; Nichols & Chen, 1981; Welner, Welner, Stewart, Palkes, & Wish, 1977) have found consistent evidence for the familiality of the condition. Although several of these studies suffer from serious methodological problems (such as nonblind diagnoses), partisans of the genetic *or environmental* positions would be surprised if they *did not* find a familial clustering of ADHD.

In spite of the formal pronouncement that family studies by themselves cannot be used as evidence of genetic transmission, several important ADHD researchers have written that the evidence from these studies suggests a genetic basis for the condition. For example, in Barkley's authoritative handbook for the diagnosis and treatment of ADHD, the author writes, "Family aggregation studies find that ADHD clusters among biological relatives of children or adults with the disorder, strongly implying a hereditary basis to this condition" (Barkley, 1998b, p. 36). While Faraone and Tsuang (1995) viewed the results from family studies as providing only the "initial hint" of genetic factors, Barkley believes that these findings "strongly imply" such an etiology.

Several ADHD family researchers have implied that their results support the genetic position. For example, Nichols and Chen (1981) concluded that the "greater risks to relatives of the severely affected children and to relatives of girls, the less frequently affected sex, provided some evidence that the familial association was determined partly by polygenic inheritance" (p. 276), and Biederman et al. (1995) have written, "Additional lines of evidence from second-degree relative, twin ... adoption, and segregation analysis studies suggest that the familial aggregation of ADHD has a substantial genetic component" (p.

432). However, a method which by itself cannot be regarded as evidence in favor of the genetic hypothesis does not become evidence when combined with the supposed findings of another type of study. As noted by Diller, Tanner, and Weil (1995), "Familial clustering, as noted in the [Biederman et al. 1995 family study] article, cannot distinguish between potential genetic and environmental etiologies. While the authors are careful to describe the new data as familial, they nevertheless discuss them only in the context of a genetic etiology" (p. 451).

There is little reason to engage in a detailed discussion of the ADHD family studies, since their results are in accordance with the expectations of environmentalists and hereditarians alike. Therefore, this article focuses on the two methods most often cited in support of the genetic basis of ADHD: twin and adoption studies.

ADHD Twin Studies

Overview

As we have seen, the finding that a trait or condition runs in families is consistent with both genetic and environmental etiologies. For this reason, the results from twin studies have been promoted as evidence in favor of the genetic position. According to Barkley (1998a), twin studies have provided "the most conclusive evidence that genetics can contribute to ADHD" (p. 68). Several ADHD twin studies have been published since 1965 (Eaves et al., 1993; Edelbrock, Rende, Plomin, & Thompson, 1995; Gilger, Pennington, & DeFries, 1992; Gillis, Gilger, Pennington, & DeFries, 1992; Gjone, Stevenson, & Sundet, 1996; Goodman & Stevenson, 1989a, 1989b; Levy, Hay, McStephen, Wood, & Waldman, 1997; Lopez, 1965; Nadder, Silberg, Eaves, Maes, & Meyer, 1998; Sherman, Iacono, & McGue, 1997; Silberg et al., 1996; Steffensson et al., 1999; Stevenson, 1992; Thapar, Hervas, & McGuffin, 1995; van den Oord, Verhulst, & Boomsma, 1996; Willerman, 1973). All of these studies utilized the so-called "classical twin method" (also known as the "twin method"), which compares the concordance rates or correlations of reared-together identical twins (also known as monozygotic or MZ) to the same measures of reared-together fraternal twins (also known as dizygotic or DZ). A significantly greater similarity or concordance of MZ twins when compared with DZs is usually cited as evidence in favor of the genetic basis for the trait or condition under study. All ADHD twin studies have investigated pairs who were reared *together;* there have been no studies of reared-apart pairs. Separated twin studies typically look at similarities in personality and cognitive ability, but have been plagued by methodological problems and questionable theoretical assumptions (see Farber, 1981; Joseph, in press-d; Kamin, 1974; Taylor, 1980).

The authors of ADHD twin studies have found consistently that identical twins are more concordant for ADHD or correlate higher for ADHD-related behaviors than fraternals, and there is little doubt that in spite of these studies' methodological problems, MZ twins are significantly more similar than DZ twins. The question which concerns us here is whether the greater phenotypic similarity of MZ twins is caused by their greater genetic similarity, as the proponents of the twin method maintain. In order to answer this question, it is necessary to examine the theoretical underpinnings of the twin method itself. So before returning to the ADHD twin studies, we must assess the validity of the most important assumption of the twin method.

The "Equal Environment Assumption" in Twin Studies

Because MZs rate more similarly on ADHD-related measures than DZs, twin studies would be considered solid evidence in favor of a genetic predisposition for ADHD were it not for one important detail: Since its inception in the mid-1920s, the twin method has been based on the theoretical assumption that identical and fraternal twins share equal environments. The equal environment assumption (EEA) must be valid in order to claim that the MZ/DZ concordance rate difference, found in most types of human behavior, can be attributed to genetic factors. According to Kendler, the most prominent contemporary defender of the equal environment assumption, "The EEA is crucial because, if the EEA is incorrect, excess resemblance of MZ twins compared with DZ twins ascribed to genetic factors could be partly or entirely due to environmental effects" (1993, p. 906). Kendler is quite right: If the EEA is false, the twin method could be measuring nothing else than the more similar environment and greater emotional bond experienced by MZ twins.

Although the validity of the EEA is crucial to the viability of the twin method, it is not often discussed in detail by its defenders. The EEA has been the subject of at least two critical reviews (Joseph, 1998b; Pam, Kemker, Ross, & Golden, 1996), whose authors concluded that the assumption is untenable.

Until the late 1950s, the assumption of equal environments between MZ and DZ pairs was taken for granted by most twin researchers, although little theoretical or empirical justification for this clearly counterintuitive assumption was offered. In 1960, Don Jackson published a critique of the five schizophrenia twin studies which had been published up to that time. Jackson pointed out that female twins were consistently more concordant than male twins, that same-sex DZs were more concordant than opposite-sex DZs, and that fraternal twins were more concordant than ordinary siblings, though they each share the same genetic relationship to each other. Jackson noted that common environment, "ego fusion," and association could explain these differences, and he implied that the MZ/DZ concordance rate difference could also be explained on this basis. As a "plausible hypothesis," Jackson (1960, p. 67) predicted that "according to the degree of likeness in siblings, we will find an increased concordance for schizophrenia, without concern for genetic similarity." (Slightly modifying Jackson's position, we might say that according to the degree of *environmental similarity* among siblings, we would expect greater behavioral similarity, without concern for genetic relationship.) The reaction of the schizophrenia twin studying world followed, for the most part, two different paths. The first was an attempt to discredit Jackson's theory by claiming that its validity rested on Jackson's hypothesis that the identical twinship itself might create conditions more conducive to schizophrenia and that we would therefore expect to find a higher rate of schizophrenia among individual MZ twins than among the single-born population. Although Rosenthal (1960) and others claimed to have provided evidence that twins are no more susceptible than nontwins, the evidence is in fact equivocal (Joseph, 1998a; Kläning, Mortensen, & Kyvik, 1996). More importantly, Jackson's "theory of identity confusion" does not require twins to be more susceptible than singletons for the trait in question. The thrust of Jackson's theory dealt with the reasons why the *second* member of a twin pair fell to schizophrenia, not the first (Joseph, in press-c).

The second way that the proponents of the twin method responded to Jackson's ideas was to concede some of his most important points while continuing to uphold the twin method as a valid instrument for the detection of genetic influences. As demonstrated elsewhere (Joseph, 1998b), the most important twin researchers of the 1960s and 1970s were in agreement that environmental similarity and association were *partly* responsible for the MZ/DZ concordance rate difference. But I ask the reader: How did they know that environmental influences were not *entirely* responsible for the difference? In fact, they didn't know —they only *hoped* that their studies had measured genetic influences. In one of the early collaborations of Gottesman and Shields (1966), we find that the authors were willing to acknowledge that the greater psychological identification of MZ twins could affect concordance rates "provided that the same proportion of potential schizophrenics are held back from overt illness by identifying with a normal twin as those who become ill by identifying with an abnormal one" (p. 55). Gottesman and Shields provided no evidence in support of their attempt to balance the ledgers of the twin method. On what grounds, one might ask, did Gottesman and Shields insist on a one-to-one correspondence between those twins who became concordant for reasons of association and those who stayed "well" for the same reason? Could we not just as easily surmise that, for reasons of identification, there are *five* twins who become concordant for every *one* who remains well? The reasoning of Gottesman and Shields constituted little more than wishful thinking in the service of keeping a theory intact.

... ADHD twin studies are based on an unsupported theoretical assumption and therefore offer, like family studies, only a "hint" about the possible genetic basis of ADHD. It is quite possible, and even likely, that these studies have recorded nothing more than the greater psychological bond and environmental similarity experienced by identical twins.

ADHD Adoption Studies

Overview

The third method used to establish the genetic basis of a condition is the study of individuals who have been adopted. In theory, the adoption method is able to disentangle a person's genetic heritage from his or her rearing environment. Of course, if the twin method could satisfactorily accomplish this task, adoption studies would hardly be necessary, since they are more difficult to perform than twin studies. The well-known Danish/American schizophrenia adoption studies were performed by Kety, Rosenthal, Wender, and others. These researchers came together on the basis of a common belief that the twin method was unable to satisfactorily separate genetic and environmental influences. For example, Kety wrote,

> Twin studies are a more compelling form of genetic data [than family studies], but even twin studies depend on the assumption that the only thing that differentiates monozygotic from dizygotic twins is their genetic relatedness, and that environmental factors are somehow canceled out or randomized. But that is not the case. Monozygotic twins share much of their environment as well as their genetic endowment. They live together; they sleep together; they are dressed alike by parents; they are paraded in a double parambulator as infants; their friends cannot distinguish one from the other. In short, they develop a certain ego identification with each other that is very hard to dissociate from the purely genetic identity with which they were born. (Kety, 1978, p. 48)

And Rosenthal (1979) concluded, "in both family and twin studies, the possible genetic and environmental factors are confounded, and one can draw conclusions about them only at considerable risk" (p. 25). Wender, of course, is well known in the ADHD field in addition to being a schizophrenia researcher. He too has doubts about genetic inferences from twin studies: "The roles of 'heredity' (nature) and 'environment' (nurture) in the etiology of ADHD (as with other psychiatric disorders) cannot be determined by adding data from twin studies to the data from family studies" (Wender, 1995, p. 93). As an important advocate of adoption studies, Wender concluded that the roles of heredity and environment in ADHD "can, however, be more conclusively separated by adoption studies, in which the parents providing the genetic constitution (the biological parents) and those who provide the psychological environment (the adoptive parents) are different people" (p. 93).

While the method of studying adoptees as a way of definitively separating genetic and environmental influences may appear straightforward, the most important psychiatric adoption studies (e.g., Heston, 1966; Kety, Rosenthal, Wender, & Schulsinger, 1968; Kety, Rosenthal, Wender, Schulsinger, & Jacobsen, 1975; Kety et al., 1994; Rosenthal, Wender, Kety, Welner, & Schulsinger, 1971; Tienari et al., 1994) were likely confounded by the selective placement of adoptees on the basis of the socioeconomic and psychiatric status of index adoptees' biological families (Joseph, 1999a, 1999b, in press-b; Lewontin, Rose, & Kamin, 1984). Like family and twin studies, adoption studies are susceptible to the confounding influence of environmental factors.

As of this writing, there have been five ADHD adoption studies (Alberts-Corush, Firestone, & Goodman, 1986; Cantwell, 1975; Morrison & Stewart, 1973; Safer, 1973; van den Oord, Boomsma, & Verhulst, 1994). In spite of the numerous flaws of the schizophrenia adoption studies, they possessed two important virtues not found in ADHD adoption studies: (1) most diagnoses were made blindly and (2) their authors studied or had information on the biological families of their adoptees. . . .

Summary and Discussion of the Findings of ADHD Adoption Studies

... The fact that ADHD adoption studies typically fail to perform blind evaluations of their participants is reason enough to question their conclusions. As a leading schizophrenia adoption researcher has noted, "With respect to all such research, in which the dependent variable is the diagnosis of relatives, it is essential that the diagnostician not know whether the individual examined is related to an index or control proband ... because it is easy to be swayed by knowledge regarding index or control status" (Rosenthal, 1975, p. 20). For Rosenthal, who had intimate knowledge of how these studies were performed, blind diagnoses are "essential" because it is "easy" to be influenced by knowledge of the group status of the participant under study. The authors of the ADHD adoption studies noted the difficulty of remaining blind to the status of their participants because details of the adoption process are usually disclosed in the interview process. Nevertheless, our understanding of the difficulties faced by these researchers does not mean that we must accept their conclusions. Summarizing the evidence in favor of the genetic basis of ADHD, Wender (1995) wrote, "What have these adoption studies added to the data on ADHD from the family and twin studies? First, they have provided more solid data showing that 'hyperactivity' (broadly defined) has genetic contributions" (p. 99). Because, as we have seen, Wender considered family and twin studies to be confounded by environmental factors, one might ask what "solid data" he was referring to. Like other genetically oriented commentators, Wender implied that the alleged findings from one research method can legitimize—or "unconfound"—the results from another. However, if family and twin studies are contaminated by environmental factors, the results from an adoption study cannot alter this finding. According to Wender, another important finding of the ADHD adoption studies was that "they have shown that some psychiatric disorders associated with conduct disorder—'alcoholism,' Antisocial Personality Disorder ('psychopathy,' 'sociopathy'), somatization disorder ('Briquet's Syndrome,' 'hysteria')—are associated with hyperactivity and are also genetically transmitted" (1995, p. 99). The authors of the original ADHD adoption studies (Cantwell, 1975; Morrison & Stewart, 1973) believed that there was a genetic link between ADHD and alcoholism, sociopathy, and hysteria on the basis of the (extremely weak) evidence in support of the genetic foundation of these diagnoses. That Wender continues to see a genetic linkage is based on two unlikely assumptions: (1) that the evidence in favor of the genetic basis of alcoholism, sociopathy, and hysteria is solid; and (2) that the mere association of psychiatric conditions is evidence for their *genetic* association. The most outstanding example of Wender's embrace of assumption 2 was his support of the questionable Danish/American "schizophrenia spectrum" concept (see Joseph, 1998a).

Psychiatric genetics has a long history of the mistaken belief that the mere association of conditions implies their genetic relationship. Kallmann's (1938) consanguinity study looked at the families of 1087 people diagnosed with schizophrenia who had been admitted to Herzberge Hospital in Berlin. In addition to finding that the relatives of his "probands" were diagnosed with schizophrenia at rates significantly higher than population expectations, he also found that patients and their relatives had died of tuberculosis at rates several times greater than in the general population. This finding led Kallmann to conclude, with certainty, that tuberculosis and schizophrenia were genetically related diseases:

> Because in our estimate of the causes of death we naturally counted only the absolutely assured deaths from tuberculosis, the assumption will have to be made for the probands that at least one third of them, and possibly even more, died of tuberculosis. Thus no doubt can remain that *within our own proband material the death rate from tuberculosis was also much higher than in the general population, and that, on the whole, a very particular significance must be assigned to tuberculosis in the entire heredity-circle of schizophrenia* [emphasis in original]. (Kallmann, 1938, p. 86)

Today it is apparent that Kallmann's "finding" was actually a textbook example of what is known as a spurious correlation, which has been defined as a "correlation that results not from any direct relationship between the variables under assessment, but because of their relationships to a third variable (or fourth, or more) that has no connecting relationship between them" (Reber, 1985, p. 161). Kallmann failed to recognize that the high rate of tuberculosis among schizophrenia patients and their relatives was the result of environmental conditions common to both schizophrenics and tuberculosis sufferers: namely that the socioeconomic and hygienic conditions of mental patients and their family members were inferior to the conditions of a typical German family. Similarly, the conclusion that alcoholism, sociopathy, and hysteria are genetically related to ADHD could be the result of a correlation as spurious as Kallmann's.

To summarize, the ADHD adoption literature reveals a handful of greatly flawed studies which, even when combined, provide (at best) inconclusive evidence in favor of either a genetic basis for ADHD or its genetic relationship to any other condition.

Summary and Conclusions

We have seen that the genetic basis of ADHD has been supported with the same types of studies cited in favor of the genetic basis of schizophrenia and other psychiatric diagnoses. There are three main ways that psychiatric geneticists and behavior geneticists have made the case for the genetic basis of ADHD: family, twin, and adoption studies. We have seen that although family studies might be able to demonstrate the familiality of ADHD, the fact that families share a common environment as well as common genes does not permit any conclusion about a genetic component for the diagnosis.

It was argued that the classical twin method is no less confounded by environmental factors than family studies because identical twins clearly share a more similar environment than fraternals. Twin researchers have attempted to defend the assumption of equal environments but have failed to provide convincing evidence that the EEA, whether using the traditional or trait-relevant definition, is valid. It is therefore likely that the greater similarity of MZ vs

DZ twins on measures related to ADHD symptoms records nothing more than the greater environmental similarity and identification of MZ twins. Typically, ADHD twin study articles discuss the EEA briefly or not at all, and in no study do the authors come out in favor of the trait-relevant EEA. The conclusions of these studies, therefore, are based on the simple assumption that MZ and DZ environments are equal when it is clear that these environments are not equal.

ADHD adoption studies are greatly inferior to the already flawed schizophrenia adoption studies which preceded them and therefore offer no important evidence in favor of the genetic position. Apart from the other methodological problems with these studies, the fact that most made non-blind diagnoses and did not assess adoptees' biological relatives invalidates any inferences of the operation of genetic factors. After an examination of the total weight of evidence in favor of a genetic basis or predisposition for ADHD, it is concluded that a role for genetic factors is not supported and that future research should be directed toward psychosocial causes.

A reevaluation of the genetic evidence is important in the context of how ADHD is viewed and what directions will be taken in future research. Proponents of the brain dysfunction model of ADHD (and other psychiatric conditions) often point to the evidence from genetic studies in support of their position, since defective genes are seen as creating associated biological defects. The belief in the biological/genetic basis of ADHD has hindered investigation into possible environmental factors (McCubbin & Cohen, 1999), but it is just this area that demands greater attention. While there is little solid evidence in support of specific environmental factors, there are theories requiring further investigation. DeGrandpre (1999) sees the condition as the result of some children's problems with impulse control in our increasingly "rapid-fire culture," leading to children's "rapid-fire consciousness":

> At the heart of the developmental problem lies the emergence of a phenomenological experience of unsettledness, characterized by feelings of restlessness, anxiety, and impulsivity. Hyperactivity and the inability to attend to mundane activities exemplify the type of escape behavior that the "sensory addicted" child or adult uses in order to maintain his or her needed stream of stimulation. (p. 32)

It is reasonable to propose that future research be directed toward psychosocial theories such as DeGrandpre's. If future studies are also able to detect genetic factors, this information could be used to identify children in need of special intervention. Unfortunately, history has shown that the results of genetic studies have often been used to stigmatize individuals and groups, to discourage the search for other relevant and necessary factors, and to support the use of psychotropic drugs to treat problems caused by social and psychological factors. This article, therefore, is a necessary counterweight to the prevailing biopsychiatric/pharmacological view of ADHD.

References

Alberts-Corush, J., Firestone, P., & Goodman, J. (1986). Attention and impulsivity characteristics of the biological and adoptive parents of hyperactive and normal control children. *American Journal of Orthopsychiatry, 56*, 413–423.

Barkley, R. (1998a, September). Attention-deficit hyperactivity disorder. *Scientific American,* 66–71.

Barkley, R. (1998b). *Attention-deficit hyperactivity disorder: A handbook for diagnosis and treatment* (2nd ed.). New York: The Guilford Press.

Biederman, J., Faraone, S., Mick, E., Spencer, T., Wilens, T., Kiely, K., Guite, J., Ablon, S., Reed, E., & Warburton, R. (1995). High risk for attention deficit hyperactivity disorder among children of parents with childhood onset of the disorder: A pilot study. *American Journal of Psychiatry, 152*, 431–435.

Biederman, J., Munir, K., Knee, D., Habelow, M., Autor, S., Hoge, S., & Waternaux, C. (1986). A family study of patients with attention deficit disorder and normal controls. *Journal of Psychiatric Research, 20*, 263–274.

Breggin, P. (1998). *Talking back to Ritalin.* Monroe, ME: Common Courage Press.

Cantwell, D. (1972). Psychiatric illness in the families of hyperactive children. *Archives of General Psychiatry, 27*, 414–417.

Cantwell, D. (1975). Genetic studies of hyperactive children: Psychiatric illness in biologic and adopting parents. In R. Fieve, D. Rosenthal, & H. Brill (Eds.), *Genetic research in psychiatry* (pp. 273–280). Baltimore: The Johns Hopkins Press.

DeGrandpre, R. (1999). *Ritalin nation.* New York: Norton.

Diller, L., Tanner, J., & Weil, J. (1995). Etiology of ADHD: Nature or Nurture? [Letter to the editor]. *American Journal of Psychiatry, 153*, 451–452.

Diller, L. (1998). *Running on Ritalin.* New York: Bantam Books.

Eaves, L., Silberg, J., Hewitt, J., Meyer, J., Rutter, M., Simonoff, E., Neale, M., & Pickles, A. (1993). Genes, personality, and psychopathology: A latent class analysis of liability to symptoms of attention-deficit hyperactivity disorder in twins. In R. Plomin & G. McClearn (Eds.), *Nature, nurture, & psychology* (pp. 285–303). Washington, DC: American Psychological Association Press.

Edelbrock, C., Rende, R., Plomin, R., & Thompson, L. (1995). A twin study of competence and problem behavior in childhood and early adolescence. *Journal of Child Psychology and Psychiatry, 36*, 775–785.

Faraone, S., Biederman, J., Keenan, K., & Tsuang, M. (1991a). A family-genetic study of girls with DSM-III attention deficit disorder. *American Journal of Psychiatry, 148*, 112–117.

Faraone, S., & Tsuang, M. (1995). Methods in psychiatric genetics. In M. Tsuang, M. Tohen, & G. Zahner (Eds.), *Textbook in psychiatric epidemiology* (pp. 81–134). New York: Wiley–Liss.

Farber, S. (1981). *Identical twins reared apart: A reanalysis.* New York: Basic Books.

Gilger, J., Pennington, B., & DeFries, J. (1992). A twin study of the etiology of co-morbidity: Attention-deficit hyperactivity disorder and dyslexia. *Journal of the American Academy of Child and Adolescent Psychiatry, 31*, 343–348.

Gillis, J., Gilger, J., Pennington, B., & DeFries, J. (1992). Attention deficit disorder in reading-disabled twins: Evidence for a genetic etiology. *Journal of Abnormal Child Psychology, 20*, 303–315.

Gjone, H., Stevenson, J., & Sundet, J. (1996). Genetic influence on parent-reported attention-related problems in a Norwegian general population twin study. *Journal of the American Academy of Child and Adolescent Psychiatry, 35*, 588–596.

Goodman, R., & Stevenson, J. (1989a). A twin study of hyperactivity: I. An examination of hyperactivity scores and categories derived from the Rutter Teacher and Parent Questionnaires. *Journal of Child Psychology and Psychiatry, 30*, 671–689.

Goodman, R., & Stevenson, J. (1989b). A twin study of hyperactivity: II. The aetiological role of genes, family relationships and perinatal adversity. *Journal of Child Psychology and Psychiatry, 30*, 691–709.

Gottesman, I. (1991). *Schizophrenia genesis.* New York: W. H. Freeman.

Gottesman, I., & Shields, J. (1966). Contributions of twin studies to perspectives on schizophrenia. In B. Maher (Ed.), *Progress in experimental personality research* (Vol. 3, pp. 1–84). New York: Academic Press.

Heston, L. (1966). Psychiatric disorders in foster home reared children of schizophrenic mothers. *British Journal of Psychiatry,* 112, 819–825.

Jackson, D. (1960). A critique of the literature on the genetics of schizophrenia. In D. Jackson (Ed.), *The etiology of schizophrenia* (pp. 37–87). New York: Basic Books.

Joseph, J. (1998a). *A critical analysis of the genetic theory of schizophrenia.* Unpublished doctoral dissertation, California School of Professional Psychology, Alameda.

Joseph, J. (1998b). The equal environment assumption of the classical twin method: A critical analysis. *Journal of Mind and Behavior,* 19, 325–358.

Joseph, J. (1999a). A critique of the Finnish Adoptive Family Study of Schizophrenia. *Journal of Mind and Behavior,* 20, 133–154.

Joseph, J. (1999b). The genetic theory of schizophrenia: A critical overview. *Ethical Human Sciences and Services,* 1, 119–145.

Joseph, J. (in press-c). Don Jackson's "A critique of the literature on the genetics of schizophrenia"—A reappraisal after 40 years. *Genetic, Social, and General Psychology Monographs.*

Joseph, J. (in press-d). Separated twins and the genetics of personality differences: A critique. *American Journal of Psychology.*

Kallmann, F. (1938). *The genetics of schizophrenia: A study of heredity and reproduction in the families of 1,087 schizophrenics.* New York: J. J. Augustin.

Kamin, L. (1974). *The science and politics of I.Q.* Potomac, MD: Erlbaum.

Kendler, K. (1993). Twin studies of psychiatric illness: Current status and future directions. *Archives of General Psychiatry,* 50, 905–915.

Kety, S. (1978). Heredity and environment. In J. Shershow (Ed.), *Schizophrenia: Science and practice* (pp. 47–68). Cambridge, MA: Harvard Univ. Press.

Kety, S., Rosenthal, D., Wender, P., & Schulsinger, F. (1968). The types and prevalence of mental illness in the biological and adoptive families of adopted schizophrenics. In D. Rosenthal & S. Kety (Eds.), *The transmission of schizophrenia* (pp. 345–362). New York: Pergamon Press.

Kety, S., Rosenthal, D., Wender, P., Schulsinger, F., & Jacobsen, B. (1975). Mental illness in the biological and adoptive families of adopted individuals who have become schizophrenic: A preliminary report based on psychiatric interviews. In R. Fieve, D. Rosenthal, & H. Brill (Eds.), *Genetic research in psychiatry* (pp. 147–165). Baltimore: The Johns Hopkins Press.

Kety, S., Wender, P., Jacobsen, B., Ingraham, L., Jansson, L., Faber, B., & Kinney, D. (1994). Mental illness in the biological and adoptive relatives of schizophrenic adoptees: Replication of the Copenhagen study to the rest of Denmark. *Archives of General Psychiatry,* 51, 442–455.

Kläning, U., Mortensen, P., & Kyvik, K. (1996). Increased occurrence of schizophrenia and other psychiatric illnesses among twins. *British Journal of Psychiatry,* 168, 688–692.

Lewontin, R., Rose, S., & Kamin, L. (1984). *Not in our genes.* New York: Pantheon.

Levy, F., Hay, D., McStephen, M., Wood, C., & Waldman, I. (1997). Attention-deficit hyperactivity disorder: A category or a continuum? Genetic analysis of a large-scale twin study. *Journal of the American Academy of Child and Adolescent Psychiatry,* 36, 737–744.

Lopez, R. (1965). Hyperactivity in twins. *Canadian Psychiatric Association Journal,* 10, 421–426.

McCubbin, M., & Cohen, D. (1999). Empirical, ethical, and political perspectives on the use of methylphenidate. *Ethical Human Sciences and Services,* 1, 81–101.

Morrison, J., & Stewart, M. (1971). A family study of the hyperactive child syndrome. *Biological Psychiatry,* 3, 189–195.

Morrison, J., & Stewart, M. (1973). The psychiatric status of the legal families of adopted hyperactive children. *Archives of General Psychiatry, 28,* 888–891.

Nadder, T., Silberg, J., Eaves, L., Maes, H., & Meyer, J. (1998). Genetic effects on ADHD symptomatology in 7–13-year-old twins: Results from a telephone survey. *Behavior Genetics, 28,* 83–99.

Nichols, P., & Chen, T. (1981). *Minimal brain dysfunction.* Hillsdale, NJ: Erlbaum.

Pam, A. (1995). Biological psychiatry: Science or pseudoscience? In C. Ross & A. Pam (Eds.), *Pseudoscience in biological psychiatry: Blaming the body* (pp. 7–84). New York: Wiley.

Pam, A., Kemker, S., Ross, C., & Golden, R. (1996). The "equal environment assumption" in MZ–DZ comparisons: An untenable premise of psychiatric genetics? *Acta Geneticae Medicae et Gemellologiae, 45,* 349–360.

Plomin, R., DeFries, J., & McClearn, G. (1990). *Behavioral genetics: A primer* (2nd ed.). New York: W. H. Freeman.

Reber, A. (1985). *The Penguin dictionary of psychology.* London: Penguin Books.

Rosenthal, D. (1960). Confusion of identity and the frequency of schizophrenia in twins. *Archives of General Psychiatry, 3,* 101–108.

Rosenthal, D. (1970). *Genetic theory and abnormal behavior.* New York: McGraw-Hill.

Rosenthal, D. (1975). The spectrum concept in schizophrenic and manic-depressive disorders. In D. Freedman (Ed.), *Biology of the major psychoses* (pp. 19–25). New York: Raven.

Rosenthal, D. (1979). Genetic factors in behavioural disorders. In M. Roth & V. Cowie (Eds.), *Psychiatry, genetics and pathography: A tribute to Eliot Slater* (pp. 22–33). London: Oxford Univ. Press.

Rosenthal, D., Wender, P., Kety, S., Welner, J., & Schulsinger, F. (1971). The adopted-away offspring of schizophrenics. *American Journal of Psychiatry, 128,* 307–311.

Rüdin, E. (1916). *Zur Vererbung und Neuentstehung der Dementia praecox.* Berlin: Springer-Verlag OHG.

Safer, D. (1973). A familial factor in minimal brain dysfunction. *Behavior Genetics, 3,* 175–186.

Sherman, D., Iacono, W., & McGue, M. (1997). Attention-deficit hyperactivity disorder dimensions: A twin study of inattention and impulsivity-hyperactivity. *Journal of the American Academy of Child and Adolescent Psychiatry, 36,* 745–753.

Silberg, J., Rutter, M., Meyer, J., Maes, H., Hewitt, J., Simonoff, E., Pickles, A., & Loeber, R. (1996). Genetic and environmental influences on the covariation between hyperactivity and conduct disturbance in juvenile twins. *Journal of Psychology and Psychiatry, 37,* 803–816.

Steffensson, B., Larsson, J., Fried, I., El-Sayed, E., Rydelius, P., & Lichtenstein, P. (1999). Genetic disposition for global maturity: An explanation for genetic effects on parental report of ADHD. *International Journal of Behavioral Development, 23,* 357–374.

Stevenson, J. (1992). Evidence for a genetic etiology in hyperactivity in children. *Behavior Genetics, 22,* 337–344.

Tannock, R. (1998). Attention deficit hyperactivity disorder: Advances in cognitive, neurobiological, and genetic research. *Journal of Child Psychology and Psychiatry, 39,* 65–99.

Taylor, H. (1980). *The IQ game: A methodological inquiry into the heredity-environment controversy.* New Brunswick, NJ: Rutgers Univ. Press.

Tienari, P., Wynne, L., Moring, J., Lahti, I., Naarala, M., Sorri, A., Wahlberg, K., Saarento, O., Seitamaa, M., Kaleva, M., & Läsky, K. (1994). The Finnish adoptive family study of schizophrenia. *British Journal of Psychiatry, 164*(Suppl. 23), 20–26.

van den Oord, E., Boomsma, D., & Verhulst, F. (1994). A study of problem behaviors in 10- to 15-year-old biologically related and unrelated international adoptees. *Behavior Genetics, 24,* 193–205.

van den Oord, E., Verhulst, F., & Boomsma, D. (1996). A genetic study of maternal and paternal ratings of problem behaviors in 3-year-old twins. *Journal of Abnormal Psychology,* **105,** 349–357.

Welner, Z., Welner, A., Stewart, M., Palkes, H., & Wish, E. (1977). A controlled study of siblings of hyperactive children. *Journal of Nervous and Mental Disease,* **165,** 110–117.

Wender, P. (1995). *Attention-deficit hyperactivity disorder in adults.* New York: Oxford Univ. Press.

Willerman, L. (1973). Activity level and hyperactivity in twins. *Child Development,* **44,** 288–293.

**Stephen V. Faraone and
Joseph Biederman**

Nature, Nurture, and Attention Deficit Hyperactivity Disorder

This commentary shows that [Jay] Joseph's... review of the genetics of attention deficit hyperactivity disorder (ADHD) contains errors of scientific logic and ignores much relevant research. Thus, we reject his conclusions. We also reject Joseph's approach of pitting nature against nurture as if these two facets of human life are at odds with one another. Instead, most scientists who study the genetics of psychiatric disorders embrace the idea that these disorders are influenced by both genes and environmental factors. In fact, the twin studies criticized by Joseph provide the strongest evidence that environmental risk factors play a substantial role in the etiology of ADHD. They do so by showing that when one identical twin has ADHD the risk to the co-twin is much less than 100%, a fact which can only be explained by environmental risk factors. We also reject the idea that genetic studies have hindered psychosocial research, stigmatized patients, or promoted psychopharmacologic treatments. Genetic studies have aimed at solving one part of the puzzle of ADHD. By testing a parsimonious theory, they have set the stage for gene discovery and the delineation of how genes and environment combine to cause this impairing disorder.

Attention deficit hyperactivity disorder (ADHD) is a childhood-onset, clinically heterogeneous disorder of inattention, hyperactivity, and impulsivity. Its impact on society is enormous in terms of its financial cost, stress to families, adverse academic and vocational outcomes, and negative effects on self-esteem (Barkley, 1998). For these reasons, discussions of the etiology of ADHD have serious implications. Because conclusions from such discussions are likely to drive future research and treatment development, how we address these issues will ultimately affect the lives of the many children, adolescents, and adults who suffer from this disorder.

For these reasons it is essential that readers carefully evaluate the controversial conclusion drawn by Joseph (2000): "After an examination of the total weight of evidence in favor of a genetic basis or predisposition for ADHD, it is concluded that a role for genetic factors is not supported and that future

From Stephen V. Faraone and Joseph Biederman, "Nature, Nurture, and Attention Deficit Hyperactivity Disorder," *Developmental Review*, vol. 20, no. 4 (December 2000). Copyright © 2000 by Academic Press. Reprinted by permission of the publisher and Stephen V. Faraone.

research should be directed toward psychosocial causes." In this commentary we show this conclusion to be wrong, not only because it runs counter to the prevailing view in the scientific community (Barkley, 1998; Faraone & Biederman, 1998; Faraone & Doyle, in press; Swanson, Castellanos, Murias, LaHoste, & Kennedy, 1998; Thapar, Holmes, Poulton, & Harrington, 1999), but also because it is based on errors in scientific logic compromised by an incomplete review of relevant data.

Joseph's Errors of Inference

Joseph's main logical error is his lack of attention to the nature of scientific theory building and hypothesis testing. The theory that genes influence ADHD is a viable theory because it makes several predictions which, *if proven wrong,* would disprove the theory. The first is that ADHD should run in families. It does (Faraone & Doyle, in press). The second is that identical twins should show a greater concordance for ADHD than fraternal twins. They do (Faraone & Doyle, in press). The third is that ADHD should be transmitted through biological, not adoptive family relationships. It is (Faraone & Doyle, in press). The fourth is that the familial transmission of ADHD should conform to genetic, not cultural transmission, models. It does (Faraone & Doyle, in press). The fifth is that molecular genetic studies should find evidence that specific genes cause ADHD. They have (Faraone & Doyle, in press).

Joseph does not claim that any of these predictions have been proven wrong. In fact, he does not even address predictions four and five. Thus, his article cannot be viewed as disproving the hypothesis that genes influence the etiology of ADHD. Instead, his argument can be boiled down to three key claims. His first claim is that studies showing ADHD runs in families are irrelevant to the question of genetic transmission because familial transmission can be caused by environmental factors. It is true that disorders can run in families due to either environmental or genetic reasons (Faraone, Tsuang, & Tsuang, 1999). But it is wrong to state that family studies are irrelevant to testing the theory that genes influence ADHD. The theory provides the testable prediction that ADHD should run in families, which has yet to be proven wrong.

The second claim made by Joseph is that twin studies of ADHD are flawed by the equal environment assumption, which holds that the trait-relevant environments of identical and fraternal twins are the same. He finds this assumption untenable for two reasons. First, several studies have shown that, compared with fraternal twins, identical twins are treated more alike, spend more time together, have more common friends, and experience greater levels of identity confusion. Second, he *infers* from these data that identical twins are more likely to be similarly exposed to "trait-relevant" environmental factors. Notably, Joseph presents no data to support his inference. Thus, readers should view it as a hypothesis to be tested rather than a conclusion to be accepted. In fact, although not mentioned by Joseph, this hypothesis was tested by Thapar et al. (1995). They found that the equal environment assumption was violated because identical twins scored significantly higher on an index of environmental sharing than did fraternal twins. But, contrary to Joseph's inference, this index of environmental sharing did not predict twin similarity for ADHD scores, i.e., it was not trait relevant.

Joseph's third claim is that adoption studies of ADHD are flawed in several ways. We agree with Joseph that no ADHD adoption study has directly compared the biological and adoptive families of the same child. These, along with the other relatively minor methodological problems detailed by Joseph, limit the strength of any inferences we can draw from these studies.

What should readers conclude about the three areas of genetic research discussed by Joseph? The standard interpretation of these data would be that the theory of genes influencing ADHD has not been disproven. We have chosen our language carefully here to correspond to the logic of scientific inference. Experiments subject theories to falsification. They can fail to falsify a theory but cannot prove that it is correct. Of course, consistent failures to falsify a theory will strengthen our belief that the theory (or parts of it) are true. Thus, most scientists find value in the theory that genes influence ADHD because it has consistently made predictions which turn out to be correct.

Joseph rejects the standard interpretation yet provides no theory of his own beyond vague assertions that psychosocial events could account for the pattern of data observed in family, twin, and adoption studies. But scientists need more than vague assertions, we need theories which make testable predictions. A testable psychosocial theory of the apparent genetic transmission of ADHD would need to specify a psychosocial causal factor that (a) is transmitted from parents to children, (b) is more likely to be shared by identical than fraternal twins, and (c) explains the elevated rates of ADHD and associated traits among the biological relatives of adopted away ADHD children. Unfortunately, Joseph does not present a testable theory that can be assessed as a potential alternative to the theory that genes influence ADHD.

Another lacuna in Joseph's argument is his failure to address the principle of parsimony when considering the value of alternative theories. This principle states that, other things being equal, a theory which makes fewer assumptions is better than one requiring more assumptions. Any genetic theory of ADHD explains the family, twin, and adoption data with a single idea, the idea that genes influence the etiology of the disorder. In contrast, Joseph must appeal to several different mechanisms to explain these findings. One mechanism must explain transmission from parent to child (perhaps modeling or cultural transmission; he does not say). Another mechanism (the idea that identical twins share a more trait-relevant environment than fraternal twins) must be invoked to account for twin data. And a third mechanism (faulty study design) must be conjured up to explain the results of adoption studies. It is, of course, *possible* that three different mechanisms have converged to produce a pattern of results that simulates genetic transmission. But such a three-factor theory is not parsimonious, especially when compared with the idea that genes account for the observed data.

Joseph's Incomplete Literature Review

Joseph's literature review ignores two domains of research into the genetics of ADHD: segregation analyses and molecular genetic studies. Segregation analysis is a mathematical method which examines evidence for genetic transmission by determining if the pattern of illness in families follows known genetic mechanisms. Morrison and Stewart (1974) concluded that polygenic inheritance was a likely mode of transmission for ADHD. Recent studies have, however, been more consistent with the idea that one gene may have a more robust effect than others (e.g., Deutsch, Matthysse, Swanson, & Farkas, 1990). Faraone et al. (1992) showed that the familial transmission of ADHD was consistent with single-gene effects but not with cultural transmission. Consistent findings have also emerged in a study of a South American sample (Lopera et al., 1999) in which the only models of inheritance that could not be rejected were those of dominant and codominant gene effects. In addition, Maher et al. (1999) found that a Mendelian model was the best explanation for the pattern of transmission of ADHD.

Because, in some of these studies (i.e., Deutsch et al., 1990; Faraone et al., 1992) the differences in fit between genetic models involving multifactorial and single gene inheritance was modest, several interpretations are possible. If ADHD had more than one genetic cause, then the evidence for any single mode of transmission might be relatively weak. Alternatively, ADHD may be caused by several interacting genes of modest effect, which is consistent with ADHD's high population prevalence (2 to 7% for ADHD) and high concordance in MZ [identical] twins but modest recurrence risks to first-degree relatives. In summary, segregation analyses have not resolved ADHD's mode of transmission, but they do implicate genetics as opposed to environmental mechanisms.

Although still in their infancy, molecular genetic studies have already implicated several genes as mediating the susceptibility to ADHD. Researchers have examined genes in catecholaminergic pathways because animal models, theoretical considerations, and the effectiveness of stimulant treatment implicate catecholaminergic dysfunction in the pathophysiology of this disorder (Faraone & Biederman, 1998).

Seven groups have reported an association between ADHD and the 7-repeat allele of the DRD4 gene (Barr et al., 2000; Comings et al., 1999; Faraone et al., 1999; LaHoste et al., 1996; Rowe et al., 1998; Smalley et al., 1998; Swanson et al., 1998). Six groups, however, could not replicate this association (Asherson et al., 1998; Castellanos et al., 1998; Comings et al., 1999; Daly, Hawi, Fitzgerald, & Gill, 1998; Eisenberg et al., 2000; Hawi, McCarron, Kirley, Fitzgerald, & Gill, 2000). Despite the negative findings, a meta-analysis of these data concluded that the DRD4 7-repeat allele was significantly associated with ADHD (Faraone, 1999).

Notably, the DRD4 7-fold repeat allele mediates a blunted response to dopamine (Asghari et al., 1995) and has been implicated in novelty seeking (Benjamin, Patterson, Greenberg, Murphy, & Hamer, 1996; Ebstein et al., 1996), a personality trait related to ADHD. When the D4 gene is disabled in a knockout mouse model, dopamine synthesis increases in the dorsal striatum and the mice show locomotor supersensitivity to ethanol, cocaine, and methamphetamine (Rubinstein et al., 1997). D4 knockout mice also show reduced novelty-related exploration (Dulawa, Grandy, Low, Paulus, & Geyer, 1999), which is consistent with human data suggesting a role for D4 in novelty-seeking behaviors.

Cook (1995) reported an association between ADHD and the 480-bp allele of the dopamine transporter (DAT) gene using a family-based association study. This finding was replicated in family-based studies of ADHD by Gill et al. (1997), Daly et al. (1998), and Waldman et al. (1998) but not in two other studies (Asherson et al., 1998; Poulton et al., 1998). The link between the DAT gene and ADHD is further supported by a study that relates this gene to poor methylphenidate response in ADHD children (Winsberg & Comings, 1999), a knockout mouse study showing that its elimination leads to hyperactivity in mice (Majzoub & Muglia, 1996), and a neuroimaging study showing DAT activity in the striatum is elevated by 70% in ADHD adults (Dougherty et al., 1999).

Four studies examined the Catechol-O-Methyltransferase (COMT) gene, the product of which is involved in the breakdown of dopamine and norepinephrine. One study (Eisenberg et al., 1999) found that ADHD was associated with the high enzyme activity COMT Val allele; three others (Barr et al., 1999; Hawi, Millar, Daly, Fitzgerald, & Gill, 2000; Tahir et al., 2000) did not. One study implicated the A1 allele of the dopamine D2 receptor gene (Comings et al., 1991) and found additive effects of DRD2, DBH, and DAT with regard to ADHD symptoms. Another study (Jiang et al., 2000) found an association with the DXS7 locus of the X chromosome, a marker for MAO which encodes enzymes that metabolize dopamine and other neurotransmitters. Finally, Comings et al. (1999) found associations and additive effects of polymorphisms at three noradrenergic genes [the adrenergic alpha 2A (ADRA2A), adrenergic alpha 2C (ADRA2C), and DBH] on an ADHD symptom score in a sample of individuals with Tourette's syndrome.

Like family, twin, and adoption studies, segregation analysis and molecular genetic studies have not disproven the theory that genes influence ADHD. Segregation studies are consistent with the idea that familial transmission follows genetic mechanisms. In contrast, they reject the idea that familial transmission can be accounted for by environmental risk factors. In addition, molecular genetic studies have implicated two genes, DRD4 and DAT, in the etiology of ADHD.

Further Considerations

Joseph's confrontational approach to psychiatric genetics misleads readers in several ways. He states that "The belief in the biological/genetic basis of ADHD has hindered investigation into possible environmental factors." This statement errs by conflating biological with genetic thus denying the potential biological nature of environmental risk factors. Moreover, even a cursory review of the literature shows that the investigation of environmental factors has not been hindered.

With regard to the biological environment, the idea that food additives cause ADHD has been studied and rejected (Conners, 1980) as has the theory that excessive sugar intake leads to ADHD (Wolraich, Wilson, & White, 1995). Some toxins have been implicated in the etiology of ADHD. Lead contamination leads to distractibility, hyperactivity, restlessness, and lower intellectual functioning (Needleman, 1982). But many ADHD children do not show lead contamination and many children with high lead exposure do not develop ADHD. Thus, lead exposure cannot account for the bulk of ADHD cases.

The literature examining the association of ADHD with pregnancy and delivery complications [PDCs] supports the idea that PDCs predispose children to ADHD (e.g., Chandola, Robling, Peters, Melville-Thomas, & McGuffin, 1992; Conners, 1975; Hartsough & Lambert, 1985; Milberger, Biederman, Faraone, Guite, & Tsuang, 1997; Nichols & Chen, 1981; Sprich-Buckminster, Biederman, Milberger, Faraone, & Krifcher Lehman, 1993). The PDCs implicated in ADHD frequently lead to hypoxia and tend to involve *chronic* exposures to the fetus, such as toxemia, rather than *acute,* traumatic events, such as delivery complications (Faraone & Biederman, 1998). Notably, maternal smoking during pregnancy predicts behavioral and cognitive impairment in children and ADHD (e.g., Denson, Nanson, & McWatters, 1975; Milberger, Biederman, Faraone, Chen, & Jones, 1996).

Researchers have also implicated the psychosocial environment in the etiology of ADHD. Rutter's (1975) classic studies of the Isle of Wight and the inner borough of London provide a compelling example of how psychosocial risk factors influence child psychopathology. This research revealed six risk factors within the family environment that correlated significantly with childhood mental disturbances: (a) severe marital discord; (b) low social class; (c) large family size; (d) paternal criminality; (e) maternal mental disorder; and (f) foster placement. Rutter found that it was the aggregate of adversity factors, rather than the presence of any single one, that impaired development. Other studies also find that as the number of adverse conditions accumulates, the risk of impaired outcome in the child increases proportionally (Blanz, Schmidt, & Esser, 1991). Biederman et al. (1995) found a positive association between Rutter's index of adversity and ADHD, measures of ADHD-associated psychopathology, impaired cognition, and psychosocial dysfunction.

Other cross-sectional and longitudinal studies have identified variables such as marital distress, family dysfunction, and low social class as risk factors for psychopathology and dysfunction in children. For example, the Ontario Child Health Study showed that family dysfunction and low income predicted persistence and onset of one or more psychiatric disorders over a 4-year follow-up period (Offord et al., 1992). Other work implicates low maternal education, low social class, and single parenthood as important adversity factors for ADHD (e.g., Nichols & Chen, 1981; Palfrey, Levine, Walker, & Sullivan, 1985). These studies suggest that the mothers of ADHD children have more negative communication patterns, more conflict with their child, and a greater intensity of anger than do control mothers.

Biederman et al. (1995) showed that chronic conflict, decreased family cohesion, and exposure to parental psychopathology, particularly maternal

psychopathology, were more common in ADHD families compared with control families. The differences between ADHD and control children could not
be accounted for by either SES or parental history of major psychopathology.
Moreover, increased levels of family-environment adversity predicted impaired
psychosocial functioning. Measures indexing chronic family conflict had a
more pernicious impact on the exposed child than those indexing exposure
to parental psychopathology. Indeed, marital discord in families has consistently predicted disruptive behaviors in boys (Institute of Medicine, 1989).
This research shows that it is the extent of discord and overt conflict, regardless of whether the parents are separated, that predicts the child's risks for
psychopathology and dysfunction (Hetherington, Cox, & Cox, 1982).

Low maternal warmth and high maternal malaise and criticism have
been previously associated with ADHD in children (Barkley, Fischer, Edlebrock, & Smallish, 1991). An epidemiologic study examining family attributes
in children who had undergone stressful experiences, found that children's
perceptions of mothers, but not fathers, differentiated stress-resilient and
stress-affected children (Wyman et al., 1992).

Another misleading conclusion from Joseph's article is his statement "Unfortunately, history has shown that the results of genetic studies have often
been used to stigmatize individuals and groups, to discourage the search for
other relevant and necessary factors...." Joseph presents no data to show that
the results of genetic studies stigmatize individuals and groups. We realize that
psychiatric genetic data had been used by the Nazis to justify eugenic steriliza-
tion and murder (Gottesman & Bertelsen, 1996), but that would not be a fair
assessment of contemporary psychiatric genetics. Today, people with mental illness are stigmatized, but we know of no data showing that genetic studies lead
to stigma. In fact, in the 19th century and earlier, long before the advent of
psychiatric genetics, patients with psychiatric disorders were stigmatized much
more than they are today (e.g., as being witches and/or possessed by the devil).

Moreover, Joseph fails to mention that psychosocial theories can stigmatize families. We recall the now-discredited theory of the schizophrenogenic
mother which burdened an entire generation of mothers of schizophrenic patients. In fact, data supporting a genetic and biological etiology of ADHD can
be used to reduce stigma by teaching patients, relatives, and the public that
ADHD is an illness which can be treated not an inadequacy to be ashamed of.

Another misleading conclusion made by Joseph is his statement that the
results of genetic studies have often been used "to support the use of psychotropic drugs to treat problems caused by social and psychological factors."
This statement confuses the etiology of a disorder with its treatment. Although
this error in logic was corrected by Meehl (1973), it periodically recurs in the
literature. Meehl used the term "therapeutic nihilism" to refer to the belief that
a genetic cause for a disorder means that psychosocial therapies will be useless.
He showed that therapeutic nihilism was wrong because the idea that genes
cause a disorder does not rule out the possibility that environmental factors
also influence its etiology or modulate its course.

In practice, most psychiatric and psychological treatment programs reject
therapeutic nihilism. For example, schizophrenia is influenced by genes and has

a strong biological basis. Yet, its medication treatment is often supplemented with psychosocial therapies (Tsuang, Faraone, & Green, 1999). Similarly, despite knowing of the genetic basis of ADHD for many years, the National Institute of Mental Health (NIMH) launched a multisite study to evaluate the efficacy of stimulant medication, psychosocial treatment, and their combination in the treatment of ADHD (Arnold et al., 1997).

Another form of therapeutic nihilism occurs with the belief that problems caused by psychological or social factors can only be treated with psychosocial therapies. Should traumatized people with severe, recurrent anxiety be denied antianxiety medication because the cause of their disorder was a psychosocial event? Should those who become depressed and suicidal in the wake of a family tragedy be denied antidepressants? Should patients with a reactive psychosis be denied antipsychotic medication?

Clearly, choosing treatment options based on the presumed psychosocial or genetic origin of a disorder can lead to serous clinical errors. Instead, we suggest that clinicians use controlled clinical trials to determine which treatments are most appropriate for their patients. For example, the recent NIMH multisite study of ADHD treatment showed that stimulant treatment was more effective than psychosocial treatment and that the combination of stimulant and psychosocial treatment did not improve outcome beyond what was found with stimulant treatment alone (Arnold et al., 1997).

Conclusions

We have shown that Joseph's review contains errors of scientific logic and ignores a substantial body of research relevant to the theory that genes influence ADHD. For these reasons, we reject his conclusions, especially since he does not provide an alternative theory that better describes the relevant data. We also encourage readers to reject Joseph's approach of pitting nature against nurture as if these two facets of human life are somehow at odds with one another. Instead, readers should recognize that most scientists who study the genetics of psychiatric disorders embrace the idea that these disorders are influenced by both genes and environmental factors. In fact, the twin studies so severely criticized by Joseph provided the strongest evidence that environmental risk factors play a substantial role in the etiology of ADHD. They do so by showing that when one identical twin has ADHD the risk to the co-twin is much less than 100%, a fact which can only be explained by environmental risk factors.

We also reject the idea that genetic studies of ADHD have hindered psychosocial research, stigmatized patients, or promoted psychopharmacologic treatments. Genetic studies have simply aimed at solving one part of the puzzle that is ADHD. By repeatedly testing a parsimonious theory, genetic studies have begun to clarify the genetic component to ADHD. By doing so they have set the stage for gene discovery and the delineation of how genes and environment combine to cause this impairing disorder.

References

Arnold, L. E., Abikoff, H. B., Cantwell, D. P., Conners, C. K., Elliot, G., Greenhill, L. L., Hechtman, L., Hinshaw, S. P., Hoza, B., Jensen, P. S., Kraemer, H. C., March, J. S., Newcorn, J. H., Pelham, W. E., Richters, J. E., Schiller, E., Severe, J. B., Swanson, J. M., Vereen, D., & Wells, K. C. (1997). National Institute of Mental Health Collaborative Multimodal Treatment Study of Children with ADHD (the MTA). Design challenges and choices. *Archives of General Psychiatry,* 54, 865–870.

Asghari, V., Sanyal, S., Buchwaldt, S., Paterson, A., Jovanovic, V., & Van Tol, H. H. (1995). Modulation of intracellular cyclic AMP levels by different human dopamine D4 receptor variants. *Journal of Neurochemistry,* 65, 1157–1165.

Asherson, P., Virdee, V., Curran, S., Ebersole, S., Freeman, B., Craig, I., Simonoff, E., Eley, T., Plomin, R., & Taylor, E. (1998). Association of DSM-IV attention deficit hyperactivity disorder and monoamine pathway genes. *American Journal of Medical Genetics, Neuropsychiatric Genetics,* 81, 548.

Barkley, R. A. (1998). *Attention Deficit Hyperactivity Disorder: A handbook for diagnosis and treatment.* New York: Guilford.

Barkley, R. A., Fischer, M., Edlebrock, C., & Smallish, L. (1991). The adolescent outcome of hyperactive children diagnosed by research criteria: III. Mother-child interactions, family conflicts and maternal psychopathology. *Journal of Child Psychology and Psychiatry,* 32, 233–255.

Barr, C. L., Wigg, K., Malone, M., Schachar, R., Tannock, R., Roberts, W., & Kennedy, J. L. (1999). Linkage study of catechol-O-methyltransferase and attention-deficit hyperactivity disorder. *American Journal of Medical Genetics,* 88, 710–713.

Barr, C. L., Wigg, K. G., Bloom, S., Schachar, R., Tannock, R., Roberts, W., Malone, M., & Kennedy, J. L. (2000). Further evidence from haplotype analysis for linkage of the dopamine D4 receptor gene and attention-deficit hyperactivity disorder. *American Journal of Medical Genetics (Neuropsychiatric Genetics),* 96(3), 244–250.

Benjamin, J., Patterson, C., Greenberg, B. D., Murphy, D. L., & Hamer, D. H. (1996). Population and familial association between the D4 dopamine receptor gene and measures of novelty seeking. *Nature Genetics,* 12, 81–84.

Biederman, J., Milberger, S., Faraone, S. V., Kiely, K., Guite, J., Mick, E., Ablon, S., Warburton, R., & Reed, E. (1995). Family-environment risk factors for attention deficit hyperactivity disorder: A test of Rutter's indicators of adversity. *Archives of General Psychiatry,* 52, 464–470.

Biederman, J., Milberger, S. V., Faraone, S., Kiely, K., Guide, J., Mick, E., Ablon, S., Warburton, R., Reed, E., & Davis, S. (1995). Impact of adversity on functioning and comorbidity in children with attention-deficit hyperactivity disorder. *Journal of the American Academy of Child and Adolescent Psychiatry,* 34, 1495–1503.

Blanz, B., Schmidt, M. H., & Esser, G. (1991). Familial adversities and child psychiatric disorders. *Journal of Child Psychology and Psychiatric Disorders,* 32, 939–950.

Castellanos, F. X., Lau, E., Tayebi, N., Lee, P., Long, R. E., Giedd, J. N., Sharp, W., Marsh, W. L., Walter, J. M., Hamburger, S. D., Ginns, E. I., Rapoport, J. L., & Sidransky, E. (1998). Lack of an association between a dopamine-4 receptor polymorphism and attention-deficit/hyperactivity disorder: Genetic and brain morphometric analyses. *Molecular Psychiatry,* 3, 431–434.

Chandola, C., Robling, M., Peters, T., Melville-Thomas, G., & McGuffin, P. (1992). Pre- and perinatal factors and the risk of subsequent referral for hyperactivity. *Child Psychology and Psychiatry,* 33, 1077–1090.

Comings, D., Gade-Andavolu, R., Gonzalez, N., Blake, H., & MacMurray, J. (1999). Additive effect of three naradenergic genes (ADRA2A, ADRA2C, DBH) on attention-deficit hyperactivity disorder and learning disabilities on Tourette syndrome subjects. *Clinical Genetics,* 55, 160–172.

Comings, D. E., Comings, B. G., Muhleman, D., Dietz, G., Shahbahrami, B., Tast, D., Knell, E., Kocsis, P., Baumgarten, R., Kovacs, B. W., Levy, D. L., Smith, M., Borison, R. L., Evans, D. D., Klein, D. N., MacMurray, J., Tosk, J. M., Sverd, J., Gysin, R., & Flanagan, S. D. (1991). The dopamine D2 receptor locus as a modifying gene in neuropsychiatric disorders. *Journal of the American Medical Association, 266,* 1793–1800.

Comings, D. E., Gonzalez, N., Wu, S., Gade, R., Muhleman, D., Saucier, G., Johnson, P., Verde, R., Rosenthal, R. J., Lesieur, H. R., Rugle, L. J., Miller, W. R., & MacMurray, J. P. (1999). Studies of the 48 bp repeat polymorphism of the DRD4 gene in impulsive, compulsive, addictive behaviors: Tourette syndrome, ADHD, pathological gambling, and substance abuse. *American Journal of Medical Genetics (Neuropsychiatric Genetics), 88,* 358–368.

Conners, C. K. (1975). Controlled trial of methylphenidate in preschool children with minimal brain dysfunction. *International Journal of Mental Health, 4,* 61–74.

Conners, C. K. (1980). *Food additives and hyperactive children.* New York: Plenum.

Cook, E. H., Stein M. A., Krasowski, M. D., Cox, N. J., Olkon, D. M., Kieffer, J. E., & Leventhal, B. L. (1995). Association of attention deficit disorder and the dopamine transporter gene. *American Journal of Human Genetics, 56,* 993–998.

Daly, G., Hawi, Z., Fitzgerald, M., & Gill, M. (1998). Attention deficit hyperactivity disorder: Association with the dopamine transporter (DATI) but not with the dopamine D4 receptor (DRD4). *American Journal of Medical Genetics, Neuropsychiatric Genetics, 81,* 501.

Denson, R., Nanson, J., & McWatters, J. (1975). Hyperkinesis and maternal smoking. *Canadian Psychiatric Association Journal, 20,* 183–187.

Deutsch, C. K., Matthysse, S., Swanson, J. M., & Farkas, L. G. (1990). Genetic latent structure analysis of dysmorphology in attention deficit disorder. *Journal of the American Academy of Child and Adolescent Psychiatry, 29,* 189–194.

Dougherty, D. D., Bonab, A. A., Spencer, T. J., Rauch, S. L., Madras, B. K., & Fischman, A. J. (1999). Dopamine transporter density is elevated in patients with ADHD. *Lancet, 354,* 2132–2133.

Dulawa, S. C., Grandy, D. K., Low, M. J., Paulus, M. P., & Geyer, M. A. (1999). Dopamine D4 receptor-knock-out mice exhibit reduced exploration of novel stimuli. *Journal of Neuroscience, 19,* 9550–9556.

Ebstein, R. P., Novick, O., Umansky, R., Priel, B., Osher, Y., Blaine, D., Bennett, E. R., Nemanov, L., Katz, M., & Belmaker, R. H. (1996). Dopamine D4 receptor (D4DR) exon III polymorphism associated with the human personality trait of novelty seeking. *Nature Genetics, 12,* 78–80.

Eisenberg, J., Mei-Tal, G., Steinberg, A., Tartakovsky, E., Zohar, A., Gritsenko, I., Nemanov, L., & Ebstein, R. P. (1999). Haplotype relative risk study of catechol-O-methyltransferase (COMT) and attention deficit hyperactivity disorder (ADHD): Association of the high-enzyme activity Val allele with ADHD impulsive-hyperactive phenotype. *American Journal of Medical Genetics, 88,* 497–502.

Eisenberg, J., Zohar, A., Mei-Tal, G., Steinberg, A., Tartakovsky, E., Gritsenko, I., Nemanov, L., & Ebstein, R. P. (2000). A haplotype relative risk study of the dopamine D4 receptor (DRD4) exon III repeat polymorphism and attention deficit hyperactivity disorder (ADHD). *American Journal of Medical Genetics (Neuropsychiatric Genetics), 96*(3), 258–261.

Faraone, S., Biederman, J., Chen, W. J., Krifcher, B., Keenan, K., Moore, C., Sprich, S., & Tsuang, M. (1992). Segregation analysis of attention deficit hyperactivity disorder: Evidence for single gene transmission. *Psychiatric Genetics, 2,* 257–275.

Faraone, S. V. (1999). A family based association study of the DAT and DRD4 genes in ADHD. Presented at the World Congress of Psychiatric Genetics. Monterey, CA.

Faraone, S. V., & Biederman, J. (1998). Neurobiology of attention-deficit hyperactivity disorder. *Biological Psychiatry, 44,* 951–958.

Faraone, S. B., Biederman, J., Weiffenbach, B., Keith, T., Chu, M. P., Weaver, A., Spencer, T. J., Wilens, T. E., Frazier, J., Cleves, M., & Sakai, J. (1999). Dopamine D4 gene 7-repeat allele and attention deficit hyperactivity disorder. *American Journal of Psychiatry,* **156,** 768–770.

Faraone, S. V., & Doyle, A. (in press). The nature and heritability of attention deficit hyperactivity disorder. In R. Todd (Ed.), *Genetic contributions to early onset psychopathology.* Philadelphia, PA: W. B. Saunders.

Faraone, S. V., Tsuang, D., & Tsuang, M. T. (1999). *Genetics and mental disorders: A guide for students, clinicians, and researchers.* New York: Guilford.

Gill, M., Daly, G., Heron, S., Hawi, Z., & Fitzgerald, M. (1997). Confirmation of association between attention deficit hyperactivity disorder and a dopamine transporter polymorphism. *Molecular Psychiatry,* **2,** 311–313.

Gottesman, I. I., & Bertelsen, A. (1996). Legacy of German psychiatric genetics: Hindsight is always 20/20. *American Journal of Medical Genetics,* **67,** 317–322.

Hartsough, C. S., & Lambert, N. M. (1985). Medical factors in hyperactive and normal children: Prenatal, developmental, and health history findings. *American Journal of Orthopsychiatry,* **55,** 191–201.

Hawi, Z., McCarron, M., Kirley, A., Fitzgerald, M., & Gill, M. (2000). No association of dopamine DRD4 receptor gene polymorphism in Attention Deficit Hyperactivity disorder in the Irish population. *American Journal of Medical Genetics (Neuropsychiatric Genetics).*

Hawi, Z., Millar, N., Daly, G., Fitzgerald, M., & Gill, M. (2000). No association between Catechol-O-methyltransferase (COMT) gene polymorphism and ADHD in an Irish sample. *American Journal of Medical Genetics (Neuropsychiatric Genetics),* **96**(3), 241–243.

Hetherington, E. M., Cox, M., & Cox, R. (1982). Effects of divorce on parents and children. In M. Lamb (Ed.), *Non-traditional families* (pp. 223–285). Hillsdale, NJ: Erlbaum.

Institute of Medicine. (1989). *Research on children and adolescents with mental, behavioral and developmental disorders.* Washington, DC: National Academy Press.

Jiang, S., Xin, R., Wu, X., Lin, S., Qian, Y., Ren, D., Tang, G., & Wang, D. (2000). Association between attention deficit disorder and the DXS7 locus. *Neuropsychiatric Genetics.*

Joseph, J. (2000). Not in their genes: A critical view of the genetics of attention deficit hyperactivity disorder. *Developmental Review,* **20,** 539–567.

LaHoste, G. J., Swanson, J. M., Wigal, S. B., Glabe, C., Wigal, T., King, N., & Kennedy, J. L. (1996). Dopamine D4 receptor gene polymorphism is associated with attention deficit hyperactivity disorder. *Molecular Psychiatry,* **1,** 121–124.

Lopera, F., Palacio, L. G., Jimenez, I., Villegas, P., Puerta, I. C., Pineda, D., Jimenez, M., & Arcos-Burgos, M. (1999). [Discrimination between genetic factors in attention deficit] *Revista de Neurologia,* **28,** 660–664.

Majzoub, J., & Muglia, L. (1996). Knockout mice. *The New England Journal of Medicine,* **334,** 904–907.

Manji, H. K., Moore, G. J., & Chen, G. (1999). Lithium at 50: Have the neuroprotective effects of this unique cation been overlooked? *Biological Psychiatry,* **46,** 929–940.

Meehl, P. E. (1973). Specific genetic etiology, psychodynamics, and therapeutic nihilism. In *Psychodiagnosis: Selected papers* (pp. 182–199). New York: Norton.

Milberger, S., Biederman, J., Faraone, S., Chen, L., & Jones, J. (1996). Is maternal smoking during pregnancy a risk factor for attention deficit hyperactivity disorder in children? *American Journal of Psychiatry,* **153,** 1138–1142.

Milberger, S., Biederman, J., Faraone, S., Guite, J., & Tsuang, M. (1997). Pregnancy delivery and infancy complications and ADHD: Issues of gene-environment interactions. *Biological Psychiatry,* **41,** 65–75.

Morrison, J. R., & Stewart, M. A. (1974). Bilateral inheritance as evidence for polygenicity in the hyperactive child syndrome. *Journal of Nervous and Mental Disease,* **158,** 226–228.

Needleman, H. L. (1982). The neuropsychiatric implications of low level exposure to lead. *Psychological Medicine,* **12,** 461–463.

Nichols, P. L., & Chen, T. C. (1981). *Minimal brain dysfunction: A prospective study.* Hillsdale, NJ: Erlbaum.

Offord, D. R., Boyle, M. H., Racine, Y. A., Fleming, J. E., Cadman, D. T., Blum, H. M., Byrne, C., Links, P. S., Lipman, E. L., & Macmillan, H. L. (1992). Outcome, prognosis and risk in a longitudinal follow-up study. *Journal of the American Academy of Child and Adolescent Psychiatry,* **31,** 916–923.

Palfrey, J. S., Levine, M. D., Walker, D. K., & Sullivan, M. (1985). The emergence of attention deficits in early childhood: A prospective study. *Developmental and Behavioral Pediatrics,* **6,** 339–348.

Poulton, K., Holmes, J., Hever, T., Trumper, A., Fitzpatrick, H., McGuffin, P., Owen, M., Worthington, J., Ollier, W., Harrington, R., & Thapar, A. (1998). A molecular genetic study of hyperkinetic disorder/attention deficit hyperactivity disorder. *American Journal of Medical Genetics, Neuropsychiatric Genetics,* **81,** 458.

Rowe, D. C., Stever, C., Giedinghagen, L. N., Gard, J. M., Cleveland, H. H., Terris, S. T., Mohr, J. H., Sherman, S., Abramowitz, A., & Waldman, I. D. (1998). Dopamine DRD4 receptor polymorphism and attention deficit hyperactivity disorder. *Molecular Psychiatry,* **3,** 419–426.

Rubinstein, M., Phillips, T. J., Bunzow, J. R., Falzone, T. L., Dziewczapolski, G., Zhang, G., Fang, Y., Larson, J. L., McDougall, J. A., Chester, J. A., Saez, C., Pugsley, T. A., Gershanik, O., Low, M. J., & Grandy, D. K. (1997). Mice lacking dopamine D4 receptors are supersensitive to ethanol, cocaine, and methamphetamine. *Cell,* **90,** 991–1001.

Rutter, M., Cox, A., Tupling, C., Berger, M., & Yule, W., (1975). Attainment and adjustment in two geographical areas: Vol. 1. The prevalence of psychiatric disorders. *British Journal of Psychiatry,* **126,** 493–509.

Smalley, S. L., Bailey, J. N., Palmer, C. G., Cantwell, D. P., McGough, J. J., Del'Homme, M. A., Asarnow, J. R., Woodward, J. A., Ramsey, C., & Nelson, S. F. (1998). Evidence that the dopamine D4 receptor is a susceptibility gene in attention deficit hyperactivity disorder. *Molecular Psychiatry,* **3,** 427–430.

Sprich-Buckminster, S., Biederman, J., Milberger, S., Faraone, S., & Krifcher Lehman, B. (1993). Are perinatal complications relevant to the manifestation of ADD? Issues of comorbidity and familiality. *Journal of the American Academy of Child and Adolescent Psychiatry,* **32,** 1032–1037.

Swanson, J., Castellanos, F., Murias, M., LaHoste, G., & Kennedy, J. (1998). Cognitive neuroscience of attention deficit hyperactivity disorder and hyperkinetic disorder. *Current Opinion in Neurobiology,* **8,** 263–271.

Swanson, J. M., Sunohara, G. A., Kennedy, J. L., Regino, R., Fineberg, E., Wigal, T., Lerner, M., Williams, L., LaHoste, G. J., & Wigal, S. (1998). Association of the dopamine receptor D4 (DRD4) gene with a refined phenotype of attention deficit hyperactivity disorder (ADHD): A family-based approach. *Molecular Psychiatry,* **3,** 38–41.

Tahir, E., Curran, S., Yazgan, Y., Ozbay, F., Cirakoglu, B., & Asherson, P. J. (2000). No association between low and high activity catecholamine-methl-transferase (COMT) and Attention deficit hyperactivity disorder (ADHD) in a sample of Turkish children. *American Journal of Medical Genetics (Neuropsychiatric Genetics),* **96**(3), 285–288.

Thapar, A., Hervas, A., & McGuffin, P. (1995). Childhood hyperactivity scores are highly heritable and show sibling competition effects: Twin study evidence. *Behavior Genetics,* **25,** 537–544.

Thapar, A., Holmes, J., Poulton, K., & Harrington, R. (1999). Genetic basis of attention deficit and hyperactivity. *British Journal of Psychiatry,* **174,** 105–111.

Tsuang, M. T., Faraone, S. V., & Green, A. L. (1999). Schizophrenia and other psychotic disorders. In M. Amand & J. Nicholi (Eds.), *The Harvard guide to psychiatry.* Cambridge, MA: Harvard Univ. Press.

Waldman, I. D., Rowe, D. C., Abramowitz, A., Kozel, S. T., Mohr, J. H., Sherman, S. L., Cleveland, H. H., Sanders, M. L., Gard, J. M., & Stever, C. (1998). Association and linkage of the dopamine transporter gene and attention-deficit hyperactivity disorder in children: Heterogeneity owing to diagnostic subtype and severity. *American Journal of Human Genetics, 63,* 1767–1776.

Winsberg, B. G., & Comings, D. E. (1999). Association of the dopamine transporter gene (DAT1) with poor methylphenidate response [see comments]. *Journal of the American Academy of Child and Adolescent Psychiatry, 38,* 1474–1477.

Wolraich, M., Wilson, D., & White, W. (1995). The effect of sugar on behavior or cognition in children. *Journal of the American Medical Association, 274,* 1617–1621.

Wyman, P. A., Cowen, E. L., Work, W. C., Raoof, A., Gribble, P. A., Parker, G. R., & Wannon, M. (1992). Interviews with children who experienced major life stress: Family and child attributes that predict resilient outcomes. *Journal of the American Academy of Child and Adolescent Psychiatry, 31,* 904–911.

CHALLENGE QUESTIONS

Are Genetic Explanations of Attention Deficit Hyperactivity Disorder Faulty?

1. What do you think is the best way for parents to view their ADHD children, from Joseph's perspective or from Faraone and Biederman's perspective? What are the advantages and disadvantages of each perspective from the viewpoint of a parent?
2. A pivotal point in this issue is the presence (or absence) of a mind/body connection. What is the current thinking on this connection in medicine? In philosophy? In psychology?
3. What do you think about the movement toward biological explanations in psychology? What are the advantages and disadvantages of this trend in psychology?
4. What implications does this issue have for the free will and determinism of ADHD children? That is, would a perspective that says ADHD is genetically caused (even if it is also caused by the environment) mean that the actions of ADHD children are determined (not within their control)? If so, what implications would a lack of control have?

ISSUE 5

Is Love a Mechanism of Evolution?

YES: Helen Fisher, from "The Nature of Romantic Love," *The Journal of NIH Research* (April 1994)

NO: Jeffrey S. Reber and Marissa S. Beyers, from "Love Is Not an Evolutionarily Derived Mechanism," An Original Essay Written for This Volume (January 2000)

ISSUE SUMMARY

YES: Anthropologist Helen Fisher contends that love is a chemical mechanism through which natural selection initiates and sustains human pair-bonds. Furthermore, she maintains that serial monogamy has adaptive advantages and is visible in worldwide patterns of divorce.

NO: Freelance writers Jeffrey S. Reber and Marissa S. Beyers contend that love is not merely biological but also fundamentally relational, social, and psychological. Additionally, they argue that Fisher's commitment to an evolutionary perspective leads to a biased interpretation of the evidence.

Many people would argue that of all the human emotions, love is the most universal and important. It is an emotion shared by almost every culture, present and past, and it is the subject of countless tales, poems, and songs. Given its pervasiveness and significance to human beings, love is a vital area of psychological investigation. Indeed, psychologists have been concerned with providing a full understanding of this emotion, both as it originates and as it is experienced.

Evolutionary psychologists argue that the powerful emotion of love can be understood in terms of selective pressures. According to the renowned naturalist Charles Darwin, who formalized and popularized the theory of evolution during the nineteenth century, natural selection has directed the progression and development of all living organisms. Therefore, love is like any other attribute of living organisms. It has evolved because it ensures the progression of the species; thus, feelings of love are adaptive.

Consistent with this evolutionary perspective, Helen Fisher proposes in the following selection that all aspects of love—from attachment to detachment

—can be explained in terms of evolutionarily driven, biochemical determinants. She cites patterns of divorce and other statistics to bolster her case. Her evolutionary understanding of love is best exemplified through the sexual strategy of serial monogamy, wherein intimate relationships exist to produce viable offspring. Love is the mechanism through which these relationships are formed, and it exists at least until the successful production of viable offspring is accomplished.

In the second selection, Jeffrey S. Reber and Marissa S. Beyers take issue with Fisher's assertion that love can be adequately understood in terms of evolutionarily driven, biochemical determinants. They argue that the notion of chemically derived emotions negates the possibility of other defining features that are necessary to fully understand love. Furthermore, Reber and Beyers assert that divorce statistics are not evidence that serial monogamy is a human sexual strategy. They contend that Fisher's work is guided more by her commitment to evolutionary theory than by a commitment to a full account of how humans truly experience love.

POINT

- Love can be explained in terms of biochemical components.

- Serial monogamy is the primary sexual strategy of human beings as evidenced by divorce statistics and shared evolutionary origins.

- Cultural forces and free will may influence human pair-bonding.

- Attachment patterns support love's role in evolution.

COUNTERPOINT

- Love is not merely biological but also fundamentally social, relational, and psychological.

- Serial monogamy is not the primary sexual strategy of human beings; Fisher misinterprets divorce statistics and relies on badly fitted animal analogues to support the contention that it is.

- Fisher's perspective reduces cultural forces and free will to mere functions of natural selection; their roles in feelings of love are actually much more profound.

- Divorce and remarriage rates do not support an evolutionary account of love.

Helen Fisher

 **YES**

The Nature of Romantic Love

Oh eyes be strong, you cherish people and then they're gone." Safia, a middle-aged Bedouin woman of Egypt's Western Desert, recited this short poem about lost love. She is not the only human being who has felt the angst or ecstasy of romance. In 1992, anthropologists William Jankowiak and Edward Fischer surveyed 166 societies and found evidence of romantic love in 88.5 percent of them. In some cultures, people sang love songs. Some eloped. Some informants recounted their anguish to the anthropologists, who lived among them. And the mythology of many societies portrayed romantic entanglements. So Jankowiak and Fischer concluded that romantic love, which they equate with "passionate love," constitutes a human universal. They attributed the absence of evidence for romantic love in the balance of these cultures to "ethnographic oversight," or lack of access to the folklore of the culture.

What is this thing called love? From the responses to a series of questionnaires administered at and around the University of Bridgeport, Conn., psychologist Dorothy Tennov identified a constellation of psychological characteristics common to the condition of "limerence," her term for being in love. Limerence, she notes, begins the moment another individual takes on "special meaning"; the other person could be a stranger or an old friend seen in a new perspective. But as one informant put it, "My whole world had been transformed. It had a new center, and that center was Marilyn."

... Why is it that scientists have failed to study such a profound and universal emotional state? Affiliative behavior plays a crucial role in the mating process of all birds and mammals—and mating is the single most important act of any individual of any sexually reproducing species. Yet in the 1970s, Sen. William Proxmire gave the Golden Fleece Award (for wasting public funds) to a group of psychologists studying romantic behavior.

Perhaps we think love is too private, too intangible, or too frivolous for scientific investigation. First, humankind studied the stars, plants, and animals; only in the past two centuries have the fields of psychology, sociology, and anthropology developed to examine human behavior systematically. Even now, as scientists explore the biochemistry of the basic emotions, investigations focus on the physiology of aggression, dominance, depression, and anxiety. Studies are just beginning on the biochemistry of affiliation.

From Helen Fisher, "The Nature of Romantic Love," *The Journal of NIH Research*, vol. 6 (April 1994). Copyright © 1994 by Medical Economics. Reprinted by permission. References omitted.

The Chemistry of Attraction and Attachment

In seminal research done in the 1980s, psychiatrist Michael Liebowitz divided human romantic love into two basic stages, attraction and attachment, and he proposed that specific physiological events in the brain were involved in each. After analyzing the effects of antidepressant drugs that inhibit monoamine oxidase (MAO) that were administered to lovesick patients, Liebowitz concluded that the exhiliration of attraction is associated with phenylethylamine (PEA), which is chemically related to the amphetamines, and/or with the action of the monoamine neurotransmitters norepinephrine, dopamine, and serotonin in the limbic system and associated areas of the brain.

Liebowitz attributed the second stage of romantic love, attachment, and its concomitant feelings of tranquility and peace to heightened production of the endorphins, peptide neurotransmitters that are chemically related to morphine. Newer data suggest that oxytocin and vasopressin, peptide neurotransmitters that play central roles in male-female bonding, group bonding, and mother-infant bonding in other mammalian species, may also be involved in human attachment.

Moreover, human attraction and attachment have analogues in birds and other mammals—suggesting that these emotions evolved. Birds and mammals distinguish among potential mates, judge which would make better breeding partners, and exhibit interest in some individuals more than others. Much like humans, chimpanzees, gorillas, baboons, elephants, wolves, and many other social mammals express attraction with an array of pats, rubs, taps, gazes, licks, and nibbles, as well as with close body contact, play gestures and tolerance of one another. And while courting, many mammals are energized....

Does a male elephant feel attraction as he strokes a female's back with his trunk just before he mounts her? Does a male wolf feel attachment as he nudges a chunk of meat toward his hungry mate while she is nursing in their den? Questions about the animal correlates of the human emotions remain. But the... data suggest that attraction and attachment are emotions as primitive and universal as fear, anger, and surprise, which are (at least in part) psychopharmacological events arising from arousal circuits located primarily in the limbic system and surrounding regions of avian and mammalian brains.

I think these emotions evolved in birds and mammals to initiate mating and sustain male-female associations long enough to ensure reproduction and survival of the young. (Because each species has a distinctive breeding system, the brain anatomy and physiology for these emotions undoubtedly vary to correspond with each species-specific mating cycle.) Then, with the evolution of the cerebral cortex among the first hominids, our ancestors began to build on this core of primitive emotions associated with reproduction, eventually developing complex romantic feelings and elaborate traditions to celebrate and curb what European cultures would come to call romantic love.

How Love Progresses

"When two people are first together, their hearts are on fire and their passion is very great. After a while, the fire cools and that's how it stays. They continue to love each other, but it's in a different way—warm and dependable." So said Nisa, a !Kung San woman of the Kalahari Desert of southern Africa to anthropologist Marjorie Shostak in her 1981 book, *Nisa: The Life and Words of a !Kung Woman.* At some point, that magic wanes. Tennov measured the duration of limerence from the moment infatuation hit to the moment a "feeling of neutrality" for one's love object began. She concluded that the most frequent duration of "being in love," as well as the average, was between approximately 18 months and three years. Sexologist John Money agrees, proposing that once you begin to see your sweetheart regularly, the elation typically lasts two to three years.

Liebowitz has hypothesized that the transition from attraction to the second stage of romantic love, attachment, is also grounded in brain physiology; either neurons in the limbic system become habituated to the brain's natural stimulants or concentrations of PEA and/or other endogenous amphetamine-like substances begin to drop. Then, the endorphin system begins to take over, giving partners feelings of safety, stability, tranquility, and peace. Perhaps as feelings of attachment grow, the production of oxytocin and/or vasopressin or the sensitivity of the receptor sites for these peptides increases as well.

No one has examined how long human attachment lasts, but clearly many mateships end. So, for some men and women, there is a third stage of romantic love, detachment. To my knowledge, the physiology of detachment has not been explored. But in trying to explain why birds abandon their nests at the end of the breeding season to join a flock and why many creatures leave the safety of their natal home after infancy, ethologist Norbert Bischof has theorized that an animal gets an "excess of security," to which it responds by withdrawing from the object of attachment. The same phenomenon may occur in humans. At some point in some long relationships, the brain's receptor sites for the endorphins, oxytocin, vasopressin, and/or other neurochemicals may become desensitized. Thus attachment wanes and sets up the mind for separation.

None of the above is meant to suggest that men and women are biologically *compelled* to fall in love, to attach or detach from one another. Cultural forces play a powerful role in directing behavior, as does one's idiosyncratic perspective—what philosophers have long called "free will." But marriage is a cultural universal and divorce is common in societies around the world. Moreover, worldwide data on marriage and the timing of divorce suggest that, like attraction and attachment, the physiology of detachment evolved to direct the ebb and flow of our ancestral hominid mating system (discussed below).

Human Reproductive Strategies

Records going back to the mid-1800s indicate that over 90 percent of American men and women in every birth cohort marry. The 1982 *Demographic Yearbook of the United Nations* lists the number of men and women who have married by age 49 in 97 industrial and agricultural countries: Between 1972 and

1981, an average of 93.1 percent of women and 91.8 percent of men married in these 97 countries. These figures have not changed significantly since then. Although no worldwide tabulations have been made on the percentage of men and women who marry in horticultural and hunter-gatherer cultures, the ethnographic literature confirms that marriage is a pancultural custom; in nonindustrial communities, men and women who have never married are rare.

Moreover, most men and women are monogamous; they wed only one individual at a time. What is permissible to each gender varies, however. In 99.5 percent of 853 cultures for which anthropologists have data, women are permitted to marry only one man at a time, monandry. Each woman forms a social and economic relationship that entails sexual rights and privileges with only that one man.

... [D]ata on monogamy does not suggest that human beings are sexually faithful to their spouses, however. Extra-pair copulations are commonly seen in monogamous species of birds and mammals; adultery is clearly a secondary *opportunistic* reproductive strategy in humans. However, this article addresses only the primary human reproductive strategy: monogamy, specifically *serial* monogamy, because human pairing displays several patterns of decay that are relevant to understanding the evolution and nature of human romantic love.

Human Divorce Patterns

With a few exceptions, peoples from Amazonia to Siberia divorce. Several patterns of divorce have purely cultural explanations, but four of these patterns do not correlate with the divorce rate. These four patterns, I think, evolved in humans and resulted in the characteristic ebb and flow of human romantic love.

The first pattern is reflected in the duration of marriage that ends in divorce. Data from the demographic yearbooks of the United Nations on 62 available industrial and agricultural societies for all obtainable years between 1947 and 1989 (188 graphs, or cases, each showing the divorce profile for a specific country, area, or ethnic group in a specific year) indicate that divorces exhibit a skewed distribution, characterized by the occurrence of the mode (or divorce peak) during and around the fourth year, followed by a gradual, long-tailed decline in divorce counts. Divorces peak during and around four years after marriage.

The second common aspect of human divorce patterns evident in the demographic yearbooks of the United Nations is the age at which divorce occurs. Age at highest divorce risk was tabulated for 24 available societies in selected years (80 cases each showing the divorce profile for a specific country in a specific year) between 1966 and 1989. Divorce risk was highest among men in the age category 25 to 29; divorce risk for women was equally highest in age categories 20 to 24 and 25 to 29. Across the 62 sampled societies (188 cases), the mean percent of divorces that involved women under age 45 was 81 percent; the mean percent of divorces that involved men under age 45 was 74 percent. Thus, in the above cross-cultural sample, divorce risk was greatest at the height of reproductive and parenting years.

The third pattern is seen in the number of children per couple who divorce. In the 59 societies recorded between 1950 and 1989, 39 percent of divorces occurred among couples with no dependent children, 26 percent occurred among those with one dependent child, 19 percent occurred among couples with two dependent children, 7 percent occurred among those with three children, 3 percent occurred among couples with four young, and couples with five or more dependent young rarely split. Hence, divorce counts were highest among couples with no children and one dependent child, and they decreased with increasing numbers of dependent young. (The demographic yearbooks of the United Nations do not provide comparative cross-cultural data sufficient to establish divorce risk by number of dependent young.)

The fourth pattern of human pair-bonding concerns remarriage. The U.S. Census Bureau reports that approximately 75 percent of American women and 80 percent of American men who divorce remarry, and one-half of the American remarriages take place within three years of a divorce. Moreover, most remarriages occur during reproductive years: 76.3 percent of American women who divorce during their 20s remarry; 56.2 percent of those who divorce in their 30s remarry; and 32.4 percent of those who divorce in their 40s remarry. In 1979, the modal age at remarriage for American men was 30 to 34 years, and the modal age at remarriage for American women was 25 to 29 years.

Cross-culturally, remarriage by divorced individuals also peaks among men and women of reproductive age. Among the 98 peoples surveyed by the United Nations between 1971 and 1982, the modal age at remarriage among men was 30 to 34 years; women who remarried after a divorce were modal age of 25 to 29 years. The United Nations Statistical Office does not tabulate the percent of divorced individuals who remarry. Remarriage is frequent, however, in those places for which data are available, and remarriage rates are highest for men and women of reproductive age.

Human marriages, then, have several general patterns of decay. They tend to disband during and around the fourth year of existence. Men and women around the world tend to divorce while in their twenties—the height of reproductive and parenting years. Men and women regularly abandon a partnership that has produced no children or one dependent child. Most divorced individuals of reproductive age remarry. And the longer a mateship lasts, the older the spouses get, and/or the more children they bear, the more likely a couple is to remain together.

Why Love Ends—and Begins Again

Why do human beings pair up, establish a home base, build networks of business associates, family, and friends, and bear and nurture children—only to leave each other and pair anew? From a Darwinian perspective, it is remarkable that we pair at all. Monogamy is rare in mammals; only 3 percent pair up, and they do so only under specific circumstances. Many of these circumstances may have contributed to the evolution of monogamy in hominids. But a factor proposed by [D. G.] Kleiman is particularly relevant. She writes that monogamy is favored in evolution "whenever more than a single individual (the female) is needed to rear the young."

Canid species are good examples. The female red fox bears as many as five altricial kits that need to be fed almost continuously, so she must stay in the den to attend to them; she needs a mate to bring her food. For the male fox, polygyny is impractical because resources are usually spread out; he cannot acquire enough food to feed a harem. So, a male and female fox form a pair-bond in midwinter and raise their young together during the spring and early summer. But the pair-bond lasts only through the breeding season; as the kits become independent, mates part company. Serial monogamy in conjunction with a breeding season is also a common reproductive strategy among birds. In at least 50 percent of the 9,000 or so avian species, individuals pair at the beginning of the mating season, rear their chicks together until the young are fledged, and then part to join a flock. Some pair together at the beginning of the next breeding season, while others choose new mates.

Homo sapiens shares traits with seasonally parenting foxes and birds. The modal duration of marriage that ends in divorce, four years, conforms to the traditional period between human successive births, four years. So, I propose that the human tendency to pair up and remain together for a modal duration of about four years reflects an ancestral hominid reproductive strategy to pair and remain together throughout the infancy of a single highly dependent child. Once a child living in a hunter-gatherer society could join a multi-age play group at about age 4, however, and be raised by other members of the band, a pair-bond broke up—enabling both partners to choose new mates and bear more varied young. And I think the physiologically based emotions associated with romantic love—specifically attraction, attachment, and restlessness during long relationships—evolved to stimulate this ancestral *cyclic* breeding system, serial monogamy. . . .

Despite the social disruption that detachment entails in humans (and many other species), serial monogamy may have had several genetic benefits in our prehistoric past. Variety in one's lineage has been mentioned. Furthermore, males who dissolved one partnership for another acquired the opportunity to select a younger mate more likely to produce more viable offspring. Ancestral females who dissolved an unsatisfactory relationship, on the other hand, acquired the opportunity to choose a mate who provided better protection, food, and nurturance for her, her children, and her forthcoming infants. So, regardless of the social complexities inherent in changing partners, serial monogamy *during reproductive years* became an adaptive reproductive strategy, leaving this legacy not only in contemporary worldwide patterns of divorce and remarriage but in our universal struggle with primitive, powerful, and often transitory reproductive emotions that many associate with romantic love.

Nature, Culture, and Romantic Love

Someone once asked Margaret Mead why all of her marriages failed. Mead reportedly replied, "I beg your pardon, I had three marriages and none of them was a failure." Most Americans do not view marriage so pragmatically. Even fewer are willing to consider the possibility of genetic components to divorce—largely because this perspective threatens their concept of free will. Many scientists resist exploring the biological bases of attraction, attachment, and divorce for an historical reason. Soon after Darwin proposed the concept of natural selection by survival of the fittest, these ideas were marshaled by conservatives to vindicate the social hierarchy of Victorian England. Women, poor people, immigrants, colonized peoples, and the outcasts of society were dismissed as "less fit." This credo led to a bitter reaction by the 1920s and ushered in several decades of "cultural determinism." Today, many lay people and scientists still hold that love is a purely cultural phenomenon, outside the realm of scientific inquiry.

But romantic love is an elegant example of the complex mixture of environment and heredity. Culture, for example, plays an essential role in one's *choice* of partner and the *timing* and *process* of courting. As children, for example, we develop specific likes and dislikes in response to family, friends, and experiences. So, by the teenage years, each individual carries within him or her an unconscious mental template, or "love map," a group of physical, psychological, and behavioral traits that he or she finds attractive in a mate. People fall in love when they are ready. Barriers (such as geographic or social constraints) enhance infatuation, as does novelty and unfamiliarity. And cultural beliefs regularly tie partners together. In fact, 50 percent of Americans marry for life—an excellent example, I believe, of the triumph of culture and personal commitment over nature.

So, culture plays a crucial role in *whom* you find attractive, *when* you court, *where* you woo, *how* you pursue a potential partner, *how* you resolve your problems, and (depending on economic factors) *how many* people stay together. But beliefs, traditions, family, friends, books, songs, and other cultural phenomena do not teach one *what to feel* as one falls in love, becomes attached to a mate, or becomes restless in a long relationship. Instead, these emotions are generated by brain-body physiology. They evolved long ago to direct the ebb and flow of our primary reproductive strategy, serial monogamy, and they came across the eons to invigorate and complicate our lives.

NO

Jeffrey S. Reber and Marissa S. Beyers

Love Is Not an Evolutionarily Derived Mechanism

$\mathbf{M}$any Greek tragedies, Shakespeare's sonnets, and countless other pieces of literature, art, music, and poetry are all based on love. This overflow of artistic expression is a testament to the profound meaning that all of us associate with love and intimate relationships. Yet, in Helen Fisher's article, "The Nature of Romantic Love," she seems content to explain love in such a way that its profound meaning is irrelevant and impossible. Granted, this irrelevancy and impossibility are not immediately apparent in her article. In fact, Fisher begins with the feelings and emotions involved in the meaningful experience of love. However, because she attributes this experience to an evolutionarily adaptive strategy, she ultimately renders love meaningless.

The problem is that Fisher's evolutionary perspective assumes that all human behaviors are the product of natural selection and biology. Fisher speaks about the importance of culture and free will but she does not consider them primary in her explanation of love. They are instead the byproducts of natural selection and biology. Fisher argues that these conclusions are forced on her by scientific evidence. However, we will show how the research findings she reports do not necessitate an evolutionary/biological explanation. Indeed, the correlations she cites between biochemical substances in the brain and feelings of love, or between animals and humans, can be accounted for by a number of alternative, equally viable, explanations. For this reason, we contend that Fisher's evolutionary perspective fails to prove that love is the product of natural selection and biology. We also argue that her evolutionary/biological account negates the rich and profound meaning of love as well as the primary role of culture and free will in that meaning.

Can we account for love in a way that preserves its meaning? Herein we offer an alternative account that gives sufficient weight to free will and culture. According to this alternative, human beings are not merely biological; they are also fundamentally relational, social, and psychological. Although we hold that biology is very much a part of human experience and thus, the experience of love, this biology does not constitute or cause love. On the contrary, we propose that love, culture, free will, and the meaning we attach to intimate relationships *give rise to* the biological experience of love. Because love is rooted in the meaningful experience of intimate relationships, rather than in our biology or any universalized sexual strategy, natural laws and forces cannot and do not determine love. The relationships and meanings themselves determine love.

Love Is Not Merely Biological

Fisher's assertion that feelings of love arise out of brain chemicals, structures, and processes cannot offer a sufficient account of love. We agree that love has its physiological correlates. Anyone who has experienced love can attest to the butterflies in the stomach, the dry mouth, and racing heart that accompany it. But to say that biological activity is associated with love is not the same thing as Fisher's assertion that feelings of love originate in our biology. It is our contention that Fisher's assertion that feelings associated with love and intimacy arise from neurological brain patterns is mistaken. We will argue that a full accounting of love cannot be possible using *solely* biological correlates. The focus of this section, then, is twofold: 1) we will illustrate how an understanding of the biological activity associated with love fails to provide a sufficient explanation for the rich and full meaning of love as experienced in intimate relationships; and 2) we will argue that biology doesn't produce love, but that the special meaning we attach to a person and a relationship actually gives rise to biological activity.

For Fisher, the psychological experience of love is *really just* biological activity. She contends that our "complex romantic feelings and elaborate traditions" stem from a core of primitive emotions that arise from arousal circuits located in the brain. In other words, the rich meaning of love that is expressed in literature, music, and especially between lovers ultimately reduces to primitive brain structures and neurotransmitters such as vasopressin and oxytocin. Any particular accounting of love, such as the one Fisher refers to: "My whole world had been transformed. It had a new center, that center was Marilyn," is explainable in terms of "particular brain chemistry for attachment." This perspective replaces an experience of love that is rich with psychological, social, relational, and biological components with one made up of *solely* biological components. As a result, the psychological, social, and relational components of love become merely by-products or secondary manifestations of what is *really* going on. For Fisher, all of the rich meaning and emotion shared in loving relationships, the cultural traditions and rituals of marriage, and the sense of satisfaction and fulfillment that accompanies child-rearing exist *only* as the byproducts of neuronal activity.

At this point it is important to ask whether there is anything wrong with a completely biological account of love and intimate relationships. We are, after all, biologically embodied. Isn't it therefore reasonable to assume that love arises from our bodies? It is our contention that although such an assumption may seem reasonable, it is, in fact, impossible. That is, a completely biological account of love fails because it reduces love to neurotransmitters and peptides that in and of themselves are meaningless and can tell us nothing of the rich variety of thoughts and feelings that are central to loving relationships. Vasopressin has no inherent meaning; nor can oxytocin love anything at all! Chemical components cannot create a poem or a love song. Neurotransmitters do not love other neurotransmitters. Rather, we contend that they are part of a greater psychological process wherein biological components receive their meaning from people in particular contexts or relationships. A racing heart, for example, means very different things in the context of a mugging, where it is associated with fear, or in a fight, where it is understood in terms of anger, or in an embrace, wherein it is assigned the meaning of love. In short, the biological activity described by Fisher can tell us very little about ourselves without being connected to the meaningful context of our experience.

Biological activity, then, must be understood within a greater context. We contend that biology depends on the human experience of love for its meaning. That is, it isn't until we assign meaning and importance to a person that the biological activities are relevant or even begin. We don't get butterflies in the stomach, a racing heart, and increased endorphin production for just anyone or anything. We reserve such responses for that one person who is important to us, that particular person who "takes on special meaning." Hence, love originates not in our biology, but in a relationship between two people that is sufficiently meaningful to engage the whole person—mind and body. That is, the meaning we assign to a person not only affects our thoughts and feelings, but also our very physiology. The person with whom we are in love means so much to us that even the chemicals in the deepest recesses of our brain respond. So yes, we agree that love has its biological components, but those components are not solely responsible for love—they do not give rise to love.

The evolutionary perspective Fisher advocates identifies all aspects of life as arising from biology and consequently, Fisher misinterprets the causal nature of the biological activity associated with love. In so doing, she has blinded herself to the possibility—indeed, we would claim, the very reality—that love gives rise to biology; not in the sense that love creates the biology, but in the sense that without love the biology would be meaningless and its activity dormant. There would be no racing heart or increased endorphins were it not for the special meaning that is assigned to a particular person and one's relationship to that person. Because Fisher's account fails to acknowledge this centrality of meaning, we find her biological explanation of love to be neither sufficient nor compelling.

Love Has No Meaning If It Is Determined by Evolutionary Forces

Fisher's endorsement of evolutionary theory negates a meaningful account of love. We propose that this meaninglessness occurs because, according to the evolutionary philosophy undergirding Fisher's account, persons are not directing their behavior, natural forces are. Consequently, feelings of love for another or behaving lovingly can be about as meaningful as a rock rolling down a hill. A rock rolling down a hill merely reacts to forces acting upon it (i.e., gravity). The rock does not decide to roll down the hill, nor can it choose to stop; its rolling and the direction that rolling takes are completely determined by the natural forces acting upon it. Hence, there can be no meaning attached to the rock's "behavior" because the rock has no ability to intervene or behave differently.

In a similar fashion, natural forces are thought to determine human behavior. Specifically, Fisher's account rests on the assumption that loving behavior is determined by natural selection. That is, because the evolutionary perspective views human beings as natural organisms that are essentially the same as other natural organisms (e.g., mammals, birds, insects, etc.), and because natural laws determine the actions of natural organisms, human beings are determined by natural laws. Accordingly, because natural selection is a natural law, human beings are determined by natural selection. As a result our behavior is not really our behavior. Rather, for Fisher, we, like the rock, are objects that can be moved and shaped according to natural pressures and forces that exist to progress the species. Hence, we love because love leads to mating, we mate because mating leads to offspring—the spread of our genetic material—and we care for our offspring to ensure the survival of our genes. This is the agenda of natural selection, and, as a natural law, natural selection *is* the ultimate cause of love and intimate relationships.

If, as Fisher's argument demands, we are *not* the arbiters of our own behaviors, then it becomes all too clear that our own behaviors are devoid of meaning. Sure, we may assign meaning to our relationships and loved ones. We may call them special or our reason for living. We may share rich cultural traditions with them, like marriage, where we express publicly our undying love. But through it all, it is natural selection, not our own will, which causes us to do those things. A groom may think he chooses his bride because he feels a meaningful connection to her, but according to this perspective, she is *really just* a satisfactory target for reproduction. That is, she is sufficiently young, healthy, and hardy to produce viable offspring and raise them to survive. The meaning in this marriage exists *only* as a function of the ever-present agenda of natural selection that governs behavior just as gravity governs the behavior of a rock rolling down a hill.

In light of this determinism, Fisher's claims regarding the influence of culture and free will sound hollow. Cultural forces and free will cannot "play a powerful role in directing behavior" in any genuine sense. They cannot ultimately "triumph over nature" because they too are the products of nature and are governed by natural law. That is, culture exists only because it facilitates specific human mating rituals that ensure genetic fitness and viable offspring. Similarly, free will is not free, as it too must fall under the reign of natural selection. Like the experience of love, culture and any feelings of free will are byproducts or manifestations of selection. Neither has causal power in and of itself, but like biological mechanisms, each ultimately serves as a tool to bring about evolutionary ends.

Because Fisher's argument denies culture, free will, and love any real status or influence and because her account renders irrelevant any meaning that we might attach to other people and our loving relationships, we cannot accept her explanation of love. We do agree that there are natural aspects to human beings and that humans share some biological commonality with other nat-

NO / Reber and Beyers

NO / Reber and Beyers   **97**

ural organisms, but we cannot agree that we are *merely* natural organisms. In the previous section we showed how the meaning we attach to our relationships actually gives rise to our biology, proving that, although love may have its biological components, it is more fundamentally relational. As a result, we contend that love is not under the governance of natural selection. If it were, why would we ever love people with whom we do not mate? Why would we care for children that share no biological make-up with us whatsoever?

From an evolutionary perspective, wherein we are merely natural organisms determined by natural selection, these questions are not easily answered. However, when we recognize that we are not merely natural organisms, but that also and more fundamentally, we are relational beings, the answers to these questions become clear. It is the meaning that we assign to a person and our willingness to commit ourselves to them that causes us to love our partner and care for our children, regardless of any evolutionary agenda. So, just as gravity may affect our bodies, but cannot affect our minds or our feelings, natural selection cannot affect the non-natural, non-biological activity of relational beings. When it comes to human relationships and love, natural selection simply is not relevant.

Human Beings Are Not Serially Monogamous

Fisher does not show serial monogamy to be the primary sexual strategy of human beings. Serial monogamy requires the detachment phase and, as we will show, the evidence she provides does not support her assertion regarding this phase of love. According to Fisher, monogamous relationships are inconsistent with evolutionary theory, as they do not allow for the widest spread of genetic material and progression of the species. Serial monogamy, however, allows for the increased genetic fitness and progression required by natural selection. To stay consistent with her evolutionary perspective then, Fisher asserts that serial monogamy is the primary sexual strategy for human beings. In order for serial monogamy to be *primary* however, detachment, as a necessary stage of serial monogamy, must be universal to the majority of human beings across relationships and cultures. If detachment is not universal, then serial monogamy cannot be primary, because it would mean that most couples do not transition out of the attachment stage.

Current marriage and divorce statistics do not reflect a universal detachment phase in the majority of intimate relationships. Consequently, there is no compelling reason to conclude that serial monogamy is the primary sexual strategy of human beings. It is our contention then, that Fisher's assertion is more an expression of her evolutionary bias (wherein serial monogamy is adaptive and monogamy is not) than an objective report of the evidence. Fisher's assertions regarding detachment, though consistent with the assumptions of evolutionary theory, simply are not supported by the evidence she provides.

Consider as an example her discussion regarding divorce. According to the most recent report of the United Nations, which investigated divorce rates in a sample of 36 countries, more couples stay together than divorce. Yet Fisher bases her discussion only on those individuals who do divorce. Conveniently, she skips right to this population, never indicating to the reader that this population itself is a very small subset of the population to which she refers. Remember, her claims of the universality of love (and its three stages) are thought by her to apply to *all* people in *all* cultures. However, the divorce rates in most countries are low, varying between .15 to 3.36 per 1,000 people. Even in the United States where divorce rates are among the highest in the world (4.95 per 1,000), the incidence of divorce is no higher than 40%. Mathematically speaking, her explanations and proposals regarding both the incidence of detachment and serial monogamy are only applicable to 40% of the people in this country and considerably fewer people in the rest of the world.

On this point alone, Fisher's explanatory justification loses much of its power. She seems less interested in understanding love and intimate relationships and more interested in supporting her evolutionary account. Unfortunately, this misdirected focus leads her to misrepresent the data on marriage and divorce. Consequently, she runs the risk of misleading the reader into believing that serial monogamy is the primary sexual strategy of human beings, when it clearly is not. Although we agree that detachment and serial monogamy occur, they are not universal experiences. They don't even capture the majority of human beings. A true account of love would be based on what most people do, which is marry and stay married.

Love as Meaningful Experience

At this point we must conclude that Fisher fails to illuminate the nature of romantic love. Her claim that love exists and is universal because it is the product of some universal force or law (i.e., natural selection) reduces love to meaningless biological activity that is always in the service of evolutionary ends. According to her account, vasopressin and endorphins replace intimacy and passion. She demeans our experience by equating it with the behavior of red foxes, elephants, and birds. She denies culture and free will any genuine status or influence. Last but not least, her account turns children and partners into tools of genetic proliferation, in whom we are invested only to secure the progress of the species.

Fisher's explanatory strategies and their consequences remove love from its context (i.e., the human realm) wherein it is experienced and is meaningful. Once removed from the human realm love no longer connects to human experience. In this transition, love loses the characteristics and qualities that comprise its very nature. Consequently, Fisher has to rely on badly fitted animal analogues (e.g., red foxes), flimsy correlational evidence, and even irrelevant statistics (e.g., divorce rates) to uphold an explanation that has become more important than what she is trying to explain. Fisher moves directly to an evolutionary/biological accounting of love, not because the evidence demands it, but because of her evolutionary assumptions about human life. In so doing, she disregards a number of other, equally feasible explanations that would adequately explain the data *and* preserve the rich meaning and culture of love and intimate relationships.

Paradoxically, in all her efforts to explain love, Fisher has essentially explained it away. However, the meaningful experience of love cannot be explained away. Love cannot be transformed into a principle or force in any meaningful way, and as we have argued, any effort to do so, changes it so fundamentally that it no longer connects to human experience. Hence, love must be understood in terms of love, an experience that is universal to being human. But it is not just the universality of love that makes it worthy of investigation. As discussed initially, love and intimate relationships are fundamental to human life. Love is universal because it defines us, because it is so important to us. If it were universally present, but unimportant, few if any would be concerned with it. But it is perhaps the most meaningful aspect of our lives. Given its centrality and the necessity of understanding it as it is experienced in the human realm, the meaningful experience of love must be fundamental.

Once the meaningful experience of love is understood as fundamental, the focus of investigation changes completely. The relationship and the feelings of the people involved become central to an understanding of love. Love remains full of possibility and cannot be captured by any singular account or explanation. Literature, art, music, and other expressions of love play an important role in understanding the full and rich meaning of this experience. For example, the phrase, "My whole world had been transformed. It had a new center and that center was Marilyn," is taken as the reality and is studied in terms of the meaning it expresses. In this quote, the man clearly feels changed by Marilyn so completely that she now has become the most important thing in his life. She seems to have created in him feelings of love so penetrating that he can do nothing but think of her. He does not conceive of Marilyn as a target for mating. She cannot be relegated to the status of an object to be used and then discarded after she fulfills her role in this evolutionary scheme. On the contrary, she is central to this man's world. She is more important to him than anything else. She is part of a relationship that is filled with passion, intimacy, and commitment, not because it satisfies some evolutionary goal, but because she, together with the man, created it and because they both care about it and each other.

CHALLENGE QUESTIONS

Is Love a Mechanism of Evolution?

1. Describe how evolutionary explanations have become so popular in psychological theory, both historically and logically. Why do you suppose this is an attractive thesis?
2. Why is it difficult for Fisher to account for culture as a separate influence if she endorses an evolutionary explanation of love? What effects follow from the assumption that human emotions and behavior are caused by our genes?
3. How do Reber and Beyers account for biological correlates without assuming a causal relationship? How might you explain other emotions, such as anger and depression, with the same thesis?
4. Research other aspects of evolutionary psychology. What strengths and weaknesses do you find in this research?

On the Internet . . .

American Academy of Child & Adolescent Psychiatry

At this site of the American Academy of Child & Adolescent Psychiatry (AACAP), you will find information on child and adolescent psychiatry, fact sheets for parents and caregivers, AACAP membership, current research, practice guidelines, managed care information, awards and fellowship descriptions, meeting information, and much more.

http://www.aacap.org

The No-Spanking Page

This site is devoted to positive, nonpunitive approaches to childrearing.

http://www.cei.net/~rcox/index.html

Corporal Punishment of Children

This page provides links and references to research on corporal punishment of children in the home and critiques of the antispanking research. Some of these critiques illustrate methodological flaws that can occur in psychological research.

http://people.biola.edu/faculty/paulp/

CRETV: Center for Research on the Effects of Television

Based at Ithica College, the Center for Research on the Effects of Television has an archive of television content and a research lab conducting studies of the content of television and its effects on viewers.

http://www.ithaca.edu/cretv/

The State of Censorship: Studies & Research

This Libertus.net page contains links to studies and research on the effects of portrayals of violence in the electronic media, as well as reviews, analyses, and commentaries on that research.

http://libertus.net/censor/studies.html

PART 3

Human Development

*T*he goal of developmental psychologists is to document the course of our physical, social, and intellectual changes over a life span. Considerable attention has been paid to the childhood part of that life span because this period of development seems to set the stage for later periods. Two potential influences on childhood are debated here: spanking and television.

- Does Spanking Lead Children to Become More Violent?

- Does Viewing Television Increase Aggression?

ISSUE 6

Does Spanking Lead Children to Become More Violent?

YES: Murray A. Straus, from *Beating the Devil Out of Them: Corporal Punishment in American Families and Its Effects on Children* (Lexington Books, 1994)

NO: Den A. Trumbull and S. DuBose Ravenel, from "Spare the Rod?" *Family Policy* (September–October 1996)

ISSUE SUMMARY

YES: Professor of sociology Murray A. Straus argues that several studies show a link between childhood spanking and aggressive behavior in later life because spanking teaches a child violence.

NO: Pediatricians Den A. Trumbull and S. DuBose Ravenel, of the Family Research Council, argue that the current research on spanking fails to distinguish between spanking and physical abuse and, thus, leads to inaccurate results about parents who appropriately spank their children.

T he impact of early childhood events is a topic of primary significance to developmental psychologists. The psychoanalyst Sigmund Freud would say that the lessons that a child learns in the first few years set the pattern for the rest of his or her life. If that is true, then a heavy burden is placed upon the young and inexperienced parent. Even experienced parents may feel the burden of shaping their children's futures. Making the wrong choices, saying the wrong words, or using the wrong disciplinary techniques are just a few of the mistakes that parents fear may permanently damage the psychological well-being of their children.

Discipline is a special concern in this regard. Everyone seems to have an opinion about how people should discipline their children, from the family pediatrician to the children's grandparents. One concern is the use of spanking to discipline children. Critics argue that spanking emotionally confuses children, teaching them that anger allows people to hit others, even loved ones. If you were spanked as a child, do you remember being confused or believing that it was okay to hit others because your parents hit you?

According to Murray A. Straus, in the first of the following selections, this is the conclusion that many children draw when their loving parents hit them in anger. He presents and then attempts to refute several beliefs about spanking that he maintains allows parents to justify spanking as an acceptable form of punishment. He argues that spanking is not only ineffective but also results in violent adult behavior and child abuse later in life.

Den A. Trumbull and S. DuBose Ravenel, in the second selection, contend that appropriate spanking is effective and does not lead to violence. These authors also present several arguments in support of spanking and attempt to refute them. They argue that much of the current spanking research fails to distinguish between appropriate spanking and physical abuse. This blurred distinction leads to inappropriate conclusions about the results of appropriate spanking.

POINT

- Research studies show that spanking children leads to later violent behavior.

- Spanking weakens the bond between parent and child.

- Spanking, like verbal abuse, should never be considered an acceptable form of punishment.

- Because the myths about spanking are so strongly held in American culture, laws protecting children from this abuse will never be passed.

COUNTERPOINT

- Methodological flaws, such as failing to distinguish spanking from physical abuse, leads to invalid results about spanking.

- There is no evidence that proper disciplinary spanking is harmful to the parent-child relationship.

- Spanking and other forms of negative consequences, when combined with reasoning, effectively decrease the frequency of misbehavior.

- The Swedish ban on spanking resulted in a fourfold increase in child abuse and a sixfold increase in teen violence in 10 years.

Murray A. Straus  **YES**

Ten Myths That Perpetuate Corporal Punishment

[H]itting children is legal in every state of the United States and 84 percent of a survey of Americans agreed that it is sometimes necessary to give a child a good hard spanking.... [A]lmost all parents of toddlers act on these beliefs. Study after study shows that almost 100 percent of parents with toddlers hit their children. There are many reasons for the strong support of spanking. Most of them are myths.

Myth 1: Spanking Works Better

There has been a huge amount of research on the effectiveness of corporal punishment of animals, but remarkably little on the effectiveness of spanking children. That may be because almost no one, including psychologists, feels a need to study it because it is assumed that spanking is effective. In fact, what little research there is on the effectiveness of corporal punishment of children agrees with the research on animals. Studies of both animals and children show that punishment is *not* more effective than other methods of teaching and controlling behavior. Some studies show it is less effective.

Ellen Cohn and I asked 270 students at two New England colleges to tell us about the year they experienced the most corporal punishment. Their average age that year was eight, and they recalled having been hit an average of six times that year. We also asked them about the percent of the time they thought that the corporal punishment was effective. It averaged a little more than half of the times (53 percent). Of course, 53 percent also means that corporal punishment was *not* perceived as effective about half the time it was used.

LaVoie (1974) compared the use of a loud noise (in place of corporal punishment) with withdrawal of affection and verbal explanation in a study of first- and second-grade children. He wanted to find out which was more effective in getting the children to stop touching certain prohibited toys. Although the loud noise was more effective initially, there was no difference over a longer period of time. Just explaining was as effective as the other methods.

A problem with LaVoie's study is that it used a loud noise rather than actual corporal punishment. That problem does not apply to an experiment by Day and Roberts (1983). They studied three-year-old children who had been given "time out" (sitting in a corner). Half of the mothers were assigned to use spanking as the mode of correction if their child did not comply and left the corner. The other half put their non-complying child behind a low plywood barrier and physically enforced the child staying there. Keeping the child behind the barrier was just as effective as the spanking in correcting the misbehavior that led to the time out.

A study by Larzelere (in press) also found that a combination of *non*-corporal punishment and reasoning was as effective as corporal punishment and reasoning in correcting disobedience.

Crozier and Katz (1979), Patterson (1982), and Webster-Stratton et al. (1988, 1990) all studied children with serious conduct problems. Part of the treatment used in all three experiments was to get parents to stop spanking. In all three, the behavior of the children improved after spanking ended. Of course, many other things in addition to no spanking were part of the intervention. But, as you will see, parents who on their own accord do not spank also do many other things to manage their children's behavior. It is these other things, such as setting clear standards for what is expected, providing lots of love and affection, explaining things to the child, and recognizing and rewarding good behavior, that account for why children of non-spanking parents tend to be easy to manage and well-behaved. What about parents who do these things and also spank? Their children also tend to be well-behaved, but it is illogical to attribute that to spanking since the same or better results are achieved without spanking, and also without adverse side effects.

Such experiments are extremely important, but more experiments are needed to really understand what is going on when parents spank. Still, what Day and Roberts found can be observed in almost any household. Let's look at two examples.

In a typical American family there are many instances when a parent might say, "Mary! You did that again! I'm going to have to send you to your room again." This is just one example of a non-spanking method that did *not* work.

The second example is similar: A parent might say, "Mary! You did that again! I'm going to have to spank you again." This is an example of spanking that did *not* work.

The difference between these two examples is that when spanking does not work, parents tend to forget the incident because it contradicts the almost-universal American belief that spanking is something that works when all else fails. On the other hand, they tend to remember when a *non*-spanking method did not work. The reality is that nothing works all the time with a toddler. Parents think that spanking is a magic charm that will cure the child's misbehavior. It is not. There is no magic charm. It takes many interactions and many repetitions to bring up children. Some things work better with some children than with others.

Parents who favor spanking can turn this around and ask, If spanking doesn't work any better, isn't that the same as saying that it works just as well? So what's wrong with a quick slap on the wrist or bottom? There are at least three things that are wrong:

- Spanking becomes less and less effective over time and when children get bigger, it becomes difficult or impossible.
- For some children, the lessons learned through spanking include the idea that they only need to be good if Mommy or Daddy is watching or will know about it.
- ... [T]here are a number of very harmful side effects, such as a greater chance that the child will grow up to be depressed or violent. Parents don't perceive these side effects because they usually show up only in the long run.

Myth 2: Spanking Is Needed as a Last Resort

Even parents and social scientists who are opposed to spanking tend to think that it may be needed when all else fails. There is no scientific evidence supporting this belief, however. It is a myth that grows out of our cultural and psychological commitment to corporal punishment. You can prove this to yourself by a simple exercise with two other people. Each of the three should, in turn, think of the most extreme situation where spanking is necessary. The other two should try to think of alternatives. Experience has shown that it is very difficult to come up with a situation for which the alternatives are not as good as spanking. In fact, they are usually better.

Take the example of a child running out into the street. Almost everyone thinks that spanking is appropriate then because of the extreme danger. Although spanking in that situation may help *parents* relieve their own tension and anxiety, it is not necessary or appropriate for teaching the child. It is not necessary because spanking does not work better than other methods, and it is not appropriate because of the harmful side effects of spanking. The only physical force needed is to pick up the child and get him or her out of danger, and, while hugging the child, explain the danger.

Ironically, if spanking is to be done at all, the "last resort" may be the worst. The problem is that parents are usually very angry by that time and act impulsively. Because of their anger, if the child rebels and calls the parent a name or kicks the parent, the episode can escalate into physical abuse. Indeed, most episodes of physical abuse started as physical punishment and got out of hand (see Kadushin and Martin, 1981). Of course, the reverse is not true, that is, most instances of spanking do not escalate into abuse. Still, the danger of abuse is there, and so is the risk of psychological harm.

The second problem with spanking as a last resort is that, in addition to teaching that hitting is the way to correct wrongs, hitting a child impulsively teaches another incorrect lesson—that being extremely angry justifies hitting.

Myth 3: Spanking Is Harmless

When someone says, I was spanked and I'm OK, he or she is arguing that spanking does no harm. This is contrary to almost all the available research. One reason the harmful effects are ignored is because many of us (including those of us who are social scientists) are reluctant to admit that their own parents did something wrong and even more reluctant to admit that we have been doing something wrong with our own children. But the most important reason may be that it is difficult to see the harm. Most of the harmful effects do not become visible right away, often not for years. In addition, only a relatively small percentage of spanked children experience obviously harmful effects....

Another argument in defense of spanking is that it is not harmful if the parents are loving and explain why they are spanking. The research does show that the harmful effects of spanking are reduced if it is done by loving parents who explain their actions. However,... a study by Larzelere (1986) shows that although the harmful effects are reduced, they are not eliminated. The ... harmful side effects include an increased risk of delinquency as a child and crime as an adult, wife beating, depression, masochistic sex, and lowered earnings.

In addition to having harmful psychological effects on children, hitting children also makes life more difficult for parents. Hitting a child to stop misbehavior may be the easy way in the short run, but in the slightly longer run, it makes the job of being a parent more difficult. This is because spanking reduces the ability of parents to influence their children, especially in adolescence when they are too big to control by physical force. Children are more likely to do what the parents want if there is a strong bond of affection with the parent. In short, being able to influence a child depends in considerable part on the bond between parent and child (Hirschi, 1969). An experiment by Redd, Morris, and Martin (1975) shows that children tend to avoid caretaking adults who use punishment. In the natural setting, of course, there are many things that tie children to their parents. I suggest that each spanking chips away at the bond between parent and child....

Contrary to the "spoiled child" myth, children of non-spanking parents are likely to be easier to manage and better behaved than the children of parents who spank. This is partly because they tend to control their own behavior on the basis of what their own conscience tells them is right and wrong rather than to avoid being hit. This is ironic because almost everyone thinks that spanking "when necessary" makes for better behavior.

Myth 4: One or Two Times Won't Cause Any Damage

The evidence in this book indicates that the greatest risk of harmful effects occurs when spanking is very frequent. However, that does not necessarily mean that spanking just once or twice is harmless. Unfortunately, the connection between spanking once or twice and psychological damage has not been addressed by most of the available research. This is because the studies seem to be based on this myth. They generally cluster children into "low" and "high" groups in terms of the frequency they were hit. This prevents the "once or twice is harmless" myth from being tested scientifically because the low group may include parents who spank once a year or as often as once a month. The few studies that did classify children according to the number of times they were hit by their parents . . . show that even one or two instances of corporal punishment are associated with a slightly higher probability of later physically abusing your own child, slightly more depressive symptoms, and a greater probability of violence and other crime later in life. The increase in these harmful side effects when parents use only moderate corporal punishment (hit only occasionally) may be small, but why run even that small risk when the evidence shows that corporal punishment is no more effective than other forms of discipline in the short run, and less effective in the long run.

Myth 5: Parents Can't Stop Without Training

Although everyone can use additional skills in child management, there is no evidence that it takes some extraordinary training to be able to stop spanking. The most basic step in eliminating corporal punishment is for parent educators, psychologists, and pediatricians to make a simple and unambiguous statement that hitting a child is wrong and that a child *never,* ever, under any circumstances except literal physical self-defense, should be hit.

That idea has been rejected almost without exception everytime I suggest it to parent educators or social scientists. They believe it would turn off parents and it could even be harmful because parents don't know what else to do. I think that belief is an unconscious defense of corporal punishment. I say that because I have never heard a parent educator say that before we can tell parents to never *verbally* attack a child, parents need training in alternatives. Some do need training, but everyone agrees that parents who use *psychological* pain as a method of discipline, such as insulting or demeaning, the child, should stop immediately. But when it comes to causing *physical* pain by spanking, all but a small minority of parent educators say that before parents are told to stop spanking, they need to learn alternative modes of discipline. I believe they should come right out, as they do for verbal attacks, and say without qualification that a child should *never* be hit. . . .

This can be illustrated by looking at one situation that almost everyone thinks calls for spanking: when a toddler who runs out into the street. A typical parent will scream in terror, rush out and grab the child, and run to safety, telling the child, No! No! and explaining the danger—all of this accompanied by one or more slaps to the legs or behind.

The same sequence is as effective or more effective *without the spanking.* The spanking is not needed because even tiny children can sense the terror in the parent and understand, No! No! Newborn infants can tell the difference between when a mother is relaxed and when she is tense (Stern, 1977). Nevertheless, the fact that a child understands that something is wrong does not guarantee never again running into the street; just as spanking does not guarantee the child will not run into the street again. . . .

Of course, when the child misbehaves again, most spanking parents do more than just repeat the spanking or spank harder. They usually also do things such as explain the danger to the child before letting the child go out again or warn the child that if it happens again, he or she will have to stay in the house for the afternoon, and so on. The irony is that when the child finally does learn, the parent attributes the success to the spanking, not the explanation.

Myth 6: If You Don't Spank, Your Children Will Be Spoiled or Run Wild

It is true that some non-spanked children run wild. But when that happens it is not because the parent didn't spank. It is because some parents think the alternative to spanking is to ignore a child's misbehavior or to replace spanking with verbal attacks such as, Only a dummy like you can't learn to keep your toys where I won't trip over them. The best alternative is to take firm action to correct the misbehavior without hitting. Firmly condemning what the child has done and explaining why it is wrong are usually enough. When they are not, there are a host of other things to do, such as requiring a time out or depriving the child of a privilege, neither of which involves hitting the child.

Suppose the child hits another child. Parents need to express outrage at this or the child may think it is acceptable behavior. The expression of outrage and a clear statement explaining why the child should never hit another person, except in self-defense, will do the trick in most cases. That does not mean one such warning will do the trick, any more than a single spanking will do the trick. It takes most children a while to learn such things, whatever methods the parents use.

The importance of how parents go about teaching children is clear from a classic study of American parenting—*Patterns of Child Rearing* by Sears, Maccoby, and Levin (1957). This study found two actions by parents that are linked to a high level of aggression by the child: permissiveness of the child's aggression, namely ignoring it when the child hits them or another child, and spanking to correct misbehavior. The most aggressive children . . . are children of parents who permitted aggression by the child and who also hit them for a variety of misbehavior. The least aggressive children are . . . children of parents who clearly condemned acts of aggression and who, by not spanking, acted in a way that demonstrated the principle that hitting is wrong.

There are other reasons why, on the average, the children of parents who do not spank are better behaved than children of parents who spank:

- Non-spanking parents pay more attention to their children's behavior, both good and bad, than parents who spank. Consequently, they are more likely to reward good behavior and less likely to ignore misbehavior.

- Their children have fewer opportunities to get into trouble because they are more likely to child-proof the home. For older children, they have clear rules about where they can go and who they can be with.
- Non-spanking parents tend to do more explaining and reasoning. This teaches the child how to use these essential tools to monitor his or her own behavior, whereas children who are spanked get less training in thinking things through.
- Non-spanking parents treat the child in ways that tend to bond the child to them and avoid acts that weaken the bond. They tend to use more rewards for good behavior, greater warmth and affection, and fewer verbal assaults on the child (see Myth 9). By not spanking, they avoid anger and resentment over spanking. When there is a strong bond, children identify with the parent and want to avoid doing things the parent says are wrong. The child develops a conscience and lets that direct his or her behavior. That is exactly what Sears et al. found.

Myth 7: Parents Spank Rarely or Only for Serious Problems

Contrary to this myth, parents who spank tend to use this method of discipline for almost any misbehavior. Many do not even give the child a warning. They spank before trying other things. Some advocates of spanking even recommend this. At any supermarket or other public place, you can see examples of a child doing something wrong, such as taking a can of food off the shelf. The parent then slaps the child's hand and puts back the can, sometimes without saying a word to the child. John Rosemond, the author of *Parent Power* (1981), says, "For me, spanking is a first resort. I seldom spank, but when I decide ... I do it, and that's the end of it."

The high frequency of spanking also shows up among the parents [studied]. The typical parent of a toddler told us of about 15 instances in which he or she had hit the child during the previous 12 months. That is surely a minimum estimate because spanking a child is generally such a routine and unremarkable event that most instances are forgotten. Other studies, such as Newson and Newson (1963), report much more chronic hitting of children. My tabulations for mothers of three- to five-year-old children in the National Longitudinal Study of Youth found that almost two-thirds hit their children during the week of the interview, and they did it more then three times in just that one week. As high as that figure may seem, I think that daily spanking is not at all uncommon. It has not been documented because the parents who do it usually don't realize how often they are hitting their children.

Myth 8: By the Time a Child Is a Teenager, Parents Have Stopped

As we have seen, parents of children in their early teens are also heavy users of corporal punishment, although at that age it is more likely to be a slap on the face than on the behind.... [M]ore than half of the parents of 13- to 14-year-old children in our two national surveys hit their children in the previous 12 months. The percentage drops each year as children get older, but even at age 17, one out of five parents is still hitting. To make matters worse, these are minimum estimates.

Of the parents of teenagers who told us about using corporal punishment, 84 percent did it more than once in the previous 12 months. For boys, the average was seven times and for girls, five times. These are minimum figures because we interviewed the mother in half the families and the father in the other half. The number of times would be greater if we had information on what the parent who was not interviewed did.

Myth 9: If Parents Don't Spank, They Will Verbally Abuse Their Child

The scientific evidence is exactly the opposite. Among the nationally representative samples of parents [surveyed], those who did the least spanking also engaged in the least verbal aggression.

It must be pointed out that non-spanking parents are an exceptional minority. They are defying the cultural prescription that says a good parent should spank if necessary. The depth of their involvement with their children probably results from the same underlying characteristics that led them to reject spanking. There is a danger that if more ordinary parents are told to never spank, they might replace spanking by ignoring misbehavior or by verbal attacks. Consequently, a campaign to end spanking must also stress the importance of avoiding verbal attacks as well as physical attacks, and also the importance of paying attention to misbehavior.

Myth 10: It Is Unrealistic to Expect Parents to Never Spank

It is no more unrealistic to expect parents to never hit a child than to expect that husbands should never hit their wives, or that no one should go through a stop sign, or that a supervisor should never hit an employee. Despite the legal prohibition, some husbands hit their wives, just as some drivers go through stop signs, and a supervisor occasionally may hit an employee.

If we were to prohibit spanking, as is the law in Sweden (see Deley, 1988; and Haeuser, 1990), there still would be parents who would continue to spank. But that is not a reason to avoid passing such a law here. Some people kill even though murder has been a crime since the dawn of history. Some husbands continue to hit their wives even though it has been more than a century since the courts stopped recognizing the common law right of a husband to "physically chastise an errant wife" (Calvert, 1974).

A law prohibiting spanking is unrealistic only because spanking is such an accepted part of American culture. That also was true of smoking. Yet in less than a generation we have made tremendous progress toward eliminating smoking. We can make similar progress toward eliminating spanking by showing parents that spanking is dangerous, that their children will be easier to bring up if they do not spank, and by clearly saying that a child should *never*, under any circumstances, be spanked.

Spare the Rod?

Opposition to parents spanking their children has been growing significantly in elite circles over the past 15 years.[1] No doubt much of this opposition springs from a sincere concern for the well-being of children. Child abuse is a reality, and stories of child abuse are horrifying. But while loving and effective discipline is quite definitely *not* harsh and abusive, neither is it weak and ineffectual. Indeed, disciplinary spanking can fall well within the boundaries of loving discipline and need not be labeled abusive violence.[2]

Or so most Americans seem to think. According to a recent Voter/Consumer Research poll commissioned by the Family Research Council, 76 percent of the more than 1,000 Americans surveyed said that spanking was an effective form of discipline in their home when they were children.[3] These results are made all the more impressive by the fact that nearly half of those who answered otherwise grew up in homes in which they were never spanked. Taken together, more than four out of five Americans who were actually spanked by their parents as children say that it was an effective form of discipline.

In addition, Americans perceive lack of discipline to be the biggest problem in public education today, according to a recent Gallup poll.[4] Several studies show strong public support for corporal punishment by parents.[5]

Critics claim that spanking a child is abusive and contributes to adult dysfunction. These allegations arise from studies that fail to distinguish appropriate spanking from other forms of punishment. Abusive forms of physical punishment such as kicking, punching, and beating are commonly grouped with mild spanking. Furthermore, the studies usually include, and even emphasize, corporal punishment of adolescents, rather than focusing on preschool children, where spanking is more effective. This blurring of distinctions between spanking and physical abuse, and between children of different ages, gives critics the illusion of having data condemning all disciplinary spanking.

There are several arguments commonly leveled against disciplinary spanking. Interestingly, most of these arguments can be used against other forms of discipline. Any form of discipline (time-out, restriction, etc.), when used inappropriately and in anger, can result in distorting a child's perception of justice and harming his emotional development. In light of this, let us examine some of the unfounded arguments promoted by spanking opponents.

From Den A. Trumbull and S. DuBose Ravenel, "Spare the Rod?" *Family Policy*, vol. 9, no. 5 (September–October 1996). Copyright © 1996 by The Family Research Council. Reprinted by permission of *Family Policy,* a publication of The Family Research Council, Washington, DC.

Argument #1: Many psychological studies show that spanking is an improper form of discipline.

Counterpoint: Researchers John Lyons, Rachel Anderson and David Larson of the National Institute of Healthcare Research recently conducted a systematic review of the research literature on corporal punishment.[6] They found that 83 percent of the 132 identified articles published in clinical and psychosocial journals were merely opinion-driven editorials, reviews or commentaries, devoid of new empirical findings. Moreover, most of the empirical studies were methodologically flawed by grouping the impact of abuse with spanking. The best studies demonstrated beneficial, not detrimental, effects of spanking in certain situations. Clearly, there is insufficient evidence to condemn parental spanking and adequate evidence to justify its proper use.

Argument #2: Physical punishment establishes the moral righteousness of hitting other persons who do something which is regarded as wrong.

Counterpoint: The "spanking teaches hitting" belief has gained in popularity over the past decade, but is not supported by objective evidence. A distinction must be made between abusive hitting and nonabusive spanking. A child's ability to discriminate hitting from disciplinary spanking depends largely upon the parents' attitude with spanking and the parents' procedure for spanking. There is no evidence in the medical literature that a mild spank to the buttocks of a disobedient child by a loving parent teaches the child aggressive behavior.

The critical issue is *how* spanking (or, in fact, any punishment) is used more so than *whether* it is used. Physical abuse by an angry, uncontrolled parent will leave lasting emotional wounds and cultivate bitterness and resentment within a child. The balanced, prudent use of disciplinary spanking, however, is an effective deterrent to aggressive behavior with some children.

Researchers at the Center for Family Research at Iowa State University studied 332 families to examine both the impact of corporal punishment and the quality of parental involvement on three adolescent outcomes—aggressiveness, delinquency, and psychological well-being. The researchers found a strong association between the quality of parenting and each of these three outcomes. Corporal punishment, however, was *not* adversely related to any of these outcomes. This study proves the point that quality of parenting is the chief determinant of favorable or unfavorable outcomes.[7] Remarkably, childhood aggressiveness has been more closely linked to maternal permissiveness and negative criticism than to even abusive physical discipline.[8]

It is unrealistic to expect that children would never hit others if their parents would only exclude spanking from their discipline options. Most children in their toddler years (long before they are ever spanked) naturally attempt to hit others when conflict or frustration arises. The continuation of this behavior is largely determined by how the parent or caregiver responds. If correctly disciplined, the hitting will become less frequent. If ignored or ineffectively disciplined, the hitting will likely persist and even escalate. Thus, instead of contributing to greater violence, spanking can be a useful component in an overall plan to effectively teach a child to stop aggressive hitting.

Argument #3: Since parents often refrain from hitting until the anger or frustration reaches a certain point, the child learns that anger and frustration justify the use of physical force.

Counterpoint: A study published in *Pediatrics* indicates that most parents who spank do not spank on impulse, but purposefully spank their children with a belief in its effectiveness.[9] Furthermore, the study revealed no significant correlation between the frequency of spanking and the anger reported by mothers. Actually, the mothers who reported being angry were not the same parents who spanked.

Reactive, impulsive hitting after losing control due to anger is unquestionably the wrong way for a parent to use corporal punishment. Eliminating all physical punishment in the home, however, would not remedy such explosive scenarios. It could even increase the problem. When effective spanking is removed from a parent's disciplinary repertoire, he or she is left with nagging, begging, belittling, and yelling, once the primary disciplinary measures—such as time-out and logical consequences—have failed. By contrast, if proper spanking is proactively used in conjunction with other disciplinary measures, better control of the particularly defiant child can be achieved, and moments of exasperation are less likely to occur.

Argument #4: Physical punishment is harmful to a child.

Counterpoint: Any disciplinary measure, physical, verbal or emotional, carried to an extreme can harm a child. Excessive scolding and berating of a child by a parent is emotionally harmful. Excessive use of isolation (time-out) for unreasonable periods of time can humiliate a child and ruin the measure's effectiveness. Obviously, excessive or indiscriminate physical punishment is harmful and abusive. However, an appropriately administered spanking of a forewarned disobedient child is not harmful when administered in a loving, controlled manner. Without the prudent use of spanking for the particularly defiant child, a parent runs the risk of being inconsistent and rationalizing the child's behavior. This inconsistent manner of parenting is confusing and harmful to the child and is damaging to the parent-child relationship. There is no evidence that proper disciplinary spanking is harmful to the child.

Argument #5: Physical punishment makes the child angry at the parent.

Counterpoint: All forms of punishment initially elicit a frustrated, angry response from a child. Progression of this anger is dependent primarily upon the parent's attitude during and after the disciplinary event, and the manner of its application. Any form of punishment administered angrily for purposes of retribution, rather than calmly for purposes of correction, can create anger and resentment in a child. Actually, a spanking can break the escalating rage of a rebellious child and more quickly restore the relationship between parent and child.

> *Argument #6: Spanking teaches a child that "might makes right," that power and strength are most important and that the biggest can force their will upon the smallest.*

Counterpoint: Parental power is commonly exerted in routine child rearing and spanking is only one example. Other situations where power and restraint are exercised by the average parent include:

- The young child who insists on running from his parent in a busy mall or parking lot.
- The toddler who refuses to sit in his car seat.
- The young patient who refuses to hold still as a vaccination is administered, or as a laceration is repaired.

Power and control over the child are necessary at times to ensure safety, health and proper behavior. Classic child rearing studies have shown that some degree of power, assertion,[10] and firm control[11] is essential for optimal child rearing. When power is exerted in the context of love and for the child's benefit, the child will not perceive it as bullying or demeaning.

A Closer Look

Distinguishing Spanking From Abuse

Corporal punishment is often defined broadly as *bodily punishment of any kind.* Since this definition includes spanking as well as obviously abusive acts such as kicking, punching, beating, face slapping, and even starvation, more specific definitions must be used to separate appropriate versus inappropriate corporal punishment.

Spanking is one of many disciplinary responses available to parents intended to shape appropriate behavior in the developing toddler and child. It is an adjunctive corrective measure, to be used in combination with primary responses such as restraint, natural and logical consequences, time-out, and restriction of privileges.

Child development experts believe spanking should be used mainly as a back-up to primary measures, and then independently to correct deliberate and persistent problem behavior that is not remedied with milder measures. It is most useful with toddlers and preschoolers from 18 months to 6 years of age, when reasoning is less persuasive.

Moreover, child development experts say that spanking should always be a planned action by a parent, not an impulsive reaction to misbehavior. The child should be forewarned of the spanking consequence for each of the designated problem behaviors. Spanking should always be administered in private. It should consist of one or two spanks to the child's buttocks, followed by a calm review of the offense and the desired behavior.

Table 1

	Spanking	Physical Abuse
The Act	Spanking: One or two spanks to the buttocks	Beating: To strike repeatedly (also kick, punch, choke)
The Intent	Training: To correct problem behavior	Violence: Physical force intended to injure or abuse
The Attitude	With love and concern	With anger and malice
The Effects	Behavioral correction	Emotional and physical injury

Argument #7: Spanking is violence.

Counterpoint: Spanking, as recommended by most primary care physicians,[12] is not violence by definition ("exertion of physical force so as to injure or abuse").[13] Parents who properly spank do not injure or abuse their child.

   The use of this term "violence" in the spanking debate only serves to deepen the confusion. Why do anti-spanking authors repeatedly fail to distinguish between abusive violence and mild spanking? The distinction is so fundamental and obvious that its omission suggests that these authors use such terminology for its propaganda value, not to clarify issues.

Argument #8: Spanking is an ineffective solution to misbehavior.

Counterpoint: Though the specific use of appropriate spanking has rarely been studied, there is evidence of its short-term and long-term effectiveness. When combined with reasoning, the use of negative consequences (including spanking) does effectively decrease the frequency of misbehavior recurrences with preschool children.[14] In clinical field trials where parental spanking has been studied, it has consistently been found to reduce the subsequent frequency of noncompliance with time-out.[15] Spanking, as an effective enforcer of time-out, is a component of several well-researched parent training programs[16] and popular parenting texts.[17]

Dr. Diana Baumrind of the Institute for Human Development at the University of California-Berkeley, conducted a decade-long study of families with children 3 to 9 years old.[18] Baumrind found that parents employing a balanced disciplinary style of firm control (including spanking) and positive encouragement experienced the most favorable outcome in their children. Parents taking extreme approaches to discipline (authoritarian-types using excessive punishment with less encouragement or permissive-types using little punishment and no spanking) were less successful.

Baumrind concluded that evidence from this study "did not indicate that negative reinforcement or corporal punishment per se were harmful or ineffective procedures, but rather the total patterns of parental control determined the effects on the child of these procedures."

This approach of balanced parenting, employing the occasional use of spanking, is advocated by several child rearing experts.[19] In the hands of loving parents, a spanking to the buttocks of a defiant toddler in appropriate settings is a powerful motivator to correct behavior and an effective deterrent to disobedience.

Argument #9: Adults who were spanked as children are at risk for using violence as a means of resolving conflicts as adults.

Counterpoint: This theory comes from work done by Murray Straus of the Family Research Lab at the University of New Hampshire. Straus' conclusions are based upon theoretical models and survey results of adults recalling spankings as teenagers. His work is not clinical research, and many experts believe that his conclusions go far beyond his data. As with most of Straus' survey research, teenage spanking is the focus, not the selective use of spanking of young children by reasonable parents. The evidence for his conclusion disappears when parental spanking is measured between the ages of 2 and 8 years, and when childhood aggression is measured at a later age.

In a 1994 review article on corporal punishment, Dr. Robert E. Larzelere, a director of research at Boys Town, Nebraska, presents evidence supporting a parent's selective use of spanking of children, particularly those 2 to 6 years old.[20] After thoroughly reviewing the literature, Larzelere concludes that any association between spanking and antisocial aggressiveness in children is insignificant and artifactual.

After a decade of longitudinal study of children beginning in third grade, Dr. Leonard Eron found no association between punishment (including spanking) and later aggression. Eron, a clinical psychologist at the Univeristy of Michigan's Institute for Social Research, concluded, "Upon follow-up 10 years after the original data collection, we found that punishment of aggressive acts at the earlier age was no longer related to current aggression, and instead, other variables like parental nurturance and children's identification with their parents were more important in predicting later aggression."[21]

Again, it is the total pattern of parenting that determines the outcome of a parent's efforts.

Argument #10: Spanking leads a parent to use harmful forms of corporal punishment which lead to physical child abuse.

Counterpoint: The abuse potential when loving parents use appropriate disciplinary spanking is very low. Since parents have a natural affection for their children, they are more prone to underutilize spanking than to overutilize it. Both empirical data and professional opinion oppose the concept of a causal relationship between spanking and child abuse.

Surveys indicate that 70 to 90 percent of parents of preschoolers use spanking,[22] yet the incidence of physical child abuse in America is only about 5 percent. Statistically, the two practices are far apart. Furthermore, over the past decade reports of child abuse have steadily risen while approval for parental spanking has steadily declined.[23]

More than 70 percent of primary care pediatricians reject the idea that spanking sets the stage for parents to engage in forms of physical abuse.[24]

Teaching parents appropriate spanking may actually reduce child abuse, according to Larzelere, in his 1994 review article on corporal punishment.[25] Parents who are ill-equipped to control their child's behavior, or who take a more permissive approach (refusing to use spanking), may be more prone to anger[26] and explosive attacks on their child.[27]

Parental child abuse is an interactive process involving parental competence, parental and child temperaments, and situational demands.[28] Abusive parents are more angry, depressed and impulsive, and emphasize punishment as the predominant means of discipline. Abused children are more aggressive and less compliant than children from nonabusive families. There is less interaction between family members in abusive families and abusive mothers display more negative than positive behavior. The etiology of abusive parenting is multifactorial with emphasis on the personalities involved, and cannot be simply explained by a parent's use of spanking.

In a letter to the editor in a 1995 issue of Pediatrics, Drs. Lawrence S. Wissow and Debra Roter of Johns Hopkins University's pediatrics department acknowledge that a definitive link between spanking and child abuse has yet to be established.[29]

Finally, the Swedish experiment to reduce child abuse by banning spanking seems to be failing. In 1980, one year after this ban was adopted, the rate of child beatings was twice that of the United States.[30] According to a 1995 report from the government organization Statistics Sweden, police reports of child abuse by family members rose four-fold from 1984 to 1994, while reports of teen violence increased nearly six-fold.[31]

Most experts agree that spanking and child abuse are not on the same continuum, but are very different entities. With parenting, it is the "user" and how a measure is used much more than the measure used that determines the outcome of the disciplinary effort. Clearly, spanking can be safely used in the discipline of young children with an excellent outcome. The proper use of spanking may actually reduce a parent's risk of abusing the child.

Argument #11: Spanking is never necessary.

Counterpoint: All children need a combination of encouragement and correction as they are disciplined to become socially responsible individuals. In order for correction to deter disobedient behavior, the consequence imposed upon the child must outweigh the pleasure of the disobedient act. For very compliant children, milder forms of correction will suffice and spanking may never be necessary. For more defiant children who refuse to comply with or be persuaded by milder consequences such as time-out, spanking is useful, effective, and appropriate.

Conclusion

The subject of disciplinary spanking should be evaluated from a factual and philosophical perspective. It must be distinguished from abusive, harmful forms of corporal punishment. Appropriate disciplinary spanking can play an important role in optimal child development, and has been found in prospective studies to be a part of the parenting style associated with the best outcomes. There is no evidence that mild spanking is harmful. Indeed, spanking is supported by history, research, and a majority of primary care physicians.

ET CETERA, ET CETERA: GUIDELINES FOR DISCIPLINARY SPANKING

The following are guidelines that Dr. Den Trumbull has used to advise the parents he serves in disciplining children. These guidelines should help policymakers appreciate the legitimacy of disciplinary spanking.

1. Spanking should be used selectively for clear, deliberate misbehavior, particularly that which arises from a child's persistent defiance of a parent's instruction. It should be used only when the child receives at least as much encouragement and praise for good behavior as correction for problem behavior.
2. Milder forms of discipline, such as verbal correction, time-out, and logical consequences, should be used initially, followed by spanking when noncompliance persists. Spanking has shown to be an effective method of enforcing time-out with the child who refuses to comply.
3. Only a parent (or in exceptional situations, someone else who has an intimate relationship of authority with the child) should administer a spanking.
4. Spanking should not be administered on impulse or when a parent is out of control. A spanking should always be motivated by love for the purpose of teaching and correcting, never for revenge.
5. Spanking is inappropriate before 15 months of age and is usually not necessary until after 18 months. It should be less necessary after 6 years, and rarely, if ever, used after 10 years of age.
6. After 10 months of age, one slap to the hand of a stubborn crawler or toddler may be necessary to stop serious misbehavior when distraction and removal have failed. This is particularly the case when the forbidden object is immovable and dangerous, such as a hot oven door or an electrical outlet.

7. Spanking should always be a planned action, not a reaction, by the parent and should follow a deliberate procedure.

   - The child should be forewarned of the spanking consequence for designated problem behaviors.
   - Spanking should always be administered in private (bedroom or restroom) to avoid public humiliation or embarassment.
   - One or two spanks should be administered to the buttocks. This is followed by embracing the child and calmly reviewing the offense and the desired behavior in an effort to reestablish a warm relationship.

8. Spanking should leave only transient redness of the skin and should never cause physical injury.
9. If properly administered spankings are ineffective, other appropriate disciplinary responses should be tried, or the parent should seek professional help. Parents should never increase the intensity of spankings.

Notes

1. Fathman, Dr. Robert E. "Corporal Punishment Fact Sheet." July 1994.
2. Lyons, Dr. John S., Anderson, Rachel L., and Larson, Dr. David B., memo.
3. Voter/Consumer Research Poll, National Values. Commissioned by the Family Research Council, 1994.
4. "School Poll." *The Washington Times.* Aug. 28, 1995, p. A-2.
5. Flynn, Clifton P. "Regional Differences in Attitudes Toward Corporal Punishment." *Journal of Marriage and the Family.* 56 (May 1994): 314–324.
6. Lyons, Dr. John S., Anderson, Rachel L., and Larson, Dr. David B. "The Use and Effects of Physical Punishment in the Home: A Systematic Review." Presentation to the Section on Bio-Ethics of the American Academy of Pediatrics at annual meeting, Nov. 2, 1993.
7. Simons, Ronald L., Johnson, Christine, and Conger, Rand D. "Harsh Corporal Punishment versus Quality of Parental Involvement as an Explanation of Adolescent Maladjustment." *Journal of Marriage and Family.* 1994; 56:591–607.
8. Olweus, Dan. "Familial and Tempermental Determinants of Aggressive Behavior in Adolescent Boys: A Causal Analysis." *Developmental Psychology.* 1980; 16:644–660.
9. Socolar, Rebecca R. S., M.D. and Stein, Ruth E.K., M.D. "Spanking Infants and Toddlers: Maternal Belief and Practice." *Pediatrics.* 1995; 95:105–111.
10. Hoffman, Martin. "Parental Discipline and Child's Moral Development." *Journal of Personal Social Psychology.* 1967; 5:45–57.
11. Baumrind, Diana, Ph.D. "Rearing Competent Children." Damon, W. (Ed.) *Child Development Today and Tomorrow.* 1989; pp. 349–378. San Francisco, Calif.: Jossey-Bass.
12. McCormick, Kenelm F., M.D. "Attitudes of Primary Care Physicians Toward Corporal Punishment." *Journal of the American Medical Association.* 1992; 267:3161–3165.
13. *Webster's Ninth New Collegiate Dictionary.* 1987; p. 1316. Massachusetts: Merriam-Webster, Inc.
14. Larzelere, Dr. Robert E. and Merenda, Dr. J.A. "The Effectiveness of Parental Discipline for Toddler Misbehavior at Different Levels of Child Distress." *Family Relations.* 1994; 43 (4).

15. Roberts, Mark W. and Powers, Scott W. "Adjusting Chair Time-out Enforcement Procedures for Oppositional Children." *Behavioral Therapy.* 1990; 21:257–271, and Bean, Arthur W. and Roberts, Mark W. "The Effect of Time-out Release Contingencies on Changes in Child Noncompliance." *Journal of Abnormal Child Psychology.* 1981; 9:95–105.

16. Forehand, R.L. and McMahon, R.J. *Helping the Noncompliant Child.* 1981; pp. 79–80. New York: Guilford Press.

17. Clark, Lynn C. *SOS! Help for Parents.* 1985; pp. 181–185. Kentucky: Parents Press.

18. Baumrind, Dr. Diana. "The Development of Instrumental Competence Through Socialization. *Minnesota Symposia on Child Psychology.* 1973; 7:3–46.

19. Austin, Glenn. *Love and Power: How to Raise Competent, Confident Children.* 1988. California: Robert Erdmann Publishing. Also, Dobson, Dr. James. *The Strong-Willed Child.* 1985. Illinois: Tyndale House Publishers, and Coopersmith, Stanley. *The Antecedents of Self-Esteem.* 1967. New York: W.H. Freeman & Co. Reprinted 1981. California: Consulting Psychologists Press, Inc.

20. Larzelere, Dr. Robert E. "Should the Use of Corporal Punishment by Parents be Considered Child Abuse?" Mason, M., Gambrill, E. (Eds.) *Debating Children's Lives.* 1994; pp. 204–209. California: SAGE Publications.

21. Eron, Dr. Leonard D. "Theories of Aggression: From Drives to Cognitions." Huesmann, L.R. (Ed.) *Aggressive Behavior, Current Perspectives.* 1994; pp. 3–11. New York: Plenum Press.

22. Straus, Murray A. "Discipline and Deviance: Physical Punishment of Children and Violence and Other Crime in Adulthood." *Social Problems.* 1991; 38:133–152.

23. National Committee to Prevent Child Abuse. *Memorandum.* May 1995; 2(5).

24. White, Kristin. "Where Pediatricians Stand on Spanking." *Pediatric Management.* September 1993: 11–15.

25. Larzelere, Dr. Robert E., *op. cit.*

26. Socolar, Rebecca R.S., M.D. and Stein, Ruth E.K., M.D., *op. cit.*

27. Baumrind, Dr. Diana, *op. cit.*

28. Wolfe, David A. "Child-Abusive Parents: An Empirical Review and Analysis." *Psychological Bulletin.* 1985; 97(3): 462–482.

29. Wissow, Dr. Lawrence S. and Roter, Dr. Debra. Letter to the editor, in reply to corporal punishment letter. *Pediatrics.* 1995; 96(4): 794–795.

30. Larzelere, Dr. Robert E., *op. cit.*

31. Statistics Sweden. *K R Info.* May 1995; pp. 1–6. Stockholm, Sweden.

CHALLENGE QUESTIONS

Does Spanking Lead Children to Become More Violent?

1. How did your parents discipline you? Describe how you think your parents' disciplinary practices affected you, positively and negatively. Relate these observations to the remarks of the authors.
2. How have the selections affected how you plan to discipline your own children?
3. How do you explain the results of the Swedish ban on spanking, as described by Trumbull and Ravenel? How would Straus explain these results?
4. Should spanking be made illegal? Why, or why not? How might such a law be enforced?

ISSUE 7

Does Viewing Television Increase Aggression?

YES: Brandon S. Centerwall, from "Television and Violent Crime," *The Public Interest* (Spring 1993)

NO: Brian Siano, from "Frankenstein Must Be Destroyed: Chasing the Monster of TV Violence," *The Humanist* (January/February 1994)

ISSUE SUMMARY

YES: Brandon S. Centerwall, an epidemiologist, argues that children act out the violence they see on television and carry the violent behaviors into adulthood.

NO: Brian Siano, a writer and researcher, contends that children with nonnurturing parents, regardless of the children's television viewing habits, tend to be more aggressive than children who closely identify with either parent.

Survey after survey shows that one of the primary concerns of contemporary society is violence. The popular perception is that violence is on the rise. Indeed, some people believe that violence is like some contagious disease that has spread to epidemic proportions. What is the reason for this seeming "epidemic"? Why does the current generation appear to be more prone to violence than previous generations? How is today different from the "good old days"?

Many people would sum up that difference in one word—television. Television now occupies a place (or two or three) in almost every home in the United States, regardless of the inhabitants' race or level of income. And television has been cited time and again by the U.S. surgeon general, by members of the U.S. Congress, and by psychological researchers as a medium filled with many kinds of violence. It seems only natural for parents to wonder about television's impact on small children, who average over 20 hours of television viewing per week. Indeed, some have suggested that a child witnesses over 100,000 acts of violence on television before graduating from elementary school. How do these acts of violence affect a child's development?

In the following selection, Brandon S. Centerwall asserts that televised violence leads to an increase in a child's aggression, referring to numerous published studies to support this assertion. He theorizes that children have an instinctive desire to imitate behavior. Unfortunately, however, children are not born with an instinct for evaluating the appropriateness of certain actions. This means that children naturally model what they see on television and do not typically think about whether or not they *should* model what they see. Consequently, even when clearly antisocial behaviors are depicted on television, children are still likely to learn and imitate them. Centerwall believes that the danger to a child's development is so great that he advocates making television violence a part of the public health agenda.

In the second selection, Brian Siano contends that factors other than television are more influential on a child's tendency for violent actions. He points to research that contradicts Centerwall's views. For example, one study found that boys who watch nonviolent shows tend to be more aggressive than boys who watch violent television. Siano argues that style of parenting is a better indicator of the development of violent behavior. Children of nonnurturing parents and children who do not identify with their parents are the ones who are most likely to exhibit violence. Although Siano is an advocate of quality programming, he is reluctant to indiscriminately censor all violence from television, particularly when effective parenting can counter any possible ill effects.

POINT

- Research indicates that parents who watched more television as children punished their own children more severely.
- Children are incapable of discriminating between what they should and should not imitate.
- Limiting all children's exposure to television violence should become part of the public health agenda.
- Many studies demonstrate a positive relationship between television exposure and physical aggression.
- For children to be safe, television violence must be eliminated.

COUNTERPOINT

- Boys who watch nonviolent shows tend to be more aggressive than boys who watch violent shows.
- Good parents teach children how to discriminate among their behaviors.
- Violence can be used in television shows for pro-social reasons.
- Parental identification can change the way children interpret physical punishment on television.
- Indiscriminate censorship of all violence is too high a price to pay for the minimal influence of television.

Brandon S. Centerwall

 **YES**

Television and Violent Crime

Children are born ready to imitate adult behavior. That they can, and do, imitate an array of adult facial expressions has been demonstrated in newborns as young as a few hours old, before they are even old enough to know that they have facial features. It is a most useful instinct, for the developing child must learn and master a vast repertoire of behavior in short order.

But while children have an instinctive desire to imitate, they do not possess an instinct for determining whether a behavior ought to be imitated. They will imitate anything, including behavior that most adults regard as destructive and antisocial. It may give pause for thought, then, to learn that infants as young as fourteen months demonstrably observe and incorporate behavior seen on television.

The average American preschooler watches more than twenty-seven hours of television per week. This might not be bad if these young children understood what they were watching. But they don't. Up through ages three and four, most children are unable to distinguish fact from fantasy on TV, and remain unable to do so despite adult coaching. In the minds of young children, television is a source of entirely factual information regarding how the world works. There are no limits to their credulity. To cite one example, an Indiana school board had to issue an advisory to young children that, no, there is no such thing as Teenage Mutant Ninja Turtles. Children had been crawling down storm drains looking for them.

Naturally, as children get older, they come to know better, but their earliest and deepest impressions are laid down at an age when they still see television as a factual source of information about the outside world. In that world, it seems, violence is common and the commission of violence is generally powerful, exciting, charismatic, and effective. In later life, serious violence is most likely to erupt at moments of severe stress—and it is precisely at such moments that adolescents and adults are most likely to revert to their earliest, most visceral sense of the role of violence in society and in personal behavior. Much of this sense will have come from television.

From Brandon S. Centerwall, "Television and Violent Crime," *The Public Interest,* no. 111 (Spring 1993), pp. 56–71. Copyright © 1993 by National Affairs, Inc. Reprinted by permission.

The Seeds of Aggression

In 1973, a remote rural community in Canada acquired television for the first time. The acquisition of television at such a late date was due to problems with signal reception rather than any hostility toward TV. As reported in *The Impact of Television* (1986), Tannis Williams and her associates at the University of British Columbia investigated the effect of television on the children of this community (which they called "Notel"), taking for comparison two similar towns that already had television.

The researchers observed forty-five first- and second-graders in the three towns for rates of inappropriate physical aggression before television was introduced into Notel. Two years later, the same forty-five children were observed again. To prevent bias in the data, the research assistants who collected the data were kept uninformed as to why the children's rates of aggression were of interest. Furthermore, a new group of research assistants was employed the second time around, so that the data gatherers would not be biased by recollections of the children's behavior two years earlier.

Rates of aggression did not change in the two control communities. By contrast, the rate of aggression among Notel children increased 160 percent. The increase was observed in both boys and girls, in those who were aggressive to begin with and in those who were not. Television's enhancement of noxious aggression was entirely general and not limited to a few "bad apples."

In another Canadian study, Gary Granzberg and his associates at the University of Winnipeg investigated the impact of television upon Indian communities in northern Manitoba. As described in *Television and the Canadian Indian* (1980), forty-nine third-, fourth-, and fifth-grade boys living in two communities were observed from 1973, when one town acquired television, until 1977, when the second town did as well. The aggressiveness of boys in the first community increased after the introduction of television. The aggressiveness of boys in the second community, which did not receive television then, remained the same. When television was later introduced in the second community, observed levels of aggressiveness increased there as well.

In another study conducted from 1960 to 1981, Leonard Eron and L. Rowell Huesmann (then of the University of Illinois at Chicago) followed 875 children living in a semirural U.S. county. Eron and Huesmann found that for both boys and girls, the amount of television watched at age eight predicted the seriousness of criminal acts for which they were convicted by age thirty. This remained true even after controlling for the children's baseline aggressiveness, intelligence, and socioeconomic status. Eron and Huesmann also observed second-generation effects. Children who watched much television at age eight later, as parents, punished their own children more severely than did parents who had watched less television as children. Second- and now third-generation effects are accumulating at a time of unprecedented youth violence.

All seven of the U.S. and Canadian studies of prolonged childhood exposure to television demonstrate a positive relationship between exposure and physical aggression. The critical period is preadolescent childhood. Later exposure does not appear to produce any additional effect. However, the aggression-enhancing effect of exposure in pre-adolescence extends into adolescence and adulthood. This suggests that any interventions should be designed for children and their caregivers rather than for the general adult population.

These studies confirmed the beliefs of most Americans. According to a Harris poll at the time of the studies, 43 percent of American adults believe that television violence "plays a part in making America a violent society." An additional 37 percent think it might. But how important is television violence? What is the effect of exposure upon entire populations? To address this question, I took advantage of an historical accident—the absence of television in South Africa prior to 1975.

The South African Experience

White South Africans have lived in a prosperous, industrialized society for decades, but they did not get television until 1975 because of tension between the Afrikaner- and English-speaking communities. The country's Afrikaner leaders knew that a South African television industry would have to rely on British and American shows to fill out its programming schedule, and they felt that this would provide an unacceptable cultural advantage to English-speaking South Africans. So, rather than negotiate a complicated compromise, the government simply forbade television broadcasting. The entire population of two million whites—rich and poor, urban and rural, educated and uneducated—was thus excluded from exposure to television for a quarter century after the medium was introduced in the United States.

In order to determine whether exposure to television is a cause of violence, I compared homicide rates in South Africa, Canada, and the United States. Since blacks in South Africa live under quite different conditions than blacks in the United States, I limited the comparison to white homicide rates in South Africa and the United States, and the total homicide rate in Canada (which was 97 percent white in 1951).[1] I chose the homicide rate as a measure of violence because homicide statistics are exceptionally accurate.

From 1945 to 1974, the white homicide rate in the United States increased 93 percent. In Canada, the homicide rate increased 92 percent. In South Africa, where television was banned, the white homicide rate declined by 7 percent.

Controlling for Other Factors

Could there be some explanation other than television for the fact that violence increased dramatically in the U.S. and Canada while dropping in South Africa? I examined an array of alternative explanations. None is satisfactory:

- **Economic growth.** Between 1946 and 1974, all three countries experienced substantial economic growth. Per capita income increased by 75 percent in the United States, 124 percent in Canada, and 86 percent in South Africa. Thus differences in economic growth cannot account for the different homicide trends in the three countries.

- **Civil unrest.** One might suspect that anti-war or civil-rights activity was responsible for the doubling of the homicide rate in the United States during this period. But the experience of Canada shows that this was not the case, since Canadians suffered a doubling of the homicide rate without similar civil unrest.

Other possible explanations include changes in age distribution, urbanization, alcohol consumption, capital punishment, and the availability of firearms. As discussed in *Public Communication and Behavior* (1989), none provides a viable explanation for the observed homicide trends.

In the United States and Canada, there was a lag of ten to fifteen years between the introduction of television and a doubling of the homicide rate. In South Africa, there was a similar lag. Since television exerts its behavior-modifying effects primarily on children, while homicide is primarily an adult activity, this lag represents the time needed for the "television generation" to come of age.

The relationship between television and the homicide rate holds *within* the United States as well. Different regions of the U.S., for example, acquired television at different times. As we would expect, while all regions saw increases in their homicide rates, the regions that acquired television first were also the first to see higher homicide rates.

Similarly, urban areas acquired television before rural areas. As we would expect, urban areas saw increased homicide rates several years before the occurrence of a parallel increase in rural areas.

The introduction of television also helps explain the different rates of homicide growth for whites and minorities. White households in the U.S. began acquiring television sets in large numbers approximately five years before minority households. Significantly, the white homicide rate began increasing in 1958, four years before a parallel increase in the minority homicide rate.

Of course, there are many factors other than television that influence the amount of violent crime. Every violent act is the result of a variety of forces coming together—poverty, crime, alcohol and drug abuse, stress—of which childhood TV exposure is just one. Nevertheless, the evidence indicates that if, hypothetically, television technology had never been developed, there would today be 10,000 fewer homicides each year in the United States, 70,000 fewer rapes, and 700,000 fewer injurious assaults. Violent crime would be half what it is.

The Television Industry Takes a Look

The first congressional hearings on television and violence were held in 1952, when not even a quarter of U.S. households owned television sets. In the years since, there have been scores of research reports on the issue, as well as several major government investigations. The findings of the National Commission on the Causes and Prevention of Violence, published in 1969, were particularly significant. This report established what is now the broad scientific consensus: Exposure to television increases rates of physical aggression.

Television industry executives were genuinely surprised by the National Commission's report. What the industry produced was at times unedifying, but physically harmful? In response, network executives began research programs that collectively would cost nearly a million dollars.

CBS commissioned William Belson to undertake what would be the largest and most sophisticated study yet, an investigation involving 1,565 teenage boys. In *Television Violence and the Adolescent Boy* (1978), Belson controlled for one hundred variables, and found that teenage boys who had watched above-average quantities of television violence before adolescence were committing acts of serious violence (e.g., assault, rape, major vandalism, and abuse of animals) at a rate 49 percent higher than teenage boys who had watched below-average quantities of television violence. Despite the large sum of money they had invested, CBS executives were notably unenthusiastic about the report.

ABC commissioned Melvin Heller and Samuel Polsky of Temple University to study young male felons imprisoned for violent crimes (e.g, homicide, rape, and assault). In two surveys, 22 and 34 percent of the young felons reported having consciously imitated crime techniques learned from television programs, usually successfully. The more violent of these felons were the most likely to report having learned techniques from television. Overall, the felons reported that as children they had watched an average of six hours of television per day—approximately twice as much as children in the general population at that time.

Unlike CBS, ABC maintained control over publication. The final report, *Studies in Violence and Television* (1976), was published in a private, limited edition that was not released to the general public or the scientific community.

NBC relied on a team of four researchers, three of whom were employees of NBC. Indeed, the principal investigator, J. Ronald Milavsky, was an NBC vice president. The team observed some 2,400 schoolchildren for up to three years to see if watching television violence increased their levels of physical aggressiveness. In *Television and Aggression* (1982), Milavsky and his associates reported that television violence had no effect upon the children's behavior. However, every independent investigator who has examined their data has concluded that, to the contrary, their data show that television violence did cause a modest increase of about 5 percent in average levels of physical aggressiveness. When pressed on the point, Milavsky and his associates conceded that their findings were consistent with the conclusion that television violence increased physical aggressiveness "to a small extent." They did not concede that television violence actually caused an increase, but only that their findings were consistent with such a conclusion.

The NBC study results raise an important objection to my conclusions. While studies have repeatedly demonstrated that childhood exposure to television increases physical aggressiveness, the increase is almost always quite minor. A number of investigators have argued that such a small effect is too weak to account for major increases in rates of violence. These investigators, however, overlook a key factor.

Homicide is an extreme form of aggression—so extreme that only one person in 20,000 committed murder each year in the United States in the mid-1950s. If we were to rank everyone's degree of physical aggressiveness from the least aggressive (Mother Theresa) to the most aggressive (Jack the Ripper), the large majority of us would be somewhere in the middle and murderers would be virtually off the chart. It is an intrinsic property of such "bell curve" distributions that small changes in the average imply major changes at the extremes. Thus, if exposure to television causes 8 percent of the population to shift from below-average aggression to above-average aggression, it follows that the homicide rate will double. The findings of the NBC study and the doubling of the homicide rate are two sides of the same coin.

After the results of these studies became clear, television industry executives lost their enthusiasm for scientific research. No further investigations were funded. Instead, the industry turned to political management of the issue.

The Television Industry and Social Responsibility

The television industry routinely portrays individuals who seek to influence programming as un-American haters of free speech. In a 1991 letter sent to 7,000 executives of consumer product companies and advertising agencies, the president of the Network Television Association explained:

> Freedom of expression is an inalienable right of all Americans vigorously supported by ABC, CBS, and NBC. However, boycotts and so-called advertiser "hit lists" are attempts to manipulate our free society and democratic process.

The letter went on to strongly advise the companies to ignore all efforts by anyone to influence what programs they choose to sponsor. By implication, the networks themselves should ignore all efforts by anyone to influence what programs they choose to produce.

But this is absurd. All forms of public discourse are attempts to "manipulate" our free society and democratic process. What else could they be? Consumer boycotts are no more un-American than are strikes by labor unions. The Network Television Association is attempting to systematically shut down all discourse between viewers and advertisers, and between viewers and the television industry. Wrapping itself in patriotism, the television industry's response to uppity viewers is to put them in their place. If the industry and advertisers were to actually succeed in closing the circle between them, the only course they would leave for concerned viewers would be to seek legislative action.

In the war against tobacco, we do not expect help from the tobacco industry. If someone were to call upon the tobacco industry to cut back production as a matter of social conscience and concern for public health, we would regard that person as simple-minded, if not frankly deranged. Oddly enough, however, people have persistently assumed that the television industry is somehow different—that it is useful to appeal to its social conscience. This was true in 1969 when the National Commission on the Causes and Prevention of Violence published its recommendations for the television industry. It was equally true in 1989 when the U.S. Congress passed an anti-violence bill that granted television industry executives the authority to hold discussions on the issue of television violence without violating antitrust laws. Even before the law was passed, the four networks stated that there would be no substantive changes in their programming. They have been as good as their word.

For the television industry, issues of "quality" and "social responsibility" are peripheral to the issue of maximizing audience size—and there is no formula more tried and true than violence for generating large audiences. To television executives, this is crucial. For if advertising revenue were to decrease by just 1 percent, the television industry would stand to lose $250 million in revenue annually. Thus, changes in audience size that appear trivial to most of us are regarded as catastrophic by the industry. For this reason, industry spokespersons have made innumerable protestations of good intent, but nothing has happened. In the more than twenty years that levels of television violence have been monitored, there has been no downward movement. There are no recommendations to make to the television industry. To make any would not only be futile but could create the false impression that the industry might actually do something constructive.

On December 11, 1992, the networks finally announced a list of voluntary guidelines on television violence. Curiously, reporters were unable to locate any network producers who felt the new guidelines would require changes in their programs. That raises a question: Who is going to bell the cat? Who is going to place his or her career in jeopardy in order to decrease the amount of violence on television? It is hard to say, but it may be revealing that when Senator Paul Simon held the press conference announcing the new inter-network agreement, no industry executives were present to answer questions.

Meeting the Challenge

Television violence is everybody's problem. You may feel assured that your child will never become violent despite a steady diet of television mayhem, but you cannot be assured that your child won't be murdered or maimed by someone else's child raised on a similar diet.

The American Academy of Pediatrics recommends that parents limit their children's television viewing to one to two hours per day. But why wait for a pediatrician to say it? Limiting children's exposure to television violence should become part of the public health agenda, along with safety seats, bicycle helmets, immunizations, and good nutrition. Part of the public health approach should be to promote child-care alternatives to the electronic babysitter, especially among the poor.

Parents should also guide what their children watch and how much. This is an old recommendation that can be given new teeth with the help of modern technology. It is now feasible to fit a television set with an electronic lock that permits parents to preset the channels and times for which the set will be available; if a particular program or time of day is locked, the set will not operate then. Time-channel locks are not merely feasible; they have already been designed and are coming off the assembly line.

The model for making them widely available comes from closed-captioning circuitry, which permits deaf and hard-of-hearing persons access to television. Market forces alone would not have made closed-captioning available to more than a fraction of the deaf and hard-of-hearing. To remedy this problem, Congress passed the Television Decoder Circuitry Act in 1990, which requires that virtually all new television sets be manufactured with built-in closed-captioning circuitry. A similar law should require that all new television sets be manufactured with built-in time-channel lock circuitry—and for a similar reason. Market forces alone will not make this technology available to more than a fraction of households with children and will exclude most poor families, the ones who suffer the most from violence. If we can make television technology available to benefit twenty-four million deaf and hard-of-hearing Americans, surely we can do no less for the benefit of fifty million American children.

A final recommendation: Television programs should be accompanied by a violence rating so that parents can judge how violent a program is without having to watch it. Such a rating system should be quantitative, leaving aesthetic and social judgments to the viewers. This approach would enjoy broad popular support. In a *Los Angeles Times* poll, 71 percent of adult Americans favored the establishment of a TV violence rating system. Such a system would not impinge on artistic freedom since producers would remain free to produce programs with high violence ratings. They could even use high violence ratings in the advertisements for their shows.

None of these recommendations would limit freedom of speech. That is as it should be. We do not address the problem of motor vehicle fatalities by calling for a ban on cars. Instead, we emphasize safety seats, good traffic signs, and driver education. Similarly, to address the problem of television-inspired violence, we need to promote time-channel locks, program rating systems, and viewer education about the hazards of violent programming. In this way we can protect our children and our society.

Note

1. The "white homicide rate" refers to the rate at which whites are the victims of homicide. Since most homicide is intra-racial, this closely parallels the rate at which whites commit homicide.

References

William A. Belson, *Television Violence and the Adolescent Boy.* Westmead, England: Saxon House (1978).

Brandon S. Centerwall, "Exposure to Television as a Cause of Violence," *Public Communication and Behavior,* Vol. 2. Orlando, Florida: Academic Press (1989), pp. 1–58.

Leonard D. Eron and L. Rowell Huesmann, "The Control of Aggressive Behavior by Changes in Attitudes, Values, and the Conditions of Learning," *Advances in the Study of Aggression*. Orlando, Florida: Academic Press (1984), pp. 139–171.

Gary Granzberg and Jack Steinbring (eds.), *Television and the Canadian Indian*. Winnipeg, Manitoba: University of Winnipeg (1980).

L. Rowell Huesmann and Leonard D. Eron, *Television and the Aggressive Child*. Hillsdale, New Jersey: Lawrence Erlbaum Associates (1986), pp. 45–80.

Candace Kruttschnitt, et al., "Family Violence, Television Viewing Habits, and Other Adolescent Experiences Related to Violent Criminal Behavior," *Criminology*, Vol. 24 (1986), pp. 235–267.

Andrew N. Meltzoff, "Memory in Infancy," *Encyclopedia of Learning and Memory*. New York: Macmillan (1992), pp. 271–275.

J. Ronald Milavsky, et al., *Television and Aggression*. Orlando, Florida: Academic Press (1982).

Jerome L. Singer, et al., "Family Patterns and Television Viewing as Predictors of Children's Beliefs and Aggression," *Journal of Communication*, Vol. 34, No. 2 (1984), pp. 73–89.

Tannis M. Williams (ed.), *The Impact of Television*. Orlando, Florida: Academic Press (1986).

NO

Brian Siano

Frankenstein Must Be Destroyed: Chasing the Monster of TV Violence

Here's the scene: Bugs Bunny, Daffy Duck, and a well-armed Elmer Fudd are having a stand-off in the forest. Daffy the rat-fink has just exposed Bugs' latest disguise, so Bugs takes off the costume and says, "That's right, Doc, I'm a wabbit. Would you like to shoot me now or wait until we get home?"

"Shoot him now! Shoot him now!" Daffy screams.

"You keep out of this," Bugs says. "He does not have to shoot you now."

"He does *so* have to shoot me now!" says Daffy. Full of wrath, he storms up to Elmer Fudd and shrieks, "And I *demand* that you shoot me now!"

Now, if you *aren't* smiling to yourself over the prospect of Daffy's beak whirling around his head like a roulette wheel, stop reading right now. This one's for a very select group: those evil degenerates (like me) who want to corrupt the unsullied youth of America by showing them violence on television.

Wolves' heads being conked with mallets in Tex Avery's *Swing Shift Cinderella*. Dozens of dead bodies falling from a closet in *Who Killed Who?* A sweet little kitten seemingly baked into cookies in Chuck Jones' *Feed the Kitty*. And best of all, Wile E. Coyote's unending odyssey of pain in *Fast and Furrious* and *Hook, Line, and Stinker*. God, I love it. The more explosions, crashes, gunshots, and defective ACME catapults there are, the better it is for the little tykes.

Shocked? Hey, I haven't even gotten to "The Three Stooges" yet.

The villagers are out hunting another monster—the Frankenstein of TV violence. Senator Paul Simon's hearings in early August 1993 provoked a fresh round of arguments in a debate that's been going on ever since the first round of violent kids' shows—"Sky King," "Captain Midnight," and "Hopalong Cassidy"—were on the air. More recently, Attorney General Janet Reno has taken a hard line on TV violence. "We're fed up with excuses," she told the Senate, arguing that "the regulation of violence is constitutionally permissible" and that, if the networks don't do it, "government should respond." . . .

From Brian Siano, "Frankenstein Must Be Destroyed: Chasing the Monster of TV Violence," *The Humanist*, vol. 54, no. 1 (January/February 1994). Copyright © 1994 by Brian Siano. Reprinted by permission.

Simon claims to have become concerned with this issue because, three years ago, he turned on the TV in his hotel room and was treated to the sight of a man being hacked apart with a chainsaw.... This experience prompted him to sponsor a three-year antitrust exemption for the networks, which was his way of encouraging them to voluntarily "clean house." But at the end of that period, the rates of TV violence hadn't changed enough to satisfy him, so Simon convened open hearings on the subject in 1993.

If Simon was truly concerned with the content of television programming, the first question that comes to mind is why he gave the networks an antitrust exemption in the first place. Thanks to Reagan-era deregulation, ownership of the mass media has become steadily more concentrated in the hands of fewer and fewer corporations. For example, the Federal Communications Commission used to have a "seven-and-seven" rule, whereby no company was allowed to own more than seven radio and seven television stations. In 1984, this was revised to a "12-and-12-and-12" rule: 12 FM radio stations, 12 AM radio stations, and 12 TV stations. It's a process outlined by Ben Bagdikian in his fine book *The Media Monopoly.* The net result is a loss of dissident, investigative, or regional voices; a mass media that questions less; and a forum for public debate that includes only the powerful.

This process could be impeded with judicious use of antitrust laws and stricter FCC controls—a return to the "seven-and-seven" rule, perhaps. But rather than hold hearings on this subject—a far greater threat to the nation's political well-being than watching *Aliens* on pay-per-view—Simon gave the networks a three-year *exemption* from antitrust legislation....

The debate becomes even more impassioned when we ask how children might be affected. The innocent, trusting little tykes are spending hours bathed in TV's unreal colors, and their fantasy lives are inhabited by such weirdos as Wolverine and Eek the Cat. Parents usually want their kids to grow up sharing their ideals and values, or at least to be well-behaved and obedient. Tell parents that their kids are watching "Beavis and Butt-head" in their formative years and you set off some major alarms.

There are also elitist, even snobbish, attitudes toward pop culture that help to rationalize censorship. One is that the corporate, mass-market culture of TV isn't important enough or "art" enough to deserve the same free-speech protection as James Joyce's *Ulysses* or William Burrough's *Naked Lunch.* The second is that rational, civilized human beings are supposed to be into Shakespeare and Scarlatti, not Pearl Jam and "Beavis and Butt-head." Seen in this "enlightened" way, the efforts of Paul Simon are actually for *our own good.* And so we define anything even remotely energetic as "violent," wail about how innocent freckle-faced children are being defiled by such fare as "NYPD Blue," and call for a Council of Certified Nice People who will decide what the rest of us get to see. A recent *Mother Jones* article by Carl Cannon (July/August 1993) took just this hysterical tone, citing as proof "some three thousand research studies of this issue."

Actually, there aren't 3,000 studies. In 1984, the *Psychological Bulletin* published an overview by Jonathan Freedman of research on the subject. Referring to the "2,500 studies" figure bandied about at the time (it's a safe bet that 10 years would inflate this figure to 3,000), Freedman writes:

> The reality is more modest. The large number refers to the complete bibliography on television. References to television and aggression are far fewer, perhaps around 500.... The actual literature on the relation between television violence and aggression consists of fewer than 100 independent studies, and the majority of these are laboratory experiments. Although this is still a substantial body of work, it is not vast, and there are only a small number of studies dealing specifically with the effects of television violence outside the laboratory.

The bulk of the evidence for a causal relationship between television violence and violent behavior comes from the research of Leonard Eron of the University of Illinois and Rowell Huesmann of the University of Michigan. Beginning in 1960, Eron and his associates began a large-scale appraisal of how aggression develops in children and whether or not it persists into adulthood. (The question of television violence was, originally, a side issue to the long-term study.) Unfortunately, when the popular press writes about Eron's work, it tends to present his methodology in the simplest of terms: *Mother Jones* erroneously stated that his study "followed the viewing habits of a group of children for twenty-two years." It's this sort of sloppiness, and overzealousness to prove a point, that keeps people from understanding the issues or raising substantial criticisms. Therefore, we must discuss Eron's work in some detail.

The first issue in Eron's study was how to measure aggressiveness in children. Eron's "peer-nominated index" followed a simple strategy: asking each child in a classroom questions about which kids were the main offenders in 10 different categories of classroom aggression (that is, "Who pushes or shoves children?"). The method is consistent with other scales of aggression, and its one-month test/retest reliability is 91 percent. The researchers also tested the roles of four behavioral dimensions in the development of aggression: *instigation* (parental rejection or lack of nurturance), *reinforcement* (punishment versus reward), *identification* (acquiring the parents' behavior and values), and *sociocultural norms*.

Eron's team selected the entire third-grade population of Columbia County, New York, testing 870 children and interviewing about 75 to 80 percent of their parents. Several trends became clear almost immediately. Children with less nurturing parents were more aggressive. Children who more closely identified with either parent were less aggressive. And children with low parental identification who were punished tended to be *more* aggressive (an observation which required revision of the behavioral model).

Ten years later, Eron and company tracked down and re-interviewed about half of the original sample. (They followed up on the subjects in 1981 as well.) Many of the subjects—now high-school seniors—demonstrated a persistence in aggression over time. Not only were the "peer-nominated" ratings roughly consistent with the third-grade ratings, but the more aggressive kids were three times as likely to have a police record by adulthood.

Eron's team also checked for the influences on aggression which they had previously noted when the subjects were eight. The persistent influences were parental identification and socioeconomic variables. Some previously important influences (lack of nurturance, punishment for aggression) didn't seem to affect the subjects' behavior as much in young adulthood. Eron writes of these factors:

> Their effect is short-lived and other variables are more important in predicting later aggression. Likewise, contingencies and environmental conditions can change drastically over 10 years, and thus the earlier contingent response becomes irrelevant.

It's at this stage that Eron mentions television as a factor:

> One of the best predictors of how aggressive a young man would be at age 19 was the violence of the television programs he preferred when he was 8 years old. Now, because we had longitudinal data, we could say with more certainty, on the basis of regression analysis, partial correlation, path analysis, and so forth, that there indeed was a cause-and-effect relation. *Continued research, however, has indicated that the causal effect is probably bidirectional: Aggressive children prefer violent television, and the violence on television causes them to be more aggressive.* [italics added]

Before we address the last comment, I should make one thing clear. Eron's research is sound. The methods he used to measure aggression are used by social scientists in many other contexts. His research does not ignore such obvious factors as the parents' socioeconomic status. And, as the above summary makes clear, Eron's own work makes a strong case for the positive or negative influence of parents in the development of their children's aggressiveness.

Now let's look at this "causal effect" business. Eron's data reveals that aggressive kids who turn into aggressive adults like aggressive television. But this is a correlation; it is not proof of a causal influence. If aggressive kids liked eating strawberry ice cream more often than the class wusses did, that too would be a predictor, and one might speculate on some anger-inducing chemical in strawberries.

Of course, the relation between representational violence and its influence on real life isn't as farfetched as that. The problem lies in determining precisely the nature of that relation, as we see when we look at the laboratory studies conducted by other researchers. Usually, the protocol of these experiments involves providing groups of individuals with entertainment calibrated for violent content, and studying some aspect of behavior after exposure—response to a behavioral test, which toys the children choose to play with, and so forth. But the results of these tests have been somewhat mixed. Sometimes the results are at variance with other studies, and many have methodological problems. For example, which "violent" entertainment is chosen? Bugs Bunny and the "Teenage Mutant Ninja Turtles" present action in very different contexts, and in one study, the Adam West "Batman" series was deemed nonviolent, despite those *Pow! Bam! Sock!* fistfights that ended every episode.

Many of the studies report that children do demonstrate higher levels of interpersonal aggression shortly after watching violent, energetic entertainment. But a 1971 study by Feshbach and Singer had boys from seven schools watch preassigned violent and nonviolent shows for six weeks. The results were not constant from school to school—and the boys watching the *nonviolent* shows tended to be more aggressive. Another protocol, carried out in Belgium as well as the United States, separated children into cottages at an institutional school and exposed certain groups to violent films. Higher aggression was noted in *all* groups after the films were viewed, but it returned to a near-baseline level after a week or so. (The children also rated the less violent films as less exciting, more boring, and sillier than the violent films—indicating that maybe kids *like* a little rush now and then.) Given the criticisms of the short-term-effects studies, and the alternate interpretations of the longitudinal studies, is this matter really settled?

Eron certainly thinks so. Testifying before Simon's committee in August, he declared that "the scientific debate is over" and called upon the Senate to reduce TV violence. His statement did not include any reference to such significant factors as parental identification—which, as his own research indicates, can change the way children interpret physical punishment. And even though Rowell Huesmann concurred with Eron in similar testimony before a House subcommittee, Huesmann's 1984 study of 1,500 youths in the United States, Finland, Poland, and Australia argued that, assuming a causal influence, television might be responsible for 5 percent of the violence in society. At *most.*

This is where I feel one has to part company with Leonard Eron. He is one of the most respected researchers in his field, and his work points to an imperative for parents in shaping and sharing their children's lives. But he has lent his considerable authority to such diversionary efforts as Paul Simon's and urged us to address, by questionable means, what only *might* be causing a tiny portion of real-life violence.

Some of Eron's suggestions for improving television are problematic as well. In his Senate testimony, Eron proposed restrictions on televised violence from 6:00 AM to 10:00 PM—which would exclude pro football, documentaries about World War II, and even concerned lawperson Janet Reno's proudest moments. Or take Eron's suggestion that, in televised drama, "perpetrators of violence should not be rewarded for violent acts." I don't know what shows Eron's been watching, but all of the cop shows I remember usually ended with the bad guys getting caught or killed. And when Eron suggests that "gratuitous violence that is not necessary to the plot should be reduced or abandoned," one has to ask just *who* decides that it's "not necessary"? Perhaps most troubling is Eron's closing statement:

> For many years now Western European countries have had monitoring of TV and films for violence by government agencies and have *not* permitted the showing of excess violence, especially during child viewing hours. And I've never heard complaints by citizens of those democratic countries that their rights have been violated. If something doesn't give, we may have to

institute some such monitoring by government agencies here in the U.S.A. If the industry does not police itself, then there is left only the prospect of official censorship, distasteful as this may be to many of us.

e·⟨⊙⟩·⟩

The most often-cited measure of just how violent TV programs are is that of George Gerbner, dean of the Annenberg School of Communications at the University of Pennsylvania. Few of the news stories about TV violence explain how this index is compiled, the context in which Gerbner has conducted his studies, or even some criticisms that could be raised.

Gerbner's view of the media's role in society is far more nuanced than the publicity given the violence profile may indicate. He sees television as a kind of myth-structure/religion for modern society. Television dramas, situation comedies, news shows, and all the rest create a shared culture for viewers, which "communicates much about social norms and relationships, about goals and means, about winners and losers." One portion of Gerbner's research involves compiling "risk ratios" in an effort to discern which minority groups— including children, the aged, and women—tend to be the victims of the aggressors in drama. This provides a picture of a pecking order within society (white males on top, no surprise there) that has remained somewhat consistent over the 20-year history of the index.

In a press release accompanying the 1993 violence index, Gerbner discusses his investigations of the long-term effects of television viewing. Heavy viewers were more likely to express feelings of living in a hostile world. Gerbner adds, "Violence is a demonstration of power. It shows who can get away with what against whom."

In a previous violence index compiled for cable-television programs, violence is defined as a "clear-cut and overt episode of physical violence—hurting or killing or the threat of hurting and/or killing—in any context." An earlier definition reads: "The overt expression of physical force against self or other compelling action against one's will on pain of being hurt or killed, or actually hurting or killing." These definitions have been criticized for being too broad; they encompass episodes of physical comedy, depiction of accidents in dramas, and even violent incidents in documentaries. They also include zany cartoon violence; in fact, the indexes for Saturday-morning programming tend to be substantially higher than the indexes for prime-time programming. Gerbner argues that, since he is analyzing cultural norms and since television entertainment is a deliberately conceived expression of these norms, his definition serves the purposes of his study.

The incidents of violence (total number = R) in a given viewing period are compiled by Gerbner's staff. Some of the statistics are easy to derive, such as the percentage of programs with violence, the number of violent scenes per hour, and the actual duration of violence, in minutes per hour. The actual violence index is calculated by adding together the following stats:

$\%P$—the *percentage* of programs in which there is violence;

$2(R/P)$—twice the number of violent episodes per program;

$2(R/H)$—twice the number of violent episodes per *hour;*

%*V*—percentage of *leading characters* involved in violence, either as victim or perpetrator; and

%*K*—percentage of leading characters involved in an actual *killing,* either as victim or perpetrator.

But if these are the factors used to compile the violence profile, it's difficult to see how they can provide a clear-cut mandate for the specific content of television drama. For example, two of the numbers used are averages; why are they arbitrarily doubled and then added to percentages? Also, because the numbers are determined by a definition which explicitly separates violence from dramatic context, the index says little about actual television content outside of a broad, overall gauge. One may imagine a television season of nothing but slapstick comedy with a very high violence profile.

This is why the violence profile is best understood within the context of Gerbner's wider analysis of media content. It does not lend itself to providing specific conclusions or guidelines of the sort urged by Senator Paul Simon. (It is important to note that, even though Simon observed little change in prime-time violence levels during his three-year antitrust exemption, the index for all three of those years was *below* the overall 20-year score.)

Finally, there's the anecdotal evidence—loudly trumpeted as such by Carl Cannon in *Mother Jones*—where isolated examples of entertainment-inspired violence are cited as proof of its pernicious influence. Several such examples have turned up recently. A sequence was edited out of the film *The Good Son* in which McCaulay Culkin drops stuff onto a highway from an overhead bridge. (As we all know, nobody ever did this before the movie came out.) The film *The Program* was re-edited when some kids were killed imitating the film's characters, who "proved their courage" by lying down on a highway's dividing line. Perhaps most notoriously, in October 1993 a four-year-old Ohio boy set his family's trailer on fire, killing his younger sister; the child's mother promptly blamed MTV's "Beavis and Butt-head" for setting a bad example. But a neighbor interviewed on CNN reported that the family didn't even have cable television and that the kid had a local rep as a pyromaniac months before. This particular account was not followed up by the national media, which, if there were no enticing "Beavis and Butt-head" angle, would never have mentioned this fire at a low-income trailer park to begin with.

Numerous articles about media-inspired violence have cited similar stories—killers claiming to be Freddy Kreuger, kids imitating crimes they'd seen on a cop show a few days before, and so forth. In many of these cases, it is undeniably true that the person involved took his or her inspiration to act from a dramatic presentation in the media—the obvious example being John Hinckley's fixation on the film *Taxi Driver....* But stories of media-inspired violence are striking mainly because they're so *atypical* of the norm; the vast majority of people don't take a movie or a TV show as a license to kill. Ironically, it is the *abnormality* of these stories that ensures they'll get widespread dissemination and be remembered long after the more mundane crimes are forgotten.

Of course, there are a few crazies out there who will be unfavorably influenced by what they see on TV. But even assuming that somehow the TV show (or movie or record) shares some of the blame, how does one predict what future crazies will take for inspiration? What guidelines would ensure that people write, act, or produce something that *will not upset a psychotic*? Not only is this a ridiculous demand, it's insulting to the public as well. We would all be treated as potential murderers in order to gain a hypothetical 5 percent reduction in violence.

⋅⊙⋅

In crusades like this—where the villagers pick up their torches and go hunting after Frankenstein—people often lose sight of what they're defending. I've read reams of statements from people who claim to know what television does to kids; but what do *kids* do with television? Almost none of what I've read gives kids any credit for thinking. None of these people seems to remember what being a kid is like.

When *Jurassic Park* was released, there was a huge debate over whether or not children should be allowed to see it. Kids like to see dinosaurs, people argued, but this movie might scare them into catatonia.... These objections were actually taken seriously. But kids like dinosaurs because they're big, look really weird, and scare the hell out of everything around them. Dinosaurs *kick ass.* What parent would tell his or her child that dinosaurs were *cute*? . . .

Along the same lines, what kid hasn't tried to gross out everyone at the dinner table by showing them his or her chewed-up food? Or tried using a magnifying glass on an anthill on a hot day? Or clinically inspected the first dead animal he or she ever came across? Sixty years ago, adults were terrified of *Frankenstein* and fainted at the premiere of *King Kong*. But today, *Kong* is regarded as a fantasy story, *Godzilla* can be shown without the objections of child psychologists, and there are breakfast cereals called Count Chocula and Frankenberry. Sadly, there are few adults who seem to remember how they identified more with the monsters. Who wanted to be one of those stupid villagers waving torches at Frankenstein? That's what our *parents* were like.

But it's not just an issue of kids liking violence, grossness, or comic-book adventure. About 90 percent of the cartoon shows I watched as a child were the mass-produced sludge of the Hanna-Barbera Studios—like "Wacky Races," "The Jetsons," and "Scooby Doo, Where Are You?" I can't remember a single memorable moment from any of them. But that Bugs Bunny sequence at the beginning of this article (from *Rabbit Seasoning,* 1952, directed by Chuck Jones) was done from memory, and I have no doubt that it's almost verbatim.

I know that, even at the age of eight or nine, I had some rudimentary aesthetic sense about it all. There was something hip and complex about the Warner Bros. cartoons, and some trite, insulting *sameness* to the Hanna-Barbera trash, although I couldn't quite understand it then. Bugs Bunny clearly wasn't made for kids according to some study on social-interaction development. Bugs Bunny was meant to make adults laugh as much as children. Kids can also enjoy entertainment ostensibly created for adults—in fact, that's often the most rewarding kind. I had no trouble digesting *Jaws,* James Bond, and Clint Eastwood "spaghetti westerns" in my preteen years. And I'd have no problems with showing a 10-year-old *Jurassic Park,* because I know how much he or she would love it. . . .

I don't enjoy bad television with lots of violence, but I'd rather not lose *decent* shows that use violence for good reason. Shows like "Star Trek," "X-Men," or the spectacular "Batman: The Animated Series" can give kids a sense of adventure while teaching them about such qualities as courage, bravery, and heroism. Even better, a healthy and robust spirit of irreverence can be found in Bugs Bunny, "Ren and Stimpy," and "Tiny Toons." Some of these entertainments—like adventure stories and comic books of the past—can teach kids how to be really *alive.*

Finally, if we must have a defense against the pernicious influence of the mass media, it cannot be from the Senate's legislation or the pronouncements of social scientists. It must begin with precisely the qualities I described above —especially irreverence. One good start is Comedy Central's "Mystery Science Theater 3000," where the main characters, forced to watch horrendous movies, fight back by heckling them. Not surprisingly, children love the show, even though most of the jokes go right over their curious little heads. They recognize a kindred spirit in "MST 3000." Kids want to stick up for themselves, maybe like Batman, maybe like Bugs Bunny, or even like Beavis and Butt-head—but always against a world made by adults.

You know, *adults*—those doofuses with the torches, trying to burn up Frankenstein in the old mill.

CHALLENGE QUESTIONS

Does Viewing Television Increase Aggression?

1. Pretend that you have two young children, ages 5 and 7. After reading the selections by Centerwall and Siano, how would you handle television for your youngsters, and why?
2. Centerwall seems to imply that children have no choice but to imitate adults; imitation is instinctive. How does this explanation involve the issues of free choice and determinism? If children are truly determined by their environments and their instincts, can they be held responsible for their actions? Why, or why not?
3. Whose view does most of the research on this issue support, Centerwall's or Siano's? Review the research at your library to help you form a judgment.
4. There is considerable research on children who watch television with their parents. One set of findings indicates that parents who actively comment upon and engage their children in discussions about television programs minimize the impact of television's ill effects. How might such research affect the debate between Centerwall and Siano?

On the Internet ...

Cognitive Science Society

This is the home page for the Cognitive Science Society.

    http://www.cognitivesciencesociety.org

Psychology Tutorials

A collection of interactive tutorials and simulations, primarily in the areas of sensation and perception, is available at this site.

    http://psych.hanover.edu/Krantz/tutor.html

Cognitive Science Archive

This Finnish source contains articles on various fields of cognitive science.

    http://www.helsinki.fi/hum/kognitiotiede/archive.html

Multiple Intelligences Links

This site provides a "cream of the crop" list of multiple intelligence links identified via extensive site searches and examinations.

    http://www.clat.psu.edu/homes/bxb11/mi/MILinks.htm

About: Memory Repression and Recovery

This site provides information about the repression and recovery of traumatic memories and memory research from perspectives of different sides of the controversy.

    http://incestabuse.about.com/msubmem.htm?once=true&

Behavior Analysis Resources

Those who are interested in the behaviorist approach to human development should check out the links at this site.

    http://www.coedu.usf.edu/behavior/bares.htm

PART 4

Cognitive Processes

*T*he nature and limitation of our mental (or cognitive) processes pose fundamental questions for psychologists. Are mental capacities, such as intelligence, determined at birth? Is it even valid to speak of intelligence as one entity, or are there multiple intelligences? Also, can we trust our memories? For example, are memories of early sexual abuse always reliable? Can they be trusted enough to bring alleged abusers to trial? Finally, what is the nature of learning? Do external forces, such as rewards, affect learning?

- Should Psychology Adopt a Theory of Multiple Intelligences?

- Do Adults Repress Childhood Sexual Abuse?

- Do Rewards Facilitate Learning?

ISSUE 8

Should Psychology Adopt a Theory of Multiple Intelligences?

YES: Howard Gardner, from "A Multiplicity of Intelligences," *Scientific American Presents* (Winter 1998)

NO: Linda S. Gottfredson, from "The General Intelligence Factor," *Scientific American Presents* (Winter 1998)

ISSUE SUMMARY

YES: Psychologist Howard Gardner argues that humans are better understood as having eight or nine different kinds of intelligence rather than as having one general intelligence.

NO: Psychologist Linda S. Gottfredson contends that despite some popular assertions, a single factor for intelligence can be measured with IQ tests and is predictive of success in life.

Most people who have seen Michael Jordan play professional basketball have been amazed by his grace and poise. Even when ill, he can outscore most other players. What is the source of his abilities? Does his being so good at playing basketball necessarily imply that he is good at other activities? In addition to being an outstanding basketball player, Jordan is generally acknowledged as being bright, articulate, and socially skilled. On the other hand, his attempt to play baseball at the major league level was less than successful. Can people only be really good at one thing and not any others, or is some general ability—some general intelligence—involved?

The traditional view of intelligence is that there is a single factor, often called *g*, that underlies most other abilities. Most tests of intelligence yield a single score, which emphasizes the idea that intelligence is a single, measurable entity. However, Howard Gardner is noted for having challenged this traditional view. Gardner has argued that intelligence is best understood as a number of distinct and relatively independent abilities, such as musical intelligence and bodily-kinesthetic intelligence.

In the following selection, Gardner argues that the single-factor theory of intelligence is outdated and should be replaced by a theory of multiple intelligences. He argues that individuals have profiles reflecting both strengths and weaknesses in different areas of intelligence. He also contends that when people have strokes, often only one ability (e.g., memory) is affected while others (e.g., musical abilities) are completely spared. This type of evidence leads Gardner to postulate the existence of multiple intelligences.

In the second selection, Linda S. Gottfredson contends that a general theory of intelligence explains most differences among individuals. She sees the *g* factor as the apex of a hierarchical model that reflects all the combined abilities. For example, Michael Jordan may indeed have a type of kinesthetic intelligence or ability, but the *g* factor reflects all his other abilities, including his logical and cognitive abilities. Gottfredson cites research that suggests that highly intelligent people have quicker reaction times and faster brain processing than less intelligent people. She also asserts that the *g* factor is useful in predicting job performance as well as academic ability.

POINT

- Humans are best understood as having a number of relatively independent intellectual faculties.
- Psychometric tests devalue capacities such as musical or bodily-kinesthetic intelligences as talents but not intelligence.
- Different factors are developed, prized, or ignored in different cultures.

- Recent neuroscience and evolutionary psychology support a multiple intelligence concept.

COUNTERPOINT

- The overlap among cognitive skills suggests that there is one global element of intelligence.
- Psychometric tests are the best way to measure human intelligence.

- The general factor (*g*) of intelligence exists in all cultures and is not a social artifact.
- Biological studies of brain waves support the general factor theory.

Howard Gardner

A Multiplicity of Intelligences

As a psychologist, I was surprised by the huge public interest in *The Bell Curve,* the 1994 book on human intelligence by the late Harvard University psychologist Richard J. Herrnstein and policy analyst Charles Murray. Most of the ideas in the book were familiar not only to social scientists but also to the general public. Indeed, educational psychologist Arthur R. Jensen of the University of California at Berkeley as well as Herrnstein had written popularly about the very same ideas in the late 1960s and the early 1970s. Perhaps, I reasoned, every quarter-century a new generation of Americans desires to be acquainted with "the psychologist's orthodoxy" about intelligence—namely, that there is a single, general intelligence, often called *g,* which is reflected by an individual's intelligence quotient, or IQ.

This concept stands in contrast to my own view developed over the past decades: that human intelligence encompasses a far wider, more universal set of competencies. Currently I count eight intelligences, and there may be more. They include what are traditionally regarded as intelligences, such as linguistic and logical-mathematical abilities, but also some that are not conventionally thought of in that way, such as musical and spatial capacities. These intelligences, which do not always reveal themselves in paper-and-pencil tests, can serve as a basis for more effective educational methods.

Defining Brainpower

The orthodox view of a single intelligence, widely, if wrongly, accepted today in the minds of the general population, originated from the energies and convictions of a few researchers, who by the second decade of this century had put forth its major precepts. In addition to its basic assumption, the orthodoxy also states that individuals are born with a certain intelligence or potential intelligence, that this intelligence is difficult to change and that psychologists can assess one's IQ using short-answer tests and, perhaps, other "purer" measures, such as the time it takes to react to a sequence of flashing lights or the presence of a particular pattern of brain waves.

Soon after this idea had been proposed—I like to call it "hedgehog orthodoxy"—more "foxlike" critics arose. From outside psychology, commentators

From Howard Gardner, "A Multiplicity of Intelligences," *Scientific American Presents* (Winter 1998).

such as American newspaper columnist Walter Lippmann challenged the criteria used to assess intelligence, contending that it was more complex and less fixed than the psychometricians had proposed.

From within psychology, scientists questioned the notion of a single, overarching intelligence. According to their analyses, intelligence is better thought of as a set of several factors. In the 1930s Louis L. Thurstone of the University of Chicago said it makes more sense to think of seven, largely independent "vectors of the mind." In the 1960s Joy P. Guilford of the University of Southern California enunciated 120 factors, later amended to 150. Scottish investigator Godfrey Thomson of the University of Edinburgh spoke around the 1940s of a large number of loosely coupled faculties. And in our own day, Robert J. Sternberg of Yale University has proposed a triarchic theory of intellect. These arches comprise a component that deals with standard computational skill, a component that is sensitive to contextual factors and a component that is involved with novelty.

Somewhat surprisingly, all these commentators—whether in favor of or opposed to the notion of single intelligence—share one conviction. They all believe that the nature of intelligence will be determined by testing and analyzing the data thus secured. Perhaps, reason orthodox defenders like Herrnstein and Murray, performance on a variety of tests will yield a strong general factor of intelligence. And indeed, there is evidence for such a "positive manifold," or high correlation, across tests. Perhaps, counter pluralists like Thurstone and Sternberg, the right set of tests will demonstrate that the mind consists of a number of relatively independent factors, with strength in one area failing to predict strength or weakness in other areas.

But where is it written that intelligence needs to be determined on the basis of tests? Were we incapable of making judgments about intellect before Sir Francis Galton and Alfred Binet cobbled together the first set of psychometric items a century ago? If the dozens of IQ tests in use around the world were suddenly to disappear, would we no longer be able to assess intellect?

Break From Orthodoxy

Nearly 20 years ago, posing these very questions, I embarked on quite a different path into the investigation of intellect. I had been conducting research primarily with two groups: children who were talented in one or more art form and adults who had suffered from strokes that comprised specific capacities while sparing others. Every day I saw individuals with scattered profiles of strengths and weaknesses, and I was impressed by the fact that a strength or a deficit could cohabit comfortably with distinctive profiles of abilities and disabilities across the variety of humankind.

On the basis of such data, I arrived at a firm intuition: human beings are better thought of as possessing a number of relatively independent faculties, rather than as having a certain amount of intellectual horsepower, or IQ, that can be simply channeled in one or another direction. I decided to search for a better formulation of human intelligence. I defined an intelligence as "a psychobiological potential to solve problems or to fashion products that are valued in at least one cultural context." In my focus on fashioning products and cultural values, I departed from orthodox psychometric approaches, such as those adopted by Herrnstein, Murray and their predecessors.

CRITERIA FOR AN INTELLIGENCE

1. *Potential isolation by brain damage.* For example, linguistic abilities can be compromised or spared by strokes.
2. *The existence of prodigies, savants and other exceptional individuals.* Such individuals permit the intelligence to be observed in relative isolation.
3. *An identifiable core operation or set of operations.* Musical intelligence, for instance, consists of a person's sensitivity to melody, harmony, rhythm, timbre and musical structure.
4. *A distinctive developmental history within an individual, along with a definable nature of expert performance.* One examines the skills of, say, an expert athlete, salesperson or naturalist, as well as the steps to attaining such expertise.
5. *An evolutionary history and evolutionary plausibility.* One can examine forms of spatial intelligence in mammals or musical intelligence in birds.
6. *Support from tests in experimental psychology.* Researchers have devised tasks that specifically indicate which skills are related to one another and which are discrete.
7. *Support from psychometric findings.* Batteries of tests reveal which tasks reflect the same underlying factor and which do not.
8. *Susceptibility to encoding in a symbol system.* Codes such as language, arithmetic, maps and logical expression, among others, capture important components of respective intelligences.

To proceed from an intuition to a definition of a set of human intelligences, I developed criteria that each of the candidate intelligences had to meet *[see box]*. These criteria were drawn from several sources:

- Psychology: The existence of a distinct developmental history for a capacity through which normal and gifted individuals pass as they grow to adulthood; the existence of correlations (or the lack of correlations) between certain capacities.
- Case studies of learners: Observations of unusual humans, including prodigies, savants or those suffering from learning disabilities.
- Anthropology: Records of how different abilities are developed, ignored or prized in different cultures.
- Cultural studies: The existence of symbol systems that encode certain kinds of meanings—language, arithmetic and maps, for instance.

- Biological sciences: Evidence that a capacity has a distinct evolutionary history and is represented in particular neural structures. For instance, various parts of the left hemisphere dominate when it comes to motor control of the body, calculation and linguistic ability; the right hemisphere houses spatial and musical capacities, including the discrimination of pitch.

The Eight Intelligences

Armed with the criteria, I considered many capacities, ranging from those based in the senses to those having to do with planning, humor and even sexuality. To the extent that a candidate ability met all or most of the criteria handily, it gained plausibility as an intelligence. In 1983 I concluded that seven abilities met the criteria sufficiently well: linguistic, logical-mathematical, musical, spatial, bodily-kinesthetic (as exemplified by athletes, dancers and other physical performers), interpersonal (the ability to read other people's moods, motivations and other mental states), and intrapersonal (the ability to access one's own feelings and to draw on them to guide behavior). The last two can generally be considered together as the basis for emotional intelligence (although in my version, they focus more on cognition and understanding than on feelings). Most standard measures of intelligence primarily probe linguistic and logical intelligence; some survey spatial intelligence. The other four are almost entirely ignored. In 1995, invoking new data that fit the criteria, I added an eighth intelligence—that of the naturalist, which permits the recognition and categorization of natural objects. Examples are Charles Darwin, John James Audubon and Rachel Carson. I am currently considering the possibility of a ninth: existential intelligence, which captures the human proclivity to raise and ponder fundamental questions about existence, life, death, finitude. Religious and philosophical thinkers such as the Dalai Lama and Søren A. Kierkegaard exemplify this kind of ability. Whether existential intelligence gets to join the inner sanctum depends on whether convincing evidence accrues about the neural basis for it.

The theory of multiple intelligences (or MI theory, as it has come to be called) makes two strong claims. The first is that all humans possess all these intelligences: indeed, they can collectively be considered a definition of *Homo sapiens,* cognitively speaking. The second claim is that just as we all look different and have unique personalities and temperaments, we also have different profiles of intelligences. No two individuals, not even identical twins or clones, have exactly the same amalgam of profiles, with the same strengths and weaknesses. Even in the case of identical genetic heritage, individuals undergo different experiences and seek to distinguish their profiles from one another.

Within psychology, the theory of multiple intelligences has generated controversy. Many researchers are nervous about the movement away from standardized tests and the adoption of a set of criteria that are unfamiliar and less open to quantification. Many also balk at the use of the word "intelligence" to describe some of the abilities, preferring to define musical or bodily-kinesthetic intelligences as talents. Such a narrow definition, however, devalues those capacities, so that orchestra conductors and dancers are talented but not smart. In my view, it would be all right to call those abilities talents, so long as logical reasoning and linguistic facility are then also termed talents.

Some have questioned whether MI theory is empirical. This criticism, however, misses the mark. MI theory is based completely on empirical evidence. The number of intelligences, their delineation, their subcomponents are all subject to alteration in the light of new findings. Indeed, the existence of the naturalist intelligence could be asserted only after evidence had accrued that parts of the temporal lobe are dedicated to the naming and recognition of natural things, whereas others are attuned to human-made objects. (Good evidence for a neural foundation comes from clinical literature, which reported instances in which brain-damaged individuals lost the capacity to identify living things but could still name inanimate objects. Experimental findings by Antonio R. Damasio of the University of Iowa, Elizabeth Warrington of the Dementia Research Group at National Hospital in London and others have confirmed the phenomenon.)

Much of the evidence for the personal intelligences has come from research in the past decade on emotional intelligence and on the development in children of a "theory of mind"—the realization that human beings have intentions and act on the basis of these intentions. And the intriguing finding by Frances H. Rauscher of the University of Wisconsin—Oshkosh and her colleagues of the "Mozart effect"—that early musical experiences may enhance spatial capacities—raises the possibility that musical and spatial intelligences draw on common abilities.

It is also worth noting that the movement toward multiple intelligences is quite consistent with trends in related sciences. Neuroscience recognizes the modular nature of the brain; evolutionary psychology is based on the notion that different capacities have evolved in specific environments for specific purposes; and artificial intelligence increasingly embraces expert systems rather than general problem-solving mechanisms. Within science, the believers in a single IQ or general intelligence are increasingly isolated, their positions more likely to be embraced by those, like Herrnstein and Murray, who have an ideological ax to grind.

If some psychologists expressed skepticism about the theory of multiple intelligences, educators around the world have embraced it. MI theory not only comports with their intuitions that children are smart in different ways; it also holds out hope that more students can be reached more effectively if their favored ways of knowing are taken into account in curriculum, instruction and assessment. A virtual cottage industry has arisen to create MI schools, classrooms, curricula, texts, computer systems and the like. Most of this work is well intentioned, and some of it has proved quite effective in motivating students and in giving them a sense of involvement in intellectual life.

Various misconceptions, however, have arisen: for example, that every topic should be taught in seven or eight ways or that the purpose of school is to identify (and broadcast) students' intelligences, possibly by administering an octet of new standardized tests. I have begun to speak out against some of these less advisable beliefs and practices.

My conclusion is that MI theory is best thought of as a tool rather than as an educational goal. Educators need to determine, in conjunction with their communities, the goals that they are seeking. Once these goals have been articulated, then MI theory can provide powerful support. I believe schools should strive to develop individuals of a certain sort—civic-minded, sensitive to the arts, deeply rooted in the disciplines. And schools should probe pivotal topics with sufficient depth so that students end up with a comprehensive understanding of them. Curricular and assessment approaches founded on MI theory, such as Project Spectrum at the Eliot-Pearson Preschool at Tufts University, have demonstrated considerable promise in helping schools to achieve these goals.

The Future of MI

Experts have debated various topics in intelligence—including whether there is one or more—for nearly a century, and it would take a brave seer to predict that these debates will disappear. (In fact, if past cycles repeat themselves, a latter-day Herrnstein and Murray will author their own *Bell Curve* around 2020.) As the person most closely associated with the theory of multiple intelligences, I record three wishes for this line of work.

The first is a broader but not infinitely expanded view of intelligence. It is high time that intelligence be widened to incorporate a range of human computational capacities, including those that deal with music, other persons and skill in deciphering the natural world. But it is important that intelligence not be conflated with other virtues, such as creativity, wisdom or morality.

I also contend that intelligence should not be so broadened that it crosses the line from description to prescription. I endorse the notion of emotional intelligence when it denotes the capacity to compute information about one's own or others' emotional life. When the term comes to encompass the kinds of persons we hope to develop, however, then we have crossed the line into a value system—and that should not be part of our conception of intelligence. Thus, when psychologist and *New York Times* reporter Daniel Goleman emphasizes in his recent best-seller, *Emotional Intelligence,* the importance of empathy as part of emotional intelligence, I go along with him. But he also urges that individuals care for one another. The possession of the capacity to feel another's suffering is not the same as the decision to come to her aid. Indeed, a sadistic individual might use her knowledge of another's psyche to inflict pain.

My second wish is that society shift away from standardized, short-answer proxy instruments to real-life demonstrations or virtual simulations. During a particular historical period, it was perhaps necessary to assess individuals by administering items that were themselves of little interest (for example, repeating numbers backward) but that were thought to correlate with skills or habits of importance. Nowadays, however, given the advent of computers and virtual technologies, it is possible to look directly at individuals' performances—to see how they can argue, debate, look at data, critique experiments, execute works of art, and so on. As much as possible, we should train students directly in these valued activities, and we should assess how they carry out valued performances under realistic conditions. The need for ersatz instruments, whose relation to real-world performance is often tenuous at best, should wane.

My third wish is that the multiple-intelligences idea be used for more effective pedagogy and assessment. I have little sympathy with educational efforts that seek simply to "train" the intelligences or to use them in trivial ways (such as singing the math times tables or playing Bach in the background while one is doing geometry). For me, the educational power of multiple intelligences is exhibited when these faculties are drawn on to help students master consequential disciplinary materials.

I explain how such an approach might work in my book, *A Well-Disciplined Mind*... (1999). I focus on three rich topics: the theory of evolution (as an example of scientific truth), the music of Mozart (as an example of artistic beauty), and the Holocaust (as an example of immorality in recent history). In each case, I show how the topic can be introduced to students through a variety of entry points drawing on several intelligences, how the subject can be made more familiar through the use of analogies and metaphors drawn from diverse domains, and how the core ideas of the topic can be captured not merely through a single symbolic language but rather through a number of complementary model languages or representations.

Pursuing this approach, the individual who understands evolutionary theory, for instance, can think of it in different ways: in terms of a historical narrative, a logical syllogism, a quantitative examination of the size and dispersion of populations in different niches, a diagram of species delineation, a dramatic sense of the struggle among individuals (or genes or populations), and so on. The individual who can think of evolution in only one way—using only one model language—actually has only a tenuous command of the principal concepts of the theory.

The issue of who owns intelligence has been an important one in our society for some time—and it promises to be a crucial and controversial one for the foreseeable future. For too long, the rest of society has been content to leave intelligence in the hands of psychometricians. Often these test makers have a narrow, overly scholastic view of intellect. They rely on a set of instruments that are destined to valorize certain capacities while ignoring those that do not lend themselves to ready formulation and testing. And those with a political agenda often skirt close to the dangerous territory of eugenics.

MI theory represents at once an effort to base the conception of intelligence on a much broader scientific basis, one that offers a set of tools to educators that will allow more individuals to master substantive materials in an effective way. Applied appropriately, the theory can also help each individual achieve his or her human potential at the workplace, in avocations and in the service of the wider world.

NO

Linda S. Gottfredson

The General Intelligence Factor

No subject in psychology has provoked more intense public controversy than the study of human intelligence. From its beginning, research on how and why people differ in overall mental ability has fallen prey to political and social agendas that obscure or distort even the most well-established scientific findings. Journalists, too, often present a view of intelligence research that is exactly the opposite of what most intelligence experts believe. For these and other reasons, public understanding of intelligence falls far short of public concern about it. The IQ experts discussing their work in the public arena can feel as though they have fallen down the rabbit hole into Alice's Wonderland.

The debate over intelligence and intelligence testing focuses on the question of whether it is useful or meaningful to evaluate people according to a single major dimension of cognitive competence. Is there indeed a general mental ability we commonly call "intelligence," and is it important in the practical affairs of life? The answer, based on decades of intelligence research, is an unequivocal yes. No matter their form or content, tests of mental skills invariably point to the existence of a global factor that permeates all aspects of cognition. And this factor seems to have considerable influence on a person's practical quality of life. Intelligence as measured by IQ tests is the single most effective predictor known of individual performance at school and on the job. It also predicts many other aspects of well-being, including a person's chances of divorcing, dropping out of high school, being unemployed or having illegitimate children.

By now the vast majority of intelligence researchers take these findings for granted. Yet in the press and in public debate, the facts are typically dismissed, downplayed or ignored. This misrepresentation reflects a clash between a deeply felt ideal and a stubborn reality. The ideal, implicit in many popular critiques of intelligence research, is that all people are born equally able and that social inequality results only from the exercise of unjust privilege. The reality is that Mother Nature is no egalitarian. People are in fact unequal in intellectual potential—and they are born that way, just as they are born with different potentials for height, physical attractiveness, artistic flair, athletic prowess and other traits. Although subsequent experience shapes this potential, no amount of social engineering can make individuals with widely divergent mental aptitudes into intellectual equals.

Of course, there are many kinds of talent, many kinds of mental ability and many other aspects of personality and character that influence a person's chances of happiness and success. The functional importance of general mental ability in everyday life, however, means that without onerous restrictions on individual liberty, differences in mental competence are likely to result in social inequality. This gulf between equal opportunity and equal outcomes is perhaps what pains Americans most about the subject of intelligence. The public intuitively knows what is at stake: when asked to rank personal qualities in order of desirability, people put intelligence second only to good health. But with a more realistic approach to the intellectual differences between people, society could better accommodate these differences and minimize the inequalities they create.

Extracting *g*

Early in the century-old study of intelligence, researchers discovered that all tests of mental ability ranked individuals in about the same way. Although mental tests are often designed to measure specific domains of cognition—verbal fluency, say, or mathematical skill, spatial visualization or memory—people who do well on one kind of test tend to do well on the others, and people who do poorly generally do so across the board. This overlap, or intercorrelation, suggests that all such tests measure some global element of intellectual ability as well as specific cognitive skills. In recent decades, psychologists have devoted much effort to isolating that general factor, which is abbreviated *g*, from the other aspects of cognitive ability gauged in mental tests.

The statistical extraction of *g* is performed by a technique called factor analysis. Introduced at the turn of the century by British psychologist Charles Spearman, factor analysis determines the minimum number of underlying dimensions necessary to explain a pattern of correlations among measurements. A general factor suffusing all tests is not, as is sometimes argued, a necessary outcome of factor analysis. No general factor has been found in the analysis of personality tests, for example; instead the method usually yields at least five dimensions (neuroticism, extraversion, conscientiousness, agreeableness and openness to ideas), each relating to different subsets of tests. But, as Spearman observed, a general factor does emerge from analysis of mental ability tests, and leading psychologists, such as Arthur R. Jensen of the University of California at Berkeley and John B. Carroll of the University of North Carolina at Chapel Hill, have confirmed his findings in the decades since. Partly because of this research, most intelligence experts now use *g* as the working definition of intelligence.

The general factor explains most differences among individuals in performance on diverse mental tests. This is true regardless of what specific ability a test is meant to assess, regardless of the test's manifest content (whether words, numbers or figures) and regardless of the way the test is administered (in written or oral form, to an individual or to a group). Tests of specific mental abilities do measure those abilities, but they all reflect g to varying degrees as well. Hence, the g factor can be extracted form scores on any diverse battery of tests.

Conversely, because every mental test is "contaminated" by the effects of specific mental skills, no single test measures only g. Even the scores from IQ tests—which usually combine about a dozen subtests of specific cognitive skills —contain some "impurities" that reflect those narrower skills. For most purposes, these impurities make no practical difference, and g and IQ can be used interchangeably. But if they need to, intelligence researchers can statistically separate the g component of IQ. The ability to isolate g has revolutionized research on general intelligence, because it has allowed investigators to show that the predictive value of mental tests derives almost entirely from this global factor rather than from the more specific aptitudes measured by intelligence tests.

In addition to quantifying individual differences, tests of mental abilities have also offered insight into the meaning of intelligence in everyday life. Some tests and test items are known to correlate better with g than others do. In these items the "active ingredient" that demands the exercise of g seems to be complexity. More complex tasks require more mental manipulation, and this manipulation of information—discerning similarities and inconsistencies, drawing inferences, grasping new concepts and so on—constitutes intelligence in action. Indeed, intelligence can best be described as the ability to deal with cognitive complexity.

This description coincides well with lay perceptions of intelligence. The g factor is especially important in just the kind of behaviors that people usually associate with "smarts": reasoning, problem solving, abstract thinking, quick learning. And whereas g itself describes mental aptitude rather than accumulated knowledge, a person's store of knowledge tends to correspond with his or her g level, probably because that accumulation represents a previous adeptness in learning and in understanding new information. The g factor is also the one attribute that best distinguishes among persons considered gifted, average or retarded.

Several decades of factor-analytic research on mental tests have confirmed a hierarchical model of mental abilities. The evidence, summarized most effectively in Carroll's 1993 book, *Human Cognitive Abilities*, puts g at the apex in this model, with more specific aptitudes arrayed at successively lower levels: the so-called group factors, such as verbal ability, mathematical reasoning, spatial visualization and memory, are just below g, and below these are skills that are more dependent on knowledge or experience, such as the principles and practices of a particular job or profession.

Some researchers use the term "multiple intelligences" to label these sets of narrow capabilities and achievements. Psychologist Howard Gardner of Harvard University, for example, has postulated that eight relatively autonomous "intelligences" are exhibited in different domains of achievement. He does not dispute the existence of g but treats it as a specific factor relevant chiefly to academic achievement and to situations that resemble those of school. Gardner does not believe that tests can fruitfully measure his proposed intelligences; without tests, no one can at present determine whether the intelligences are

Figure 1

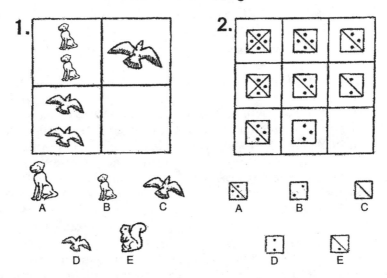

Matrix Reasoning

Number Series

3. 2, 4, 6, 8, _, _

4. 3, 6, 3, 6, _, _

5. 1, 5, 4, 2, 6, 5, _, _

6. 2, 4, 3, 9, 4, 16, _, _

Analogies

7. brother: sister ⟶ father: _____
A. child   B. mother   C. cousin   D. friend

8. joke: humor ⟶ law: _____
A. lawyer   B. mercy   C. courts   D. justice

Answers: 1. A; 2. D; 3. 10, 12; 4. 3, 6; 5. 3, 7; 6. 5, 25; 7. B; 8. D

Sample IQ Items resembling those on current tests require the test taker to fill in the empty spaces based on the pattern in the images, numbers or words. Because they can vary in complexity, such tasks are useful in assessing *g* level.

indeed independent of *g* (or each other). Furthermore, it is not clear to what extent Gardner's intelligences tap personality traits or motor skills rather than mental aptitudes.

Other forms of intelligence have been proposed; among them, emotional intelligence and practical intelligence are perhaps the best known. They are probably amalgams either of intellect and personality or of intellect and informal experience in specific job or life settings, respectively. Practical intelligence like "street smarts," for example, seems to consist of the localized knowledge and know-how developed with untutored experience in particular everyday settings and activities—the so-called school of hard knocks. In contrast, general intelligence is not a form of achievement, whether local or renowned. Instead the g factor regulates the rate of learning: it greatly affects the rate of return in knowledge to instruction and experience but cannot substitute for either.

The Biology of g

Some critics of intelligence research maintain that the notion of general intelligence is illusory: that no such global mental capacity exists and that apparent "intelligence" is really just a by-product of one's opportunities to learn skills and information valued in a particular cultural context. True, the concept of intelligence and the way in which individuals are ranked according to this criterion could be social artifacts. But the fact that g is not specific to any particular domain of knowledge or mental skill suggests that g is independent of cultural content, including beliefs about what intelligence is. And tests of different social groups reveal the same continuum of general intelligence. This observation suggests either that cultures do not construct g or that they construct the same g. Both conclusions undercut the social artifact theory of intelligence.

Moreover, research on the physiology and genetics of g has uncovered biological correlates of this psychological phenomenon. In the past decade, studies by teams of researchers in North America and Europe have linked several attributes of the brain to general intelligence. After taking into account gender and physical stature, brain size as determined by magnetic resonance imaging is moderately correlated with IQ (about 0.4 on a scale of 0 to 1). So is the speed of nerve conduction. The brains of bright people also use less energy during problem solving than do those of their less able peers. And various qualities of brain waves correlate strongly (about 0.5 to 0.7) with IQ: the brain waves of individuals with higher IQs, for example, respond more promptly and consistently to simple sensory stimuli such as audible clicks. These observations have led some investigators to posit that differences in g result from differences in the speed and efficiency of neural processing. If this theory is true, environmental conditions could influence g by modifying brain physiology in some manner.

Studies of so-called elementary cognitive tasks (ECTs), conducted by Jensen and others, are bridging the gap between the psychological and the physiological aspects of g. These mental tasks have no obvious intellectual content and are so simple that adults and most children can do them accurately in less than a second. In the most basic reaction-time tests, for example, the subject must react when a light goes on by lifting her index finger off a home button and immediately depressing a response button. Two measurements are taken: the number of milliseconds between the illumination of the light and the subject's release of the home button, which is called decision time, and the number of milliseconds between the subject's release of the home button and pressing of the response button, which is called movement time.

In this task, movement time seems independent of intelligence, but the decision times of higher-IQ subjects are slightly faster than those of people with lower IQs. As the tasks are made more complex, correlations between average decision times and IQ increase. These results further support the notion that intelligence equips individuals to deal with complexity and that its influence is greater in complex tasks than in simple ones.

The ECT-IQ correlations are comparable for all IQ levels, ages, genders and racial-ethnic groups tested. Moreover, studies by Philip A. Vernon of the University of Western Ontario and others have shown that the ECT-IQ overlap results almost entirely from the common g factor in both measures. Reaction times do not reflect differences in motivation or strategy or the tendency of some individuals to rush through tests and daily tasks—that penchant is a personality trait. They actually seem to measure the speed with which the brain apprehends, integrates and evaluates information. Research on ECTs and brain physiology has not yet identified the biological determinants of this processing speed. These studies do suggest, however, that g is as reliable and global a phenomenon at the neural level as it is at the level of the complex information processing required by IQ tests and everyday life.

The existence of biological correlates of intelligence does not necessarily mean that intelligence is dictated by genes. Decades of genetics research have shown, however, that people are born with different hereditary potentials for intelligence and that these genetic endowments are responsible for much of the variation in mental ability among individuals. [Recently] an international team of scientists headed by Robert Plomin of the Institute of Psychiatry in London announced the discovery of the first gene linked to intelligence. Of course, genes have their effects only in interaction with environments, partly by enhancing an individual's exposure or sensitivity to formative experiences. Differences in general intelligence, whether measured as IQ or, more accurately, as g are both genetic and environmental in origin—just as are all other psychological traits and attitudes studied so far, including personality, vocational interests and societal attitudes. This is old news among the experts. The experts have, however, been startled by more recent discoveries.

One is that the heritability of IQ rises with age—that is to say, the extent to which genetics accounts for differences in IQ among individuals increases as people get older. Studies comparing identical and fraternal twins, published in the past decade by a group led by Thomas J. Bouchard, Jr., of the University of Minnesota and other scholars, show that about 40 percent of IQ differences among preschoolers stems from genetic differences but that heritability rises to 60 percent by adolescence and to 80 percent by late adulthood. With age, differences among individuals in their developed intelligence come to mirror more closely their genetic differences. It appears that the effects of environment on intelligence fade rather than grow with time. In hindsight, perhaps this should have come as no surprise. Young children have the circumstances of their lives imposed on them by parents, schools and other agents of society, but as people get older they become more independent and tend to seek out the life niches that are most congenial to their genetic proclivities.

A second big surprise for intelligence experts was the discovery that environments shared by siblings have little to do with IQ. Many people still mistakenly believe that social, psychological and economic differences among families create lasting and marked differences in IQ. Behavioral geneticists refer to such environmental effects as "shared" because they are common to siblings who grow up together. Research has shown that although shared environments do have a modest influence on IQ in childhood, their effects dissipate by adolescence. The IQs of adopted children, for example, lose all resemblance to those of their adoptive family members and become more like the IQs of the biological parents they have never known. Such findings suggest that siblings either do not share influential aspects of the rearing environment or do not experience them in the same way. Much behavioral genetics research currently focuses on the still mysterious processes by which environments make members of a household less alike.

g on the Job

Although the evidence of genetic and physiological correlates of *g* argues powerfully for the existence of global intelligence, it has not quelled the critics of intelligence testing. These skeptics argue that even if such a global entity exists, it has no intrinsic functional value and becomes important only to the extent that people treat it as such: for example, by using IQ scores to sort, label and assign students and employees. Such concerns over the proper use of mental tests have prompted a great deal of research in recent decades. This research shows that although IQ tests can indeed be misused, they measure a capability that does in fact affect many kinds of performance and many life outcomes, independent of the tests' interpretations or applications. Moreover, the research shows that intelligence tests measure the capability equally well for all native-born English-speaking groups in the U.S.

If we consider that intelligence manifests itself in everyday life as the ability to deal with complexity, then it is easy to see why it has great functional or practical importance. Children, for example, are regularly exposed to complex tasks once they begin school. Schooling requires above all that students learn, solve problems and think abstractly. That IQ is quite a good predictor of differences in educational achievement is therefore not surprising. When scores on both IQ and standardized achievement tests in different subjects are averaged over several years, the two averages correlate as highly as different IQ tests from the same individual do. High-ability students also master material at many times the rate of their low-ability peers. Many investigations have helped quantify this discrepancy. For example, a 1969 study done for the U.S. Army by the Human Resources Research Office found that enlistees in the bottom fifth of the ability distribution required two to six times as many teaching trials and prompts as did their higher-ability peers to attain minimal proficiency in rifle assembly, monitoring signals, combat plotting and other basic military tasks. Similarly, in school settings the ratio of learning rates between "fast" and "slow" students is typically five to one.

The scholarly content of many IQ tests and their strong correlations with educational success can give the impression that *g* is only a narrow academic ability. But general mental ability also predicts job performance, and in more

Figure 2

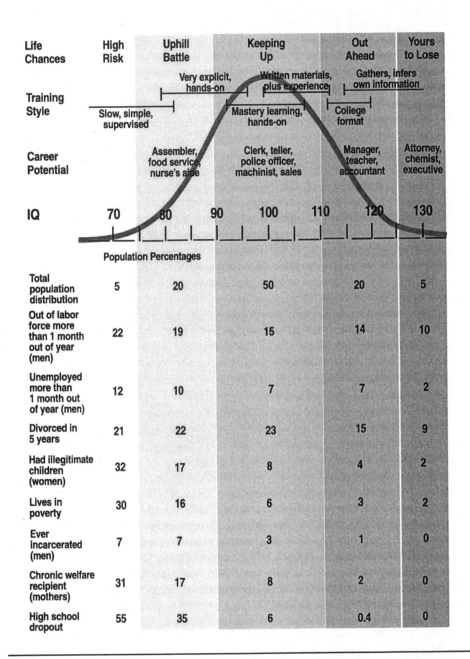

	High Risk	Uphill Battle	Keeping Up	Out Ahead	Yours to Lose
Life Chances	High Risk	Uphill Battle	Keeping Up	Out Ahead	Yours to Lose
Training Style	Slow, simple, supervised	Very explicit, hands-on	Written materials, plus experience / Mastery learning, hands-on	Gathers, infers own information / College format	
Career Potential		Assembler, food service, nurse's aide	Clerk, teller, police officer, machinist, sales	Manager, teacher, accountant	Attorney, chemist, executive
IQ	70	80	90 100	110 120	130

Population Percentages

Total population distribution	5	20	50	20	5
Out of labor force more than 1 month out of year (men)	22	19	15	14	10
Unemployed more than 1 month out of year (men)	12	10	7	7	2
Divorced in 5 years	21	22	23	15	9
Had illegitimate children (women)	32	17	8	4	2
Lives in poverty	30	16	6	3	2
Ever incarcerated (men)	7	7	3	1	0
Chronic welfare recipient (mothers)	31	17	8	2	0
High school dropout	55	35	6	0.4	0

Correlation of IQ scores with occupational achievement suggests that *g* reflects an ability to deal with cognitive complexity. Scores also correlate with some social outcomes (the percentages apply to young white adults in the U.S.).

Adapted from *Intelligence*, Vol. 24, No. 1: January/February 1997. Reprinted by permission of John Mengel, Ponzi & Weill, Inc.

complex jobs it does so better than any other single personal trait, including education and experience. The army's Project A, a seven-year study conducted in the 1980s to improve the recruitment and training process, found that general mental ability correlated strongly with both technical proficiency and soldiering in the nine specialties studied, among them infantry, military police and medical specialist. Research in the civilian sector has revealed the same pattern. Furthermore, although the addition of personality traits such as conscientiousness can help hone the prediction of job performance, the inclusion of specific mental aptitudes such as verbal fluency or mathematical skill rarely does. The predictive value of mental tests in the work arena stems almost entirely from their measurement of g, and that value rises with the complexity and prestige level of the job.

Half a century of military and civilian research has converged to draw a portrait of occupational opportunity along the IQ continuum. Individuals in the top 5 percent of the adult IQ distribution (above IQ 125) can essentially train themselves, and few occupations are beyond their reach mentally. Persons of average IQ (between 90 and 110) are not competitive for most professional and executive-level work but are easily trained for the bulk of jobs in the American economy. In contrast, adults in the bottom 5 percent of the IQ distribution (below 75) are very difficult to train and are not competitive for any occupation on the basis of ability. Serious problems in training low-IQ military recruits during World War II led Congress to ban enlistment from the lowest 10 percent (below 80) of the population, and no civilian occupation in modern economies routinely recruits its workers from that range. Current military enlistment standards exclude any individual whose IQ is below about 85.

The importance of g in job performance, as in schooling, is related to complexity. Occupations differ considerably in the complexity of their demands, and as that complexity rises, higher g levels become a bigger asset and lower g levels a bigger handicap. Similarly, everyday tasks and environments also differ significantly in their cognitive complexity. The degree to which a person's g level will come to bear on daily life depends on how much novelty and ambiguity that person's everyday tasks and surroundings present and how much continual learning, judgment and decision making they require. As gamblers, employers and bankers know, even marginal differences in rates of return will yield big gains—or losses—over time. Hence, even small differences in g among people can exert large, cumulative influences across social and economic life.

In my own work, I have tried to synthesize the many lines of research that document the influence of IQ on life outcomes. As [Figure 2] shows, the odds of various kinds of achievement and social pathology change systematically across the IQ continuum, from borderline mentally retarded (below 70) to intellectually gifted (above 130). Even in comparisons of those of somewhat below average (between 76 and 90) and somewhat above average (between 111 and 125) IQs, the odds for outcomes having social consequence are stacked against the less able. Young men somewhat below average in general mental ability, for example, are more likely to be unemployed than men somewhat above average. The lower-IQ woman is four times more likely to bear illegitimate children than the higher-IQ woman; among mothers, she is eight times more likely to become a chronic welfare recipient. People somewhat below average are 88 times more likely to drop out of high school, seven times more likely to be jailed and five times more likely as adults to live in poverty than people of somewhat above-average IQ. Below-average individuals are 50 percent more likely to be divorced than those in the above-average category.

These odds diverge even more sharply for people with bigger gaps in IQ, and the mechanisms by which IQ creates this divergence are not yet clearly understood. But no other single trait or circumstance yet studied is so deeply implicated in the nexus of bad social outcomes—poverty, welfare, illegitimacy and educational failure—that entraps many low-IQ individuals and families. Even the effects of family background pale in comparison with the influence of IQ. As shown most recently by Charles Murray of the American Enterprise Institute in Washington, D.C., the divergence in many outcomes associated with IQ level is almost as wide among siblings from the same household as it is for strangers of comparable IQ levels. And siblings differ a lot in IQ—on average, by 12 points, compared with 17 for random strangers.

An IQ of 75 is perhaps the most important threshold in modern life. At that level, a person's chances of mastering the elementary school curriculum are only 50–50, and he or she will have a hard time functioning independently without considerable social support. Individuals and families who are only somewhat below average in IQ face risks of social pathology that, while lower, are still significant enough to jeopardize their well-being. High-IQ individuals may lack the resolve, character or good fortune to capitalize on their intellectual capabilities, but socioeconomic success in the postindustrial information age is theirs to lose.

What Is Versus What Could Be

The foregoing findings on g's effects have been drawn from studies conducted under a limited range of circumstances—namely, the social, economic and political conditions prevailing now and in recent decades in developed countries that allow considerable personal freedom. It is not clear whether these findings apply to populations around the world, to the extremely advantaged and disadvantaged in the developing world or, for that matter, to people living under restrictive political regimes. No one knows what research under different circumstances, in different eras or with different populations might reveal. But we do know that, wherever freedom and technology advance, life is an uphill battle for people who are below average in proficiency at learning, solving problems and mastering complexity. We also know that the trajectories of mental development are not easily deflected. Individual IQ levels tend to remain unchanged from adolescence onward, and despite strenuous efforts over the past half a century, attempts to raise g permanently through adoption or educational means have failed. If this is a reliable, ethical way to raise or equalize levels of g, no one has found it.

Some investigators have suggested that biological interventions, such as dietary supplements of vitamins, may be more effective than educational ones in raising *g* levels. This approach is based in part on the assumption that improved nutrition has caused the puzzling rise in average levels of both IQ and height in the developed world during this century. Scientists are still hotly debating whether the gains in IQ actually reflect a rise in *g* or are caused instead by changes in less critical, specific mental skills. Whatever the truth may be, the differences in mental ability among individuals remain, and the conflict between equal opportunity and equal outcome persists. Only by accepting these hard truths about intelligence will society find humane solutions to the problems posed by the variations in general mental ability.

CHALLENGE QUESTIONS

Should Psychology Adopt a Theory of Multiple Intelligences?

1. What do you think intelligence testing should be used for in society? Should IQ tests be used to place students in certain kinds of classes? How might the acceptance of a multiple theory of intelligence change how IQ tests are used in society and education?

2. Gardner asserts that some intelligences are not covered by IQ tests. How might a psychologist evaluate these intelligences? What kind of test or evaluation would you use to determine an individual's musical intelligence?

3. If culture is a factor in understanding and measuring intelligence, as Gardner argues, how should psychologists go about testing the IQ of individuals who are not part of Western culture? Do prominent IQ tests have a cultural or gender bias?

4. What is the difference between talent and intelligence? Should intelligence be considered primarily a measure of cognitive and academic abilities?

ISSUE 9

Do Adults Repress Childhood Sexual Abuse?

YES: May Benatar, from "Running Away From Sexual Abuse: Denial Revisited," *Families in Society: The Journal of Contemporary Human Services* (May 1995)

NO: Susan P. Robbins, from "Wading Through the Muddy Waters of Recovered Memory," *Families in Society: The Journal of Contemporary Human Services* (October 1995)

ISSUE SUMMARY

YES: May Benatar, a clinical social worker and lecturer, asserts that recent publicity on memories of sexual abuse has focused more on the "hype" of sexual abuse rather than on the actual prevailing act of sexual abuse. She maintains that repressed memories are a common response to child sexual abuse and that they can be recovered in adulthood.

NO: Susan P. Robbins, an associate professor of graduate social work, contends that there is little support for the idea of repressed or dissociated memories of child sexual abuse in scientific studies. She also argues that outside sources can trigger or influence many inaccurate memories of child abuse.

I t is hard to imagine a more heinous crime than sexual abuse. Yet, perhaps surprisingly, it is a crime that often goes unpunished. Frequently, sexual abusers are family members and their victims are children who are too young to protest or too naive to know that they are being violated. This problem is part of the reason why memories have become so significant to the sexual abuse issue. Often it is not until the victims become adults that they realize they were abused.

Complicating the issue is that the reliability of memory itself is questionable. In the courtroom, for example, eyewitness testimony has lost much of its credibility because memories of a single occurrence can vary from witness to witness. Suggestive questions may even change the memory of a witness. More pertinent, the so-called repression or dissociation of sexual abuse memories has been called by some "false memories." Many feel that "memories" of sexual abuse are not always real; that is, memories can be changed by outside influences, such as suggestions, "trigger" questions, and hypnosis. If a therapist or another investigator is suspected of manipulating subject responses and "creating" memories of sexual abuse, then the validity of "recovered" memories becomes questionable. On the other hand, some therapists believe that there is an overemphasis on the validity of memories, sometimes referred to as "hype." Their concern is that by getting too bogged down in the "hype" of sexual memories, people are ignoring the pain of the victims.

In the following selection, May Benatar asserts that too much attention is indeed being paid to this "hype" and to the mistrust of children with memories of sexual abuse. She questions the value being placed on the welfare of children, stating, "The author asks whether we are panicking over child abuse. Is criminal prosecution tantamount to panic? And if it is, is the abuse of children not worthy of such a response?" But Benatar emphasizes that a lack of explicit memories of sexual abuse does not mean that abuse did not occur. Many times, child sexual abuse has occurred regardless of the victim's recollection of explicit details.

In the second selection, Susan P. Robbins refutes Benatar's arguments and calls for greater attention in distinguishing conjecture from fact. Robbins sides with the critics and points out that critics are skeptical of recovered memories because there is no support from reproducible scientific evidence. She states, "[The critics] contend that the growing body of research on memory has consistently shown memory to be subject to inaccuracy, distortion, and fabrication." Robbins also calls attention to the differences between child sexual abuse and the "recovered memories" of abuse, a distinction often lost on proponents of prosecuting child sexual abuse.

POINT

- Denial of child sexual abuse comes from a backlash against feminism.

- One out of every three girls and one out of every seven to ten boys is sexually abused.

- Clinicians have been trained to deny that their clients have been sexually abused because Sigmund Freud was politically pressured to abandon his theory of repressed sexual abuse.

- Traumatic memories are stored in a special part of the brain and are retrieved in response to a number of stimuli, such as suggestion.

- By focusing on cases of "false memories" of sexual abuse, society is denying the pain of its children.

COUNTERPOINT

- The real feminist issue is the victimization of clients who may have traumatic memories implanted by a therapist.

- Because statistics regarding sexual abuse are so difficult to accurately gather, they should always be viewed with caution.

- Freud never denied his clients' conscious memories of sexual abuse; he only questioned their unconscious and recovered memories.

- Memory experts agree that memory is not stored in the brain but is reconstructed meaningfully.

- Questioning the veracity of recovered or repressed memories is not the same as doubting that child sexual abuse occurs.

Running Away From Sexual Abuse: Denial Revisited

After a period of increased professional and public awareness of how pervasive the sexual maltreatment of children is in our society, we appear to be in danger of vaulting away from hard-won insights into this major public health issue. Both propounding and expressing the prejudices of the culture, the press and other media have taken to indicting the veracity of traumatic memories of survivors of sexual abuse, minimizing the toxic long-term effects of the sexual maltreatment of children, and casting doubt on both the skill and good intentions of clinicians treating both child victims and adult survivors. We have seen front-page articles on the purported "false" memories of adult survivors of abuse; examples of "false" accusations of innocent parents, grandparents, or teachers; or speculations that therapists, many of whom are survivors themselves, intentionally or unintentionally suggest events to their patients that never took place.

A 1993 *Newsweek* cover photograph showed a middle-age couple convicted of molesting their grandchildren. The caption asks: "When does the fight to protect our kids go too far?" Does this strange juxtaposition of material imply that convicting child molesters is "going too far?" The article inside (Shapiro, 1993) reviews a few recent court cases and one reversal and addresses the issue of child testimony; the author asks whether we are panicking over child abuse. Is criminal prosecution tantamount to panic? And if it is, is the abuse of children not worthy of such a response?

In the *New Yorker*, Wright (1993a, 1993b) wrote a two-part article on the case of a Washington state deputy sheriff, who, after being accused of child abuse by his two daughters, confessed to sexually abusing them, prostituting them to family friends, and being part of a satanic cult. The case unraveled when it was discovered that at least some of the accusations and confessions by both parents resulted from overzealous questioning and suggestions by police interrogators on what were alleged to be highly suggestible subjects. The article clearly implies that this case represents one of many instances of modern-day witch hunts—the innocent "witches" in this case being those accused of perpetrating unthinkable crimes such as ritual sexual abuse, torture, and murder.

In *Mother Jones,* a well-regarded if somewhat off-beat publication, Watters (1993) also expressed concern about false memories and false accusations in a report of a young woman's delayed discovery of childhood abuse. The woman entered therapy following a severe depressive episode and while in therapy recovered memories of sexual abuse. Although the facts of the case neither exculpate the accused nor affirm the victim's accusations, the author uses this case to propose that "a substantial segment of the therapy community has charged ahead, creating a *growth* industry around the concept of recovered memories."

Even Carol Tavris (1993), a noted feminist author, cast a skeptical eye on what she termed the "incest-survivor machine," an umbrella term for therapists working with adult survivors, writers of self-help books for survivors, and the grass-roots recovery movement of adult survivors.

For clinicians working with patients to address the post-traumatic effects of childhood sexual abuse and for adult survivors struggling to take their own stories seriously and understand the difficulties of their adult lives as sequelae of and adaptation to violations that occurred during childhood, this emphasis on the "hype" of sexual abuse is deeply troubling.

Child Abuse: Past and Present Findings

The reality of child abuse is well established. Why then is it currently acceptable, even fashionable, to doubt the victims, those who prosecute for them, and those who treat their post-traumatic illnesses? This backlash against sexual-abuse survivors has social, cultural, political, and psychological roots. One reading is that this backlash is a response to the evolution in law regarding the issue of incest—an evolution that now allows some adult survivors to seek legal redress many years, even decades, after the commission of crimes. Another reason for this backlash may be related to the cultural mysogyny that Faludi (1991) documents in her book *Backlash,* which refers to the social forces that thwart the gains that women have achieved in society. On another level of analysis, we may understand this phenomenon of denial of social realities as "cultural dissociation." As a society we are unable to accept the reality of the cruelty, sadism, neglect, and narcissism that adults inflict upon children. In a world where some people still debate the reality of Nazi death camps, it is not surprising that we have difficulties acknowledging that 1 of every 3 girls and 1 of 7 to 10 boys are "used" by an adult in a manner that brings great harm to them for the rest of their lives.

The epidemiology of child sexual abuse has been carefully documented. Kinsey found in the early 1950s that 24% of his female sample of 4,000 women reported sexual abuse in childhood (before the age of puberty) (Brownmiller, 1975). Dozens of studies have confirmed this finding. Thirty years later, Russell (1986) carefully surveyed a nonclinical population of nearly 1,000 women. She reported that 38% of the sample reported being molested before the age of 18 and 28% before puberty. In addition, she found that most abusers are known to the child as trusted individuals who occupy a position of authority over the child.

In another significant study, Herman and Schatzow (1987) discussed recall of traumatic memories from childhood often dissociated by the child in an effort to maintain secrecy and safety. Fifty-three female patients in group psychotherapy reported delayed recall of traumatic memory; 74% of the women confirmed their memories of abuse by obtaining independent corroborating evidence—physical evidence, diaries, pictures, confirmation by perpetrators and/ or corroboration by other family members who had also been victimized. This study appears to strengthen Russell's and Kinsey's data. Even those with delayed recall, when seeking confirmation of the reality of their memories many years after the fact, are able to confirm the memory. To my knowledge, no comparable study demonstrates *false* recall of childhood-abuse memories.

Interestingly, the conflict between the reality of child abuse and the voices of disbelief and disavowal is not unique to the 1990s; a century ago western psychiatry experienced a similar struggle and process. Masson (1984), in *The Assault on Truth,* presented important work done in 19th-century France regarding the criminal brutalization and sexual abuse of children. In setting the stage for his explanation of why Freud first adopted and later abandoned the "seduction theory" to explain the origins of hysterical neurosis, Masson discusses child abuse in Europe during that period. Forensic psychiatrists uncovered shocking facts about child abuse. Ambrose Tardieu, a professor and dean of forensic medicine at the University of Paris and president of the Academy of Medicine in Paris in 1860, published "A Medico-Legal Study of Cruelty and Brutal Treatment Inflicted on Children." He presented case after case of detailed medical evidence indicating severe child abuse, including the sexual abuse of children. He indicated that the phenomenon was not rare and that perpetrators were often parents and that victims were often very young and primarily girls.

Paul Brouardel, Tardieu's successor to the chair of legal medicine in Paris and also a contemporary of Freud, described perpetrators as "excellent family men" who were often the fathers of the victims. Brouardel was a collaborator of Jean-Martin Charcot, a neurologist who demonstrated the efficacy of hypnosis in the treatment of psychiatric patients, particularly female hysterics. Freud was fascinated by Charcot's work and came to Paris to study with him. Masson argues that Freud and his contemporaries were more than likely aware of the work of Tardieu, Brouardel, and other forensic psychiatrists in France through their studies with Charcot. Freud's early struggles to understand the underpinnings of neurosis suggest his awareness of the traumatic origins of psychic disturbance as well as the influence that the French pioneers had on his clinical awareness. In the late 1890s Freud (1984) wrote movingly and persuasively in *The Aetiology of Hysteria* about 18 cases of hysterical neurosis in which an early experience of sexual abuse had led to hysterical symptoms in adult life— symptoms similar to what we categorize today as post-traumatic stress disorder or dissociative disorder.

However, it was Pierre Janet, another visitor to Charcot's seminars, who developed both a complex theoretical understanding and efficacious treatment model for hysteria. Janet published many of his findings the year before Freud's *Aetiology of Hysteria* appeared, but unlike Freud he held fast to the trauma model that Freud renounced. Janet described many cases of what we have come to understand as dissociative disorders and multiple personality disorder. Janet understood his patients' symptoms, much as trained clinicians do today, as ingenious and creative adaptations to overwhelming childhood stress such as physical and/or sexual abuse. He saw hysterical symptoms, not as compromise formations of drive derivatives or expressions of drive conflicts, but rather as fossils from the past, derivatives of traumatic memory, communications of early betrayals and overwhelming affects (van der Kolk & van der Hart, 1989).

Yet for most of the 20th century, Janet was *not* studied and *not* employed in our attempts to understand mental life. Freud's development of psychoanalysis obliterated Janet's work. To read Janet today, 100 years later, is to be struck with how little modern trauma psychology and our understandings of traumatic memory can add to his understandings, how clearly he explicated what we have come to rediscover in the past decade and a half, and how brilliantly he anticipated modern findings on the psychophysiology of memory.

Herman (1992) and others have proposed that Freud and his students moved away from trauma theory or the "seduction theory," because the zeitgeist of the time and place could not support such conclusions. Earlier in the century, in Tardieu's and Charcot's France, the political atmosphere was one of reform: challenges to the monarchy and the church enabled a movement toward understanding mental illness as a rational, not magical, pursuit. They viewed mental illness as a sequela of early experience that could be understood and addressed by science. These sociopolitical forces ushered in an era of more humane treatment of the mentally ill that approached mental illness as trauma based. Freud's science grew in different soil—Viennese soil—where trauma-based theory was unable to take root.

For a brief period in the 1800s, clinicians and students of forensic psychiatry knew that many children were severely abused by their families and that such abuse led to dramatic effects in the mental health of adults. They also understood effective treatment of these symptoms involved revisiting early memory and processing these memories in the context of a solid therapeutic alliance. By the beginning of the 20th century, after Freud had published *The Aetiology of Hysteria,* the political winds had shifted, as had the politics of psychiatry. Traumatic etiology was relegated to the background and endogenous intrapsychic conflicts moved to the foreground. We stopped looking at the environmental surround—the maltreatment of children—and turned our scientific gaze inward toward fantasy formation and the intricate topography of the mind.

Where Do We Go Today?

It has taken us nearly a century to get back to where we started—the work of Janet. Two concurrent social movements helped to reawaken our awareness of childhood trauma. In the 1970s, the returning Vietnam War veterans became quite active in seeking validation for their catastrophic experiences during the war. They organized themselves to obtain services from veterans hospitals and recognition for their suffering from their communities. Their illnesses became the focus for legal activity and psychiatric attention. Psychiatrists rediscovered "war neurosis" and learned from their patients about the aftereffects of severe, intense, and acute traumatic experience. Post-traumatic stress disorder became a diagnostic entity and was entered into the *Diagnostic and Statistical Manual of Mental Disorders* in 1980.

The other major social change that contributed to the reemergence of our awareness of childhood sexual abuse was the women's movement in the 1970s. Women meeting in consciousness-raising groups, helping one another to name their fears, their frustrations, and their hopes, began telling stories of sexual manipulation, sexual violence, and early experiences of sexual violation at the hands of family members. Women Against Rape centers sprang up across the country; from these centers rape-crisis-counseling centers were developed. Today, a strong grass-roots recovery movement exists, carrying the message about child abuse and dissociative disorders to the public. Individuals help one another in 12-step-type recovery groups, generating art, newsletters, books, workshops, and conferences to help heal themselves as well as educate clinicians and lay individuals.

As a result of these two powerful movements for social change, survivors of childhood sexual abuse found a voice and clinicians began to listen. By the 1980s we began to see new journals devoted to exploring the effects and the treatment of individuals so affected. A whole new subspecialty in psychiatry, psychology, and social work emerged: working with dissociative disorders. Today, however, troubling signs indicate that public and political retrenchment from various interconnecting and interactive factors are contributing to renewed denial and disavowal of the prevalence of child sexual abuse. Moreover, social, legal, political, and psychological pressures are undermining all that we have learned about the etiology and sequelae of this devastating societal problem.

Factor One

In many ways, the mass media have focused more attention on survivors than has the mental health establishment. Oprah, Phil, and Sally Jesse have featured shows alerting the public to the painful experiences of adult survivors, which has led to a "Geraldoizing" effect. Despite the fact that Geraldo Rivera has actually done a couple of interesting shows on multiple personality disorder and has devoted more time and attention to the consequences of severe childhood trauma than have many mental health professionals, his and other popular talk shows tend to be associated with sensationalism and exploitation. As a result, real problems are trivialized in the public mind. If Geraldo thinks it is interesting, it must be hype. The overall effect is chilling. Clients wonder whether their memories and intense psychic, even physical, pain associated with their abuse histories are merely childish bids for attention. A client who kept her childhood rape secret for 40 years spoke of her dread of being perceived as having the "designer" affliction of our time.

Factor Two

The effect on memory is one sequela of childhood trauma that muddies the water for both the layperson and professional. How reliable is memory?

Police and prosecutors of violent crime understand that survivors of psychological trauma make very poor witnesses. Janet brilliantly described the differences between what he termed "narrative memory" and "traumatic memory" (van der Kolk & van der Hart, 1989). Narrative memory is what we generally mean when we speak of memory. It involves a complex process whereby new experiences are integrated into preexisting schema or mental categories, along with the slow evolution and expansion of those schema. Traumatic memory is different. Trauma is an event or series of events that lies outside the ordinary, expectable events of life. It is overwhelming in its affective impact on the individual. It does not easily fit into preexisting schema, nor does it evolve easily with other memories. Traumatic memories are "dissociated." To use a computer analogy, narrative memory is stored on drive C, the drive that is generally available to consciousness and voluntary control processes. Although drive C may have subdirectories of unconsciousness as well, that is, memories that are repressed but can be brought into consciousness through psychoanalysis, dream work, free association, and the like, drive B, or dissociated, memories arise unexpectedly when someone or something triggers them into actualization: therapy, a child reaching a developmental milestone, a movie, a book, a television show, a death. Dissociated memories are fragmentary, illusive, uncertain, even terrifying.

If the trauma is not verifiable and if it occurred early in life and was severe, these dissociated states act as containers for memories and pain and assume the coherence of alternative selves, that is, separate personality or ego states that hold particular memories together. During the therapeutic process, the therapist and patient attempt to understand the nature of these drive B materials, retrieve them, and integrate them into drive C consciousness. In so doing, traumatic memory is integrated and assimilated into narrative memory.

For example, a 36-year-old woman who has been in therapy for three years struggling with depression and periodic panic attacks glances at her four-year-old daughter playing at the beach and suddenly remembers being raped by her father when she was four years old. In the following days, she questions her sanity and is unable to understand what is happening to her. Her therapist may also wonder about this bewildering experience. She will likely try to forget or trivialize it.

The impulse to both know the secrets of early trauma, and to tell it most typically fight with the impulse to keep the secret: what emerges is often jumbled and contradictory. That is the nature of traumatic memory! This is why victims are poor witnesses. The most common scenarios for survivors is to want to discredit their dissociated memories, not particularly to elevate them to heroic status. False memories, or memories that are iatrogenically induced during therapy, are not that common. Although some types of memories can be distorted or implanted in the minds of individuals under certain circumstances, evidence does not indicate that this occurs frequently, or even occasionally, in psychotherapeutic work with survivors of trauma.

Factor Three

Faludi (1991) states that approximately every 30 years a cultural backlash arises against nascent feminism. Even modest status gains by women are quickly followed by a cultural response indicating that these changes and gains are not good for society or women.

Sexual abuse and sexual violence are cast as women's issues, despite the fact that children of both sexes are affected by abuse. Attacks on feminism focus energy on maintaining the *status quo* in power relationships. As a result, child victims and adult survivors may be discredited under the rubric of women's issues. Faludi points to the 1980s as a decade of government retrenchment on women's issues, disproportionate cuts in funding for women's programs, and decreased commitment in government funding for battered women's programs, despite increases in domestic violence. A dramatic rise in sexual violence against women, an increase that outstrips other types of violent crimes, has been met with indifference at all levels of government.

The retreat from renewed awareness of child-abuse problems in general and sexual abuse in particular reflects this backlash. Interestingly, patients' veracity in therapy was never an issue until we began discussing issues of sexual abuse.

Factor Four

The changing legal climate regarding prosecution in civil incest suits has also affected adult-survivor issues. In the early 1980s, legal scholars began to reconsider the problem of seeking legal redress for crimes involving sexual abuse years after the commission of these crimes and after the statute of limitations had expired. In the *Harvard Women's Law Review,* Salten (1984) persuasively argued, "Given the latent nature and belated detection of many incest related injuries, the parent's special duty of care to his [sic] child, the youth of the incest victim, and the likelihood of psychological disabilities which preclude timely action, a tort suit for latent incestuous injuries is perhaps the paradigmatic example of special circumstances requiring equitable preservation of a potential remedy" (p. 220). As a result of this and other legal arguments, several U.S. state and Canadian provincial legislatures are considering changes in the law that toll the statute of limitations for both criminal prosecution of incest (incest *is* a crime) and civil incest suits from age 21 and/or from the time the facts of the crime are discovered. These changes in the law would acknowledge both the powerlessness of children to bring suit or initiate prosecution and the problem of associative memory, whereby memories of child sexual abuse may not be available to the victim until many years after the victimization.

This "delayed discovery" approach to civil litigation has precedent in cases involving injuries from asbestos and other harmful substances. Perpetrators are now within reach of the law years, even decades, after the commission of their crimes. This evolution in the law, however, has invigorated attacks against delayed memory in adult survivors. The False Memory Syndrome Foundation is dedicated to disseminating information on what its spokepersons describe as the growing threat of false accusations of incest and sexual abuse.

Part of its mission is to provide financial assistance to families in need of legal services or legal counseling.

Conclusion

Freud anticipated the skepticism and criticism that would greet his views on sexual trauma as a cause of hysteria. Nevertheless, his views are as relevant today as they were 100 years ago. Freud discussed three aspects of work with traumatized patients:

- Patients reexperiencing an early life experience in a dissociative manner clearly demonstrate suffering, pain, shame, terror, and extreme helplessness. Suggested memories do not have this quality.
- Patients resist these memories both consciously and unconsciously and often disavow the memories immediately after the experience. People do not want to believe that they were betrayed by the adults whom they trusted for protection. Typically, such a belief requires a reorientation of one's frame of reference.
- Freud mentions that when he successfully suggested a scene to a patient, even the most compliant patients are unable to reproduce such scenes with the intensely appropriate affect and detail characteristic of dissociated memory. Although Freud did not speak of "dissociated memory" as such, he described it very sympathetically in *The Aetiology of Hysteria.*

Freud's critics had the final say, and Freud changed his mind about traumatic memories. The legacy of this intellectual struggle in psychiatry has affected tens of thousands of people whose early-life trauma has been ignored. For the past 15 years, we have struggled to reverse this legacy. We have made great strides in our understanding of female psychology, trauma, memory, and self-formation. Countervailing reactionary forces that are not grounded in scientific skepticism or informed by a spirit of inquiry would erase these gains. Both professionals and the lay public must meet this challenge by refusing to dishonor the struggles of those who refuse to forget.

References

Brownmiller, S. (1975). *Against our will: Men, women and rape.* New York: Simon and Schuster.

Faludi, S. (1991). *Backlash: The undeclared war against American women.* New York: Crown Publishers.

Freud, S. (1984). The aetiology of hysteria. In J. M. Masson (Ed.), *Freud: The assault on truth* (pp. 251–282). London: Faber and Faber.

Herman, J. L. (1992). *Trauma and recovery: The aftermath of violence from domestic abuse to political terror.* New York: Basic Books.

Herman, J. L., & Schatzow, E. (1987). Recovery and verification of memories of childhood sexual trauma. *Psychoanalytic Psychology, 4,* 1–14.

Masson, J. (1984). *Freud: The assault on truth.* London: Faber and Faber.

Russell, D. (1986). *The secret trauma: Incest in the lives of girls and women.* New York: Basic Books.

Salten, M. (1984). Statutes of limitations in civil incest suits: Preserving the victim's remedy. *Harvard Women's Law Journal, 7,* 189–220.

Shapiro, L. (1993, April 19). Rush to judgment. *Newsweek,* 54–60.

Tavris, C. (1993, January 3). Beware the incest-survivor machine. *New York Times,* Sect. 7, p. 1.

van der Kolk, B., & van der Hart, O. (1989). Pierre Janet and the breakdown of adaptation. *American Journal of Psychiatry, 146,* 1530–1540.

Watters, E. (1993, January–February). Doors of memory. *Mother Jones,* p. 24.

Wright, L. (1993a, May 17). Remembering Satan, part I. *New Yorker,* pp. 60–81.

Wright, L. (1993b, May 24). Remembering Satan, part II. *New Yorker,* pp. 54–76.

Susan P. Robbins

Wading Through the Muddy Waters of Recovered Memory

In her essay "Running Away from Sexual Abuse: Denial Revisited" Benatar (1995) addresses a timely and important topic—recovered memories of childhood sexual abuse. Delayed recovery of memories of traumatic events and the nature, validity, and accuracy of these memories have been at the center of a controversial and bitter debate among mental health professionals and researchers (see Berliner & Williams, 1994; Butler, 1995; Byrd, 1994; Ewen, 1994; Gleaves, 1994; Gold, Hughes, & Hohnecker, 1994; Gutheil, 1993; Lindsay & Read 1994; Loftus & Ketcham, 1994; Peterson, 1994; Pezdek 1994; Pope & Hudson, 1995; Slovenko, 1993; Wylie, 1993; Yapko, 1994a, 1994b).

Proponents of recovered memory believe that many victims of repeated childhood sexual abuse repress or dissociate all memory of their trauma as a mechanism for coping. Although conscious memory of the trauma is not available to the victim, it nonetheless is believed to affect one's social and psychological functioning in adulthood. Seeking therapy for various problems such as substance abuse, eating disorders, depression, or marital difficulties, unhappy adults (primarily white, middle- and upper-class women in their thirties and forties) report memories of abuse that usually surface during the course of therapy. Such memories may also surface while participating in recovery groups, attending self-help conferences, reading incest-recovery books, or as the result of a specific trigger event. These memories typically appear as terrifying images or flashbacks that proponents believe are genuine, if not precise, memories of earlier abuse. Professional knowledge about recovered memory is derived primarily from clinical case reports, and most proponents accept these case studies as confirming evidence.

Critics are skeptical of recovered memories because no reproducible scientific evidence supports these claims. They contend that the growing body of research on memory has consistently shown memory to be subject to inaccuracy, distortion, and fabrication. They have also raised serious questions about the therapeutic methods used to help clients "recover" memories, and some claim that the real feminist issue is the victimization of clients by their therapists who, either knowingly or unconsciously, are suggesting, implanting, and reinforcing memories of abuse that never happened. Many critics have expressed concern that indiscriminate acceptance of recovered memories will lead to a serious backlash of disbelief in authentic cases of abuse.

In the past five years, a rapidly growing body of literature has supported both sides of this contentious debate. Although social workers are often cited as central figures in this debate, leading social work journals have not previously addressed this controversy. Benatar's essay, although timely, adds little to this debate and is a prime example of practice prescriptions based on ideology and theoretical conjecture. In addition to a woefully inadequate review of the current literature in this area, the essay suffers from a lack of conceptual clarity, unwarranted assumptions, and factual inaccuracy.

At the outset, the issue of child sexual abuse is confused with that of "recovered memories" of abuse. These are, in fact, two different issues that have recently come to be associated with each other. The former deals with a well-documented phenomenon—the sexual abuse of children by parents, relatives, other adult caretakers, friends, acquaintances, and strangers. The latter involves the debate about traumatic memory, including the repression of traumatic events and delayed recovery of these memories. According to Loftus and Ketcham (1994), this is a debate about memory and not a debate about childhood sexual abuse.

Benatar expresses disdain for the popular media's skeptical stance about delayed memory, the techniques used to uncover such memories, and the growing incest-survivor industry. Casting this skepticism as an antifeminist backlash against sexual-abuse survivors, she discounts the crucial issue of "false memories" and asserts that those who even question the veracity of traumatic memories are eroding the important gains made in our recognition of childhood abuse. Throughout, she improperly equates skepticism about recovered memories with denial of child sexual abuse.

Adding to this conceptual confusion, Benatar fails to draw distinctions among children who are current victims of abuse, adults who have always remembered traumatic incidents of childhood abuse, and those who have only recently recovered previously amnesic memories. Because this important point is neither addressed nor explored, all client reports of childhood abuse (which she refers to as "their own stories") are inferentially cast as being equally valid descriptions of historical events.

Child Abuse: Past and Present Findings

Benatar correctly notes that "the reality of child abuse is well established." Given the increasing empirical evidence substantiating the reality of child abuse, it is most unfortunate that her ensuing discussion is based on specious analogies, incomplete data, and the use of unverified historical theories.

For example, labeled as "cultural dissociation," she equates the denial of the reality of Nazi death camps to what she believes is a prevalent societal denial of child abuse. In comparing the widely discredited beliefs of a relative few to a broader cultural misogyny that disavows child abuse, she engages in fallacious and distorted logic based on improper generalization and false analogy (see Fischer, 1970).

More problematic is the narrow sample of studies Benatar cites to support her discussion on the epidemiology of child sexual abuse, a problem further compounded by the lack of any critical analysis or discussion of the methodological limitations of these studies. A more thorough review of the literature reveals a broad range in the estimated prevalence of childhood sexual abuse. Although studies on child sexual abuse date back to 1929, few systematic studies utilizing careful statistical analyses were done before the late 1970s and early 1980s (see Demause, 1991). Retrospective surveys have reported base rates ranging from 6% to 62% for women (Burnam, cited in Peters, Wyatt, & Finkelhor, 1986; Wyatt, 1985) and between 3% and 31% for men (Landis, 1956; National Committee for the Prevention of Child Abuse, cited in Goldstein & Farmer, 1994). Researchers attribute the wide disparity in prevalence rates to the varying methodologies and definitions of sexual abuse used in each study. Studies that broadly define sexual abuse to include verbal propositions, for example, yield much higher estimates than do those using narrower definitions that only include forced sexual contact. Other definitions have included exposure, peeping, masturbation, unwanted kissing, and fondling (see Baker & Duncan, 1985; Finkelhor, Hotaling, Lewis, & Smith, 1990; Lindsay & Read, 1994; Russell, 1986, 1988; Williams & Finkelhor, 1992). Further complicating this problem, some studies fail to clarify the definition of sexual abuse being used (see Wassil-Grimm, 1995).

Because the primary focus of Benatar's essay is on recovered memories of abuse, the data she cites are also shaded by her failure to distinguish between incestuous and nonincestuous abuse. This is a critical point because the pathogenic and traumagenic nature of child sexual abuse has been linked in numerous studies to incest by a biological parent in general and, more specifically, to repeated molestation by fathers involving contact abuse and the use of force specifically (see Conte & Berliner, 1988; Elliott & Briere, 1992; Herman, 1981; Russell, 1986). Significantly, recovered memories typically involve repeated incest (see Bass & Davis, 1994).

It is difficult to obtain reliable data on incest because most studies do not make sufficient distinctions in their categorization of abusers. Based on a small number of retrospective studies, estimates indicate that approximately 4% to 5% of girls have reported being abused by a father, adoptive father, or stepfather before the age of 18 (Wassil-Grimm, 1995). Data from Williams and Finkelhor (1992) and Russell (1986) indicate that between 1% to 2.8% of girls are abused by a biological father. The rates are higher, of course, when abuse by other family members is included. Further, most cases of sexual abuse involve exhibition, masturbation, and both nongenital and genital touching rather than forced penetration (Lindsay & Read, 1994; Wakefield & Underwager, 1992). Russell's (1986) data showed a marked trend toward stepfathers abusing more frequently, using verbal threats, and being more severely abusive.

Two separate reviews of retrospective studies of childhood sexual abuse (Lindsay & Read, 1994; Wassil-Grimm, 1995) concluded that the preponderance of surveys indicate that the prevalence of intrafamilial incest is lower than the rates reported in the memory-recovery literature. In contrast, Demause (1991) contended that the known rates should be increased by 50% in order to correct for factors that lead to underreporting, including repression. Although the factors he cited are valid, his figures are based on pure speculation. Likewise, Bradshaw (1992) claimed that approximately 60% of all incest is repressed. To date, no replicable scientific evidence supports these claims. In a critique of what she sees as a "cycle of misinformation, faulty statistics, and unvalidated assertions" by incest-recovery authors, Tavris (1993) noted that inaccurate and sometimes concocted statistics are "traded like baseball cards, reprinted in every book and eventually enshrined as fact."

Another issue that is rarely discussed in the recovery literature is that not all children who are sexually abused experience the abuse as traumatic or develop psychological problems as an adult (Browne & Finkelhor, 1986; Kendall-Tacket, Williams, & Finkelhor, 1993; Russell, 1986). A review of recent empirical studies by Kendall-Tacket et al. (1993) found that many women are totally asymptomatic. Contradictory evidence also surrounds the relationship of sexual abuse to high levels of dissociation and multiple personality disorder (see Beitchman, Zucker, Heed, deCosta, & Cassavia, 1992; Brier & Elliott, 1993; Hacking, 1995; Kluft, 1985; Lindsay & Read, 1994; Nash, Hulsey, Sexton, Herralson, & Lambert, 1993a, 1993b). These findings should not minimize the severe trauma and psychological distress that some abuse victims experience; rather, they should alert us to the fact that the sequelae of childhood sexual abuse is not the same for all victims. Not surprisingly, those who demonstrate higher levels of traumatization and psychopathology are more often found in clinical samples than in the population in general (Russell, 1986).

It should be clear from the above discussion that *all* statistics on child sexual abuse should be interpreted very cautiously. Because of its hidden nature, child sexual abuse is seriously underreported. However, data from clinical samples, especially those samples undergoing therapy for childhood sexual abuse, are likely to overestimate its prevalence. Conversely, underestimates are likely if the data are based on retrospective surveys of adults in the general population, because some may choose not to report their abuse and some may not remember it. Despite discrepancies in the data, it is painfully clear that sexual abuse of children is a serious and pervasive problem that occurs more often than previously believed. As Pope and Hudson (1995) have astutely pointed out, even when conservative estimates of 10% for women and 5% for men are used, this means that 14,000,000 adults in the United States are former victims.

Revisiting Freud and Janet

Benatar gives a brief description of Freud and Janet's theories of repressed or dissociated trauma, supported only by historical case studies. Although case studies are an important source of information, they should not be confused with scientific findings. Despite a widespread belief in the validity of case reports that show repression or dissociation to be a common response to sexual abuse (see Blume, 1990; Chu & Dill, 1990; Courtois, 1988, 1992; Ellenson, 1989;

Erdelyi & Goldberg, 1979; Fredrickson, 1992; Kluft, 1985; Mennen & Pearlmut-
ter, 1993), little support for this belief can be found in empirical studies. In a
review of 60 years of research, Holmes (1990) could not find any controlled
studies that supported the concept of repression.

The few studies that were initially thought to provide possible evidence of
repression (Briere & Conte, 1993; Herman & Schatzow, 1987; Loftus, Polonsky,
& Fullilove, 1994; Williams, 1994) have yielded divergent results, with rates
ranging from 18% to 59%. Methodological limitations, however, restrict the
ability of any of these studies to support fully the mechanism of repression or
dissociation (see Lindsay & Read, 1994; Loftus, 1993; Pope & Hudson, 1995).
Despite Benatar's assertion that the Herman and Schatzow study supports the
claim of delayed traumatic recall, this study has received widespread criticism
because of its nonrepresentative sample, lack of specification of methodology
(including criteria for confirmation of abuse), the use of composites of cases,
little or no amnesia in the majority of cases, and the possibility of suggestion
during therapy (see Lindsay & Read, 1994; Pope & Hudson, 1995; Wassil-Grimm,
1995). In short, Herman and Schatzow's study is far from conclusive.

Studies have shown to the contrary that people typically remember their
past abuse. Loftus, Polonsky, and Fullilove (1994) found that in their sample of
105 women involved in outpatient treatment for substance abuse, the majority
(54%) reported a history of childhood sexual abuse; the vast majority (81%) had
always remembered their abuse. In Williams's (1994) study of 100 women with
documented histories of sexual abuse, the majority (62%) acknowledged their
abuse when asked by the researcher. Because no follow-up interview was conducted in either of these studies, it is impossible to know whether those failing
to report their past abuse did so due to repression, ordinary forgetting, normal
childhood amnesia, or the desire not to disclose a painful event. Femina, Yeager,
and Lewis's (1990) longitudinal study of 69 adults with documented histories
of child abuse (primarily physical) found no evidence of total amnesia. The majority (62%) readily reported their abuse to the interviewer. Those who initially
denied or minimized their abuse acknowledged in a follow-up "clarification"
interview that they did, in fact, remember their abuse but chose to withhold the
information for various reasons.

In order for us to validate the clinical impressions gained from current and
historical case histories, we need carefully designed studies to test the repres-
sion/dissociation hypothesis. Pope and Hudson (1995) suggested that the design
of the Williams study is a useful starting point. Strict criteria for inclusion and
the use of clarification interviews, similar to those used by Femina et al. (1990)
would be a necessary addition to the study design. Pope and Hudson proposed
that a series of case reports could be used to present preliminary evidence if they
strictly adhered to the research criteria. They noted that given the high prevalence of repression suggested by many authors, this area "begs further carefully
designed studies to resolve one of its most critical questions." In sum, both the
existence and prevalence of repression have yet to be scientifically validated; the
same is true for the type of dissociative amnesia hypothesized in the recovery
literature.

Traumatic Memory

In her discussion of traumatic memory, Benatar exhibits a serious misunderstanding of memory, in general, and memory organization, storage, and retrieval, in particular. Based on a narrow and inaccurate reading of van der Kolk and van der Hart's (1989) article, she presents an oversimplified typology of memory and compounds it with a misleading computer analogy.

Memory researchers widely accept that memory is *constructive* and *reconstructive,* not reproductive (Loftus, 1993; Loftus & Ketcham, 1994; Rose, 1992; Squire, 1987). Neuroscientist Steven Rose (1992) cautioned against the use of a flawed brain/computer metaphor:

> Brains do not work with information in the computer sense, but with *meaning* [which] is a historically and developmentally shaped process . . . because each time we remember, we in some senses do work on and transform our memories; they are not simply being called up from store. . . . Our memories are recreated each time we remember [emphasis added].

In their review of current research on memory processing, encoding, and state-dependent learning, van der Kolk and van der Hart (1989) reappraise Janet's early theory of psychopathological dissociation in an attempt to link it with recent findings. However, in contrast with Benatar's firm assertion that "traumatic memory is different," this is not what the authors conclude. They state that

> [Janet's notion] that traumatic memories are stored in memory in ways different from ordinary events is as challenging today as it was . . . almost 100 years ago. One century later, much remains to be learned about how memories are stored and keep on affecting emotions and behavior.

Likewise, in her ensuing discussion of trauma, dissociation, and memory, Benatar confuses theory with fact, stating that "if the trauma is verifiable and if it occurred early in life and was severe, these dissociated states act as containers for memories and pain and assume the coherence of alternate selves." Numerous studies on verifiable traumas (Leopold & Dillon, 1963; Malmquist, 1986; Pynoos & Nader, 1989; Strom et al., 1962; Terr, 1979, 1983) have shown to the contrary that vivid (although not necessarily accurate) recall of traumatic events is common. No subjects in these studies repressed the event or developed dissociative amnesia. Post-traumatic symptomatology most commonly involves intrusive images, flashbacks, nightmares, and anxiety attacks, such as those seen in Vietnam veterans.

It is also well established that adults rarely have recall of any events prior to the age of two or three and only sketchy memories up until age five (Fivush & Hudson, 1990; Loftus & Ketcham, 1994; Pendergast, 1995; Usher & Neisser, 1993). This normal "infantile amnesia" is developmentally based and is not due to trauma. Traumatic amnesia in adults is a well-documented phenomenon and involves either large portions of the memory (one's name, address, and other personal information) or circumscribed traumatic events, with good recall of everything prior to and subsequent to the event. In both cases, people are *aware* of the fact that they have amnesia (see Loftus & Ketcham, 1994).

In the last decade, with the revival of Freud's seduction theory and Janet's theory of dissociation, some clinicians and researchers have begun *theorizing* that traumatic memories of *repeated* childhood sexual abuse are encoded differently from other traumas and result in a total loss of awareness of not only the events but of the amnesia itself (see Herman, 1992; Terr, 1991, 1994). The idea that these painful memories are somehow "split off" or dissociated into compartmentalized areas of the mind remains an untested hypothesis. To date, attempts to establish a link between dissociated or repressed trauma and current findings in the neurobiology of memory have been speculative at best. Despite her personal conviction that traumatic memories and ordinary memories are qualitatively different, Herman (1992) acknowledged that "the biological factors underlying... traumatic dissociation remain an enigma." To paraphrase Klein (1977), we must avoid confusing what a theorist has merely claimed or believed with what she or he has actually proved or demonstrated. Even van der Kolk and van der Hart (1989) conceded that "we can neither confirm or [sic] contradict most of Janet's observations on memory disturbances following traumatization."

Veracity of Client Reports

Benatar is partly correct in her assertion that "veracity in therapy was never an issue until we began discussing issues of sexual abuse." However, this conclusion is based on the faulty premise that acceptance of a client's narrative truth is presumed to be an accurate historical account of events, which is not necessarily the case. In most cases, the veracity of a client's narrative report of life events is not an issue unless the therapist becomes aware of contradictions. It is important to note that allegations of sexual abuse, when made by children or adolescents, are now routinely subjected to extensive collateral verification by an independent investigator (Faller, 1988).

Although psychoanalysts since Freud have been trained to believe that memories of seduction and sexual abuse are incestuous wishes (Masson, 1990), the response on the part of most mental health professionals has been to ignore, minimize, or avoid the topic of sexual abuse (Craine, Henson, Colliver, & MacLean 1988; Jacobson, Koehler, & Jones-Brown, 1987; Post, Willett, Franks, House, & Weissberg, 1980; Rose, Peabody, & Stratigeas, 1991). Whether this is a result of disbelief is, according to Rose et al. (1991), a topic of endless debate. The fact that clinicians have routinely failed to inquire about or respond to reports of sexual abuse represents a serious omission, especially given the prevalence of abuse found in clinical populations.

Contrary to Masson's (1984) and Miller's (1984) assertions that Freud abandoned his theory about the primacy of incest in the etiology of hysteria, Demause (1991) argued that an unbiased reading of Freud shows that he continued to believe in his patients' spontaneous reports of *conscious* memories of abuse. Freud concluded that only *unconscious* memories of early infantile scenes of seduction were "phantasies which my patients had made up or which myself had perhaps forced on them" (cited in Demause, 1991). If Demause is correct, it would appear that even Freud came to question the veracity of *recovered* memories of sexual abuse but did not doubt those memories that were always remembered. In a similar vein, Hacking (1995) noted that Janet revised his early formulations and dropped the concept of dissociation in his later writings. He eventually came to believe that double (or multiple) personality was a special and rare case of bipolar disorder, which he termed "les circulaires." It is interesting that the proponents of recovered memory extensively cite his earlier work while ignoring his later ideas.

It is widely acknowledged that it is impossible to verify charges of sexual abuse in the absence of external corroboration. Because of its hidden nature and the tendency for perpetrators to deny their guilt, it is sometimes difficult to find the necessary corroboration, especially decades after the alleged abuse occurred. But we must be clear that clinical judgment alone is not a sufficient predictor of veracity. In his discussion of the child sexual abuse accommodation syndrome, Summit (1983, 1992) acknowledged that "there is no clinical method available to distinguish valid claims from those that should be treated as fantasy or deception." He further cautioned that "the capacity to listen and the willingness to believe . . . is not an admonition to interrogate or assume that every disclosure is real" (Summit, 1992). Clearly, we must be open to listening to our clients and willing to help them explore issues of past abuse. However, we must be cautious about accepting a client's narrative truth as historical fact in the absence of corroboration. This is especially true in the case of recovered memories; some memories may be fully accurate, some may be partly accurate, and some may be totally false. This does not imply that we should disbelieve our clients but rather that we maintain a neutral stance about historical accuracy. Historical accuracy becomes mandatory, however, when this debate is moved from the therapist's office into the courtroom (see Gutheil, 1993; Slovenko, 1993).

A more controversial but intricately related issue that Benatar fails to address is that of recovered memories of satanic ritual abuse, alien abductions, past lives, preverbal body memories, in *utero* trauma, and cellular memory (see Goldstein & Farmer, 1993, 1994; Mack, 1994; Mulhern, 1991; Pendergrast, 1995; Richardson, Best, & Bromley, 1991; Robbins, 1995; Smith, 1995; Victor, 1993). These memories raise interesting questions regarding both the veracity of client reports and the therapeutic methods used to retrieve or recover them: Are all such memories possible? If not, which ones are? Where do we draw the line? Based on what criteria? How can we determine their accuracy? These questions are significant because a growing number of therapists involved in memory-recovery therapy believe in the validity and accuracy of all recovered memories (Loftus, Garry, Brown, & Rader, 1994; Smith, 1995; Yapko, 1994a, 1994b). Not surprisingly, their clients come to believe in them as well.

False Memories: Fact or Fiction?

Skepticism about "false memories" is often voiced by proponents of recovered memory because it is seen as a backlash to the discovery of childhood sexual abuse and an attempt to silence the victims; as such, false memories are equated with "denial" of abuse (Bloom, 1995; Rockwell, 1995). In the past several years this has become the subject of debate in scholarly journals and professional conferences. Because these issues become tangled and confused, it is important once again to make the distinction between the debate about memory and the documented reality of abuse; the false-memory debate is not about the latter.

A growing body of research has shown that partially and wholly inaccurate memories are not an unusual phenomenon. Because memory is extremely malleable, it is influenced by various factors, and false memories can be created through exposure to misinformation (Loftus, 1993; Terr, 1994). According to Terr, a false memory can be "a strongly imagined memory, a totally distorted memory, a lie, or a misconstructed impression." Numerous studies have shown that people can be led to construct not only inaccurate and confabulated details of past events, but detailed memories of entire events that never happened (see Haugaard, Reppucci, Laurd, & Nauful, 1991; Loftus, 1993; Loftus & Ketcham, 1994; Neisser & Harsch, 1992; Pynoos & Nader, 1989; Spanos, Menary, Gabora, DuBreuil, & Dewhirst, 1991).

Evidence about erroneous memory has sparked concern that memories of abuse are being created by therapists who, through well-intentioned but misguided therapeutic methods, may directly or indirectly evoke specious memories with the use of hypnosis, guided visualization, "truth" drugs, abreactive therapy, dream and body memory interpretation, or suggestive questioning (Byrd, 1994; Gangelhoff, 1995; Gutheil, 1993; Lindsay & Read, 1994; Loftus, 1993; Ofshe & Watters, 1994; Pendergast, 1995; Yapko, 1994a). Although proponents of recovered memory therapy incorrectly believe that false or suggested memories cannot be experienced with the same emotional intensity as can recovered memories of real trauma, evidence suggests otherwise (see Loftus & Ketcham, 1994; Yapko, 1994a). As Loftus and Ketcham noted, reconstructed memories, once adopted, come to be believed in as strongly as genuine memories. Concern about false memory is bolstered by detailed accounts of coercive therapy and lawsuits filed by "retractors"—hundreds of women who have left therapy and recanted their allegations of abuse (see Goldstein & Farmer, 1993, 1994; Pendergrast, 1995).

Studies documenting distorted and confabulated memory in children and adults have been discounted by some proponents of memory recovery because they do not speak directly to the issue of false memories of childhood sexual abuse. Benatar echoes this position along with reservations similar to those noted by Berliner and Williams (1994) and Pezdek (1994) that little scientific evidence supports the claim that false memories of abuse are common or that memory-recovery therapy is widespread. Because little research has been done in this area, this is an accurate appraisal of our lack of scientific knowledge about false memories induced in therapy. However, it is noteworthy that many who accept the "truth" of recovered memories of childhood victimization are not willing to extend the same credibility to those who claim they were victimized by their therapists. Nonetheless, methodologically sound studies are necessary to validate the phenomena of false memory as well as recovered memory; we must rely on the same standard of proof for both.

Where Do We Go From Here?

Clearly, the reluctance of clinicians to address the reality of child sexual abuse poses a serious barrier to accurate and effective assessment and treatment. Rose et al. (1991) noted that "short- and long-term sequelae result not only from sexual and physical abuse, but from inappropriate treatment and nonrecognition of the abuse." Given social work's commitment to multidimensional assessment and holistic, nondichotomous thinking (see Compton & Galaway, 1989; Haynes & Holmes, 1994; Hepworth & Larsen, 1993; Morales & Sheafor, 1995), it is critical that clinical practitioners gather accurate information about their client's past and present biopsychosocial functioning, strengths and resources, developmental history, significant life events, and reactions to and feelings about these events. In this holistic context, it would be unconscionable to fail to inquire about physical and sexual abuse—past or present. We must be sensitive to the fact that clients may choose initially not to disclose their abuse until a level of trust is developed in the therapeutic relationship. Failure to disclose should not *automatically* be assumed to be due to repression or dissociation.

We must also be cautious about hastily attributing a laundry list of non-specific symptoms to prior abuse, as this defeats the purpose of a multidimensional assessment. When a previously repressed history of sexual abuse is revealed, it is especially important to consider the use of collateral sources of information because clients may themselves be confused about these memories. However, collateral sources should never be used without the client's express permission. The use of collateral sources does not imply that the social workers should take on the dual roles of investigator and therapist, because doing so represents a serious conflict of interest (Mason, 1991). Instead, collateral information should be used to help both the practitioner and the client gain a well-rounded picture of the situation. Hepworth and Larsen (1993) noted that important factors that may otherwise be overlooked can often be identified by persons close to the client. According to van der Kolk and van der Hart (1989), Janet frequently interviewed his patients' family members and acquaintances in order to get as complete a picture as possible.

Conclusion

Social workers who work with victims of childhood sexual abuse, especially those whose claim is based solely on recovered memories, should become acquainted with the full range of clinical and social scientific literature on the topic. Clinical case studies must be balanced with scientific findings; both are crucial sources of knowledge. Many clinicians receive only training or information that supports a narrow ideology and practice methodology. As I have suggested elsewhere (Robbins, 1995), social workers must be fully informed in order to "evaluate critically these disparate ideological positions and the adequacy of the research that supports them." This is especially important because a recent study by Feld (1995) found that few social workers are provided with any content about memory or memory retrieval in their academic programs.

In addition, social workers need to be fully aware of their own personal biases in order to prevent them from interfering with assessment and treatment. Preconceived beliefs about repression, dissociation, and recovered memories may lead to an ideological stance that inhibits thorough and accurate assessment. It is imperative that we recognize the serious consequences for our clients and their families when our personal biases lead us to either underdiagnose or overdiagnose childhood sexual abuse. Further, we must remember that the imposition of our personal values and beliefs is antithetical to our deeply held value of client self-determination (Hepworth & Larsen, 1993).

As a result of the lack of scientific verification and the polemical debate shaping research and practice, we must wade cautiously through the muddy waters of recovered memory. Social workers may feel caught between two conflicting sets of claims that demand allegiance to one side or the other. It is doubtful, however, that positioning ourselves at the extremes of this debate will lead to a stance that is in the best interests of our clients. Amid the black and white positions of what Loftus and Ketcham (1994) call the "true believers" and "skeptics," a middle-ground stance is often hard to find, despite the grey areas of uncertainty and ambiguity that exist. Acknowledgment of these grey areas does not mean, however, that one is in "denial" or is uncaring or negligent as a practitioner. We must be open to new findings in this area but we must also be cautious in distinguishing between conjecture and fact.

Finally, when skepticism about the ideology of the recovery movement is based on a thorough review of valid, scientific findings, it must not be cast as antifeminist backlash. As Klein (1977) aptly noted, "Scientific questions are to be settled by appeals to evidence rather than by appeals to authority—even the authority of a Freud."

CHALLENGE QUESTIONS

Do Adults Repress Childhood Sexual Abuse?

1. Find out what Sigmund Freud believed about childhood memories. Do you believe that Freud's theories on memories of child sexual abuse are relevant today? Why, or why not?
2. Referring to the selection by Robbins, how would you account for the wide disparity in prevalence rates of child sexual abuse? How might data gathering be improved to settle the disparity?
3. If you were a therapist and your client claimed to suddenly remember being sexually abused at an early age, how would you discern whether or not your client had actually been abused? What evidence would you need?
4. What does cognitive research say about the storage and retrieval of memories? What does this research imply about traumatic memories?

ISSUE 10

Do Rewards Facilitate Learning?

YES: Paul Chance, from "The Rewards of Learning," *Phi Delta Kappan* (November 1992)

NO: Alfie Kohn, from "Rewards Versus Learning: A Response to Paul Chance," *Phi Delta Kappan* (June 1993)

ISSUE SUMMARY

YES: Paul Chance, a teacher at James H. Groves Adult High School in Georgetown, Delaware, asserts that using reinforcement is the most effective way to help people learn.

NO: Alfie Kohn, a writer and lecturer on psychological and educational issues, argues that using external reinforcers actually decreases an individual's interest in learning.

Johnny, a third grader, is having trouble staying still and studying for his upcoming test. In order to help Johnny study, his teacher proposes to give him a piece of candy if he gets at least a B on the test. Is it acceptable to offer external rewards for learning? Would you study harder for some candy? Probably not, but would you study harder for $10? How about $100?

Behaviorism, elaborated by psychologists such as B. F. Skinner and E. L. Thorndike, proposes that we learn with the help of reinforcements. If the results of our actions are pleasing, or reinforcing, then we are more likely to repeat those actions. If, on the other hand, our actions lead to unpleasant results, then we are less likely to repeat the behavior. Behaviorists draw upon experimental evidence to support this theory. Using reinforcements, psychologists have been able to train pigeons to do unusual things. When the animal performs the desired behavior, it is reinforced—that is, it is given a reward, such as food. Presumably, the animal repeats the behavior in hopes of receiving another reward.

Although most experimental evidence concerns animal learning, most behaviorists believe that these same training techniques can be used to bring about desired behavior in people. In the case of Johnny, for example, the teacher should be able to train him to study for his test through some reward or reinforcement system.

Paul Chance argues for this behavioral viewpoint in the following selection. He contends that reinforcement is necessary to help people learn. Indeed, Chance maintains that the lack of success in American schools is due to the absence of a systematic application of reinforcement. He likens trying to teach children without extrinsic rewards to trying to teach children to become artists by blindfolding them—it just will not work.

In the second selection, Alfie Kohn responds to Chance, arguing that the use of external rewards *decreases* student interest in learning. As long as one is learning for an extrinsic reward, he says, one will only learn as long as the reward lasts. Learning becomes a nuisance that must be done in order to get the reward. In this sense, external rewards may bring about short-term compliance, but they will eventually lead to long-term negative consequences. A student must be motivated intrinsically for long-term educational success, concludes Kohn.

POINT

- Reinforcement improves both class conduct and rate of learning.
- Extrinsic rewards motivate a child to learn.
- Intrinsic rewards are not enough for efficient learning—extrinsic rewards must be used.

- Intrinsic rewards are often too remote to be effective.

COUNTERPOINT

- Reinforcement impedes performance.
- Extrinsic rewards undermine a student's motivation to learn.
- Extrinsic rewards make learning a means to an end (the reward). As such, learning will only occur as long as the reward is available.
- Effective teaching makes learning concrete and intrinsic rewards available.

Paul Chance  **YES**

The Rewards of Learning

Aman is seated at a desk. Before him lie a pencil and a large stack of blank paper. He picks up the pencil, closes his eyes, and attempts to draw a four-inch line. He makes a second attempt, a third, a fourth, and so on, until he has made well over a hundred attempts at drawing a four-inch line, all without ever opening his eyes. He repeats the exercise for several days, until he has drawn some 3,000 lines, all with his eyes closed. On the last day, he examines his work. The question is, How much improvement has there been in his ability to draw a four-inch line? How much has he learned from his effort?

E. L. Thorndike, the founder of educational psychology and a major figure in the scientific analysis of learning, performed this experiment years ago, using himself as subject.[1] He found no evidence of learning. His ability to draw a four-inch line was no better on the last day than it had been on the first.

The outcome of this experiment may seem obvious to us today, but it was an effective way of challenging a belief widely held earlier in this century, a belief that formed the very foundation of education at the time: the idea that "practice makes perfect."

It was this blind faith in practice that justified countless hours of rote drill as a standard teaching technique. Thorndike's experiment demonstrated that practice in and of itself is not sufficient for learning. Based on this and other, more formal studies, Thorndike concluded that practice is important only insofar as it provides the opportunity for reinforcement.

To reinforce means to strengthen, and among learning researchers *reinforcement* refers to a procedure for strengthening behavior (that is, making it likely to be repeated) by providing certain kinds of consequences. These consequences, called *reinforcers,* are usually events or things a person willingly seeks out. For instance, we might teach a person to draw a four-inch line with his eyes closed merely by saying "good" each time the effort is within half an inch of the goal. Most people like to succeed, so this positive feedback should be an effective way of reinforcing the appropriate behavior.

Hundreds of experimental studies have demonstrated that systematic use of reinforcement can improve both classroom conduct and the rate of learning. Yet the systematic use of reinforcement has never been widespread in American schools. In *A Place Called School,* John Goodlad reports that, in the elementary grades, an average of only 2% of class time is devoted to reinforcement; in the high schools, the figure falls to 1%.[2]

The Costs of Reward

There are probably many reasons for our failure to make the most of reinforcement. For one thing, few schools of education provide more than cursory instruction in its use. Given Thorndike's finding about the role of practice in learning, it is ironic that many teachers actually use the term *reinforcement* as a synonym for *practice*. ("We assign workbook exercises for reinforcement.") If schools of education do not teach future teachers the nature of reinforcement and how to use it effectively, teachers can hardly be blamed for not using it.

The unwanted effects of misused reinforcement have led some teachers to shy away from it. The teacher who sometimes lets a noisy class go to recess early will find the class getting noisier before recess. If high praise is reserved for long-winded essays, students will develop wordy and redundant writing styles. And it should surprise no one if students are seldom original in classrooms where only conventional work is admired or if they are uncooperative in classrooms where one can earn recognition only through competition. Reinforcement is powerful stuff, and its misuse can cause problems.

Another difficulty is that the optimal use of reinforcement would mean teaching in a new way. Some studies suggest that maximum learning in elementary and middle schools might require very high rates of reinforcement, perhaps with teachers praising someone in the class an average of once very 15 seconds.[3] Such a requirement is clearly incompatible with traditional teaching practices.

Systematic reinforcement can also mean more work for the teacher. Reinforcing behavior once every 15 seconds means 200 reinforcements in a 50-minute period—1,000 reinforcements in a typical school day. It also implies that, in order to spot behavior to reinforce, the teacher must be moving about the room, not sitting at a desk marking papers. That may be too much to ask. Some studies have found that teachers who have been taught how to make good use of reinforcement often revert to their old style of teaching. This is so even though the teachers acknowledge that increased use of reinforcement means fewer discipline problems and a much faster rate of learning.[4]

Reinforcement also runs counter to our Puritan traditions. Most Americans have always assumed—occasional protestations to the contrary notwithstanding—that learning should be hard work and at least slightly unpleasant. Often the object of education seems to be not so much to teach academic and social skills as to "build character" through exposure to adversity. When teachers reinforce students at a high rate, the students experience a minimum of adversity and actually enjoy learning. Thus some people think that reinforcement is bad for character development.

All of these arguments against reinforcement can be countered effectively. Schools of education do not provide much instruction in the practical use of reinforcement, but there is no reason why they cannot do so. Reinforcement can be used incorrectly and with disastrous results, but the same might be said of other powerful tools. Systematic use of reinforcement means teaching in a new way, but teachers can learn to do so.[5] A great deal of reinforcement is needed for optimum learning, but not all of the reinforcement needs to come from the teacher. (Reinforcement can be provided by computers and other teaching devices, by teacher aides, by parents, and by students during peer teaching and cooperative learning.) No doubt people do sometimes benefit from adversity, but the case for the character-building properties of adversity is very weak.[6]

However, there is one argument against reinforcement that cannot be dismissed so readily. For some 20 years, the claim has been made that systematic reinforcement actually undermines student learning. Those few teachers who make extensive use of reinforcement, it is claimed, do their students a disservice because reinforcement reduces interest in the reinforced activity.

Not all forms of reinforcement are considered detrimental. A distinction is made between reinforcement involving intrinsic reinforcers—or rewards, as they are often called—and reinforcement involving extrinsic rewards.[7] Only extrinsic rewards are said to be harmful. An *intrinsic reward* is ordinarily the natural consequence of behavior, hence the name. We learn to throw darts by seeing how close the dart is to the target; learn to type by seeing the right letters appear on the computer screen; learn to cook from the pleasant sights, fragrances, and flavors that result from our culinary efforts; learn to read from the understanding we get from the printed word; and learn to solve puzzles by finding solutions. The Japanese say, "The bow teaches the archer." They are talking about intrinsic rewards, and they are right.

Extrinsic rewards come from an outside source, such as a teacher. Probably the most ubiquitous extrinsic reward (and one of the most effective) is praise. The teacher reinforces behavior by saying "good," "right," "correct," or "excellent" when the desired behavior occurs. Other extrinsic rewards involve nonverbal behavior such as smiles, winks, thumbs-up signs, hugs, congratulatory handshakes, pats on the back, or applause. Gold stars, certificates, candy, prizes, and even money have been used as rewards, but they are usually less important in teaching—and even in the maintenance of good discipline—than those mentioned earlier.

The distinction between intrinsic and extrinsic rewards is somewhat artificial. Consider the following example. You put money into a vending machine and retrieve a candy bar. The behavior of inserting money into a vending machine has been reinforced, as has the more general behavior of interacting with machines. But is the food you receive an intrinsic or an extrinsic reward? On the one hand, the food is the automatic consequence of inserting money and pressing buttons, so it would appear to be an intrinsic reward. On the other hand, the food is a consequence that was arranged by the designer of the machine, so it would seem to be an extrinsic reward.

Though somewhat contrived, the distinction between intrinsic and extrinsic rewards has been maintained partly because extrinsic rewards are said to be damaging.[8] Are they? First, let us be clear about the charge. The idea is that— if teachers smile, praise, congratulate, say "thank you" or "right," shake hands, hug, give a pat on the back, applaud, provide a certificate of achievement or attendance, *or in any way provide a positive consequence (a reward) for student behavior*—the student will be less inclined to engage in that behavior when the reward is no longer available.

For example, teachers who offer prizes to students for reading books will, it is said, make the children less likely to read when prizes are no longer available. The teacher who reads a student's story aloud to the class as an example of excellent story writing actually makes the student less likely to write stories in the future, when such public approval is not forthcoming. When teachers (and students) applaud a youngster who has given an excellent talk, they make that student disinclined to give talks in the future. The teacher who comments favorably on the originality of a painting steers the young artist away from painting. And so on. This is the charge against extrinsic rewards.

No one disputes the effectiveness of extrinsic rewards in teaching or in maintaining good discipline. Some might therefore argue that extrinsic rewards should be used, even if they reduce interest in learning. Better to have students who read only when required to do so, some might say, than to have students who cannot read at all.

But if rewards do reduce interest, that fact is of tremendous importance. "The teacher may count himself successful," wrote B. F. Skinner, "when his students become engrossed in his field, study conscientiously, and do more than is required of them, but *the important thing is what they do when they are no longer being taught*" (emphasis added).[9] It is not enough for students to learn the three R's and a little science and geography; they must be prepared for a lifetime of learning. To reduce their interest in learning would be a terrible thing—even if it were done in the interest of teaching them effectively.

The question of whether rewards adversely affect motivation is not, then, of merely academic or theoretical importance. It is of great practical importance to the classroom teacher.

More than 100 studies have examined this question.[10] In a typical experiment, Mark Lepper and his colleagues observed 3- to 5-year-old nursery school children playing with various kinds of toys.[11] The toys available included felt tip pens of various colors and paper to draw on. The researchers noted the children's inclination to draw during this period. Next the researchers took the children aside and asked them to draw with the felt tip pens. The researchers promised some children a "Good Player Award" for drawing. Other children drew pictures without receiving an award.

Two weeks later, the researchers returned to the school, provided felt tip pens and paper, and observed the children's inclination to draw. They found that children who had been promised an award spent only half as much time drawing as they had originally. Those students who had received no award showed no such decline in interest.

Most studies in this area follow the same general outline: 1) students are given the opportunity to participate in an activity without rewards; 2) they are given extrinsic rewards for participating in the activity; and 3) they are again given the opportunity to participate in the activity without rewards.

The outcomes of the studies are also fairly consistent. Not surprisingly, there is usually a substantial increase in the activity during the second stage, when extrinsic rewards are available. And, as expected, participation in the activity declines sharply when rewards are no longer available. However, interest sometimes falls below the initial level, so that students are less interested in the activity than they had been before receiving rewards. It is this net loss of motivation that is of concern.

Researchers have studied this decline in motivation and found that it occurs only under certain circumstances. For example, the effect is most likely to occur when the initial interest in the activity is very high, when the rewards used are *not* reinforcers, and when the rewards are held out in advance as incentives.[12]

But perhaps the best predictor of negative effects is the nature of the "reward contingency" involved. (The term *reward contingency* has to do with the nature of the relationship between behavior and its reward.) Alyce Dickinson reviewed the research literature in this area and identified three kinds of reward contingency:[13]

Task-contingent rewards are available for merely participating in an activity, without regard to any standard of performance. Most studies that find a decline in interest in a rewarded activity involve task-contingent rewards. In the Lepper study described above, for instance, children received an award for drawing *regardless of how they drew.* The reward was task-contingent.

Performance-contingent rewards are available only when the student achieves a certain standard. Performance-contingent rewards sometimes produce negative results. For instance, Edward Deci offered college students money for solving puzzles, $1 for each puzzle solved. The rewarded students were later less inclined to work on the puzzles than were students who had not been paid. Unfortunately, these results are difficult to interpret because the students sometimes failed to meet the reward standard, and failure itself is known to reduce interest in an activity.[14]

Success-contingent rewards are given for good performance and might reflect either success or progress toward a goal. Success-contingent rewards do not have negative effects; in fact, they typically *increase* interest in the rewarded activity. For example, Ross Vasta and Louise Stirpe awarded gold stars to third- and fourth-graders each time they completed a kind of math exercise they enjoyed. After seven days of awards, the gold stars stopped. Not only was there no evidence of a loss in interest, but time spent on the math activity actually increased. Nor was there any decline in the quality of the work produced.[15]

Dickinson concludes that the danger of undermining student motivation stems not from extrinsic rewards, but from the use of inappropriate reward contingencies. Rewards reduce motivation when they are given without regard to performance or when the performance standard is so high that students frequently fail. When students have a high rate of success and when those successes are rewarded, the rewards *do not have negative effects.* Indeed, success-contingent rewards tend to increase interest in the activity. This finding, writes Dickinson, "is robust and consistent." She adds that "even strong opponents of contingent rewards recognize that success-based rewards do not have harmful effects."[16]

The evidence, then, shows that extrinsic rewards can either enhance or reduce interest in an activity, depending on how they are used. Still, it might be argued that, because extrinsic rewards *sometimes* cause problems, we might be wise to avoid their use altogether. The decision not to use extrinsic rewards amounts to a decision to rely on alternatives. What are those alternatives? And are they better than extrinsic rewards?

Alternatives to Rewards

Punishment and the threat of punishment are—and probably always have been—the most popular alternatives to extrinsic rewards. Not so long ago, lessons were "taught to the tune of a hickory stick," but the tune was not merely tapped on a desk. Students who did not learn their lessons were not only beaten; they were also humiliated: they sat on a stool (up high, so everyone could see) and wore a silly hat.

Gradually, more subtle forms of punishment were used. "The child at his desk," wrote Skinner, "filling in his workbook, is behaving primarily to escape from the threat of a series of minor aversive events—the teacher's displeasure, the criticism or ridicule of his classmates, an ignominious showing in a competition, low marks, a trip to the office 'to be talked to' by the principal, or a word to the parent who may still resort to the birch rod."[17] Skinner spent a lifetime inveighing against the use of such "aversives," but his efforts were largely ineffective. While extrinsic rewards have been condemned, punishment and the threat of punishment are widely sanctioned.

Punishment is popular because, in the short run at least, it gets results. This is illustrated by an experiment in which Deci and Wayne Cascio told students that, if they did not solve problems correctly within a time limit, they would be exposed to a loud, unpleasant sound. The threat worked: all the students solved all the problems within the time limit, so the threat never had to be fulfilled. Students who were merely rewarded for correct solutions did not do nearly as well.[18]

But there are serious drawbacks to the use of punishment. For one thing, although punishment motivates students to learn, it does not teach them. Or, rather, it teaches them only what *not* to do, not what *to* do. "We do not teach [a student] to learn quickly," Skinner observed, "by punishing him when he learns slowly, or to recall what he has learned by punishing him when he forgets, or to think logically by punishing him when he is illogical."[19]

Punishment also has certain undesirable side effects.[20] To the extent that punishment works, it works by making students anxious. Students get nervous before a test because they fear a poor grade, and they are relieved or anxious when they receive their report card depending on whether or not the grades received will result in punishment from their parents.[21] Students can and do avoid the anxiety caused by such punishment by cutting classes and dropping out of school. We do the same thing when we cancel or "forget" a dental appointment.

Another response to punishment is aggression. Students who do not learn easily—and who therefore cannot readily avoid punishment—are especially apt to become aggressive. Their aggression often takes the form of lying, cheating, stealing, and refusing to cooperate. Students also act out by cursing, by being rude and insulting, by destroying property, and by hitting people. Increasingly, teachers are the objects of these aggressive acts.

Finally, it should be noted that punishment has the same negative impact on intrinsic motivation as extrinsic rewards are alleged to have. In the Deci and Cascio study just described, for example, when students were given the chance to work on puzzles with the threat of punishment removed, they were less likely to do so than were students who had never worked under the threat of punishment.[22] Punishment in the form of criticism of performance also reduces interest in an activity.[23]

Punishment is not the only alternative to the use of extrinsic rewards. Teachers can also encourage students. Encouragement consists of various forms of behavior intended to induce students to perform. We encourage students when we urge them to try, express confidence in their ability to do assignments, and recite such platitudes as "A winner never quits and a quitter never wins."

In encouraging students, we are not merely urging them to perform, however; we are implicitly suggesting a relationship between continued performance and certain consequences. "Come on, Billy—you can do it" means, "If you persist at this task, you will be rewarded with success." The power of encouragement is ultimately dependent on the occurrence of the implied consequence. If the teacher tells Billy he can do it and if he tries and fails, future urging by the teacher will be less effective.

Another problem with encouragement is that, like punishment, it motivates but does not teach. The student who is urged to perform a task is not thereby taught how to perform it. Encouragement is a safer procedure than punishment, since it is less likely to provoke anxiety or aggression. Students who are repeatedly urged to do things at which they ultimately fail do, however, come to distrust the judgment of the teacher. They also come to believe that they cannot live up to the expectations of teachers—and therefore must be hopelessly stupid.

Intrinsic rewards present the most promising alternative to extrinsic rewards. Experts on reinforcement, including defenders of extrinsic rewards, universally sing the praises of intrinsic rewards. Unlike punishment and encouragement, intrinsic rewards actually teach. Students who can see that they have solved a problem correctly know how to solve other problems of that sort. And, unlike extrinsic rewards, intrinsic rewards do not depend on the teacher or some other person.

But there are problems with intrinsic rewards, just as there are with extrinsic ones. Sometimes students lack the necessary skills to obtain intrinsic rewards. Knowledge, understanding, and the aesthetic pleasures of language are all intrinsic rewards for reading, but they are not available to those for whom reading is a difficult and painful activity.

Often, intrinsic rewards are too remote to be effective. If a student is asked to add $3 + 7$, what is the intrinsic reward for answering correctly? The student who learns to add will one day experience the satisfaction of checking the accuracy of a restaurant bill, but this future reward is of no value to the youngster just learning to add. Though important in maintaining what has been learned, intrinsic rewards are often too remote to be effective reinforcers in the early stages of learning.

One problem that often goes unnoticed is that the intrinsic rewards for academic work are often weaker than the rewards available for other behavior. Students are rewarded for looking out the window, daydreaming, reading comic books, taking things from other students, passing notes, telling and listening to jokes, moving about the room, fighting, talking back to the teacher, and for all sorts of activities that are incompatible with academic learning. Getting the right answer to a grammar question might be intrinsically rewarding, but for many students it is considerably less rewarding than the laughter of one's peers in response to a witty remark.

While intrinsic rewards are important, then, they are insufficient for efficient learning.[24] Nor will encouragement and punishment fill the gap. The teacher must supplement intrinsic rewards with extrinsic rewards. This means not only telling the student when he or she has succeeded, but also praising, complimenting, applauding, and providing other forms of recognition for good work. Some students may need even stronger reinforcers, such as special privileges, certificates, and prizes.

Reward Guidelines

Yet we cannot ignore the fact that extrinsic rewards can have adverse effects on student motivation. While there seems to be little chance of serious harm, it behooves us to use care. Various experts have suggested guidelines to follow in using extrinsic rewards.[25] Here is a digest of their recommendations:

1. Use the weakest reward required to strengthen a behavior. Don't use money if a piece of candy will do; don't use candy if praise will do. The good effects of reinforcement come not so much from the reward itself as from the reward contingency: the relationship between the reward and the behavior.
2. When possible, avoid using rewards as incentives. For example, don't say, "If you do X, I'll give you Y." Instead, ask the student to perform a task and then provide a reward for having completed it. In most cases, rewards work best if they are pleasant surprises.
3. Reward at a high rate in the early stages of learning, and reduce the frequency of rewards as learning progresses. Once students have the alphabet down pat, there is no need to compliment them each time they print a letter correctly. Nor is there much need to reward behavior that is already occurring at a high rate.
4. Reward only the behavior you want repeated. If students who whine and complain get their way, expect to see a lot of whining and complaining. Similarly, if you provide gold stars only for the three best papers in the class, you are rewarding competition and should not be surprised if students do not cooperate with one another. And if "spelling doesn't count," don't expect to see excellent spelling.

5. Remember that what is an effective reward for one student may not work well with another. Some students respond rapidly to teacher attention: others do not. Some work well for gold stars: others don't. Effective rewards are ordinarily things that students seek—positive feedback, praise, approval, recognition, toys—but ultimately a reward's value is to be judged by its effect on behavior.

6. Reward success, and set standards so that success is within the student's grasp. In today's heterogeneous classrooms, that means setting standards for each student. A good way to do this is to reward improvement or progress toward a goal. Avoid rewarding students merely for participating in an activity, without regard for the quality of their performance.

7. Bring attention to the rewards (both intrinsic and extrinsic) that are available for behavior from sources *other than the teacher.* Point out, for example, the fun to be had from the word play in poetry or from sharing a poem with another person. Show students who are learning computer programming the pleasure in "making the computer do things." Let students know that it's okay to applaud those who make good presentations so that they can enjoy the approval of their peers for a job well done. Ask parents to talk with their children about school and to praise them for learning. The goal is to shift the emphasis from rewards provided by the teacher to those that will occur even when the teacher is not present.

Following these rules is harder in practice than it might seem, and most teachers will need training in their implementation. But reinforcement is probably the most powerful tool available to teachers, and extrinsic rewards are powerful reinforcers. To teach without using extrinsic rewards is analogous to asking our students to learn to draw with their eyes closed. Before you do that, we should open our own eyes.

Notes

1. E. L. Thorndike, *Human Learning* (1931; reprint ed., Cambridge, Mass.: MIT Press, 1966).

2. John I. Goodlad, *A Place Called School: Prospects for the Future* (New York: McGraw-Hill, 1984). Goodlad complains about the "paucity of praise" in schools. In doing so, he echoes B. F. Skinner, who wrote that "perhaps the most serious criticism of the current classroom is the relative infrequency of reinforcement." See B. F. Skinner, *The Technology of Teaching* (Englewood Cliffs, N.J.: Prentice Hall, 1968), p. 17.

3. Bill L. Hopkins and R. J. Conard, "Putting It All Together: Superschool," in Norris G. Haring and Richard L. Schiefelbusch, eds., *Teaching Special Children* (New York: McGraw-Hill, 1975), pp. 342–85. Skinner suggests that mastering the first four years of arithmetic instruction efficiently would require something on the order of 25,000 reinforcements. See Skinner, op. cit.

4. See, for example, Bill L. Hopkins, "Comments on the Future of Applied Behavior Analysis," *Journal of Applied Behavior Analysis,* vol. 20, 1987, pp. 339–46....

5. See, for example, Hopkins and Conard, op. cit.

6. For example, Mihaly Csikszentmihalyi found that adults who are successful and happy tend to have had happy childhoods.... See Tina Adler, "Support and Challenge: Both Key for Smart Kids," *APA Monitor,* September 1991, pp. 10–11.

7. The terms *reinforcer* and *reward* are often used interchangeably, but they are not really synonyms. A reinforcer is defined by its effects: an event that strengthens the behavior it follows is a reinforcer, regardless of what it was intended to do. A reward is defined by social convention as something desirable; it may or may not strengthen the behavior it follows. The distinction is important since some studies that show negative effects from extrinsic rewards use rewards that are *not* reinforcers. See Alyce M. Dickinson, "The Detrimental Effects of Extrinsic Reinforcement on 'Intrinsic Motivation,'" *The Behavior Analyst,* vol. 12, 1989, pp. 1–15.

8. ... See Alyce M. Dickinson, "Exploring New Vistas," *Performance Management Magazine,* vol. 9, 1991, p. 28....

9. Skinner, p. 162.

10. For reviews of this literature, see Edward L. Deci and Richard M. Ryan, *Intrinsic Motivation and Self-Determination in Human Behavior* (New York: Plenum, 1985); Dickinson, "The Detrimental Effects"; and Mark R. Lepper and David Greene, eds., *The Hidden Costs of Reward: New Perspectives on the Psychology of Human Motivation* (Hillsdale, N.J.: Erlbaum, 1978).

11. Mark R. Lepper, David Greene, and Richard E. Nisbett, "Undermining Children's Intrinsic Interest with Extrinsic Rewards," *Journal of Personality and Social Psychology,* vol. 28, 1973, pp. 129–37.

12. See, for example, Dickinson, "The Detrimental Effects"; and Mark Morgan, "Reward-Induced Decrements and Increments in Intrinsic Motivation." *Review of Educational Research,* vol. 54, 1984, pp. 5–30....

13. Dickinson, "The Detrimental Effects."

14. Edward L. Deci, "Effects of Externally Mediated Rewards on Intrinsic Motivation," *Journal of Personality and Social Psychology,* vol. 18, 1971, pp. 105–15.

15. Ross Vasta and Louise A. Stirpe, "Reinforcement Effects on Three Measures of Children's Interest in Math," *Behavior Modification,* vol. 3, 1979, pp. 223–44.

16. Dickinson, "The Detrimental Effects," p. 9. See also Morgan, op. cit.

17. Skinner, p. 15.

18. Edward L. Deci and Wayne F. Cascio, "Changes in Intrinsic Motivation as a Function of Negative Feedback and Threats," paper presented at the annual meeting of the Eastern Psychological Association, Boston, May 1972. This paper is summarized in Edward L. Deci and Joseph Porac, "Cognitive Evaluation Theory and the Study of Human Motivation," in Lepper and Greene, pp. 149–76.

19. Skinner, p. 149.

20. For more on the problems associated with punishment, see Murray Sidman, *Coercion and Its Fallout* (Boston: Authors Cooperative, Inc., 1989).

21. Grades are often referred to as rewards, but they are more often punishments. Students study not so much to receive high grades as to avoid receiving low ones.

22. Deci and Cascio, op. cit.

23. See, for example, Edward L. Deci, Wayne F. Cascio, and Judy Krusell, "Sex Differences, Positive Feedback, and Intrinsic Motivation," paper presented at the annual meeting of the Eastern Psychological Association, Washington, D.C., May 1973....

24. Intrinsic rewards are more important to the maintenance of skills once learned. An adult's skill at addition and subtraction is not ordinarily maintained by the approval of peers but by the satisfaction that comes from balancing a checkbook.

25. See, for example, Jere Brophy, "Teacher Praise: A Functional Analysis," *Review of Educational Research,* vol. 51, 1981, pp. 5–32; Hopkins and Conard, op. cit.; and Dickinson, "The Detrimental Effects."

NO

Alfie Kohn

Rewards Versus Learning:
A Response to Paul Chance

In the course of offering some suggestions for how educators can help children become more generous and empathic ("Caring Kids: The Role of the Schools," March 1991), I argued that manipulating student behavior with either punishments or rewards is not only unnecessary but counterproductive. Paul Chance, taking exception to this passage, wrote to defend the use of rewards (Backtalk, June 1991). Now, following the publication of his longer brief for behaviorism ("The Rewards of Learning," November 1992), it is my turn to raise some questions—and to continue what I hope is a constructive dialogue between us (not to mention a long overdue examination of classroom practices too often taken for granted).

To begin, I should mention two points where our perspectives converge. Neither of us favors the use of punishment, and both of us think that rewards, like other strategies, must be judged by their long-term effects, including what they do for (or to) children's motivation. Chance and I disagree, however, on the nature of those effects.

Rewards, like punishments, can usually get people to do what we want for a while. In that sense, they "work." But my reading of the research, corroborated by real-world observation, is that rewards can never buy us anything more than short-term compliance. Moreover, we—or, more accurately, the people we are rewarding—pay a steep price over time for our reliance on extrinsic motivators.

Rewards Are Inherently Controlling

Applied behaviorism, which amounts to saying, "Do this and you'll get that," is essentially a technique for controlling people. In the classroom, it is a way of doing things *to* children rather than working *with* them. Chance focuses on the empirical effects of rewards, but I feel obliged to pause at least long enough to stress that moral issues are involved here regardless of whether we ultimately endorse or oppose the use of rewards.

From Alfie Kohn, "Rewards Versus Learning: A Response to Paul Chance," *Phi Delta Kappan* (June 1993). Copyright © 1993 by Alfie Kohn. Reprinted by permission of the author. Some notes omitted.

209

By now it is not news that reinforcement strategies were developed and refined through experiments on laboratory animals. Many readers also realize that underlying the practice of reinforcement is a theory—specifically, the assumption that humans, like all organisms, are basically inert beings whose behavior must be elicited by external motivation in the form of carrots or sticks. For example, Alyce Dickinson, the author Chance cites six times and from whom he borrows the gist of his defense of rewards, plainly acknowledges the central premise of the perspective she and Chance share, which is that "all behavior is ultimately initiated by the external environment."[1] Anyone who recoils from this theoretical foundation ought to take a fresh look at the real-world practices that rest on it.

I am troubled by a model of human relationship or learning that is defined by control rather than, say, persuasion or mutual problem solving. Because the reinforcements themselves are desired by their recipients, it is easy to miss the fact that using them is simply a matter of "control[ling] through seduction rather than force."[2] Rewards and punishments (bribes and threats, positive reinforcements and "consequences"—call them what you will) are not really opposites at all. They are two sides of the same coin. The good news is that our options are not limited to variations on the theme of behavioral manipulation.

Rewards Are Ineffective

The question of how well rewards *work,* apart from what they do to children's long-term motivation, is dispatched by Chance in a single sentence: "No one disputes the effectiveness of extrinsic rewards in teaching or in maintaining good discipline" (p. 203). I found myself re-reading the paragraph in which this extraordinary claim appears, searching for signs that Chance was being ironic.

In point of fact, the evidence overwhelmingly demonstrates that extrinsic rewards are ineffective at producing lasting change in attitudes or even behaviors. Moreover, they typically do not enhance—and often actually impede —performance on tasks that are any more complex than pressing a bar. This evidence, which I have been sorting through recently for a book-length treatment of these issues (*Punished by Rewards,* scheduled for publication fall [1993]), is piled so high on my desk that I fear it will topple over. I cannot review all of it here; a few samples will have to do.

Consider first the matter of behavior change. Even behaviorists have had to concede that the token economy, a form of behavior modification once (but, mercifully, no longer) popular for controlling people in institutions, doesn't work. When the goodies stop, people go right back to acting the way they did before the program began.[3] Studies have found that rewarding people for losing weight,[4] quitting smoking,[5] or using seat belts[6] is typically less effective than using other strategies—and often proves worse than doing nothing at all.

Children whose parents make frequent use of rewards or praise are likely to be less generous than their peers.[7] On reflection, this makes perfect sense: a child promised a treat for acting responsibly has been given no reason to keep behaving that way when there is no longer a reward to be gained for doing so. The implications for behavioristic classroom management programs such as

Assertive Discipline, in which children are essentially bribed or threatened to conform to rules that the teacher alone devises, are painfully clear.

Rewards (like punishments) can get people to do what we want in the short term: buckle up, share a toy, read a book. In that sense, Chance is right that their effectiveness is indisputable. But they rarely produce effects that survive the rewards themselves, which is why behaviorists are placed in the position of having to argue that we need to keep the goodies coming or replace one kind of reward with another (e.g., candy bars with grades). The fact is that extrinsic motivators do not alter the attitudes that underlie our behaviors. They do not create an enduring *commitment* to a set of values or to learning; they merely, and temporarily, change what we do. If, like [American psychologist B. F.] Skinner, you think there is nothing to humans other than what we do, then this criticism will not trouble you. If, on the other hand, you think that our actions reflect and emerge from who we *are* (what we think and feel, expect and will), then you have no reason to expect interventions that merely control actions to work in the long run.

As for the effect on performance, I know of at least two dozen studies showing that people expecting to receive a reward for completing a task (or for doing it successfully) don't perform as well as those who expect nothing. The effect is robust for young children, older children, and adults; for males and females; for rewards of all kinds (including money, grades, toys, food, and special privileges). The tasks in these studies range from memorizing facts to engaging in creative problem solving, from discriminating between similar drawings to designing collages. In general, the more cognitive sophistication and open-ended thinking required, the worse people do when they are working for a reward.[8]

At first researchers didn't know what to make of these findings. (A good sign that one has stumbled onto something important is the phrase "contrary to hypothesis" in a research report.) "The clear inferiority of the reward groups was an unexpected result, unaccountable for by theory or previous empirical evidence," a pair of experimenters confessed in 1961.[9] Rewards "have effects that interfere with performance in ways that we are only beginning to understand," said Janet Spence (later president of the American Psychological Association) in 1971.[10] Since then, most researchers—with the exception of a small cadre of unreconstructed behaviorists—have gotten the message that, on most tasks, a Skinnerian strategy is worse than useless: it is counterproductive.

Rewards Make Learning Less Appealing

Even more research indicates that rewards also undermine *interest*—a finding with obvious and disturbing implications for the use of grades, stickers, and even praise. Here Chance concedes there may be a problem but, borrowing Dickinson's analysis, assures us that the damage is limited. Dickinson grants that motivation tends to decline when people are rewarded just for engaging in a task and also when they receive performance-contingent rewards—those "based on performance standards" (Dickinson) or "available only when the student achieves a certain standard" (Chance).

But Dickinson then proceeds to invent a new category, "success-contingent" rewards, and calls these innocuous. The term means that, when rewards are given out, "subjects are told they have received the rewards because of good performance." For Chance, though, a "success-contingent" reward is "given for good performance and might reflect either success or progress toward a goal" —a definition that appears to diverge from Dickinson's and that sounds quite similar to what is meant by "performance-contingent." As near as I can figure, the claim both Dickinson and Chance are making is that, when people come away thinking that they have done well, a reward for what they have achieved doesn't hurt. On this single claim rests the entire defense against the devastating charge that by rewarding students for their achievement we are leading them to see learning as a chore. But what does the research really say?

Someone who simply glances at the list of studies Dickinson offers to support her assertion might come away impressed. Someone who takes the time to read those studies will come away with a renewed sense of the importance of going straight to the primary source. It turns out that two of the studies don't even deal with rewards for successful performance.[11] Another one actually *disproves* the contention that success-contingent rewards are harmless: it finds that this kind of reward not only undermines intrinsic motivation but is more destructive than rewards given just for engaging in the task![12]

The rest of the studies cited by Dickinson indicate that some subjects in laboratory experiments who receive success-contingent rewards are neither more nor less interested in the task than those who get nothing at all. But Dickinson curiously omits a number of *other* studies that are also set up so that some subjects succeed (or think they succeed) at a task and are presented with a reward. These studies have found that such rewards *do* reduce interest.[13]

Such a result really shouldn't be surprising. As Edward Deci and his colleagues have been pointing out for years, adults and children alike chafe at being deprived of a sense of self-determination. Rewards usually feel controlling, and rewards contingent on performance ("If you do a good job, here's what I'll give you") are the most controlling of all. Even the good feeling produced by doing well often isn't enough to overcome that fact. To the extent that information about how well we have done *is* interest-enhancing, this is not an argument for Skinnerian tactics. In fact, when researchers have specifically compared the effects of straightforward performance feedback ("Here's how you did") and performance-contingent rewards ("Here's a goody for doing well"), the latter undermined intrinsic motivation more than the former.[14]

Finally, even if all the research really did show what Dickinson and Chance claim it does, remember that outside of the laboratory people often fail. That result is more likely to be de-motivating when it means losing out on a reward, such as an A or a bonus. This Chance implicitly concedes, although the force of the point gets lost: students do not turn off from failing per se but from failing when a reward is at stake. In learning contexts free of extrinsic motivators, students are more likely to persist at a task and to remain interested in it even when they don't do it well.

All of this means that getting children to think about learning as a way to receive a sticker, a gold star, or a grade—or, even worse, to get money or a

toy *for* a grade, which amounts to an extrinsic motivator for an extrinsic motivator—is likely to turn learning from an end into a means. Learning becomes
something that must be gotten through in order to receive the reward. Take
the depressingly pervasive program by which children receive certificates for
free pizza when they have read a certain number of books. John Nicholls of the
University of Illinois comments, only half in jest, that the likely consequence
of this program is "a lot of fat kids who don't like to read."

Educational psychologists such as Nicholls, Carol Dweck, and Carole Ames
keep finding that when children are led to concentrate on their performance,
on how well they are doing—an inevitable consequence of the use of rewards
or punishments—they become less interested in *what* they are doing. ("Do we
have to know this? Will it be on the test?") I am convinced that one of the
primary obligations of educators and parents who want to promote a lasting
commitment to learning is to do everything in their power to help students
forget that grades exist.

Rewards Ignore Curricular Questions

One last point. Chance's defense of the Skinnerian status quo might more properly have been titled "The Rewards *for* Learning." My interest is in the rewards
of learning, a concern that requires us to ask whether we are teaching something *worth* learning. This is a question that behaviorists do not need to ask;
it is enough to devise an efficient technique to reinforce the acquisition of
whatever happens to be in someone's lesson plan.

Chance addresses the matter of intrinsic motivation just long enough to
dismiss it as "too remote to be effective." He sets up a false dichotomy, with an
abstract math problem on one side (Why would a child be motivated to learn
that $7 + 3 = 10$? he wants to know) and reinforcements (the solution to this
problem) on the other. Indeed, if children are required to fill in an endless series
of blanks on worksheets or to memorize meaningless, disconnected facts, they
may *have* to be bribed to do so. But Chance seems oblivious to exciting developments in the field of education: the whole-language movement, the emphasis
on "learner-centered" learning, and the entire constructivist tradition (in which
teaching takes its cue from the way each child actively constructs meaning and
makes sense of the world rather than treating students as passive responders to
environmental stimuli).

I invite Chance to join the campaign for an engaging curriculum that
is connected to children's lives and interests, for an approach to pedagogy in
which students are given real choices about their studies, and for classrooms in
which they are allowed and helped to work with one another. Pursuing these
approaches, not manipulating children with artificial incentives, offers a *real*
alternative to boredom in school and to diminished motivation when school
lets out.

Notes

1. Alyce M. Dickinson, "The Detrimental Effects of Extrinsic Reinforcement on 'Intrinsic Motivation,'" *The Behavior Analyst,* vol. 12, 1989, p. 12. Notice the quotation marks around "intrinsic motivation," as if to question the very existence of the phenomenon—a telltale sign of Skinnerian orthodoxy.

2. Edward L. Deci and Richard M. Ryan, *Intrinsic Motivation and Self-Determination in Human Behavior* (New York: Plenum, 1985), p. 70.

3. ... See Alan E. Kazdin and Richard R. Bootzin, "The Token Economy: An Evaluative Review," *Journal of Applied Behavior Analysis,* vol. 5, 1972, pp. 359-60.... See Alan E. Kazdin, "The Token Economy: A Decade Later," *Journal of Applied Behavior Analysis,* vol. 15, 1982, pp. 435-37....

4. ... Richard A. Dienstbier and Gary K. Leak, "Overjustification and Weight Loss: The Effects of Monetary Reward," paper presented at the annual meeting of the American Psychological Association, Washington, D.C., September 1976; and F. Matthew Kramer et al., "Maintenance of Successful Weight Loss Over 1 Year: Effects of Financial Contracts for Weight Maintenance or Participation in Skills Training," *Behavior Therapy,* vol. 17, 1986, pp. 295-301.

5. ... See Susan J. Curry et al., "Evaluation of Intrinsic and Extrinsic Motivation Interventions with a Self-Help Smoking Cessation Program," *Journal of Consulting and Clinical Psychology,* vol. 59, 1991, p. 323.

6. ... See E. Scott Geller et al., "Employer-Based Programs to Motivate Safety Belt Use: A Review of Short-Term and Long-Term Effects," *Journal of Safety Research,* vol. 18, 1987, pp. 1-17.

7. Richard A. Fabes et al., "Effects of Rewards on Children's Prosocial Motivation: A Socialization Study," *Developmental Psychology,* vol. 25, 1989, pp. 509-15. Praise appears to have a similar detrimental effect; see Joan E. Grusec, "Socializing Concern for Others in the Home," *Developmental Psychology,* vol. 27, 1991, pp. 338-42. See also the studies reviewed in Alfie Kohn, *The Brighter Side of Human Nature: Altruism and Empathy in Everyday Life* (New York: Basic Books, 1990), pp. 201-4.

8. A complete bibliography will be available in my forthcoming book, *Punished by Rewards.* Readers unwilling to wait might wish to begin by reading Mark R. Lepper and David Greene, eds., *The Hidden Costs of Rewards* (Hillsdale, N.J.: Erlbaum, 1978), and some of Teresa Amabile's work from the 1980s documenting how rewards kill creativity.

9. Louise Brightwell Miller and Betsy Worth Estes, "Monetary Reward and Motivation in Discrimination Learning," *Journal of Experimental Psychology,* vol. 61, 1961, p. 503.

10. Janet Taylor Spence, "Do Material Rewards Enhance the Performance of Lower-Class Children?," *Child Development,* vol. 42, 1971, p. 1469.

11. In one of the studies, either money or an award was given to children just for taking part in the experiment—and both caused interest in the task to decline. See Rosemarie Anderson et al., "The Undermining and Enhancing of Intrinsic Motivation in Preschool Children," *Journal of Personality and Social Psychology,* vol. 34, 1976, pp. 915-22. In the other, a total of three children were simply praised ("good," "nice going") whenever they engaged in a task; no mention was made of how well they were performing. See Jerry A. Martin, "Effects of Positive and Negative Adult-Child Interactions on Children's Task Performance and Task Preferences," *Journal of Experimental Child Psychology,* vol. 23, 1977, pp. 493-502.

12. Michael Jay Weiner and Anthony M. Mander, "The Effects of Reward and Perception of Competency upon Intrinsic Motivation," *Motivation and Emotion,* vol. 2, 1978, pp. 67-73.

13. ... David Greene and Mark R. Lepper, "Effects of Extrinsic Rewards on Children's Subsequent Intrinsic Interest," *Child Development,* vol. 45, 1974, pp. 1141-1145.... James Garbarino, "The Impact of Anticipated Reward upon Cross-Age Tutoring," *Journal of Personality and Social Psychology,* vol. 32, 1975, pp. 421–28; Terry D. Orlick and Richard Mosher, "Extrinsic Awards and Participant Motivation in a Sport Related Task," *International Journal of Sport Psychology,* vol. 9, 1978, pp. 27–39; Judith M. Harackiewicz, "The Effects of Reward Contingency and Performance Feedback on Intrinsic Motivation," *Journal of Personality and Social Psychology,* vol. 37, 1979, pp. 1352–63; and Richard A. Fabes, "Effects of Reward Contexts on Young Children's Task Interest," *Journal of Psychology,* vol. 121, 1987, pp. 5–19. See too the studies cited in, and conclusions offered by, Kenneth O. McGraw, "The Detrimental Effects of Reward on Performance: A Literature Review and a Prediction Model," in Lepper and Greene, eds., p. 40; Mark R. Lepper, "Extrinsic Reward and Intrinsic Motivation," in John M. Levine and Margaret C. Wang, eds., *Teacher and Student Perceptions: Implications for Learning* (Hillsdale, N.J.: Erlbaum, 1983), pp. 304–5; and Deci and Ryan, p. 78.

14. Richard M. Ryan et al., "Relation of Reward Contingency and Interpersonal Context to Intrinsic Motivation: A Review and Test Using Cognitive Evaluation Theory," *Journal of Personality and Social Psychology,* vol. 45, 1983, pp. 736–50.

CHALLENGE QUESTIONS

Do Rewards Facilitate Learning?

1. Would you use reinforcement principles, such as those advocated by Chance, on your children? What alternatives are available?
2. If you knew that your son or daughter's teacher was using reinforcement principles in the classroom, would you be concerned? Why, or why not?
3. What would Kohn say about the people who assume that they work primarily for a type of reinforcement—specifically, a paycheck?
4. If an intrinsic motivation could be instilled (via Kohn's work) for learning and other activities, what would be the advantages for the individual and society?

On the Internet ...

Mental Health Infosource: Disorders

This no-nonsense page lists hotlinks to pages dealing with psychological disorders, including anxiety, panic, phobic disorders, schizophrenia, and violent/self-destructive behaviors.

http://www.mhsource.com/disorders/

Suicide Awareness: Voices of Education

This is the most popular suicide site on the Internet. A very thorough site, it includes information on dealing with suicide (both before and after) and material from the organization's many education sessions.

http://www.save.org

Mental Illness

Maintained by Patrick Macartney, a lecturer at the University of Leeds in Yorkshire, United Kingdom, this page provides many links to sites related to mental illness. Among the categories are Prozac Links and "Disorder" Links.

http://www.angelfire.com/ma/Socialworld/
Mentalillness.html

The International Society for the Study of Dissociation

The International Society for the Study of Dissociation is a nonprofit professional society that promotes research and training in the identification and treatment of dissociative disorders, provides professional and public education about dissociative states, and serves as a catalyst for international communication and cooperation among clinicians and researchers working in this field.

http://www.issd.org

PART 5

Mental Health

A mental disorder is often defined as a pattern of thinking or behavior that is either disruptive to others or uncomfortable for the person with the disorder. This definition seems straightforward, yet there is considerable debate about whether or not certain disordered "patterns" of thinking or behavior truly exist. Are there "multiple personalities," for example? Soap operas routinely portray this disorder, but does it really exist? Also, labels (or diagnoses) for disordered patterns have been developed. Are these diagnostic labels helpful or harmful to the treatment of these disorders?

- Classic Dialogue: Do Diagnostic Labels Hinder Treatment?

- Do Multiple Personalities Exist?

ISSUE 11

Classic Dialogue: Do Diagnostic Labels Hinder Treatment?

YES: D. L. Rosenhan, from "On Being Sane in Insane Places," *Science* (January 19, 1973)

NO: Robert L. Spitzer, from "On Pseudoscience in Science, Logic in Remission and Psychiatric Diagnosis: A Critique of 'On Being Sane in Insane Places,'" *Journal of Abnormal Psychology* (vol. 84, 1975)

ISSUE SUMMARY

YES: Psychologist D. L. Rosenhan describes an experiment that he contends demonstrates that once a patient is labeled "schizophrenic," his behavior is seen as such by mental health workers regardless of the true state of the patient's mental health.

NO: Psychiatrist Robert L. Spitzer argues that diagnostic labels are necessary and valuable and that Rosenhan's experiment has many flaws.

Traditionally, the first step in treating a disorder is to diagnose it. When a disorder is diagnosed, presumably the most effective treatment can then be applied. But diagnosis often involves classifying the person and attaching a label. Could such a label do more harm than good?

How would you think and behave if you were introduced to someone described as a high school dropout? A heroin addict? A schizophrenic? What would you think and how would you behave if, having recently taken a series of personality tests, you were told by an expert that you were schizophrenic?

Some people believe that diagnostic labels may actually serve as self-fulfilling prophecies. Labels seem to have a way of putting blinders on the way a problem is seen. Those who are labeled may behave differently toward others or develop self-concepts consistent with the diagnosis—and thereby exaggerate, or even create anew, behavior considered to be "abnormal."

In the following selection, D. L. Rosenhan asks the question, "If sanity and insanity exist, how shall we know them?" He then describes an experiment that he conducted to help answer this question. Rosenhan interprets the results of his investigation as demonstrating that "the normal are not detectably sane" by a mental hospital staff because "having once been labeled schizophrenic, there is nothing the [patient] can do to overcome this tag." He believes that mental institutions impose a specific environment in which the meaning of even normal behaviors can be construed as abnormal. If this is so, Rosenhan wonders, "How many people are sane... but not recognized as such in our psychiatric institutions?"

In the second selection, Robert L. Spitzer criticizes Rosenhan's experiment on many grounds and, in fact, contends that "a correct interpretation of his own [Rosenhan's] data contradicts his conclusions." Rosenhan's data, Spitzer contends, show that in "a psychiatric hospital, psychiatrists are remarkably able to distinguish the 'sane' from the 'insane.'" Although Spitzer recognizes some of the dangers of diagnostic classification, he argues that Rosenhan has not presented fairly the purpose and necessity of diagnoses. The misuse of diagnoses, he maintains, "is not a sufficient reason to abandon their use because they have been shown to be of value when properly used." They "enable mental health professionals to communicate with each other..., comprehend the pathological processes involved..., and control psychiatric disorders," says Spitzer.

POINT

- Psychiatric diagnoses are in the minds of the observers and do not reflect the behavior of the patients.
- A diagnosis can become a self-fulfilling prophecy for the doctor or the patient.
- In the setting of a mental institution, almost any behavior could be considered abnormal.
- Diagnostic labels serve no useful purpose, especially in view of the harm they do.

COUNTERPOINT

- A diagnosis based on real or false symptoms *is* based on a patient's behavior.
- Competent diagnoses derive from a necessary classification of the symptoms of a disorder.
- Mental patients *do* eventually get discharged when they continue to show no symptoms of behavioral pathology.
- Diagnoses enable psychiatrists to communicate, comprehend, and control disorders.

D. L. Rosenhan

 **YES**

On Being Sane in Insane Places

If sanity and insanity exist, how shall we know them?

The question is neither capricious nor itself insane. However much we may be personally convinced that we can tell the normal from the abnormal, the evidence is simply not compelling. It is commonplace, for example, to read about murder trials wherein eminent psychiatrists for the defense are contradicted by equally eminent psychiatrists for the prosecution on the matter of the defendant's sanity. More generally, there are a great deal of conflicting data on the reliability, utility, and meaning of such terms as "sanity," "insanity," "mental illness," and "schizophrenia." Finally, as early as 1934, Benedict suggested that normality and abnormality are not universal. What is viewed as normal in one culture may be seen as quite aberrant in another. Thus, notions of normality and abnormality may not be quite as accurate as people believe they are.

To raise questions regarding normality and abnormality is in no way to question the fact that some behaviors are deviant or odd. Murder is deviant. So, too, are hallucinations. Nor does raising such questions deny the existence of the personal anguish that is often associated with "mental illness." Anxiety and depression exist. Psychological suffering exists. But normality and abnormality, sanity and insanity, and the diagnoses that flow from them may be less substantive than many believe them to be.

At its heart, the question of whether the sane can be distinguished from the insane (and whether degrees of insanity can be distinguished from each other) is a simple matter: do the salient characteristics that lead to diagnoses reside in the patients themselves or in the environments and contexts in which observers find them? From Bleuler, through Kretchmer, through the formulators of the recently revised *Diagnostic and Statistical Manual* of the American Psychiatric Association, the belief has been strong that patients present symptoms, that those symptoms can be categorized, and, implicitly, that the sane are distinguishable from the insane. More recently, however, this belief has been questioned. Based in part on theoretical and anthropological considerations, but also on philosophical, legal, and therapeutic ones, the view has grown that psychological categorization of mental illness is useless at best and downright harmful, misleading, and pejorative at worst. Psychiatric diagnoses, in this view, are in the minds of the observers and are not valid summaries of characteristics displayed by the observed.

Gains can be made in deciding which of these is more nearly accurate by getting normal people (that is, people who do not have, and have never suffered, symptoms of serious psychiatric disorders) admitted to psychiatric hospitals and then determining whether they were discovered to be sane and, if so, how. If the sanity of such pseudopatients were always detected, there would be prima facie evidence that a sane individual can be distinguished from the insane context in which he is found. Normality (and presumably abnormality) is distinct enough that it can be recognized wherever it occurs, for it is carried within the person. If, on the other hand, the sanity of the pseudopatients were never discovered, serious difficulties would arise for those who support traditional modes of psychiatric diagnosis. Given that the hospital staff was not incompetent, that the pseudopatient had been behaving as sanely as he had been outside of the hospital, and that it had never been previously suggested that he belonged in a psychiatric hospital, such an unlikely outcome would support the view that psychiatric diagnosis betrays little about the patient but much about the environment in which an observer finds him.

This article describes such an experiment. Eight sane people gained secret admission to 12 different hospitals. Their diagnostic experiences constitute the data of the first part of this article; the remainder is devoted to a description of their experiences in psychiatric institutions. Too few psychiatrists and psychologists, even those who have worked in such hospitals, know what the experience is like. They rarely talk about it with former patients, perhaps because they distrust information coming from the previously insane. Those who have worked in psychiatric hospitals are likely to have adapted so thoroughly to the settings that they are insensitive to the impact of the experience. And while there have been occasional reports of researchers who submitted themselves to psychiatric hospitalization, these researchers have commonly remained in the hospitals for short periods of time, often with the knowledge of the hospital staff. It is difficult to know the extent to which they were treated like patients or like research colleagues. Nevertheless, their reports about the inside of the psychiatric hospital have been valuable. This article extends those efforts.

Pseudopatients and Their Settings

The eight pseudopatients were a varied group. One was a psychology graduate student in his 20s. The remaining seven were older and "established." Among them were three psychologists, a pediatrician, a psychiatrist, a painter, and a housewife. Three pseudopatients were women, five were men. All of them employed pseudonyms, lest their alleged diagnoses embarrass them later. Those who were in mental health professions alleged another occupation in order to avoid the special attentions that might be accorded by staff, as a matter of courtesy or caution, to ailing colleagues. With the exception of myself (I was the first pseudopatient and my presence was known to the hospital administrator and chief psychologist and, so far as I can tell, to them alone), the presence of pseudopatients and the nature of the research program was not known to the hospital staffs.

The settings were similarly varied. In order to generalize the findings, admission into a variety of hospitals was sought. The 12 hospitals in the sample are located in five different states on the East and West coasts. Some were old and shabby, some were quite new. Some were research-oriented, others not. Some had good staff-patient ratios, others were quite understaffed. Only one was a strictly private hospital. All the others were supported by state or federal funds or, in one instance, by university funds.

After calling the hospital for an appointment, the pseudopatient arrived at the admissions office complaining that he had been hearing voices. Asked what the voices said, he replied that they were often unclear, but as far as he could tell they said "empty," "hollow," and "thud." The voices were unfamiliar and were of the same sex as the pseudopatient. The choice of these symptoms was occasioned by their apparent similarity to existential symptoms. Such symptoms were alleged to arise from painful concerns about the perceived meaninglessness of one's life. It is as if the hallucinating person were saying, "My life is empty and hollow." The choice of these symptoms was also determined by the *absence* of a single report of existential psychoses in the literature.

Beyond alleging the symptoms and falsifying name, vocation, and employment, no further alterations of person, history, or circumstances were made. The significant events of the pseudopatient's life history were presented as they had actually occurred. Relationships with parents and siblings, with spouse and children, with people at work and in school, consistent with the aforementioned exceptions, were described as they were or had been. Frustrations and upsets were described along with joys and satisfactions. These facts are important to remember. If anything, they strongly biased the subsequent results in favor of detecting sanity, since none of their histories or current behaviors were seriously pathological in any way.

Immediately upon admission to the psychiatric ward, the pseudopatient ceased simulating *any* symptoms of abnormality. In some cases, there was a brief period of mild nervousness and anxiety, since none of the pseudopatients really believed that they would be admitted so easily. Indeed their shared fear was that they would be immediately exposed as frauds and greatly embarrassed. Moreover, many of them had never visited a psychiatric ward; even those who had, nevertheless had some genuine fears about what might happen to them. Their nervousness, then, was quite appropriate to the novelty of the hospital setting, and it abated rapidly.

Apart from that short-lived nervousness, the pseudopatient behaved on the ward as he "normally" behaved. The pseudopatient spoke to patients and staff as he might ordinarily. Because there is uncommonly little to do on a psychiatric ward, he attempted to engage others in conversation. When asked by staff how he was feeling, he indicated that he was fine, that he no longer experienced symptoms. He responded to instructions from attendants, to calls for medication (which was not swallowed), and to dining-hall instructions. Beyond such activities as were available to him on the admissions ward, he spent his time writing down his observations about the ward, its patients, and the staff.

Initially these notes were written "secretly," but as it soon became clear that no one much cared, they were subsequently written on standard tablets of paper in such public places as the dayroom. No secret was made of these activities.

The pseudopatient, very much as a true psychiatric patient, entered a hospital with no foreknowledge of when he would be discharged. Each was told that he would have to get out by his own devices, essentially by convincing the staff that he was sane. The psychological stresses associated with hospitalization were considerable, and all but one of the pseudopatients desired to be discharged almost immediately after being admitted. They were, therefore, motivated not only to behave sanely, but to be paragons of cooperation. That their behavior was in no way disruptive is confirmed by nursing reports, which have been obtained on most of the patients. These reports uniformly indicate that the patients were "friendly," "cooperative," and "exhibited no abnormal indications."

The Normal Are Not Detectably Sane

Despite their public "show" of sanity, the pseudopatients were never detected. Admitted, except in one case, with a diagnosis of schizophrenia each was discharged with a diagnosis of schizophrenia "in remission." The label "in remission" should in no way be dismissed as a formality, for at no time during any hospitalization had any question been raised about any pseudopatient's simulation. Nor are there any indications in the hospital records that the pseudopatient's status was suspect. Rather, the evidence is strong that, once labeled schizophrenic, the pseudopatient was stuck with that label. If the pseudopatient was to be discharged, he must naturally be "in remission"; but he was not sane, nor, in the institution's view, had he ever been sane.

The uniform failure to recognize sanity cannot be attributed to the quality of the hospitals, for, although there were considerable variations among them, several are considered excellent. Nor can it be alleged that there was simply not enough time to observe the pseudopatients. Length of hospitalization ranged from 7 to 52 days, with an average of 19 days. The pseudopatients were not, in fact, carefully observed, but this failure clearly speaks more to traditions within psychiatric hospitals than to lack of opportunity.

Finally, it cannot be said that the failure to recognize the pseudopatients' sanity was due to the fact that they were not behaving sanely. While there was clearly some tension present in all of them, their daily visitors could detect no serious behavioral consequences—nor, indeed, could other patients. It was quite common for the patients to "detect" the pseudopatients' sanity. During the first three hospitalizations, when accurate counts were kept, 35 of a total of 118 patients on the admissions ward voiced their suspicions, some vigorously. "You're not crazy. You're a journalist, or a professor [referring to the continual note-taking]. You're checking up on the hospital." While most of the patients were reassured by the pseudopatient's insistence that he had been sick before he came in but was fine now, some continued to believe that the pseudopatient was sane throughout his hospitalization. The fact that the patients often recognized normality when staff did not raises important questions.

Failure to detect sanity during the course of hospitalization may be due to the fact that physicians operate with a strong bias toward what statisticians call the type 2 error. This is to say that physicians are more inclined to call a healthy person sick (a false positive, type 2) than a sick person healthy (a false negative, type 1). The reasons for this are not hard to find: it is clearly more dangerous to mis-diagnose illness than health. Better to err on the side of caution, to suspect illness even among the healthy.

But what holds for medicine does not hold equally well for psychiatry. Medical illnesses, while unfortunate, are not commonly pejorative. Psychiatric diagnoses, on the contrary, carry with them personal, legal, and social stigmas. It was therefore important to see whether the tendency toward diagnosing the sane insane could be reversed. The following experiment was arranged at a research and teaching hospital whose staff had heard these findings but doubted that such an error could occur in their hospital. The staff was informed that at some time during the following 3 months, one or more pseudopatients would attempt to be admitted into the psychiatric hospital. Each staff member was asked to rate each patient who presented himself at admissions or on the ward according to the likelihood that the patient was a pseudopatient. A 10-point scale was used, with a 1 and 2 reflecting high confidence that the patient was a pseudopatient.

Judgments were obtained on 193 patients who were admitted for psychiatric treatment. All staff who had had sustained contact with or primary responsibility for the patient—attendants, nurses, psychiatrists, physicians, and psychologists—were asked to make judgments. Forty-one patients were alleged, with high confidence, to be pseudopatients by at least one member of the staff. Twenty-three were considered suspect by at least one psychiatrist. Nineteen were suspected by one psychiatrist *and* one other staff member. Actually, no genuine pseudopatient (at least from my group) presented himself during this period.

The experiment is instructive. It indicates that the tendency to designate sane people as insane can be reversed when the stakes (in this case, prestige and diagnostic acumen) are high. But what can be said of the 19 people who were suspected of being "sane" by one psychiatrist and another staff member? Were these people truly "sane," or was it rather the case that in the course of avoiding the type 2 error the staff tended to make more errors of the first sort— calling the crazy "sane"? There is no way of knowing. But one thing is certain: any diagnostic process that lends itself so readily to massive errors of this sort cannot be a very reliable one.

The Stickiness of Psychodiagnostic Labels

Beyond the tendency to call the healthy sick—a tendency that accounts better for diagnostic behavior on admission than it does for such behavior after a lengthy period of exposure—the data speak to the massive role of labeling in psychiatric assessment. Having once been labeled schizophrenic, there is nothing the pseudopatient can do to overcome this tag. The tag profoundly colors others' perceptions of him and his behavior.

From one viewpoint, these data are hardly surprising, for it has long been known that elements are given meaning by the context in which they occur. Gestalt psychology made this point vigorously, and Asch demonstrated that there are "central" personality traits (such as "warm" versus "cold") which are so powerful that they markedly color the meaning of other information in forming an impression of a given personality.

"Insane," "schizophrenic," "manic-depressive," and "crazy" are probably among the most powerful of such central traits. Once a person is designated abnormal, all of his other behaviors and characteristics are colored by that label. Indeed, that label is so powerful that may of the pseudopatients' normal behaviors were overlooked entirely or profoundly misinterpreted. Some examples may clarify this issue.

Earlier I indicated that there were no changes in the pseudopatient's personal history and current status beyond those of name, employment, and, where necessary, vocation. Otherwise, a veridical description of personal history and circumstances was offered. Those circumstances were not psychotic. How were they made consonant with the diagnosis of psychosis? Or were those diagnoses modified in such a way as to bring them into accord with the circumstances of the pseudopatient's life, as described by him?

As far as I can determine, diagnoses were in no way affected by the relative health of the circumstances of a pseudopatient's life. Rather, the reverse occurred: the perception of his circumstances was shaped entirely by the diagnosis. A clear example of such translation is found in the case of a pseudopatient who had had a close relationship with his mother but was rather remote from his father during his early childhood. During adolescence and beyond, however, his father became a close friend, while his relationship with his mother cooled. His present relationship with his wife was characteristically close and warm. Apart from occasional angry exchanges, friction was minimal. The children had rarely been spanked. Surely there is nothing especially pathological about such a history. Indeed, many readers may see a similar pattern in their own experiences, with no markedly deleterious consequences. Observe, however, how such a history was translated in the psycho-pathological context, this from the case summary prepared after the patient was discharged:

> This white 39-year-old male ... manifests a long history of considerable ambivalence in close relationships, which begins in early childhood. A warm relationship with his mother cools during his adolescence. A distant relationship to his father is described as becoming very intense. Affective stability is absent. His attempts to control emotionality with his wife and children are punctuated by angry outbursts and, in the case of the children, spankings. And while he says that he has several friends, one senses considerable ambivalence embedded in these relationships also....

The facts of the case were unintentionally distorted by the staff to achieve consistency with a popular theory of the dynamics of a schizophrenic reaction. Nothing of an ambivalent nature had been described in relations with parents, spouse, or friends. To the extent that ambivalence could be inferred, it was probably not greater than is found in all human relationships. It is true the pseudopatient's relationships with his parents changed over time, but in the ordinary context that would hardly be remarkable—indeed, it might very well be expected. Clearly, the meaning ascribed to his verbalizations (that is, ambivalence, affective instability) was determined by the diagnosis: schizophrenia. An entirely different meaning would have been ascribed if it were known that the man was normal.

All pseudopatients took extensive notes publicly. Under ordinary circumstances, such behavior would have raised questions in the minds of observers, as, in fact, it did among patients. Indeed, it seemed so certain that the notes would elicit suspicion that elaborate precautions were taken to remove them from the ward each day. But the precautions proved needless. The closest any staff member came to questioning these notes occurred when one pseudopatient asked his physician what kind of medication he was receiving and began to write down the response. "You needn't write it," he was told gently. "If you have trouble remembering, just ask me again."

If no questions were asked of the pseudopatients, how was their writing interpreted? Nursing records for three patients indicate that the writing was seen as an aspect of their pathological behavior. "Patient engages in writing behavior" was the daily nursing comment on one of the pseudopatients who was never questioned about his writing. Given that the patient is in the hospital, he must be psychologically disturbed. And given that he is disturbed, continuous writing must be a behavioral manifestation of that disturbance, perhaps a subset of the compulsive behaviors that are sometimes correlated with schizophrenia.

One tacit characteristic of psychiatric diagnosis is that it locates the sources of aberration within the individual and only rarely within the complex of stimuli that surrounds him. Consequently, behaviors that are stimulated by the environment are commonly misattributed to the patient's disorder. For example, one kindly nurse found a pseudopatient pacing the long hospital corridors. "Nervous, Mr. X?" she asked. "No, bored," he said.

The notes kept by pseudopatients are full of patient behaviors that were misinterpreted by well-intentioned staff. Often enough, a patient would go "berserk" because he had, wittingly or unwittingly, been mistreated by, say, an attendant. A nurse coming upon the scene would rarely inquire even cursorily into the environmental stimuli of the patient's behavior. Rather, she assumed that his upset derived from his pathology, not from his present interactions with other staff members. Occasionally, the staff might assume that the patient's family (especially when they had recently visited) or other patients had stimulated the outburst. But never were the staff found to assume that one of themselves or the structure of the hospital had anything to do with a patient's behavior. One psychiatrist pointed to a group of patients who were sitting outside the cafeteria entrance half an hour before lunchtime. To a group of young residents he indicated that such behavior was characteristic of the oral-acquisitive nature of the syndrome. It seemed not to occur to him that there were very few things to anticipate in a psychiatric hospital besides eating.

A psychiatric label has a life and an influence of its own. Once the impression has been formed that the patient is schizophrenic, the expectation is that he will continue to be schizophrenic. When a sufficient amount of time has passed, during which the patient has done nothing bizarre, he is considered to be in remission and available for discharge. But the label endures beyond discharge, with the unconfirmed expectation that he will behave as a schizophrenic again. Such labels, conferred by mental health professionals, are as influential on the patient as they are on his relatives and friends, and it should not surprise anyone that the diagnosis acts on all of them as a self-fulfilling prophecy. Eventually, the patient himself accepts the diagnosis, with all of its surplus meanings and expectations, and behaves accordingly.

The inferences to be made from these matters are quite simple. Much as Zigler and Phillips have demonstrated that there is enormous overlap in the symptoms presented by patients who have been variously diagnosed, so there is enormous overlap in the behaviors of the sane and the insane. The sane are not "sane" all of the time. We lose our tempers "for no good reason." We are occasionally depressed or anxious, again for no good reason. And we may find it difficult to get along with one or another person—again for no reason that we can specify. Similarly, the insane are not always insane. Indeed, it was the impression of the pseudopatients while living with them that they were sane for long periods of time—that the bizarre behaviors upon which their diagnoses were allegedly predicated constituted only a small fraction of their total behavior. If it makes no sense to label ourselves permanently depressed on the basis of an occasional depression, then it takes better evidence than is presently available to label all patients insane or schizophrenic on the basis of bizarre behaviors or cognitions. It seems more useful, as Mischel has pointed out, to limit our discussions to *behaviors,* the stimuli that provoke them, and their correlates.

It is not known why powerful impressions of personality traits, such as "crazy" or "insane," arise. Conceivably, when the origins of and stimuli that give rise to a behavior are remote or unknown, or when the behavior strikes us as immutable, trait labels regarding the *behaver* arise. When, on the other hand, the origins and stimuli are known and available, discourse is limited to the behavior itself. Thus, I may hallucinate because I am sleeping, or I may hallucinate because I have ingested a peculiar drug. These are termed sleep-induced hallucinations, or dreams, and drug-induced hallucinations, respectively. But when the stimuli to my hallucinations are unknown, that is called craziness, or schizophrenia—as if that inference were somehow as illuminating as the others.

The Experience of Psychiatric Hospitalization

The term "mental illness" is of recent origin. It was coined by people who were humane in their inclinations and who wanted very much to raise the station of (and the public's sympathies toward) the psychologically disturbed from that of witches and "crazies" to one that was akin to the physically ill. And they were at least partially successful, for the treatment of the mental ill *has* improved considerably over the years. But while treatment has improved, it is doubtful that people really regard the mentally ill in the same way that they view the physically ill. A broken leg is something one recovers from, but mental illness allegedly endures forever. A broken leg does not threaten the observer, but a crazy schizophrenic? There is by now a host of evidence that attitudes toward the mentally ill are characterized by fear, hostility, aloofness, suspicion, and dread. The mentally ill are society's lepers.

That such attitudes infect the general population is perhaps not surprising, only upsetting. But that they affect the professionals—attendants, nurses, physicians, psychologists, and social workers—who treat and deal with the mentally ill is more disconcerting, both because such attitudes are self-evidently pernicious and because they are unwitting. Most mental health professionals would insist that they are sympathetic toward the mentally ill, that they are neither avoidant nor hostile. But it is more likely that an exquisite ambivalence characterizes their relations with psychiatric patients, such that their avowed impulses are only part of their entire attitude. Negative attitudes are there too and can easily be detected. Such attitudes should not surprise us. They are the natural offspring of the labels patients wear and the places in which they are found.

Consider the structure of the typical psychiatric hospital. Staff and patients are strictly segregated. Staff have their own living space, including their dining facilities, bathrooms and assembly places. The glassed quarters that contain the professional staff, which the pseudopatients came to call "the cage," sit out on every dayroom. The staff emerge primarily for caretaking purposes—to give medication, to conduct a therapy or group meeting, to instruct or reprimand a patient. Otherwise, staff keep to themselves, almost as if the disorder that afflicts their charges is somehow catching.

So much is patient-staff segregation the rule that, for four public hospitals in which an attempt was made to measure the degree to which staff and patients mingle, it was necessary to use "time out of the staff cage" as the operational measure. While it was not the case that all time spent out of the cage was spent mingling with patients (attendants, for example, would occasionally emerge to watch television in the dayroom), it was the only way in which one could gather reliable data on time for measuring.

The average amount of time spent by attendants outside of the cage was 11.3 percent (range, 3 to 52 percent). This figure does not represent only time spent mingling with patients, but also includes time spent on such chores as folding laundry, supervising patients while they shave, directing ward clean-up, and sending patients to off-ward activities. It was the relatively rare attendant who spent time talking with patients or playing games with them. It proved impossible to obtain a "percent mingling time" for nurses, since the amount of time they spent out of the cage was too brief. Rather, we counted instances of emergence from the cage. On the average, daytime nurses emerged from the cage 11.5 times per shift, including instances when they left the ward entirely (range, 4 to 39 times). Late afternoon and night nurses were even less available, emerging on the average 9.4 times per shift (range, 4 to 41 times). Data on early morning nurses, who arrived usually after midnight and departed at 8 a.m., are not available because patients were asleep during most of this period.

Physicians, especially psychiatrists, were even less available. They were rarely seen on the wards. Quite commonly, they would be seen only when they arrived and departed, with the remaining time being spent in their offices or in the cage. On the average, physicians emerged on the ward 6.7 times per day (range 1 to 17 times). It proved difficult to make an accurate estimate in this regard, since physicians often maintained hours that allowed them to come and go at different times.

The hierarchical organization of the psychiatric hospital has been commented on before, but the latent meaning of that kind of organization is worth noting again. Those with the most power have least to do with patients, and those with the least power are most involved with them. Recall, however, that the acquisition of role-appropriate behaviors occurs mainly through the observation of others, with the most powerful having the most influence. Consequently, it is understandable that attendants not only spend more time with patients than do any other members of the staff—that is required by their station in the hierarchy—but also, insofar as they learn from their superiors' behavior, spend as little time with patients as they can. Attendants are seen mainly in the cage, which is where the models, the action, and the power are.

I turn now to a different set of studies, these dealing with staff response to patient-initiated contact. It has long been known that the amount of time a person spends with you can be an index of your significance to him. If he initiates and maintains eye contact, there is reason to believe that he is considering your requests and needs. If he pauses to chat or actually stops and talks, there is added reason to infer that he is individuating you. In four hospitals, the pseudopatient approached the staff member with a request which took the following form: "Pardon me, Mr. [or Dr. or Mrs.] X, could you tell me when I will be eligible for grounds privileges?" (or " . . . when I will be presented at the staff meeting?" or " . . . when I am likely to be discharged?"). While the content of the question varied according to the appropriateness of the target and the pseudopatient's (apparent) current needs, the form was always a courteous and relevant request for information. Care was taken never to approach a particular member of the staff more than once a day, lest the staff member become suspicious or irritated. In examining these data, remember that the behavior of the pseudopatients was neither bizarre nor disruptive. One could indeed engage in good conversation with them.

The data for these experiments are shown in Table 1, separately for physicians (column 1) and for nurses and attendants (column 2). Minor differences between these four institutions were overwhelmed by the degree to which staff avoided continuing contacts that patients had initiated. By far, their most common response consisted of either a brief response to the question offered while they were "on the move" and with head averted, or no response at all.

The encounter frequently took the following bizarre form: (pseudopatient) "Pardon me, Dr. X. Could you tell me when I am eligible for grounds privileges?" (physician) "Good morning Dave. How are you today?" (moves off without waiting for a response).

It is instructive to compare these data with data recently obtained at Stanford University. It has been alleged that large and eminent universities are characterized by faculty who are so busy that they have no time for students. For this comparison, a young lady approached individual faculty members who

Table 1

Self-Initiated Contact by Pseudopatients With Psychiatrists and Nurses and Attendants, Compared With Other Groups

Contact	Psychiatric hospitals		University campus (nonmedical)	University medical center Physicians		
	(1) Psychiatrists	(2) Nurses and attendants	(3) Faculty	(4) "Looking for a psychiatrist"	(5) "Looking for an internist"	(6) No additional comment
Responses						
Moves on, head averted (%)	71	88	0	0	0	0
Makes eye contact (%)	23	10	0	11	0	0
Pauses and chats (%)	2	2	0	11	0	0
Stops and talks (%)	4	0.5	100	78	100	90
Mean number of questions answered (out of 6)	*	*	6	3.8	4.8	4.5
Respondents (No.)	13	47	14	18	15	10
Attempts (No.)	185	1283	14	18	15	10

*Not applicable

seemed to be walking purposefully to some meeting or teaching engagement and asked them the following questions.

1. "Pardon me, could you direct me to Encina Hall?" (at the medical school: "... to the Clinical Research Center?").
2. "Do you know where Fish Annex is?" (there is no Fish Annex at Stanford).
3. "Do you teach here?"
4. "How does one apply for admission to the college?" (at the medical school: "... to the medical school?").
5. "Is it difficult to get in?"
6. "Is there financial aid?"

Without exception, as can be seen in Table 1 (column 3), all of the questions were answered. No matter how rushed they were, all respondents not only maintained eye contact, but stopped to talk. Indeed, many of the respondents went out of their way to direct or take the questioner to the office she was seeking, to try to locate "Fish Annex," or to discuss with her the possibilities of being admitted to the university.

Similar data, also shown in Table 1 (columns 4, 5, and 6), were obtained in the hospital. Here too, the young lady came prepared with six questions. After the first question, however, she remarked to 18 of her respondents (column 4), "I'm looking for a psychiatrist," and to 15 others (column 5), "I'm looking for an internist." Ten other respondents received no inserted comment (column 6). The general degree of cooperative responses is considerably higher for these university groups than it was for pseudopatients in psychiatric hospitals. Even so, differences are apparent with the medical school setting. Once having indicated that she was looking for a psychiatrist, the degree of cooperation elicited was less than when she sought an internist.

Powerlessness and Depersonalization

Eye contact and verbal contact reflect concern and individuation: their absence, avoidance and depersonalization. The data I have presented do not do justice to the rich daily encounters that grew up around matters of depersonalization and avoidance. I have records of patients who were beaten by staff for the sin of initiating verbal contact. During my own experience, for example, one patient was beaten in the presence of other patients for having approached an attendant and told him, "I like you." Occasionally, punishment meted out to patients for misdemeanors seemed so excessive that it could not be justified by the most radical interpretations of psychiatric canon. Nevertheless, they appeared to go unquestioned. Tempers were often short. A patient who had not heard a call for medication would be roundly excoriated, and the morning attendants would often wake patients with, "Come on, you m— f—s, out of bed!"

Neither anecdotal nor "hard" data can convey the overwhelming sense of powerlessness which invades the individual as he is continually exposed to the depersonalization of the psychiatric hospital. It hardly matters *which* psychiatric hospital—the excellent public ones and the very plush private hospital were better than the rural and shabby ones in this regard, but again, the features that psychiatric hospitals had in common overwhelmed by far their apparent differences.

Powerlessness was evident everywhere. The patient is deprived of many of his legal rights by dint of his psychiatric commitment. He is shorn of credibility by virtue of his psychiatric label. His freedom of movement is restricted. He cannot initiate contact with the staff, but may only respond to such overtures as they make. Personal privacy is minimal. Patient quarters and possessions can be entered and examined by any staff member, for whatever reason. His personal history and anguish are available to any staff member (often including the "grey lady" and "candy striper" volunteer) who chooses to read his folder, regardless of their therapeutic relationship to him. His personal hygiene and waste evacuation are often monitored. The water closets may have no doors.

At times, the depersonalization reached such proportions that pseudopatients had the sense that they were invisible, or at least unworthy of account. Upon being admitted, I and other pseudopatients took the initial physical examination in a semipublic room, where staff members went about their own business as if we were not there.

On the ward, attendants delivered verbal and occasionally serious physical abuse to patients in the presence of other observing patients, some of whom (the pseudopatients) were writing it all down. Abusive behavior, on the other hand, terminated quite abruptly when other staff members were known to be coming. Staff are credible witnesses. Patients are not.

A nurse unbuttoned her uniform to adjust her brassiere in the presence of an entire ward of viewing men. One did not have the sense that she was being seductive. Rather, she didn't notice us. A group of staff persons might point to a patient in the dayroom and discuss him animatedly, as if he were not there.

One illuminating instance of depersonalization and invisibility occurred with regard to medications. All told, the pseudopatients were administered nearly 2100 pills, including Elavil, Stelazine, Compazine, and Thorazine, to name but a few. (That such a variety of medications should have been administered to patients presenting identical symptoms is itself worthy of note.) Only two were swallowed. The rest were either pocketed or deposited in the toilet. The pseudopatients were not alone in this. Although I have no precise records on how many patients rejected their medications, the pseudopatients frequently found the medications of other patients in the toilet before they deposited their own. As long as they were cooperative, their behavior and the pseudopatients' own in this matter, as in other important matters, went unnoticed throughout.

Reactions to such depersonalization among pseudopatients were intense. Although they had come to the hospital as participant observers and were fully aware that they did not "belong," they nevertheless found themselves caught up in and fighting the process of depersonalization. Some examples: a graduate student in psychology asked his wife to bring his textbooks to the hospital so he could "catch up on his homework"—this despite the elaborate precautions taken to conceal his professional association. The same student, who had trained for quite some time to get into the hospital, and who had looked forward to the experience, "remembered" some drag races that he had wanted to see on the weekend and insisted that he be discharged by that time. Another pseudopatient attempted a romance with a nurse. Subsequently, he informed the staff that he was applying for admission to graduate school in psychology and was very likely to be admitted, since a graduate professor was one of his regular hospital visitors. The same person began to engage in psychotherapy with other patients —all of this as a way of becoming a person in an impersonal environment.

The Sources of Depersonalization

What are the origins of depersonalization? I have already mentioned two. First, are attitudes held by all of us toward the mentally ill—including those who treat them—attitudes characterized by fear, distrust, and horrible expectations on the other. Our ambivalence leads us, in this instance as in others, to avoidance.

Second, and not entirely separate, the hierarchical structure of the psychiatric hospital facilitates depersonalization. Those who are at the top have least to do with patients, and their behavior inspires the rest of the staff. Average daily contact with psychiatrists, psychologists, residents, and physicians combined ranged from 3.9 to 25.1 minutes, with an overall mean of 6.8 (six pseudopatients over a total of 129 days of hospitalization). Included in this average are time spent in the admissions interview, ward meetings in the presence of a senior staff member, group and individual psychotherapy contacts, case presentation conferences, and discharge meetings. Clearly, patients do not spend much time in interpersonal contact with doctoral staff. And doctoral staff serve as models for nurses and attendants.

There are probably other sources. Psychiatric installations are presently in serious financial straits. Staff shortages are pervasive, staff time at a premium. Something has to give, and that something is patient contact. Yet, while financial stresses are realities, too much can be made of them. I have the impression that the psychological forces that result in depersonalization are much stronger than the fiscal ones and that the addition of more staff would not correspondingly improve patient care in this regard. The incidence of staff meetings and the enormous amount of record-keeping on patients, for example, have not been as substantially reduced as has patient contact. Priorities exist, even during hard times. Patient contact is not a significant priority in the traditional psychiatric hospital, and fiscal pressures do not account for this. Avoidance and depersonalization may.

Heavy reliance upon psychotropic medication tacitly contributes to depersonalization by convincing staff that treatment is indeed being conducted and that further patient contact may not be necessary. Even here, however, caution needs to be exercised in understanding the role of psychotropic drugs. If patients were powerful rather than powerless, if they were viewed as interesting individuals rather than diagnostic entities, if they were socially significant rather than social lepers, if their anguish truly and wholly compelled our sympathies and concerns, would we not *seek* contact with them, despite the availability of medications? Perhaps for the pleasure of it all?

The Consequences of Labeling and Depersonalization

Whenever the ratio of what is known to what needs to be known approaches zero, we tend to invent "knowledge" and assume that we understand more than we actually do. We seem unable to acknowledge that we simply don't know. The needs for diagnosis and remediation of behavioral and emotional problems are enormous. But rather than acknowledge that we are just embarking on understanding, we continue to label patients "schizophrenic," "manic-depressive," and "insane," as if in those words we had captured the essence of understanding. The facts of the matter are that we have known for a long time that diagnoses are often not useful or reliable, but we have nevertheless continued to use them. We now know that we cannot distinguish insanity from sanity. It is depressing to consider how that information will be used.

Not merely depressing, but frightening. How many people, one wonders, are sane but not recognized as such in our psychiatric institutions? How many have been needlessly stripped of their privileges of citizenship, from the right to vote and drive to that of handling their own accounts? How many have feigned insanity in order to avoid the criminal consequences of their behavior, and, conversely, how many would rather stand trial than live interminably in a psychiatric hospital—but are wrongly thought to be mentally ill? How many have been stigmatized by well-intentioned, but nevertheless erroneous, diagnoses? On the last point, recall again that a "type 2 error" in psychiatric diagnosis does not have the same consequences it does in medical diagnosis. A diagnosis of cancer that has been found to be in error is cause for celebration. But psychiatric diagnoses are rarely found to be in error. The label sticks, a mark of inadequacy forever.

Finally, how many patients might be "sane" outside the psychiatric hospital but seem insane in it—not because craziness resides in them, as it were, but because they are responding to a bizarre setting, one that may be unique to institutions which harbor nether people? Goffman calls the process of socialization to such institutions "mortification"—an apt metaphor that includes the processes of depersonalization that have been described here. And while it is impossible to know whether the pseudopatients' responses to these processes are characteristic of all inmates—they were after all, not real patients—it is difficult to believe that these processes of socialization to a psychiatric hospital provide useful attitudes or habits of response for living in the "real world."

Summary and Conclusions

It is clear that we cannot distinguish the sane from the insane in psychiatric hospitals. The hospital itself imposes a special environment in which the meanings of behavior can easily be misunderstood. The consequences to patients hospitalized in such an environment—the powerlessness, depersonalization, segregation, mortification, and self-labeling—seem undoubtedly countertherapeutic.

I do not, even now, understand this problem well enough to perceive solutions. But two matters seem to have some promise. The first concerns the proliferation of community mental health facilities, of crisis intervention centers, of the human potential movement, and of behavior therapies that, for all of their own problems, tend to avoid psychiatric labels, to focus on specific problems and behaviors, and to retain the individual in a relatively nonpejorative environment. Clearly, to the extent that we refrain from sending the distressed to insane places, our impressions of them are less likely to be distorted. (The risk of distorted perceptions, it seems to me, is always present, since we are much more sensitive to an individual's behaviors and verbalizations than we are to the subtle contextual stimuli that often promote them. At issue here is a matter of magnitude. And, as I have shown, the magnitude of distortion is exceedingly high in the extreme context that is a psychiatric hospital).

The second matter that might prove promising speaks to the need to increase the sensitivity of mental health workers and researchers to the *Catch-22* position of psychiatric patients. Simply reading materials in this area will be of help to some such workers and researchers. For others, directly experiencing the impact of psychiatric hospitalization will be of enormous use. Clearly, further research into the social psychology of such total institutions will both facilitate treatment and deepen understanding.

I and the other pseudopatients in the psychiatric setting had distinctly negative reactions. We do not pretend to describe the subjective experiences of true patients. Theirs may be different from ours, particularly with the passage of time and the necessary process of adaptation to one's environment. But we can and do speak to the relatively more objective indices of treatment within the hospital. It could be a mistake, and a very unfortunate one, to consider that what happened to us derived from malice or stupidity on the part of the staff. Quite the contrary, our overwhelming impression of them was of people who really cared, who were committed and who were uncommonly intelligent. Where they failed, as they sometimes did painfully, it would be more accurate to attribute those failures to the environment in which they too, found themselves than to personal callousness. Their perceptions and behavior were controlled by the situation, rather than being motivated by a malicious disposition. In a more benign environment, one that was less attached to global diagnosis, their behaviors and judgments might have been more benign and effective.

Robert L. Spitzer

 NO

On Pseudoscience in Science, Logic in Remission and Psychiatric Diagnosis

S ome foods taste delicious but leave a bad aftertaste. So it is with Rosenhan's study, "On Being Sane in Insane Places" (Rosenhan, 1973a), which, by virtue of the prestige and wide distribution of *Science*, the journal in which it appeared, provoked a furor in the scientific community. That the *Journal of Abnormal Psychology*, at this late date, chooses to explore the study's strengths and weaknesses is a testament not only to the importance of the issues that the study purports to deal with but to the impact that the study has had in the mental health community.

Rosenhan apparently believes that psychiatric diagnosis is of no value. There is nothing wrong with his designing a study the results of which might dramatically support this view. However, "On Being Sane in Insane Places" is pseudoscience presented as science. Just as his pseudopatients were diagnosed at discharge as "schizophrenia, in remission," so a careful examination of this study's methods, results, and conclusions leads me to a diagnosis of "logic, in remission."

Let us summarize the study's central question, the methods used, the results reported, and Rosenhan's conclusions. Rosenhan (1973a) states the basic issue simply: "Do the salient characteristics that lead to diagnoses reside in the patients themselves or in the environments and contexts in which observers find them?" Rosenhan proposed that by getting normal people who had never had symptoms of serious psychiatric disorders admitted to psychiatric hospitals "and then determining whether they were discovered to be sane" was an adequate method of studying this question. Therefore, eight "sane" people, pseudopatients, gained secret admission to 12 different hospitals with a single complaint of hearing voices. Upon admission to the psychiatric ward, the pseudopatients ceased simulating any symptoms of abnormality.

The diagnostic results were that 11 of the 12 diagnoses on admission were schizophrenia and 1 was manic-depressive psychosis. At discharge, all of the patients were given the same diagnosis, but were qualified as "in remission."[1]

From Robert L. Spitzer, "On Pseudoscience in Science, Logic in Remission and Psychiatric Diagnosis: A Critique of 'On Being Sane in Insane Places,'" *Journal of Abnormal Psychology*, vol. 84 (1975), pp. 442–452. Copyright © 1975 by The American Psychological Association. Reprinted by permission.

Despite their "show of sanity" the pseudopatients were never detected by any of the professional staff, nor were any questions raised about their authenticity during the entire hospitalization.

Rosenhan (1973a) concluded: "It is clear that we cannot distinguish the sane from the insane in psychiatric hospitals" (p. 257). According to him, what is needed is the avoidance of "global diagnosis," as exemplified by such diagnoses as schizophrenia or manic-depressive psychosis, and attention should be directed instead to "behaviors, the stimuli that provoke them, and their correlates."

The Central Question

One hardly knows where to begin. Let us first acknowledge the potential importance of the study's central research question. Surely, if psychiatric diagnoses are, to quote Rosenhan, "only in the minds of the observers," and do not reflect any characteristics inherent in the patient, then they obviously can be of no use in helping patients. However, the study immediately becomes confused when Rosenhan suggests that this research question can be answered by studying whether or not the "sanity" of pseudopatients in a mental hospital can be discovered. Rosenhan, a professor of law and psychology, knows that the terms "sane" and "insane" are legal, not psychiatric, concepts. He knows that no psychiatrist makes a diagnosis of "sanity" or "insanity" and that the true meaning of these terms, which varies from state to state, involves the inability to appreciate right from wrong—an issue that is totally irrelevant to this study.

Detecting the Sanity of a Pseudopatient

However, if we are forced to use the terms "insane" (to mean roughly showing signs of serious mental disturbance) and "sane" (the absence of such signs), then clearly there are three possible meanings to the concept of "detecting the sanity" of a pseudopatient who feigns mental illness on entry to a hospital, but then acts "normal" throughout his hospital stay. The first is the recognition, when he is first seen, that the pseudopatient is feigning insanity as he attempts to gain admission to the hospital. This would be detecting sanity in a sane person simulating insanity. The second would be the recognition, after having observed him acting normally during his hospitalization, that the pseudopatient was initially feigning insanity. This would be detecting that the currently sane never was insane. Finally, the third possible meaning would be the recognition, during hospitalization, that the pseudopatient, though initially appearing to be "insane," was no longer showing signs of psychiatric disturbance.

These elementary distinctions of "detecting sanity in the insane" are crucial to properly interpreting the results of the study. The reader is misled by Rosenhan's implication that the first two meanings of detecting the sanity of the pseudopatient to be a fraud, are at all relevant to the central research question. Furthermore, he obscures the true results of his study—because they fail to support his conclusion—when the third meaning of detecting sanity is considered, that is, a recognition that after their admission as "insane," the pseudopatients were not psychiatrically disturbed while in the hospital.

Let us examine these three possible meanings of detecting the sanity of the pseudopatient, their logical relation to the central question of the study, and the actual results obtained and the validity of Rosenhan's conclusions.

The Patient Is No Longer "Insane"

We begin with the third meaning of detecting sanity. It is obvious that if the psychiatrists judged the pseudopatients as seriously disturbed while they acted "normal" in the hospital, this would be strong evidence that their assessments were being influenced by the context in which they were making their examination rather than the actual behavior of the patient, which is the central research question. (I suspect that many readers will agree with Hunter who, in a letter to *Science* (Hunter, 1973), pointed out that, "The pseudopatients did *not* behave normally in the hospital. Had their behavior been normal, they would have walked to the nurses' station and said, 'Look, I am a normal person who tried to see if I could get into the hospital by behaving in a crazy way or saying crazy things. It worked and I was admitted to the hospital, but now I would like to be discharged from the hospital'" [p. 361].)

What were the results? According to Rosenhan, all the patients were diagnosed at discharge as "in remission."[2] The meaning of "in remission" is clear: It means without signs of illness. Thus, all of the psychiatrists apparently recognized that all of the pseudopatients were, to use Rosenhan's term, "sane." However, lest the reader appreciate the significance of these findings, Rosenhan (1973a) quickly gives a completely incorrect interpretation: "If the pseudopatient was to be discharged, he must naturally be 'in remission'; but he was not sane, nor, in the institution's view, had he ever been sane" (p. 252). Rosenhan's implication is clear: The patient was diagnosed "in remission" not because the psychiatrist correctly assessed the patient's hospital behavior but only because the patient had to be discharged. Is this interpretation warranted?

I am sure that most readers who are not familiar with the details of psychiatric diagnostic practice assume, from Rosenhan's account, that it is common for schizophrenic patients to be diagnosed "in remission" when discharged from a hospital. As a matter of fact, it is extremely unusual. The reason is that a schizophrenic is rarely completely asymptomatic at discharge. Rosenhan does not report any data concerning the discharge diagnoses of the real schizophrenic patients in the 12 hospitals used in his study. However, I can report on the frequency of a discharge diagnosis of schizophrenia "in remission" at my hospital, the New York State Psychiatric Institute, a research, teaching, and community hospital where diagnoses are made in a routine fashion, undoubtedly no different from the 12 hospitals of Rosenhan's study. I examined the official book that the record room uses to record the discharge diagnoses and their statistical codes for all patients. Of the over 300 patients discharged in the last year with a diagnosis of schizophrenia, not one was diagnosed "in remission." It is only possible to code a diagnosis of "in remission" by adding a fifth digit (5) to the 4-digit code number for the subtype of schizophrenia (e.g., paranoid schizophrenia is coded as 295.3, but paranoid schizophrenia "in remission" is coded as 295.35). I therefore realized that a psychiatrist might intend to make a discharge diagnosis of "in remission" but fail to use the fifth digit, so that the official recording of the diagnosis would not reflect his full assessment. I therefore had research assistants read the discharge summaries of the last 100 patients whose discharge diagnosis was schizophrenia to see how often the term "in remission," "recovered," "no longer ill," or "asymptomatic" was used, even if not recorded by use of the fifth digit in the code number. The result was that only one patient, who was diagnosed paranoid schizophrenia, was described in the summary as being "in remission" at discharge. The fifth digit code was not used.

To substantiate my view that the practice at my hospital of rarely giving a discharge diagnosis of schizophrenia "in remission" is not unique, I had a research assistant call the record room librarians of 12 psychiatric hospitals, chosen catch as catch can.[3] They were told that we were interested in knowing their estimate of how often, at their hospital, schizophrenics were discharged "in remission" (or "no longer ill" or "asymptomatic"). The calls revealed that 11 of the 12 hospitals indicated that the term was either never used or, at most, used for only a handful of patients in a year. The remaining hospital, a private hospital, estimated that the terms were used in roughly 7 percent of the discharge diagnoses.

This leaves us with the conclusion that, because 11 of the 12 pseudopatients were discharged as "schizophrenia in remission," a discharge diagnosis that is rarely given to real schizophrenics, the diagnoses given to the pseudopatients were a function of the patients' behaviors and not of the setting (psychiatric hospital) in which the diagnoses were made. In fact, we must marvel that 11 psychiatrists all acted so rationally as to use at discharge the category of "in remission" or its equivalent, a category that is rarely used with real schizophrenic patients.

It is not only in his discharge diagnosis that the psychiatrist had an opportunity to assess the patient's true condition incorrectly. In the admission mental status examination, during a progress note or in his discharge note the psychiatrist could have described any of the pseudopatients as "still psychotic," "probably still hallucinating but denies it now," "loose associations," or "inappropriate affect." Because Rosenhan had access to all of this material, his failure to report such judgments of continuing serious psychopathology strongly suggests that they were never made.

All pseudopatients took extensive notes publicly to obtain data on staff and patient behavior. Rosenhan claims that the nursing records indicate that "the writing was seen as an aspect of their pathological behavior." The only datum presented to support this claim is that the daily nursing comment on one of the pseudopatients was, "Patient engaged in writing behavior." Because nursing notes frequently and intentionally comment on nonpathological activities that patients engage in so that other staff members have some knowledge of how the patient spends his time, this particular nursing note in no way supports Rosenhan's thesis. Once again, the failure of Rosenhan to provide data regarding instances where normal hospital behavior was categorized as pathological is remarkable. The closest that Rosenhan comes to providing such data is his report of an instance where a kindly nurse asked if a pseudopatient, who was pacing the long hospital corridors because of boredom, was "nervous." It was, after all, a question and not a final judgment.

Let us now examine the relation between the other two meanings of detecting sanity in the pseudopatients: the recognition that the pseudopatient was a fraud, either when he sought admission to the hospital or during this hospital stay, and the central research question.

Detecting "Sanity" Before Admission

Whether or not psychiatrists are able to detect individuals who feign psychiatric symptoms is an interesting question but clearly of no relevance to the issue of whether or not the salient characteristics that lead to diagnoses reside in the patient's behavior or in the minds of the observers. After all, a psychiatrist who believes in a pseudopatient who feigns a symptom *is* responding to the pseudopatient's behavior. And Rosenhan does not blame the psychiatrist for believing the pseudopatient's fake symptom of hallucinations. He blames him for the diagnosis of schizophrenia. Rosenhan (1973b) states:

> The issue is not that the psychiatrist believed him. Neither is it whether the pseudopatient should have been admitted to the psychiatric hospital in the first place.... The issue is the diagnostic leap that was made between the single presenting symptom, hallucinations, and the diagnosis schizophrenia (or in one case, manic-depressive psychosis). Had the pseudopatients been diagnosed "hallucinating," there would have been no further need to examine the diagnosis issue. The diagnosis of hallucinations implies only that: no more. The presence of hallucinations does not itself define the presence of "schizophrenia." And schizophrenia may or may not include hallucinations. (p. 366)

Unfortunately, as judged by many of the letters to *Science* commenting on the study (Letters to the editor, 1973), many readers, including psychiatrists, accepted Rosenhan's thesis that it was irrational for the psychiatrists to have made an initial diagnosis of schizophrenia as *the most likely condition* on the basis of a single symptom. In my judgment, these readers were wrong. Their acceptance of Rosenhan's thesis was aided by the content of the pseudopatients' auditory hallucinations, which were voices that said "empty," "hollow," and "thud." According to Rosenhan (1973a), these symptoms were chosen because of "their apparent similarity to existential symptoms [and] the *absence* of a single report of existential psychoses in the literature" (p. 251). The implication is that if the content of specific symptoms has never been reported in the literature, then a psychiatrist should somehow know that the symptom is fake. Why then, according to Rosenhan, should the psychiatrist have made a diagnosis of hallucinating? This is absurd. Recently I saw a patient who kept hearing a voice that said, "It's O.K. It's O.K." I know of no such report in the literature. So what? I agree with Rosenhan that there has never been a report of an "existential psychosis." However, the diagnoses made were schizophrenia and manic-depressive psychosis, not existential psychosis.

Differential Diagnosis of Auditory Hallucinations

Rosenhan is entitled to believe that psychiatric diagnoses are of no use and therefore should not have been given to the pseudopatients. However, it makes no sense for him to claim that within a diagnostic framework it was irrational to consider schizophrenia seriously as the most likely condition without his presenting a consideration of the differential diagnosis. Let me briefly give what I think is a reasonable differential diagnosis, based on the presenting picture of the pseudopatient when he applied for admission to the hospital.

Rosenhan says that "beyond alleging the symptoms and falsifying name, vocation, and employment, no further alterations of person, history, or circumstances were made" (p. 251). However, clearly the clinical picture includes not only the symptom (auditory hallucinations) but also the desire to enter a psychiatric hospital, from which it is reasonable to conclude that the symptom is a source of significant distress. (How often did the admitting psychiatrist suggest what would seem to be reasonable care: outpatient treatment? Did the pseudopatient have to add other complaints to justify inpatient treatment?) This, plus the knowledge that the auditory hallucinations are of 3 weeks duration,[4] establishes the hallucinations as significant symptoms of psychopathology as distinguished from so-called "pseudohallucinations" (hallucinations while falling asleep or awakening from sleep, or intense imagination with the voice heard from inside of the head).

Auditory hallucinations can occur in several kinds of mental disorders. The absence of a history of alcohol, drug abuse, or some other toxin, the absence of any signs of physical illness (such as high fever), and the absence of evidence of distractibility, impairment in concentration, memory or orientation, and a negative neurological examination all make an organic psychosis extremely unlikely. The absence of a recent precipitating stress rules out a transient situational disturbance of psychotic intensity or (to use a nonofficial category) hysterical psychosis. The absence of a profound disturbance in mood rules out an effective psychosis (we are not given the mental status findings for the patient who was diagnosed manic-depressive psychosis).

What about simulating mental illness? Psychiatrists know that occasionally an individual who has something to gain from being admitted to a psychiatric hospital will exaggerate or even feign psychiatric symptoms. This is a genuine diagnostic problem that psychiatrists and other physicians occasionally confront and is called "malingering." However, with the pseudopatients there was no reason to believe that any of them had anything to gain from being admitted into a psychiatric hospital except relief from their alleged complaint, and therefore no reason to suspect that the illness was feigned. Dear Reader: There is only one remaining diagnosis for the presenting symptom of hallucinations under these conditions in the classification of mental disorders used in this country, and that is schizophrenia.

Admittedly, there is a hitch to a definitive diagnosis of schizophrenia: Almost invariably there are other signs of the disorder present, such as poor premorbid adjustment, affective blunting, delusions, or signs of thought disorder. I would hope that if I had been one of the 12 psychiatrists presented with such a patient, I would have been struck by the lack of other signs of the disorder, but I am rather sure that having no reason to doubt the authenticity of the patients' claim of auditory hallucinations, I also would have been fooled into noting schizophrenia as the most likely diagnosis.

What does Rosenhan really mean when he objects to the diagnosis of schizophrenia because it was based on a "single symptom"? Does he believe that there are real patients with the single symptom of auditory hallucinations who are misdiagnosed as schizophrenic when they actually have some other condition? If so, what is the nature of that condition? Is Rosenhan's point that the psychiatrist should have used "diagnosis deferred," a category that is available but rarely used? I would have no argument with this conclusion. Furthermore, if he had presented data from real patients indicating how often patients are erroneously diagnosed on the basis of inadequate information and what the consequences were, it would have been a real contribution.

Until now, I have assumed that the pseudopatients presented only one symptom of psychiatric disorder. Actually, we know very little about how the pseudopatients presented themselves. What did the pseudopatients say in the study reported in *Science,* when asked as they must have been, what effect the hallucinations were having on their lives and why they were seeking admission into a hospital? The reader would be much more confident that a single presenting symptom was involved if Rosenhan had made available for each pseudopatient the actual admission work-up from the hospital record.

Detecting Sanity After Admission

Let us now examine the last meaning of detecting sanity in the pseudopatients, namely, the psychiatrist's recognition, *after* observing him act normally during his hospitalization, that the pseudopatient was initially feigning insanity and its relation to the central research question. If a diagnostic condition, by definition, is always chronic and never remits, it would be irrational not to question the original diagnosis if a patient were later found to be asymptomatic. As applied to this study, if the concept of schizophrenia did not admit the possibility of recovery, then failure to question the original diagnosis when the pseudopatients were no longer overtly ill would be relevant to the central research question. It would be an example of the psychiatrist allowing the context of the hospital environment to influence his diagnostic behavior. But neither any psychiatric textbook nor the American Psychiatric Association's *Diagnostic and Statistical Manual of Mental Disorders* (American Psychiatric Association, 1968) suggests that mental illnesses endure forever. Oddly enough, it is Rosenhan (1973a) who, without any reference to the psychiatric literature, says: "A broken leg is something one recovers from, but mental illness allegedly endures forever" (p. 254). Who, other than Rosenhan, alleges it?

As Rosenhan should know, although some American psychiatrists restrict the label of schizophrenia to mean chronic or process schizophrenia, most

American psychiatrists include an acute subtype. Thus, the *Diagnostic and Statistical Manual*, in describing the subtype, acute schizophrenic episode, states that "in many cases the patient recovers within weeks."

A similar straw man is created when Rosenhan (1973a) says,

> The insane are not always insane... the bizarre behaviors upon which their (the pseudopatients) behaviors were allegedly predicated constituted only a small fraction of their total behavior. If it makes no sense to label ourselves permanently depressed on the basis of an occasional depression, then it takes better evidence than is presently available to label all patients insane or schizophrenic on the basis of behaviors or cognitions. (p. 254)

Who ever said that the behaviors that indicate schizophrenia or any other diagnostic category comprise the total of a patient's behavior? A diagnosis of schizophrenia does not mean that all of the patient's behavior is schizophrenic anymore than a diagnosis of carcinoma of the liver means that all of the patient's body is diseased.

Does Rosenhan at least score a point by demonstrating that, although the professional staff never considered the possibility that the pseudopatient was a fraud, this possibility was often considered by other patients? Perhaps, but I am not so sure. Let us not forget that all of the pseudopatients "took extensive notes publicly." Obviously this was highly unusual patient behavior and Rosenhan's quote from a suspicious patient suggests the importance it had in focusing the other patients' attention on the pseudopatients: "You're not crazy. You're a journalist or a professor (referring to the continual note-taking). You're checking up on the hospital." (Rosenhan, 1973a, p. 252)

Rosenhan presents ample evidence, which I find no reason to dispute, that the professional staff spent little time actually with the pseudopatients. The note-taking may easily have been overlooked, and therefore they developed no suspicion that the pseudopatients had simulated illness to gain entry into the hospital. Because there were no pseudopatients who did not engage in such unusual behaviors, the reader cannot assess the significance of the patients' suspicions of fraud when the professional staff did not. I would predict, however, that a pseudopatient in a ward of patients with mixed diagnostic conditions would have no difficulty in masquerading convincingly as a true patient to both staff and patients if he did nothing unusual to draw attention to himself.

Rosenhan presents one way in which the diagnosis affected the psychiatrist's perception of the patient's circumstances: Historical facts of the case were often distorted by the staff to achieve consistency with psychodynamic theories. Here, for the first time, I believe Rosenhan has hit the mark. What he described happens all the time and often makes attendance at clinical case conferences extremely painful, especially for those with a logical mind and a research orientation. Although his observation is correct, it would seem to be more a consequence of individuals attempting to rearrange facts to comply with an unproven etiological theory than a consequence of diagnostic labeling. One could as easily imagine a similar process occurring when a weak-minded, behaviorally-oriented clinician attempts to rewrite the patient's history to account for "hallucinations reinforced by attention paid to patient by family members when patient complains of hearing voices." Such is the human condition.

One final finding requires comment. In order to determine whether "the tendency toward diagnosing the sane insane could be reversed," the staff of a research and teaching hospital was informed that at some time during the following three months, one or more pseudopatients would attempt to be admitted. No such attempt was actually made. Yet approximately 10 percent of the 193 real patients were suspected by two or more staff members (we are not told how many made judgments) to be pseudopatients. Rosenhan (1973a) concluded: "Any diagnostic process that lends itself so readily to massive errors of this sort cannot be a very reliable one" (p. 179). My conclusion is that this experimental design practically assures only one outcome.

Elementary Principles of Reliability of Classification

Some very important principles that are relevant to the design of Rosenhan's study are taught in elementary psychology courses and should not be forgotten. One of them is that a measurement or classification procedure is not reliable or unreliable in itself but only in its application to a specific population. There are serious problems in the reliability of psychiatric diagnosis as it is applied to the population to which psychiatric diagnoses are ordinarily given. However, I fail to see, and Rosenhan does not even attempt to show, how the reliability of psychiatric diagnoses applied to a population of pseudopatients (or one including the threat of pseudopatients). The two populations are just not the same. Kety (1974) has expressed it dramatically:

> If I were to drink a quart of blood and, concealing what I had done, come to the emergency room of any hospital vomiting blood, the behavior of the staff would be quite predictable. If they labeled and treated me as having a bleeding peptic ulcer, I doubt that I could argue convincingly that medical science does not know how to diagnose that condition. (p. 959)

(I have no doubt that if the condition known as pseudopatient ever assumed epidemic proportions among admittants to psychiatric hospitals, psychiatrists would in time become adept at identifying them, though at what risk to real patients, I do not know.)

Attitudes Toward the Insane

I shall not dwell on the latter part of Rosenhan's study, which deals with the experience of psychiatric hospitalization. Because some of the hospitals participated in residency training programs and were research oriented, I find it hard to believe that conditions were quite as bad as depicted, but they may well be. I have always believed that psychiatrists should spend more time on psychiatric wards to appreciate how mind dulling the experience must be for patients. However, Rosenhan does not stop at documenting the horrors of life on a psychiatric ward. He asserts, without a shred of evidence from his study, that "negative attitudes [toward psychiatric patients] are the natural offspring of the labels patients wear and the places in which they are found." This is nonsense. In recent years large numbers of chronic psychiatric patients, many of them chronic schizophrenics and geriatric patients with organic brain syndromes, have been discharged from state hospitals and placed in communities that have no facilities to deal with them. The affected communities are up in arms not primarily because they are mental patients labeled with psychiatric diagnoses (because the majority are not recognized as ex-patients) but because the behavior of some of them is sometimes incomprehensible, deviant, strange, and annoying.

There are at least two psychiatric diagnoses that are defined by the presence of single behaviors, much as Rosenhan would prefer a diagnosis of hallucinations to a diagnosis of schizophrenia. They are alcoholism and drug abuse. Does society have negative attitudes toward these individuals because of the diagnostic label attached to them by psychiatrists or because of their behavior?

The Uses of Diagnosis

Rosenhan believes that the pseudopatients should have been diagnosed as having hallucinations of unknown origin. It is not clear what he thinks the diagnosis should have been if the pseudopatients had been sufficiently trained to talk, at times, incoherently, and had complained of difficulty in thinking clearly, lack of emotion, and that their thoughts were being broadcast so that strangers knew what they were thinking. Is Rosenhan perhaps suggesting multiple diagnoses of (a) hallucinations, (b) difficulty thinking clearly, (c) lack of emotion, and (d) incoherent speech ... all of unknown origin?

It is no secret that we lack a full understanding of such conditions as schizophrenia and manic-depressive illness, but are we quite as ignorant as Rosenhan would have us believe? Do we not know, for example, that hallucinations of voices accusing the patient of sin are associated with depressed affect, diurnal mood variation, loss of appetite, and insomnia? What about hallucinations of God's voice issuing commandments, associated with euphoric affect, psychomotor excitement, and accelerated and disconnected speech? Is this not also an entirely different condition?

There is a purpose to psychiatric diagnosis (Spitzer & Wilson, 1975). It is to enable mental health professionals to (a) communicate with each other about the subject matter of their concern, (b) comprehend the pathological processes involved in psychiatric illness, and (c) control psychiatric disorders. Control consists of the ability to predict outcome, prevent the disorder from developing, and treat it once it has developed. Any serious discussion of the validity of psychiatric diagnosis, or suggestions for alternative systems of classifying psychological disturbance, must address itself to these purposes of psychiatric diagnosis.

In terms of its ability to accomplish these purposes, I would say that psychiatric diagnosis is moderately effective as a shorthand way of communicating the presence of constellations of signs and symptoms that tend to cluster together, is woefully inadequate in helping us understand the pathological processes of psychiatric disorders, but does offer considerable help in the control of many mental disorders. Control is possible because psychiatric diagnosis often yields information of value in predicting the likely course of illness (e.g., an early recovery, chronicity, or recurrent episodes) and because for many mental disorders it is useful in suggesting the best available treatment.

Let us return to the three different clinical conditions that I described, each of which had auditory hallucinations as one of its manifestations. The reader will have no difficulty in identifying the three hypothetical conditions as schizophrenia, psychotic depression, and mania. Anyone familiar with the literature on psychiatric treatment will know that there are numerous well-controlled studies (Klein & Davis, 1969) indicating the superiority of the major tranquilizers for the treatment of schizophrenia, of electroconvulsive therapy for the treatment of psychotic depression and, more recently, of lithium carbonate for the treatment of mania. Furthermore, there is convincing evidence that these three conditions, each of which is often accompanied by hallucinations, are influenced by separate genetic factors. As Kety (1974) said, "If schizophrenia is a myth, it is a myth with a strong genetic component."

Should psychiatric diagnosis be abandoned for a purely descriptive system that focuses on simple phenotypic behaviors before it has been demonstrated that such an approach is more useful as a guide to successful treatment or for understanding the role of genetic factors? I think not. (I have a vision. Traditional psychiatric diagnosis has long been forgotten. At a conference on behavioral classification, a keen research investigator proposes that the category "hallucinations of unknown etiology" be subdivided into three different groups based on associated symptomatology. The first group is characterized by depressed affect, diurnal mood variation, and so on, the second group by euphoric mood, psychomotor excitement....)

If psychiatric diagnosis is not quite as bad as Rosenhan would have us believe, that does not mean that it is all that good. What is the reliability of psychiatric diagnosis prior to 1972? Spitzer & Fleiss (1974) revealed that "reliability is only satisfactory for three categories: mental deficiencies, organic brain syndrome, and alcoholism. The level of reliability is no better than fair for psychosis and schizophrenia, and is poor for the remaining categories." So be it. But where did Rosenhan get the idea that psychiatry is the only medical specialty that is plagued by inaccurate diagnosis? Studies have shown serious unreliability in the diagnosis of pulmonary disorders (Fletcher, 1952), in the interpretation of electrocardiograms (Davis, 1958), in the interpretation of X-rays (Cochrane & Garland, 1952; Yerushalmy, 1947), and in the certification of causes of death (Markush, Schaaf, & Siegel, 1967). A review of diagnostic unreliability in other branches of physical medicine is given by Garland (1960) and the problem of the vagueness of medical criteria for diagnosis is thoroughly discussed by Feinstein (1967). The poor reliability of medical diagnosis, even when assisted by objective laboratory tests, does not mean that medical diagnosis is of no value. So it is with psychiatric diagnosis.

Recognition of the serious problems of the reliability of psychiatric diagnosis has resulted in a new approach to psychiatric diagnosis—the use of specific inclusion and exclusion criteria, as contrasted with the usually vague and ill-defined general descriptions found in the psychiatric literature and in the standard psychiatric glossary of the American Psychiatric Association. This approach was started by the St. Louis group associated with the Department of Psychiatry of Washington University (Feighner, Robins, Guze, Woodruff, Winokur, & Munoz, 1972) and has been further developed by Spitzer, Endicott, and Robins (1974) as a set of criteria for a selected group of functional psychiatric disorders, called the Research Diagnostic Criteria (RDC). The Display shows the specific criteria for a diagnosis of schizophrenia from the latest version of the RDC.[5]

Diagnostic Criteria for Schizophrenia From the Research Diagnostic Criteria

1. At least two of the following are required for definite diagnosis and one for probable diagnosis:

    a. Thought broadcasting, insertion, or withdrawal (as defined in the RDC).
    b. Delusions of control, other bizarre delusions, or multiple delusions (as defined in the RDC), of any duration as long as definitely present.
    c. Delusions other than persecutory or jealousy, lasting at least 1 week.
    d. Delusions of any type if accompanied by hallucinations of any type for at least 1 week.
    e. Auditory hallucinations in which either a voice keeps up a running commentary on the patient's behaviors or thoughts as they occur, or two or more voices converse with each other (of any duration as long as definitely present).
    f. Nonaffective verbal hallucinations spoken to the subject (as defined in this manual).
    g. Hallucinations of any type throughout the day for several days or intermittently for at least 1 month.
    h. Definite instances of formal thought disorder (as defined in the RDC).
    i. Obvious catatonic motor behavior (as defined in the RDC).

2. A period of illness lasting at least 2 weeks.
3. At no time during the active period of illness being considered did the patient meet the criteria for either probable or definite manic or depressive syndrome (Criteria 1 and 2 under Major Depressive or Manic Disorders) to such a degree that it was a prominent part of the illness.

Reliability studies using the RDC with case record material (from which all cues as to diagnosis and treatment were removed), as well as with live

patients, indicate high reliability for all of the major categories and reliability coefficients generally higher than have ever been reported (Spitzer,
Endicott, Robins, Kuriansky, & Garland, in press). It is therefore clear that
the reliability of psychiatric diagnosis can be greatly increased by the use
of specific criteria. (The interjudge reliability [chance corrected agreement,
K] for the diagnosis of schizophrenia using an earlier version of RDC criteria with 68 newly admitted psychiatric inpatients at the New York State
Psychiatric Institute was .88, which is a thoroughly respectable level of reliability). It is very likely that the next edition of the American Psychiatric
Association's *Diagnostic and Statistical Manual* will contain similar specific
criteria.

There are other problems with current psychiatric diagnosis. The recent
controversy over whether or not homosexuality per se should be considered a
mental disorder highlighted the lack of agreement within the psychiatric profession as to the definition of a mental disorder. A definition has been proposed
by Spitzer (Spitzer & Wilson, 1975), but it is not at all clear whether a consensus
will develop supporting it.

There are serious problems of validity. Many of the traditional diagnostic
categories, such as some of the subtypes of schizophrenia and of major affective
illness, and several of the personality disorders, have not been demonstrated
to be distinct entities or to be useful for prognosis or treatment assignment.
In addition, despite considerable evidence supporting the distinctness of such
conditions as schizophrenia and manic-depressive illness, the boundaries separating these conditions from other conditions are certainly not clear. Finally,
the categories of the traditional psychiatric nomenclature are of least value
when applied to the large numbers of outpatients who are not seriously ill.
It is for these patients that a more behaviorally or problem-oriented approach
might be particularly useful.

I have not dealt at all with the myriad ways in which psychiatric diagnostic labels can be, and are, misused to hurt patients rather than to help them.
This is a problem requiring serious research which, unfortunately, Rosenhan's
study does not help illuminate. However, whatever the solutions to that problem the misuse of psychiatric diagnostic labels is not a sufficient reason to
abandon their use because they have been shown to be of value when properly used.

In conclusion, there are serious problems with psychiatric diagnosis, as
there are with other medical diagnoses. Recent developments indicate that the
reliability of psychiatric diagnosis can be considerably improved. However, *even
with the poor reliability of current psychiatric diagnosis, it is not so poor that it
cannot be an aid in the treatment of the seriously disturbed psychiatric patient.*
Rosenhan's study, "On Being Sane in Insane Places," proves that pseudopatients
are not detected by psychiatrists as having simulated signs of mental illness.
This rather remarkable finding is not relevant to the real problems of the reliability and validity of psychiatric diagnosis and only serves to obscure them. A
correct interpretation of his own data contradicts his conclusions. In the setting of a psychiatric hospital, psychiatrists are remarkably able to distinguish
the "sane" from the "insane."

Notes

1. The original article only mentions that the 11 schizophrenics were diagnosed "in remission." Personal communication from D. L. Rosenhan indicates that this also applied to the single pseudopatient diagnosed as manic-depressive psychosis.

2. In personal communication D. L. Rosenhan said that "in remission" referred to a use of that term or one of its equivalents, such as recovered or no longer ill.

3. Rosenhan has not identified the hospitals used in this study because of his concern with issues of confidentiality and the potential for ad hominem attack. However, this does make it impossible for anyone at those hospitals to corroborate or challenge his account of how the pseudopatients acted and how they were perceived. The 12 hospitals used in my mini-study were: Long Island Jewish-Hillside Medical Center, New York; Massachusetts General Hospital, Massachusetts; St. Elizabeth's Hospital, Washington, D.C.; McLean Hospital, Massachusetts; UCLA, Neuropsychiatric Institute, California; Meyer-Manhattan Hospital (Manhattan State), New York; Vermont State Hospital, Vermont; Medical College of Virginia, Virginia; Emory University Hospital, Georgia; High Point Hospital, New York; Hudson River State Hospital, New York, and New York Hospital-Cornell Medical Center, Westchester Division, New York.

4. This was not in the article but was mentioned to me in personal communication by D. L. Rosenhan.

5. For what it is worth, the pseudopatient would have been diagnosed as "probable" schizophrenia using these criteria because of 1(f). In personal communication, Rosenhan said that when the pseudopatients were asked how frequently the hallucinations occurred, they said "I don't know." Therefore, Criterion 1(g) is not met.

References

American Psychiatric Association. *Diagnostic and statistical manual of mental disorders* (2nd ed.). Washington, D.C.: American Psychiatric Association, 1968.

Cochrane, A. L., & Garland, L. H. Observer error in interpretation of chest films: International Investigation. *Lancet,* 1952, 2, 505–509.

Davies, L. G. Observer variation in reports on electrocardiograms. *British Heart Journal,* 1958, 20, 153–161.

Feighner, J. P., and Robins, E., Guze, S. B., Woodruff, R. A., Winokur, G., & Munoz, R. Diagnostic criteria for use in psychiatric research. *Archives of General Psychiatry,* 1972, *26,* 57-63.

Feinstein, A. *Clinical judgment.* Baltimore, Md.: Williams & Wilkins, 1967.

Fletcher, C. M. Clinical diagnosis of pulmonary emphysema—an experimental study. *Proceedings of the Royal Society of Medicine,* 1952, *45,* 577–584.

Garland, L. H. The problem of observer error. *Bulletin of the New York Academy of Medicine,* 1960, *36,* 570–584.

Hunter, F. M. Letters to the editor. *Science,* 1973, *180,* 361.

Kety, S. S. From rationalization to reason. *American Journal of Psychiatry,* 1974, *131,* 957-963.

Klein, D., & Davis, J. *Diagnosis and drug treatment of psychiatric disorders.* Baltimore, Md.: Williams & Wilkins, 1969.

Letters to the editor. *Science,* 1973, *180,* 356–365.

Markush, R. E., Schaaf, W. E., & Siegel, D. G. The influence of the death certifier on the results of epidemiologic studies. *Journal of the National Medical Association,* 1967, *59,* 105–113.

Rosenhan, D. L. On being sane in insane places. *Science,* 1973, *179,* 250-258. (a)

Rosenhan, D. L. Reply to letters to the editor. *Science,* 1973, *180,* 365–369. (b)

Spitzer, R. L., Endicott, J., & Robins, E. *Research diagnostic criteria.* New York: Biometrics Research, New York State Department of Mental Hygiene, 1974.

Spitzer, R. L., Endicott, J., Robins, E., Kuriansky, J., & Garland, B. Preliminary report of the reliability of research diagnostic criteria applied to psychiatric case records. In A. Sudilofsky, B. Beer, & S. Gershon (Eds.), *Prediction in psychopharmacology,* New York: Raven Press, in press.

Spitzer, R. L. & Fleiss, J. L. A reanalysis of the reliability of psychiatric diagnosis. *British Journal of Psychiatry,* 1974, *125,* 341–347.

Spitzer, R. L., & Wilson, P. T. Nosology and the official psychiatric nomenclature. In A. Freedman & H. Kaplan (Eds.), *Comprehensive textbook of psychiatry.* New York: Williams & Wilkins, 1975.

Yerushalmy, J. Statistical problems in assessing methods of medical diagnosis with special reference to X-ray techniques. *Public Health Reports,* 1947, *62,* 1432–1449.

CHALLENGE QUESTIONS

Classic Dialogue: Do Diagnostic Labels Hinder Treatment?

1. Would society be better off if there were no names (such as "normal" or "abnormal") for broad categories of behavior? Why, or why not?
2. Who would you consider best qualified to judge a person's mental health: a parent, a judge, or a doctor? Why?
3. If a person at any time displays symptoms of a mental disorder, even fraudulently, is it helpful to consider that the same symptoms of disorder may appear again? Why, or why not?
4. Is there any danger in teaching the diagnostic categories of mental behavior to beginning students of psychology? Explain.

ISSUE 12

Do Multiple Personalities Exist?

YES: Frank W. Putnam, from "Response to Article by Paul R. McHugh," *Journal of the American Academy of Child and Adolescent Psychiatry* (July 1995)

NO: Paul R. McHugh, from "Resolved: Multiple Personality Disorder Is an Individually and Socially Created Artifact," *Journal of the American Academy of Child and Adolescent Psychiatry* (July 1995)

ISSUE SUMMARY

YES: Psychiatrist Frank W. Putnam defends the diagnosis of multiple personalities on the basis of research that demonstrates agreed-upon criteria of validity.

NO: Psychiatrist Paul R. McHugh rejects the notion of a multiple personality disorder and proposes that its appearance is a product of therapist suggestion.

In 1973 actress Sally Field won an Emmy Award for her performance in the movie *Sybil,* a story about a woman believed to have 16 different personalities. Much like *The Three Faces of Eve,* a movie that was released in 1957, *Sybil* had a major impact on the public perception of a phenomenon that had been relatively rare up to that point in medical history: multiple personality disorder (MPD).

Officially known today as *dissociative identity disorder,* MPD has had a love-hate relationship with mental health professionals and the American public in the last two decades. In the 1980s the diagnosis of MPD surged beyond the few cases that were previously reported, and specialty clinics opened across the United States to treat the many people who were thought to have the disorder. Many books and articles were published on the topic, and childhood abuse was proposed as the principal cause, with treatment consisting of a reintegration of "alters," or alternative personalities, into the "host personality."

In recent years, however, MPD has fallen into increasing disfavor in the eyes of the public as well as of professionals. Professional skepticism of the validity of MPD has increased because of evidence indicating that therapists can induce MPD in their clients by proposing dissociated personas as an explanation of emotional problems. In this sense, critics argue, MPD is merely a psychological fad that is currently waning in popularity.

In the first of the following selections, Frank W. Putnam disagrees with the notion that MPD is merely a fad. He reviews scientific evidence supporting the validity of MPD and contends that by meeting scientific criteria, the disorder is just as authentic as any other diagnosis. Moreover, Putnam contends that no documented cases exist in which a therapist induced a full MPD disorder.

In the second selection, Paul R. McHugh takes the opposite position. For him, MPD is no more than an iatrogenic (therapist-induced) disorder that can be explained by the same dynamics of hysteria that psychoanalyst Sigmund Freud brought to the public's attention. McHugh contends that when MPD symptoms are operationalized and included in the formal diagnostic system, psychotherapists believe that MPD must be valid and reinforce this idea in their clients through leading questions.

POINT

- MPD's clinical characteristics have been demonstrated in hundreds of cases and numerous studies.

- Research that seems to support MPD as therapist-induced is conducted in labs with role-playing students—all having little relation to actual clinical realities.
- By meeting the three basic forms of validity, MPD is a valid diagnosis.
- MPD is a long-standing disorder, crossing all sorts of psychological fads.

COUNTERPOINT

- Therapists believe that if the diagnostic system includes the disorder, it must therefore exist, and they pass this expectation on to their clients.
- Therapists have been known to induce the MPD phenomenon in their real-life clients.

- MPD is nothing more than a modern-day hysteria.
- The frequency of MPD diagnoses fluctuates with the current therapeutic fad of the day.

Frank W. Putnam    **YES**

Response to Article by Paul R. McHugh

For more than a century, the existence of multiple personality disorder (MPD) has provoked heated debate. That both the diagnosis and the controversy are still with us says something about the resiliency of both sides of the question. The similarities between the charges leveled in the current debate and those in the historical record suggest that things, unfortunately, have not changed very much in 100 years. It is unlikely that this exchange will resolve the matter, but perhaps we can move the question along to a higher level. The criticisms leveled at MPD are not credible when examined in the light of what we know about the etiologies of mental illness. Debate can be advanced by critiqueing the validity of MPD in the same manner in which the validity of other psychiatric diagnoses are assessed.

What are the criticisms of MPD? There are three basic criticisms made against this diagnosis. The first is that MPD is an iatrogenic disorder produced in patients by their psychiatrists. The second is that MPD is produced by its portrayal in the popular media. The third is that the numbers of MPD cases are increasing exponentially. The first and second charges are often lumped together and viewed as being responsible for the third.

The first accusation is historically the oldest and the most serious because it alleges therapeutic misconduct of the gravest nature. The psychiatrist's fascination with the patient's symptoms supposedly reinforces the behavior and produces the syndrome. A variation of this accusation charges that the condition is produced by the improper use of hypnosis. In either instance, the fact is that there are no cases reported in which the full clinical syndrome of MPD was induced either by fascination or by hypnosis. Experiments by Nicholas Spanos are sometimes cited as examples of the creation of MPD by role-playing students (Spanos, 1986). The reader is invited to compare the verbal responses of undergraduates responding to a staged situation with the psychiatric symptoms of MPD patients reported in the clinical literature. Two clinical studies examined the effects of using hypnosis on the symptoms and behaviors of MPD patients (Putnam et al., 1986; Ross, 1989). There were no significant differences between MPD cases diagnosed and treated with or without hypnosis. Since MPD appears in many patients with no history of hypnotic interventions, the misuse of hypnosis apparently is not responsible for the syndrome.

From Frank W. Putnam, "Response to Article by Paul R. McHugh," *Journal of the American Academy of Child and Adolescent Psychiatry*, vol. 34, no. 7 (July 1995). Copyright © 1995 by The American Academy of Child and Adolescent Psychiatry. Reprinted by permission of Lippincott Williams & Wilkins and the author.

The second allegation, that MPD is induced by media portrayals, ignores extensive research on the effects of the media on behavior. More than 30 years of research on the relation of television viewing to violence informs us of just how difficult it is to find clear-cut effects produced by exposure to specific media imagery. Certainly there are media effects, but these effects are not simple and direct identifications. Rather they are indirect, cumulative, and heavily confounded by individual and situational variables (Friedlander, 1993). The depiction of violence in the media is vastly more common (perhaps it is even the norm for movies and television) than the portrayal of MPD. Yet, the critics of MPD would have us believe that the minuscule percentage of media time devoted to MPD is directly responsible for the increase in diagnosed cases. This would be an extraordinarily specific and powerful effect—far, far beyond anything found by the thousands of studies on violence conducted by media researchers.

The first and second accusations beg an important question. Why this disorder? If these individuals are so suggestible, why don't they develop other disorders? Why should suggestion effects be unique to MPD? Psychiatrists inquire about and exhibit interest in other symptoms. We do not believe that asking about hallucinations produces them in a patient. Why should asking about the existence of "other parts" of the self produce alter personalities? What is so magical about this question? With respect to media portrayals of mental illness, a random channel-walk through the soap opera and talk show circuits will convince one that many other symptoms and disorders fill the airwaves. Eating disorders, obsessive-compulsive disorder, bipolar illness, assorted phobias, sexual dysfunctions, autism, chronic fatigue syndrome, etc., etc., are discussed in graphic detail and glamorized after their own fashion. Why don't suggestible individuals identify with these conditions? Truly, if there is such a high degree of suggestive specificity to MPD, it is worthy of intensive investigation.

The third accusation, that cases of MPD are increasing "exponentially" or "logarithmically," shows little understanding of basic mathematics. Critics often cite inflated numbers of cases without any support for their figures. I have plotted the numbers of published cases year by year, and while it is true that they have increased significantly compared to prior decades, the rise in the slope is not nearly as dramatic as the critics' hyperbole suggests. Over the same period, other disorders, e.g., Lyme disease, obsessive-compulsive disorder, and chronic fatigue syndrome, have shown equal or faster rises in the numbers of published cases. This reflects a basic process in medicine associated with the compilation and dissemination of syndromal profiles. When symptoms that were once viewed as unrelated are organized into a coherent syndromal presentation and that information is widely disseminated, physicians begin to identify the condition more frequently. The rapid rise in the number of cases of "battered child syndrome" following the classic paper by Kempe and his colleagues is a very relevant example of this process in action. A related criticism is that a few clinicians are responsible for most of the diagnosed MPD cases. Again, a review of the MPD literature demonstrates a healthy diversity of authorship comparable with that found for other conditions.

The crucial question raised by this debate is: How should the validity of a psychiatric diagnosis be judged? Considerable thought has gone into this question. (For a more complete discussion, see *The Validity of Psychiatric Diagnosis* by Robins and Barrett, 1989.) Many psychiatrists endorse the model of diagnostic validity put forth by Robins and Guze in 1970 and subsequently amplified by others (Robins and Barrett, 1989). This model requires that psychiatric diagnoses satisfy aspects of three basic forms of validity: content validity, criterion-related validity, and construct validity. Content validity is probably the most fundamental form of validity for psychiatric diagnosis. It requires that the diagnostician be able to give a specific and detailed clinical description of the disorder. Criterion-related validity requires that laboratory tests, e.g., chemical, physiological, radiological, or reliable psychological tests, are consistent with the defined clinical picture. Construct validity requires that the disorder be delimited from other disorders (discriminant validity).

The clinical phenomenology of MPD has been delineated and repeatedly replicated in a series of studies of more than 1,000 cases. A review of the best of these studies demonstrates striking similarities in the symptoms of MPD patients across different sites and investigational methodologies (Coons et al., 1988; Putnam et al., 1986; Ross et al., 1990). They should convince the interested reader that a specific, unique, and reproducible clinical syndrome is being described. A small but growing body of literature on childhood and adolescent MPD links the adult syndrome with childhood precursors, establishing a developmental continuity of symptoms and pathology (Dell and Eisenhower, 1990; Hornstein and Putnam, 1992). The well-delineated, well-replicated set of dissociative symptoms that constitute the core clinical syndrome of MPD satisfies the requirements for content validity.

MPD and its core pathological process, dissociation, can be detected and measured by reliable and valid structured interviews and scales (Carlson et al., 1993; Steinberg et al., 1991). Published data on validity compare very favorably with accepted psychological instruments and satisfy the reliability requirement imposed by Robins and Guze for the inclusion of psychological tests as measures of criterion validity. These instruments have been translated into other languages and proven to discriminate MPD in other cultures. Discriminant validity studies have been conducted for the Dissociative Experiences Scale and the Structured Clinical Interview for DSM-III-R-Dissociative Module, both of which show good receiver operating characteristic curves, a standard method for evaluating the validity of a diagnostic test (Carlson et al., 1993; Steinberg et al., 1991). MPD is well discriminated from other disorders by reliable and valid tests and thus has good criterion-related and construct validates.

Multiple personality disorder has been with us from the beginnings of psychiatry (Ellenberger, 1970). At present we conceptualize this condition as a complex form of posttraumatic dissociative disorder, highly associated with a history of severe trauma usually beginning at an early age. I believe that research demonstrates that the diagnosis of MPD meets the standards of content validity, criterion-related validity, and construct validity considered necessary for the validity of a psychiatric diagnosis. The simplistic argument that MPD is individually and socially caused "hysteria" evades the much more important question of what is the best approach to helping these patients. Denying its existence or blaming psychiatrists and television for MPD patients' symptoms is not constructive. It is important to move beyond debate about the existence of the condition to more serious discussions of therapeutic issues.

References

Carlson EB, Putnam FW, Ross CA et al. (1993), *Validity of the Dissociative Experiences Scale* in screening for multiple personality disorder: a multicenter study. *Am J Psychiatry* 150:1030–1036

Coons PM, Bowman ES, Milstein V (1988), Multiple personality disorder: a clinical investigation of 50 cases. *J Nerv Ment Dis* 176:519–527

Dell PF, Eisenhower JW (1990), Adolescent multiple personality disorder. *J Am Acad Child Adolesc Psychiatry* 29:359–366

Ellenberger HF (1970), *The Discovery of the Unconscious: The History and Evolution of Dynamic Psychiatry.* New York: Basic Books

Friedlander BZ (1993), Community violence, children's development, and mass media: in pursuit of new insights, new goals and new strategies. In: *Children and Violence,* Reiss D, Richters JE, Radke-Yarrow M, Scharff D, eds. New York: Guilford Press, pp 66–81

Hornstein NL, Putnam FW (1992), Clinical phenomenology of child and adolescent dissociative disorders. *J Am Acad Child Adolesc Psychiatry* 31:1077–1085

Putnam FW, Guroff JJ, Silberman EK, Barban L, Post RM (1986), The clinical phenomenology of multiple personality disorder: review of 100 recent cases. *J Clin Psychiatry* 47:285–293

Robins LE, Barrett JE, ed. (1989), *The Validity of Psychiatric Diagnosis.* New York: Raven Press

Ross CA (1989), Effects of hypnosis on the features of multiple personality disorder. *Am J Clin Hypn* 32:99–106

Ross CA, Miller SD, Bjornson L, Reagor P, Fraser G, Anderson G (1990), Structured interview data on 102 cases of multiple personality disorder from four centers. *Am J Psychiatry* 147:596–601

Spanos NP (1986), Hypnosis, nonvolutional responding, and multiple personality: a social psychological perspective. *Prog Exp Pers Res* 14:1–62

Steinberg M, Rounsaville B, Cicchetti D (1991), Detection of dissociative disorders in psychiatric patients by a screening instrument and a structured diagnostic interview. *Am J Psychiatry* 149:1050–1054

Paul R. McHugh

 **NO**

Resolved: Multiple Personality Disorder Is an Individually and Socially Created Artifact

W here's hysteria now that we need it? With *DSM-IV* [*Diagnostic and Statistical Manual of Mental Disorders*, 4th ed.], psychiatrists have developed a common language and a common approach to diagnosis. But in the process of operationalizing diagnoses, we may have lost some concepts about patient behavior. The term "hysteria" disappeared when *DSM-III* was published; without it, psychiatrists have been deprived of a scientific concept essential to the development of new ideas: the null hypothesis. This loss hits home with the epidemic of multiple personality disorder (MPD).

The work of Talcott Parsons (1964), David Mechanic (1978), and Isidore Pilowsky (1969) taught psychiatrists to appreciate that phenomena such as hysterical paralyses, blindness, and pseudoseizures were actually behaviors with a goal: achieving the "sick role." Inspired by Parsons, Mechanic and Pilowsky used the term "abnormal illness behavior" in lieu of hysteria. Their approach eliminated the stigma of malingering that had been implied in hysteria and indicated that patients could take on such behavior without fraudulent intent. They were describing an old reality of medical experience.

Some people—experiencing emotional distress in the face of a variety of life circumstances and conflicts—complain to doctors about physical or psychological symptoms that they claim are signs of illness. Sometimes they display gross impairments of movement or consciousness; sometimes the features are subtle and changing. These complaints prompt doctors to launch investigations in laboratories, to conduct elaborate and sometimes dangerous studies of the brain or body, and to consult with experts, who examine the patient for esoteric disease. As the investigation proceeds, the patient may become still more persuaded that an illness is at work and begin to model the signs of disorder on the subtle suggestions of the physician's inquiry. For example, a patient with complaints of occasional lapses in alertness might—in the course of investigations that include visits to the epilepsy clinic and to the EEG laboratory

From Paul R. McHugh, "Resolved: Multiple Personality Disorder Is an Individually and Socially Created Artifact," *Journal of the American Academy of Child and Adolescent Psychiatry*, vol. 34, no. 7 (July 1995). Copyright © 1995 by The American Academy of Child and Adolescent Psychiatry. Reprinted by permission of Lippincott Williams & Wilkins.

for sleep studies, photic stimulation, and nasopharyngeal leads—gradually develop the frenzied thrashing movements of the limbs that require the protective attention of several nurses and hospital aides.

Eventually, with the patient no better and the investigations proving fruitless, a psychiatric consultant alert to the concept of hysteria and its contemporary link to the "sick role" might recognize that the patient's disorder is not an epileptic but a behavioral one. The patient is displaying movements that attract medical attention and provide the privileges of patienthood.

Talcott Parsons, the Harvard sociologist, pointed out in the 1950s that medicine was an organized component of our society intended to aid, through professional knowledge, the sick and the impaired. To accomplish this, certain individuals—physicians—are licensed by society to decide not only how to manage the sick, but to choose and distinguish the sick from other impaired people. Such an identification can provide these "sick" individuals with certain social privileges, i.e., rest, freedom from employment, and support from others during the reign of the condition. The person given the appellation "sick" by the social spokesman—the physician—was assumed by the society to respond to these privileges with other actions, i.e., cooperating with the intrusions of investigators of the illness and making every effort at rehabilitation so as to return to health. The hidden assumption is that the burdens and pains of illness act to drive the patient toward these cooperative actions with the physicians and thus to be happy to relinquish the few small pleasures that can be found in being treated as a victim of sickness.

However, because there are advantages to the sick role, there are some situations in which a person might seek this role without a "ticket of admission," a disease. This is hardly a remarkable idea as almost anyone has noticed the temptation to "call in sick" when troubles are afoot. But in some patients —those with emotional conflicts, weakened self-criticism, and high suggestibility—this temptation can be transformed, usually with some prompting, into the conviction that they are infirm. This kind of patient may, in fact, use more and more information from the medical profession's activities to amplify the expression of the infirmity.

Psychiatrists have known about these matters of social and psychological dynamics for more than 100 years. They were brought vividly to attention by the distinguished pupil of Jean-Martin Charcot, Joseph Babinski (he of the plantar response). Like Sigmund Freud and Pierre Janet, Babinski had observed Charcot manage patients with, what Charcot called, "hysteroepilepsy." But Babinski was convinced that hysteroepilepsy was not a new disorder. He believed that the women at Charcot's clinic were being persuaded—and not so subtly—to take on the features of epilepsy by the interest Charcot and his assistants expressed (Babinski and Froment, 1918). Babinski also believed that these women were vulnerable to this persuasion because of distressing states of mind provoked in their life circumstances and their roles as intriguing patients and the subject of attention from many distinguished physicians who offered them a haven of care.

Babinski was bringing the null hypothesis to Charcot and with it, not a rejection of these women as legitimate victims of some problem, but an appreciation that behaving as if epileptic obscured reality and made helping their actual problem difficult. Babinski wrote that just as hysteroepilepsy rested on persuasion, so a form of counterpersuasion could correct it. He demonstrated that these patients improved when they were taken from the wards and clinics where other afflicted women—epileptic and pseudoepileptic—were housed and when the attention of the staff was turned away from their seizures and onto their lives. These measures—isolation and countersuggestion—had the advantage of limiting the rewards for the behavior and of prompting a search for and treatment of the troubles in the personal life.

All this became embedded in the concept of hysteria and needs to be reapplied in the understanding of MPD. The patients I have seen have been referred to the Johns Hopkins Health System because elsewhere they have become stuck in the process of therapy. The histories are similar. They were mostly women who in the course of some distress sought psychiatric assistance. In the course of this assistance—and often early in the process—a therapist offered them a fairly crude suggestion that they might harbor some "alter" personalities. As an example of the crudity of the suggestions to the patient, I offer this published direction of how to both make the diagnosis and elicit "alters":

> The sine qua non of MPD is a second personality who at some time comes out and takes executive control of the patient's behavior. It may happen that an alter personality will reveal itself to you during this [assessment] process, but more likely it will not. So you may have to elicit an alter personality. . . . To begin the process of eliciting an alter, you can begin by indirect questioning such as, "Have you ever felt like another part of you does things that you can't control?" If she gives positive or ambiguous responses, ask for specific examples. You are trying to develop a picture of what the alter personality is like. . . . At this point, you might ask the host personality, "Does this set of feelings have a name?" Occasionally you will get a name. Often the host personality will not know. You can then focus on a particular event or set of behaviors and follow up on those. For instance, you can ask, "Can I talk to the part of you who is taking those long drives to the country?" (Buie, 1992, p. 3).

Once the patient permits the therapist to "talk to the part . . . who is taking those long drives," the patient is committed to having MPD and is forced to act in ways consistent with this role. The patient is then placed into care on units or in services—often titled "the dissociative service"—at the institution. She meets other patients with the same compliant responses to therapists' suggestions. She and the staff begin a continuous search for other "alters." With the discovery of the first "alter," the barrier of self-criticism and self-observation is breached. No obstacles to invention remain.

Countless numbers of personalities emerge over time. What began as two or three may develop to 99 or 100. The distressing symptoms continue as long as therapeutic attention is focused on finding more alters and sustaining the view that the problems relate to an "intriguing capacity" to dissociate or fractionate the self.

At Johns Hopkins, we see patients in whom MPD has been diagnosed because symptoms of depression have continued despite therapy elsewhere. Our referrals have been few and our experience, therefore, is only now building, probably because our views—that MPD may be a therapist-induced artifact—have only recently become generally known in our community (McHugh, 1995). We seem to challenge the widely accepted view and to "turn back the clock." The referrals that come to us often arrive with obstacles to our therapeutic plans. Patients and their referring therapists often wish to stay in regular contact (two to three times weekly) and to continue their work on MPD. At the same time, we at Hopkins are expected to treat the depression or some other supposed "side issue." We, however, following the isolation and countersuggestion approach, try to bring about, at least temporarily, a separation of the patient from the staff and the support groups that sustain the focus on "alters." We refuse to talk to "alters" but rather encourage our patients to review their present difficulties, thus applying the concept of "abnormal illness behavior" to their condition.

The advocates for MPD are in the same position as Charcot was when Babinski offered his proposal of the null hypothesis. As in any scientific discussion, it is not the responsibility of the proposers of the null hypothesis to prove its likelihood. That hypothesis simply claims that nothing special has been discovered. I claim the same in this debate. The investigators proposing a new entity must demonstrate that the null hypothesis should be rejected.

In most of the discussions by champions of MPD just the opposite occurs. Not only is the null hypothesis discarded without any compelling reason, but nonrelevant information is presented to justify a uniqueness to MPD. Perhaps the most common proposal is that MPD must exist in the way proposed because it is included in *DSM-IV* and operational criteria are available to make the diagnosis. This is a misunderstanding of *DSM-IV*. It provides a way in which a diagnosis can be reliably applied to a patient, but it does not in any way validate the existence of the condition or negate a null hypothesis about it.

Charcot had quite reliable ways of diagnosing hysteroepilepsy. It just did not exist as he thought it did, but rather it was a behavior seeking the sick role. It is my opinion that MPD is another behavioral disorder—a socially created artifact—in distressed people who are looking for help. The diagnosis and subsequent procedures for exploring MPD give them a coherent posture toward themselves and others as a particular kind of patient: "sick" certainly, "victim" possibly. This posture, if sustained, will obscure the real problems in their lives and render psychotherapy long, costly, and pointless. If the customary treatments of hysteria are provided, then we can expect that the multiple personality behaviors will be abandoned and proper rehabilitative attention can be given to the patient.

Hysteria as a concept has been neglected in *DSM-III* and *DSM-IV*, but it offers just what it has always offered: a challenge to proposals of new entities in psychiatry. Some diagnoses survive and others do not. MPD has run away with itself, and its proponents must now deal with this challenge. Charcot took such a challenge from his student. Everyone learned in the process.

References

Babinski J, Froment J (1918), *Hysteria or Pithiatism and Reflex Nervous Disorders in the Neurology of War*. Rolleston JD, trans; Buzzard EF, ed. London: University of London Press

Buie SE (1992), Introduction to the diagnosis of multiple personality disorder. *Grand Rounds Rev* (4):1–3

McHugh PR (1995), Witches, multiple personalities, and other psychiatric artifacts. *Nature Med* 1:110–114

Mechanic D (1978), Effects of psychological distress on perceptions of physical health and use of medical and psychiatric facilities. *J Hum Stress* 4:26–32

Parsons T (1964), *Social Structure and Personality*. New York: Free Press

Pilowsky I (1969), Abnormal illness behaviour. *Br J Med Psychol* 42:347–351

CHALLENGE QUESTIONS

Do Multiple Personalities Exist?

1. Critics speak of MPD as "just another psychological fad." Psychological fads typically fade in and out of popularity and have approximately 15-year life spans. Do you know of any current fads in psychology? Interview a few professors and investigate the fads that they identify.
2. Research the legal cases in which MPD was used in a client's criminal defense, and describe how these cases might have influenced the public's perception and acceptance of MPD.
3. The media's portrayal of MPD has heightened awareness and the popularity of the phenomenon. Do you know of other examples in which media reports had an impact on attitudes toward mental illness? If you cannot find any literature on this, interview a few professors for leads.
4. Research Sigmund Freud's writings on hysteria. Based on the available evidence of MPD, how well does his theory of hysteria account for the existence of this phenomenon?

Psychotherapy Links

This directory of psychotherapy Web sites is sponsored by the University of Western Ontario Department of Psychiatry.

```
http://www.psychiatry.med.uwo.ca/ptherapy/
links.htm
```

Association for Gay, Lesbian, and Bisexual Issues in Counseling

This is the Web site of the Association for Gay, Lesbian, and Bisexual Issues in Counseling, a division of the American Counseling Association that works toward educating mental health service providers about issues faced by gay, lesbian, bisexual, and transgendered individuals.

```
http://www.aglbic.org
```

Sociology & Psychology Queer Links

This QueerByChoice.com page offers links to several organizations and articles related to the social and psychological bases of homosexuality.

```
http://www.queerbychoice.com/sociolinks.html
```

ECT On-Line

Dr. Carl Littlejohns, of Wrexham, North Wales, provides information on both sides of the electroconvulsive therapy debate at this site.

```
http://www.priory.co.uk/psych/ectol.htm
```

PART 6

Psychological Treatment

*C*oncerns about the expense of psychotherapy have highlighted discussions about its effectiveness. How should one go about studying the effectiveness of psychotherapy? Traditionally, effectiveness has been studied through scientific procedures, but is this always the best approach? Do these procedures introduce their own biases? What about the effectiveness of more controversial procedures? For example, can (and should) sexual orientation be changed? Can electroshock therapy cure depression? And what about the wide use of medications? Are these always as effective and problem-free as they are frequently portrayed?

- Is Treating Homosexuality Ethical and Effective?

- Does Electroshock Therapy Cure Depression?

- Are Medications for Treating Depression Harmful?

ISSUE 13

Is Treating Homosexuality Ethical and Effective?

YES: Warren Throckmorton, from "Efforts to Modify Sexual Orientation: A Review of Outcome Literature and Ethical Issues," *Journal of Mental Health Counseling* (October 1998)

NO: Barry A. Schreier, from "Of Shoes, and Ships, and Sealing Wax: The Faulty and Specious Assumptions of Sexual Reorientation Therapies," *Journal of Mental Health Counseling* (October 1998)

ISSUE SUMMARY

YES: Warren Throckmorton, director of college counseling and an associate professor of psychology at Grove City College, maintains that efforts to assist homosexually oriented individuals to modify their patterns of sexual arousal have been effective and can be conducted in an ethical manner.

NO: Barry A. Schreier, coordinator of training and a psychologist at the Counseling and Psychological Services of Purdue University, counters that homosexuality is not an illness, so there is no need to treat it.

Perhaps no issue in psychology has provoked more intense debate in the surrounding popular culture than that of homosexuality. For nearly 30 years, the governing associations of psychology, psychiatry, and counseling have worked to remove the pathological label from the lifestyles of gay and lesbian individuals. Many professionals assume that empirical research has demonstrated the biological underpinnings of sexual orientation, so many psychologists portray homosexuality as a normal alternative lifestyle and attempt to fight homophobia. Some, however, view these efforts as politically motivated and threatening to traditional religious beliefs. Others resonate with psychology's support of homosexuality as an important protection of minority rights.

One facet of this culture war is the treatment of individuals who are dissatisfied with their sexual orientation. Reorientation, or conversion therapy, as it is sometimes called, was regularly practiced before the 1970s. However, many people currently feel that it is an unethical and unproven brand of treatment. They argue that gay individuals can internalize society's pervasive homophobia and, thus, express the desire to leave the homosexual lifestyle. Others counter that no one should stand in the way of an individual's desire and that psychotherapists have an obligation to honor this desire. Of course, honoring the desire to change sexual orientation presumes that such change is possible, which is another issue in dispute.

In the following selection, Warren Throckmorton expresses discomfort with the American Counseling Association's (ACA) recent resolution against conversion therapy. He reviews the effectiveness and appropriateness of therapeutic efforts to change sexual orientation and finds several successful efforts to modify patterns of sexual arousal from multiple perspectives. Although he contends that the concept of sexual orientation has limited clinical use because it is not well defined, Throckmorton discusses the ethical obligations of psychotherapists to allow clients the choice of conversion therapy.

In the second selection, Barry A. Schreier asks why some therapists continue to insist, in the face of disconfirming scientific research, that homosexuality is an illness that needs to be cured. Schreier defends the concept of sexual orientation and states that studies supporting conversion therapy have been heavily criticized for their methodological flaws. In response to Throckmorton's ethical defense of conversion therapy, Schreier reviews the phenomenon of minority groups' struggling to accept their identities and illuminates ways in which Throckmorton's bias may underlie and skew his ethics.

POINT

- The issue of conversion therapy needs more examination before psychology's governing bodies reject them out of hand.
- The concept of sexual orientation is unclear and subjective, and it has not been tested in longitudinal research.
- Efforts to assist homosexually oriented individuals who wish to modify their patterns of sexual arousal have been shown to be empirically effective.
- Individuals who wish to modify their patterns of sexual arousal should be allowed the option of conversion therapy.
- Religious freedom may be denied if the freedom to choose conversion therapy is not affirmed.

COUNTERPOINT

- The American Psychological Association (APA) and the ACA have a long history of justified opposition to labeling homosexuality a pathology.
- Sexual orientation is a valid concept, descriptive of a natural and long-occurring characteristic.
- Research that seemingly demonstrates modified sexual orientation is methodologically flawed.
- Individuals who wish to modify their patterns of sexual arousal may have internalized society's prejudices and need help feeling validated in a minority identity.
- If conversion therapy is ineffective or damaging, then no religous freedom is denied.

Warren Throckmorton  YES

Efforts to Modify Sexual Orientation

In light of the American Counseling Association's (ACA) recent resolution expressing concerns about conversion therapy, this article reviews the effectiveness and appropriateness of therapeutic efforts to
change sexual orientation. The concept of sexual orientation is briefly
reviewed and found to be of limited clinical use. The article reviews
successful efforts to modify patterns of sexual arousal from psychoanalytic, behavioral, cognitive, group, and religious perspectives. An
ethical analysis of the ACA resolution is presented. The author concludes that efforts to assist homosexually oriented individuals who
wish to modify their patterns of sexual arousal have been effective,
can be conducted in an ethical manner, and should be available to
those clients requesting such assistance.

Since 1972, the mental health professions have been assessing and reassessing
the status of homosexuality in mental health. During the last three decades,
homosexuality has been conceptualized as a disorder, a possible disorder in the
case of the *DSM-III* [Diagnostic and Statistical Manual of Mental Disorders III]
ego-dystonic homosexuality, and most recently, as neutral as it relates to the
mental status of an individual (Rubinstein, 1995).

One impact of this openness to diverse sexual identities is the emergence
of opposition to any form of counseling to modify or to attempt to change the
sexual orientation of a client from homosexual to heterosexual. Davison (1976),
Martin (1984), and Haldeman (1994) suggest that psychotherapeutic efforts to
change sexual orientation are unethical. In 1997, after nearly 2 years of debate
and study, the American Psychological Association (APA) passed a resolution
expressing concern that clients may request conversion therapy due to "societal
ignorance and prejudice about same gender sexual orientation" and "family or
social coercion and/or lack of information" (APA, 1997; Sleek, 1997). In March
1998, the American Counseling Association (ACA) passed a similar resolution
at its annual convention in Indianapolis (ACA, 1998).

The ACA resolution was proposed by the association's Human Rights
Committee and the motion to accept was made by the representative of the
Association for Gay, Lesbian, and Bisexual Issues in Counseling (AGLBIC). The

From Warren Throckmorton, "Efforts to Modify Sexual Orientation: A Review of Outcome Literature and Ethical Issues," *Journal of Mental Health Counseling*, vol. 20 (October 1998). Copyright
© 1998 by *Journal of Mental Health Counseling*. Reprinted by permission of The American Mental
Health Counselors Association.

resolution was titled, "On Appropriate Counseling Responses to Sexual Orientation" and proposed to place the ACA in opposition to any form of conversion therapy. The proposed resolution originally read "be it further resolved that the American Counseling Association *opposes the use of so-called 'conversion or reparative' therapies in counseling individuals having a same gender sexual orientation;* opposes portrayals of lesbian, gay, and bisexual youth as mentally ill due to their sexual orientation; and supports the dissemination of accurate information about sexual orientation, mental health, and appropriate interventions in order to counteract bias that is based in ignorance or unfounded beliefs about same-gender sexual orientation." (ACA, 1998, p. 1–2). During debate over the resolution, the association's governing council deleted the phrase in italics above concerning opposition to conversion therapies (ACA, 1998). Thus, the ACA's opposition was maintained if the conversion therapy portrays "gay, lesbian or bisexual youth as mentally ill," or a counselor spreads inaccurate information or has "unfounded beliefs" about sexual orientation (ACA, 1998, p. 1–2).

As it stands, the resolution's impact is difficult to gauge. The resolution seems to discourage efforts to promote a shift from homosexual to heterosexual orientation but comes short of clear opposition. If passed as originally proposed, the resolution would have had enormous impact on practice. Mental health counselors would have been constrained to tell clients who want to modify their sexual arousal patterns that such an objective is faulty. Mental health counselors who believe homosexuality can be modified would be in danger of being charged with a violation of the ethics code. Even mental health counselors outside of the membership of ACA would be at risk, since most states adopt the ACA Code of Ethics in their counselor licensing statutes. Since most states automatically adopt subsequent revisions of that code, mental health counselors performing activities deemed unethical based on a reading of the code would be in danger of review by state licensing authorities.

This ACA resolution, along with a companion resolution supporting same-gender marriage, created immediate controversy (Lee, 1998). The association's Western Regional Assembly voted to request that the governing council rescind the motions and the Southern Regional Assembly requested the issue be reexamined (Gerst, 1998). Given the impact on counselors practicing conversion techniques and the controversy surrounding the issue, an examination of the major issues raised by the resolution is needed. The ACA resolution opposed conversion therapy on the grounds that such therapy is both ineffective and unethical. This article examines the effectiveness and ethicality of helping clients redirect their sexual orientation. First I examine the concept of sexual orientation, followed by a [brief] review of the literature concerning the modification of sexual orientation. Finally, I present an ethical analysis of the ACA resolution concerning conversion therapy....

A Word About Sexual Orientation

Haldeman (1994) suggests that before questions of change in sexual orientation are considered, clinicians and researchers should examine "the complex nature of sexual orientation and its development in the individual" (p. 222). I agree with this caution and submit that before opponents of conversion therapies attempt to eliminate sexual reorientation as an acceptable therapeutic goal, they must confront the same issue.

As Haldeman (1994) asserts, sexual orientation is not a well-defined concept. There are many suggestions in the literature concerning the proper method of defining sexual orientation. The point of departure for defining sexual orientation is often the work of Kinsey (Kinsey, Pomeroy, & Gebhard, 1948). Kinsey suggests that sexual orientation ranges along a continuum from exclusively homosexual (Kinsey rating "6") to exclusively heterosexual (Kinsey rating "0") (House & Miller, 1997). Gonsiorek, Sell, and Weinrich (1995) recommend assessing "same- and opposite-sex orientations separately, not as one continuous variable." (p. 47). They suggest treating each orientation as a continuous variable. For clinical purposes, such scales would be interesting but not terribly helpful to assess the impact of efforts to modify sexual orientation. Why? There are no norms or points along each continuum where clinicians may designate a given sexual orientation. Since researchers are mixed as to where on the continuum to declare a client truly gay or straight, how can counselors know if they are aiding clients to change from one sexual orientation to another?

Gonsiorek et al. (1995) note that the most common means of assessing sexual orientation is via self-report. However, they also note that "there are significant limitations to this method." (Gonsiorek et al., 1995, p. 44). The most obvious problem is the subjective nature of self-assessment. Being gay, lesbian, or bisexual means different things to different people. Some define their sexual orientation by their behavior or attractions or fantasies or some combination of each dimension. After summarizing the difficulties in defining sexual orientation, Gonsiorek et al. (1995) state, "Given such significant measurement problems, one could conclude there is serious doubt whether sexual orientation is a valid concept at all." (p. 46). Years earlier, Birk (1980) expressed a similar view saying "there is in fact no such unitary thing as 'homosexuality'... instead... there are many, many different homosexuals who collectively defy rigid characterization." (p. 376).

Concerning the potential for assessing change of orientation, Gonsiorek et al. (1995) note, "Perhaps the most dramatic limitation of current conceptualizations is change over time. There is essentially no research on the longitudinal stability of sexual orientation over the adult life span." (p. 46). If there is no research concerning change, how can professional associations be certain that sexual orientation cannot change? Thus, defining sexual orientation is a work in progress. Counselors ought to articulate to clients this lack of certainty in an unbiased manner.

In the absence of any sure way to define sexual orientation, assistance for questioning individuals should not be limited. Even if one accepts the presumption that sexual orientation cannot be changed, how does one know when a client's sexual orientation is settled? Without a more certain way to objectively determine sexual orientation, perhaps we should place considerable weight on the self-assessment of clients. Clients who want to change cannot reliably be told that they cannot change, since we cannot say with certainty that they have settled on a fixed trait. If any conclusions can be drawn from the literature, it is that change in sexual orientation is possible. For instance, in their review of the literature on once-married lesbians, Bridges and Croteau (1994) found that 25% to 50% of lesbians in various reports had once been in heterosexual marriages. While heterosexual marriage alone may not be a complete gauge of sexual orientation, the reasons for the marriage should offer some insight into the sexual identity of the women at the time. Kirkpatrick (1988) reports that once-married lesbian women often married because they were in love with their husbands. In examining the reasons for the shift in sexual expression, Charbonneau and Lander (1991) find two broad explanations. One group felt they had always been lesbian and were becoming true to themselves. However, another group viewed their change as a choice among sexual options. If counselors are not to assist clients in their wishes for a shift in sexual orientation, how would ACA's governing council wish for counselors to respond to such women wanting to become more settled in their choice of a lesbian identity?

More practically, I do not know with certainty if I have ever been successful in "changing" a person's sexual orientation, since I do not know how to precisely define sexual orientation or if it is even a valid clinical concept. However, I have assisted clients who were, in the beginning of mental health counseling, primarily attracted to those of the same gender but who declare they are now primarily attracted to the opposite gender. I fear that resolutions such as passed by APA and ACA will prevent such outcomes, which are viewed quite positively by the clients who have experienced them.

Efforts to Modify Sexual Orientation

Broadly, opponents of shifting sexual orientation as a therapeutic goal express doubts that sexual orientation can be changed by any means. From a gay-affirming perspective, Martin (1984) and Haldeman (1994) review studies that claimed to demonstrate change in sexual orientation. Their view is that there were no empirical studies that supported the idea that conversion therapy can change sexual orientation. However, they omitted a number of significant reports and failed to examine the outcomes of many studies that have demonstrated change.

Narrowly, the question to be addressed is: Do conversion therapy techniques work to change unwanted sexual arousal? . . . The available evidence supports the observation of many counselors—that many individuals with a same-gender sexual orientation have been able to change through a variety of counseling approaches. [Some of this evidence will be briefly addressed below, with references to additional research included.]

[The following text summarizes a lengthy section of the original article that is not included here.—Ed.]

Psychoanalytic approaches report rates of change to exclusive heterosexuality ranging from 18% to 44% of clients. (Bieber et al., 1962; Hatterer, 1970; Socarides, 1979; MacIntosh, 1994; Nicolosi, 1991, 1993). Rates for less dramatic shifts in sexual orientation are even higher in some of the reports. None of the reports document negative side effects of such efforts and, indeed, seem to show positive results for a significant number of participants, even those who do not change sexual orientation. Nicolosi, Byrd, and Potts (1998) report the results of a national survey of 882 clients engaged in sexual reorientation therapy. At the beginning of therapy, 318 of the sample rated themselves as having an exclusive same-gender sexual orientation. Posttreatment, 18% of the 318 rated themselves exclusively heterosexual, 17% rated themselves as "almost entirely heterosexual" and 12% viewed themselves as more heterosexual than gay or lesbian. Of the entire 882, only 13% remained either exclusively or almost exclusively gay or lesbian after treatment. Countering claims that reorientation therapies are harmful, the survey also asked clients concerning psychological and interpersonal adjustments both before and after therapy. The survey respondents reported significant improvements in such areas as self-acceptance, personal power, self-esteem, emotional stability, depression, and spirituality (Nicolosi et al., 1998).

Behavioral approaches to the modification of sexual orientation progressed from a reliance on aversive approaches to the use of sophisticated multimodal approaches which attempt to extinguish same-gender attraction and then provide a variety of behavioral and supportive counseling techniques to facilitate heterosexual responsiveness. (Greenspoon & Lamal, 1987; Tarlow, 1989; Barlow & Durand, 1995). Generally, the cases reported in the behavioral counseling literature support the efficacy of efforts to modify sexual orientation. (McCrady, 1973; Barlow and Agras, 1973, Phillips, Fischer, Groves & Singh, 1976)

Birk (1980) reports probably the highest success rates of any therapist. Using a combination of behavioral group and individual counseling, he reports that 100% of exclusively gay men beginning therapy with the intent to change sexual arousal were able to attain a heterosexual adaptation. Contrary to Haldeman's supposition that the men in Birk's treatment group may have had "preexisting heteroerotic tendencies" (Haldeman, 1994, p. 223), one of Birk's criteria for inclusion in this analysis is that these clients had not experienced heterosexual intercourse (Birk, 1980). Birk points to pretreatment motivation as a major key in understanding the results. Of these 14 clients who had shifted, 10 of the 14 (71%) were satisfactorily married at follow-up.

Albert Ellis, founder of Rational-Emotive Behavior Therapy (REBT), wrote in 1992 that people are free to "try a particular sexual pathway, such as homosexuality, for a time and then decide to practically abandon it for another mode, such as heterosexuality" (Ellis, 1992, p. 34). While not believing that same-gender sexual orientation is a sign of inherent emotional disturbance, Ellis recently evidenced his belief that client options should not be abridged by joining the Committee of Concerned Psychologists (CCP) (CCP, 1995). When the APA first considered a resolution to discourage the use of conversion therapies in 1995, an ad hoc group of psychologists opposed the motion. Ellis was one of more than 40 psychologists who signed a letter which urged the rejection of the motion and branded it as "illegal, unethical, unscientific, and totalitarian" (CCP, 1995, p. 4).

Finally, a number of clients report change through religiously based interventions in groups such as OneByOne, Exodus International, and Trans-

formation Ministries. While, as Haldeman (1994) documents, it is true that some ex-gays have become ex-ex-gays, the stories and research reports of individuals changing through religious interventions should not be minimized (see Pattison and Pattison 1980; Davies & Rentzel, 1994; Saia, 1988).

Ethical Principles and Conversion Therapies: Another Look

The psychological literature seems unclear about the ethics of conversion therapy. While Haldeman (1994) portrays such therapies as unethical, Garnets, Hancock, Cochran, Goodchilds, and Peplau, (1991) in the *American Psychologist* specify "biased, inadequate and inappropriate practice" and "exemplary practice" when clients present with sexual orientation issues. As an example of an exemplary response, Garnets et al. (1991) include this theme: "A therapist does not attempt to change the sexual orientation of the client without strong evidence that this is the appropriate course of action and that change is desired by the client" (p. 968). They presented as an exemplar of this theme the following comments by a survey respondent, "I had a male client who expressed a strong desire to 'go straight.' After a careful psychological assessment, his wish to become heterosexual seemed to be clearly indicated and I assisted him in that process" (Garnets et al., 1991, p. 968). This course is at odds with the proposed APA and ACA resolutions, which originally sought to deem conversion therapy unethical and therefore clinically inappropriate.

The ACA resolution begins by affirming ten principles concerning treatments to alter sexual orientation. The first is that homosexuality is not a mental disorder. While some writers who practice reparative therapy believe homosexuality is a developmental deficit (Nicolosi, 1991), it does not seem necessary to believe homosexuality is a disorder in order to offer counseling to modify sexual feelings. In fact, counseling as a profession has traditionally held that one does not need to have a disorder in order to profit from counseling. Thus, if a client requested such counseling, offering it would not require the counselor to view the client as mentally ill.

Even if one asserts that offering a mode of treatment implies a disorder, there is a condition in the *DSM-IV* that would be the proper object of conversion therapies—Sexual Disorder, Not Otherwise Specified (NOS) (American Psychiatric Association, 1994). Though the diagnosis of ego-dystonic homosexuality was removed from the *DSM-III*, Sexual Disorder, NOS remains in the *DSM-IV* with several descriptors, one of which is "persistent and marked distress about sexual orientation" (American Psychiatric Association, 1994, p. 538). Certainly, many individuals who seek conversion therapy could be described in this manner.

The second principle is that counselors should not discriminate against clients due to their sexual orientation. Contrary to this principle, banning efforts to modify sexual orientation would require the ACA to discriminate against those clients who want to change.

The third principle is that counselors will "actively attempt to understand the diverse cultural backgrounds of the clients with whom they work" (ACA,

1998). Nothing in conversion therapy negates this principle. Those requesting conversion therapy often do so because of a conflict between their homosexual feelings and the culture with which they identify. When such conflicts occur, what makes one set of loyalties more important than another set? If professional associations discredit efforts to modify sexual orientation, they may be implying that sexual arousal is more vital than any conflicting personality variables or moral convictions. The prohibition desired by proponents of the ACA resolution is an absolute one. A client's moral objection to same-gender attraction is not acknowledged by efforts to prohibit conversion approaches. On this point, I believe mental health counselors who practice conversion therapy do attempt to understand the cultural background of a client who presents in deep conflict over sexual impulses and deeply held moral convictions.

Principle four requires the counselor to inform clients concerning the "purposes, goals, techniques, procedures, limitations and potential risks and benefits of services to be performed." Nothing in this principle prohibits conversion therapy. As the above review of the literature demonstrates, it would be a violation of this point to say that there is no empirical evidence of efficacy of various conversion therapies.

The fifth principle states that "clients have the right to refuse any recommended service and be advised of the consequences of such refusal." The consensus of those finding success in shifting sexual orientation is that client's desire to change is necessary to be successful. This is true of nearly all mental health treatments.

The sixth principle supports the availability of conversion therapies. The resolution quotes the ACA Code of Ethics, section A.3.b, which states that counselors "offer clients freedom to choose whether to enter into a counseling relationship" (ACA, 1998). It is my experience that clients ask for assistance with unwanted homosexual feelings. Clients should have the freedom to choose the approaches that help them meet their goals.

The seventh principle states "when counseling minors or persons unable to give voluntary informed consent, counselors act in these clients' best interests" (ACA, 1998). Mental health counselors engaging in counseling to modify sexual orientation have a duty to act in the client's best interests whether a minor or an adult. Since it has not been shown that such counseling is intrinsically harmful, assisting a minor client who wishes to engage in such counseling does not violate this principle. When a parent's and child's counseling objectives differ, achieving a working alliance with the family requires skill in conflict resolution and family interventions no matter what kind of problem is presented.

In the eighth principle, counselors are reminded to be "aware of their own values, attitudes, beliefs, and behaviors and these apply in a diverse society and avoid imposing their values on clients" (ACA, 1998). Apparently, this point assumes that the availability of conversion therapy is an imposition of values on clients everywhere. What does the opposition to conversion therapy say? To conflicted clients who want to explore the possibility of change to a heterosexual orientation, it means that their wish is diminished, not to be taken seriously. For individuals who are morally opposed to homosexuality as a lifestyle, it means that the professions have denigrated their moral convictions. For individuals who have successfully changed, who now are heterosexual, it means that the professions have criticized their accomplishments. The existence of conversion therapy for people who want it does not require the conversion therapist to force it on someone who does not. The most appropriate response when the client's goals and the mental health counselor's skills do not match is to refer to another mental health counselor.

The ninth principle, related to the above point, is the statement from the ACA Code of Ethics (section A.6.a) that counselors "are aware of their influential positions with respect to clients, and they avoid exploiting the trust and dependency of clients." The counseling profession has been oblivious to a double standard concerning sexual orientation and religious conviction. While the ACA has opposed the modification or questioning of an individual's homosexual feelings, there has been no movement to avoid the disruption of an individual's religious convictions. For instance, Barret and Barzan (1996), in their article concerning spirituality and the gay experience, suggest that "assisting gay men and lesbians to step away from external religious authority may challenge the counselor's own acceptance of religious teachings" (p. 8). According to Barret and Barzan (1996), "most counselors will benefit from a model that helps them understand the difference between spiritual and religious authority" (p. 8)....

The last principle requires counselors to "report research accurately and in a manner that minimizes the possibility that results will be misleading." As noted above, evidence exists for the efficacy of conversion therapies. However, these findings have not been consistently reported in the counseling and psychological literature over the last two decades. A search of the *Journal of Mental Health Counseling, Journal of Counseling and Development, Counseling and Values* and the *Journal of Multicultural Counseling and Development* reveals no articles on conversion therapy. All articles concerning homosexuality espouse the gay-affirming approach to therapy. I think the information given in this article, previously unreported in counseling journals, should be widely distributed to address the issue raised in the tenth principle of the ACA resolution....

Discussion

The purpose of this review is to demonstrate that therapeutic efforts to help clients modify patterns of sexual arousal have been successful and should be available to clients wishing such assistance. I believe the available literature leaves no doubt that some degree of change is possible for some clients who wish to pursue it. The literature on therapeutic assistance for unwanted same-gender sexual arousal suddenly came to a near halt in the early 1970s, but clients wishing assistance did not cease to come to counseling. I personally have experience with clients who have wanted assistance to change their pattern of sexual arousal and due to their reports believe such change is possible.

Sexual orientation as a concept has limited clinical utility. Since the categorization of sexual orientation is somewhat arbitrary, I submit it is inappropriate to tell a client that it cannot be changed or modified. Bell and Weinberg

(1978) in their large study of homosexuality in the San Francisco area, define a homosexual as anyone with a Kinsey rating of four or higher. In the literature cited above, rates of change for individuals with Kinsey ratings of 4 and 5 were in the 57% to 78% range (Feldman, MacCulloch, & Orford, 1971; Hatterer, 1970; Mayerson & Lief, 1965). Thus, defined in the manner of the Bell and Weinberg study, an impressive majority of clients were able to change sexual orientation. Whether one can say that sexual orientation is being changed depends on how narrowly one defines sexual orientation or if it can be defined at all.

Proposed Guidelines

So what should mental health counselors do when confronted with clients who request sexual reorientation? I propose the following guidelines.

1. Neither gay-affirmative nor conversion therapy should be assumed to be the preferred approach. Generally, gay-affirmative therapy or referral to such a practitioner should be offered to those clients who want to become more satisfied with a same-gender sexual orientation. Conversion therapy or referral should be offered to clients who decide they want to modify or overcome same-gender patterns of sexual arousal. Assessment should be conducted to help clarify the strength and persistence of the client's wishes.
2. For those clients who are in distress concerning their sexual orientation and are undecided concerning reorientation, mental health counselors should not assume what approach is best. They should inform clients that many mental health professionals believe same-gender sexual orientation cannot be changed but that others believe change is possible. Clients should be informed that some mental health professionals and researchers dispute the concept of an immutable sexual orientation. Mental health counselors should explain that not all clients who participate in gay-affirming therapy are able to find satisfaction in a gay adjustment nor are all clients who seek sexual reorientation successful. When clients cannot decide which therapeutic course to pursue, mental health counselors can suggest that clients choose consistent with their values, personal convictions, and/or religious beliefs (Nicolosi et al., 1998).
3. Since religion is one of the client attributes that mental health counselors are ethically bound to respect, counselors should take great care in advising those clients dissatisfied with same-gender sexual orientation due to their religious beliefs. To accommodate such clients, counselors should develop expertise in methods of sexual reorientation or develop appropriate referral resources.

Finally, mental health counselors have an obligation to respect the dignity and wishes of all clients. ACA and other mental health associations should not attempt to limit the choices of gays and lesbians who want to change.

References

American Counseling Association. (1998, March). *On appropriate counseling responses to sexual orientation.* Adopted by the American Counseling Association Governing Council, March 27, 1998.

American Psychiatric Association. (1994). *Diagnostic and statistical manual of mental disorders* (4th ed.). Washington, DC: Author.

American Psychological Association. (1997, August). *Resolution on appropriate therapeutic responses to sexual orientation.* Adopted by the American Psychological Association Council of Representatives, August 14, 1997.

Barlow, D., & Agras, W. S. (1973). Fading to increase heterosexual responsiveness in homosexuals. *Journal of Applied Behavior Analysis, 6,* 355–366.

Barlow, D., & Durand, V. M. (1995). *Abnormal psychology: An integrative approach.* New York: Brooks/Cole Publishing.

Barret, R., & Barzan, R. (1996). Spiritual experiences of gay men and lesbians. *Counseling and Values, 41,* 4–15.

Bell, A. P., & Weinberg, M. S. (1978). *Homosexualities: A study of diversity among men and women.* New York: Simon & Schuster.

Bieber, I., Dain, H. J., Dince, P. R., Drellich, M. G., Grand, H. G., Gundlach, R. H., Kremer, M. W., Rifkin, A. H., Wilbur, C. B., & Bieber, T. B. (1962). *Homosexuality.* New York: Basic Books.

Birk, L. (1980). The myth of classical homosexuality: Views of a behavioral psychotherapist. In J. Marmor (Ed.), *Homosexual Behavior* (pp. 376–390). New York: Basic Books.

Bridges, K. L., & Croteau, J. M. (1994). Once-married lesbians: Facilitating changing life patterns. *Journal of Counseling and Development, 73,* 134–140.

Charbonneau, C., & Lander, P. S. (1991). Redefining sexuality: Women becoming lesbian in mid-life. In B. Sang, J. Warshow, & A. J. Smith (Eds.), *Lesbians at mid-life: The creative transition* (pp. 35–43). San Francisco, CA: Spinsters Book Co.

Committee of Concerned Psychologists. (1995). Letter to the American Psychological Association Council of Representatives. Quoted in *Narth Bulletin, 3*(2), 4–5.

Davies, B., & Rentzel, L. (1994). *Coming out of homosexuality.* Downers Grove, IL: InterVarsity Press.

Davison, G. C. (1976). Homosexuality: The ethical challenge. *Journal of Consulting and Clinical Psychology, 44,* 157–162.

Ellis, A. (1992, September/October). Are gays and lesbians emotionally disturbed? *The Humanist,* 33–35.

Feldman, M. P., MacCulloch, M. J., & Orford, J. F. (1971). Conclusions and speculations. In M. P. Feldman & M. J. MacCulloch, *Homosexual behaviour: Therapy and assessment* (pp. 156–188), New York: Pergamon Press.

Garnets, L., Hancock, K., Cochran, S., Goodchilds, J., & Peplau, L. (1991). Issues in psychotherapy with lesbians and gay men. *American Psychologist, 46,* 964–972.

Gerst, R. (1998, May). Letter to the editor. *Counseling Today,* 4.

Gold, S., & Neufeld, I. L. (1965). A learning approach to the treatment of homosexuality. *Behavior Research and Therapy, 2,* 201–204.

Gonsiorek, J. C., Sell, R. L., & Weinrich, J. D. (1995). Definition and measurement of sexual orientation. *Suicide and Life Threatening Behavior, 25*(Supplement), 40–51.

Greenspoon, J., & Lamal, P. (1987). A behavioristic approach. In L. Diamant (Ed.), *Male and female homosexuality: Psychological approaches.* (pp. 109–127). New York: Hemisphere Publishing.

Haldeman, D. (1994). The practice and ethics of sexual orientation conversion therapy. *Journal of Consulting and Clinical Psychology, 62,* 221–227.

Hatterer, L. (1970). *Changing homosexuality in the male.* New York: McGraw-Hill.

House, R. M., & Miller, J. L. (1997). Counseling gay, lesbian and bisexual clients. In D. Capuzzi & D. Gross (Eds.), *Introduction to the counseling profession* (2nd ed.) (pp. 397–432). Boston, MA: Allyn & Bacon.

Kinsey, A., Pomeroy, W. B., & Gebhard, P. H. (1948). *Sexual behavior in the human male*. Philadelphia: Saunders.

Kirkpatrick, M. (1988). Clinical implications of lesbian mother studies. In E. Coleman (Ed.). *Integrated identity for gay men and lesbians: Psychotherapeutic approaches for emotional well-being* (pp. 201–211). New York: Harrington Park Press.

Lee, C. (1998, May). Promoting a healthy dialogue. *Counseling Today, 5*.

McCrady, R. (1973). A forward-fading technique for increasing heterosexual responsiveness in male homosexuals. *Journal of Behavioral Therapy and Experimental Psychiatry, 4*, 257–261.

MacIntosh, H. (1994). Attitudes and experiences of psychoanalysts in analyzing homosexual patients. *Journal of the American Psychoanalytic Association, 42*, 1183–1206.

Martin, A. D. (1984). The emperor's new clothes: Modern attempts to change sexual orientation. In E. S. Hetrick & T. S. Stein (Eds.), *Psychotherapy with homosexuals* (pp. 59–74). Washington, DC: American Psychiatric Association.

Mayerson, P., & Lief, H. I. (1965). Psychotherapy of homosexuals: A follow-up study of nineteen cases. In J. Marmor (Ed.), *Sexual inversion* (pp. 302–344). New York: Basic Books.

Nicolosi, J. (1991). *Reparative therapy of male homosexuality*. Northvale, NJ: Jason Aronson.

Nicolosi, J. (1993). *Healing homosexuality*. Northvale, NJ: Jason Aronson.

Nicolosi, J., Byrd, A. D., & Potts, R. W. (1998). *Towards the ethical and effective treatment of homosexuality*. Unpublished manuscript.

Pattison, E. M., & Pattison, M. L. (1980). "Ex-gays": Religiously mediated change in homosexuals. *American Journal of Psychiatry, 137*, 1553–1562.

Phillips, D., Fischer, S. C., Groves, G. A., & Singh, R. (1976). Alternative behavioral approaches to the treatment of homosexuality. *Archives of Sexual Behavior, 5*, 223–228.

Rubinstein, G. (1995). The decision to remove homosexuality from the DSM: Twenty years later. *American Journal of Psychotherapy, 49*, 416–427.

Saia, M. R. (1988). *Counseling the homosexual*. Minneapolis, MN: Bethany House Publishers.

Sleek, S. (1997, October). Resolution raises concerns about conversion therapy. *Monitor*, 16.

Socarides, C. (1979). The psychoanalytic theory of homosexuality: With special reference to therapy. In I. Rosen (Ed.), *Sexual deviation* (2nd ed.) (pp. 243–277). New York: Oxford University Press.

Tarlow, G. (1989). *Clinical handbook of behavior therapy: Adult psychological disorders*. Brookline, MA: Brookline Books, Inc.

NO

Barry A. Schreier

Of Shoes, and Ships, and Sealing Wax

W arren Throckmorton's assumption in his article "Efforts to Modify Sexual Orientation: A Review of Outcome Literature and Ethical Issues" is that there is pathology inherent in same-sex orientations, and thus there is treatment for it. Throckmorton makes the proposal that since there is viability to this type of treatment, The American Counseling Association's (ACA) resolution "On Appropriate Counseling Responses to Sexual Orientation" (ACA, 1998) is a restriction of trade and service. This paper presents a counter position on Throckmorton's article and demonstrates why organizations such as ACA and the American Psychological Association (APA) are correctly declaring these "reorientation therapies" unethical practice. It is ethically questionable to practice treatments that are not based in empirical methodologies, that cause harm, that are based on faulty and specious assumptions, and that incorporate societal prejudice.

No Illness, No Cure

In 1998, the American Psychological Association reiterated the "long-standing official position that homosexuality and bisexuality are not mental disorders" (APA, 1998). Dr. Bryant Welch, APA's Executive Director for Professional Practice, stated, "no scientific evidence exists to support the effectiveness of any of the conversion therapies that try to change one's sexual orientation" and that "research findings suggest that efforts to 'repair' homosexuals are nothing more than social prejudice garbed in psychological accouterments" (Welch, 1990; see also Buie, 1990). The American Counseling Association's recent resolution puts ACA ethically on par with APA as well as other national health organizations including the American Psychiatric Association (1973). Even the 101st United States Congress did not include homosexuality into the Americans With Disabilities Act as it does not constitute an illness and thus cannot constitute a disability (Morin & Rothblum, 1991).

All of these organizations have adopted these policies affirming the inherent worth, dignity, and validity of same-sex orientations. These organizations have made this move because of the lack of conclusive empirical evidence supporting that same-sex orientations are any more or less mentally and physically healthy than a heterosexual orientation (Schüklenk & Ristow, 1996). In fact, the research literature has so extensively supported the nonpathological nature of same-sex orientations that the aforementioned organizations could do nothing but declassify them (Gonsiorek, 1991). And yet, some continue to insist that same-sex orientations are something of a "less than" nature and claim that if they are not desired, they can be eliminated. Hobo personality disorder was part of *Diagnostic and Statistical Manual of Mental Disorders* (American Psychiatric Association, 1952). Although it is no longer a recognized diagnosis, there do not remain advocates who are forming national associations of research and therapy for people with hobo personality disorder. Homosexuality is also no longer a diagnosis and has not been for almost 30 years (with each year bringing a further resolve and stronger evidence that it is not pathological). Yet, there continue to be those who advocate for its cure. Richard Socarides stated that "almost half of those who engage in homosexual practices have a concomitant schizophrenia, paranoia, or latent pseudoneurotic schizophrenia" (Bayer, 1987). A tremendous statement to make in light of the empirical evidence countering this and the official positions of APA and ACA.

The primary goal in responding to Throckmorton's article is to explain the logical fallacies that serve as the ground work for Throckmorton's claims. Since many of the claims are laid on untruths, the claims themselves are untruths. For instance, reorientation necessarily assumes a bipolarity in sexual orientation. This is an antiquated view of sexual orientation (Leck, 1994; Schreier, 1998; Suppe, 1985) dating back before the 1940s. Even the original American work in this area by Kinsey, Pomeroy, and Martin (1948) found that sexual orientation fell across a continuum. Sexual reorientation therapies are based on a limited understanding of sexual orientation and one that assumes a reductionistic bipolarity; one is either exclusively same-sex oriented or opposite-sex oriented.

Faulty Assumptions of Reorientation Therapy

A primary assumption Throckmorton makes is that sexual orientation is a behavioral act. Claiming that reorientation can occur by behaviorally modifying sexual arousal, as Throckmorton does, is negligent of the plethora of evidence which connotes the multimodality of sexual orientation. Sexual orientation is inclusive of behavior, cognitions, fantasy, and emotions (Golden, 1987; Isay, 1985). Even at the basic definitional level, the APA *Publication Manual* (APA, 1994) states the following, "Sexual behavior should be distinguished from sexual orientation" (p. 51). Throckmorton's behavioral definition of sexual reorientation presents a limited understanding of sexual orientation. Gonsiorek, Sell, and Weinrich (1995) define sexual orientation as an "erotic and/or affectional disposition to the same or opposite sex" (p. 41). Troiden (1989) claims a developmental model approach to defining sexual orientation. Troiden also defines a multidimensional approach that includes sexual orientation as an identity. Rothblum (1994) calls for clearer definition by the scientific community for sexual orientation and makes this call to provide more affirming mental health services for people working with sexual orientation. Throckmorton does not address this body of literature.

A further assumption Throckmorton makes is that sexual orientation may not be a valid clinical concept. Same-sex orientation is a valid concept descriptive of a naturally and long-occurring phenomenon (Ford & Beach, 1951; Gonsiorek et al., 1995; Shively & DeCecco 1977; Stein & Cohen, 1986). If Throckmorton validly uses the word *reorientation* to denote the therapy, then Throckmorton must necessarily assume the validity of the concept of sexual orientation. How can reorientation occur if orientation is not a valid concept? To support the point that sexual orientation is not a valid concept, however, Throckmorton quotes Gonsiorek et al. (1995) where they state that due to measurement problems there is doubt whether sexual orientation is a valid concept. If one reads the actual article, it is clear that Throckmorton has taken this quote out of context. The rest of the paragraph in which the quote is found discusses social constructionist and essentialism perspectives and then concludes that regardless of this debate, a predominate number of people adhere to self-definitions that clearly and distinctly conceptualize sexual orientation. Gonsiorek et al. also goes on to make the point that "there has been an increase recently in 'disinformation' about sexual orientation in the service of some political agendas, which specifically distorts measurement and definition of sexual orientation" (p. 40). This is a more accurate portrayal of the position of Gonsiorek et al. than the out-of-context quote misused by Throckmorton. Throckmorton is again negligent of the body of literature that describes the multimodality of sexual orientation. A further questioning of the validity of sexual orientation as a phenomenon has become an exercise in polemics and not a discussion of science.

The spirit of Throckmorton's argument about sexual orientation posits it as something that only people who are gay and lesbian have. The author does not discuss what heterosexuals have. It is assumed that heterosexuals have a sexual orientation, otherwise, heterosexuality too would be made as meaningless as Throckmorton has attempted to do with same-sex orientations. If heterosexuality is an orientation, is it not as "variable and unfixed" as he proposes heterosexuality to be? It would be curious to note if the author simply considers heterosexuality above discussion as a target of reorientation therapies. Throckmorton demonstrates bias by also not advocating for reorientation therapy for people who are heterosexual and are not satisfied. Throckmorton is critical about an article by Wolpe (1973) where Wolpe chose to offer religious reorientation rather than sexual reorientation. If sexual orientation is variable and fluid, is not religion as well? We know for sure that religion is a choice. Perhaps instead of sexual reorientation, individuals could seek religious reorientation to any number of major U.S. religions that are affirming of people with same-sex orientations (e.g. American Baptist Churches, Disciples of Christ, Episcopal Church, Metropolitan Community Churches, Presbyterian Church, U.S.A., Reform Judaism, Society of Friends, Unitarian Universalist Church). Not all religions are judgmental and condemning. Advocating for sexual reorientation while being critical of religious reorientation again demonstrates nothing more than bias.

Another assumption Throckmorton makes is that numerous successful re-orientations are documented in the literature. Unfortunately, these outcomes, too, are erroneously based. The author uses several studies to denote the efficacy of reorientation therapies by denoting percentages of clients who have had reorientation therapy and have "successfully and happily" changed. Articles supporting this position are rife with methodological problems that limit their generalizability and call into question their outcomes (Bieber et al., 1962; Birk, 1980; Cautela, 1967; Feldman & MacCulloch, 1965; Hadden, 1966; McConaghy, 1976; Mayerson & Lief, 1965; Mintz, 1966; and others). It is space consuming to reiterate again what many other authors have already discovered about the research supportive of reorientation therapies. As a result, the limits of this paper do not allow the space needed to delineate the problematic methodologies, participant selection criteria, statistical analyses, and outcome measures. For a detailed explanation of this, however, see Haldeman (1994); Herek (1998); Martin (1984); and Morin (1977).

Throckmorton also denotes religious-based studies demonstrating exceptional success in reorientation. Again, there are no empirical bases for these claims and many of the practices are fraught with unethical behavior, sexual abuse, deception, theological malpractice, and other highly questionable activities (see Blair, 1982; Haldeman, 1994; Lawson, 1987). Despite clear evidence time and time again that these studies are "bad science" or no science at all, Throckmorton and others continue to make use of these same studies as conclusive proof of the efficacy of reorientation studies.

A further faulty assumption is that there is only a single psychoanalytic interpretation of homosexuality. There are numerous interpretations of psychoanalytic thought some of which view same-sex orientations as healthy variations in human sexuality. Throckmorton relies on works of Nicolosi (1991; 1993) and Socarides (1979). These two authors base their work on a unitary belief in the pathology of the gay "lifestyle" (again a reductionistic term where in reality there are as many lifestyle variations as there are people with same-sex orientations). A broad review of the psychoanalytic literature reveals a rainbow of interpretations that homosexuality is a regular occurring variation in the spectrum of human sexuality. Nicolosi's National Association for Research and Therapy of Homosexuality presents a majority of work based largely on methodological ambiguities and questionable results (Haldeman, 1991) that are not supported by any empirical evidence (Edwards, 1996) nor published in refereed journals. Their theoretical suppositions are easy to make and impossible to disprove because of their tautological nature. It would be just as easy to use their interpretation of psychoanalytic theory to state that those who advocate for reorientation therapies are latent homosexuals. And because of this latency and inadequate ego strength, they must sublimate and reaction form their own same-sex orientation into advocacy for reorientation therapies. Theorists like Nicolosi ignore the lack of empirical support for their illness model and ignore the wide breadth of literature that consistently validates the nonpathological view of same-sex orientations (Haldeman, 1994; Gonsiorek, 1991). Ferguson (1994) and Isay (1985) state that many psychoanalysts are simply biased toward homosexuality and guide their analyses via their personally held value systems.

These psychoanalysts appear unable to factor out their own values. Their value bias aids their claims of success in reorientation therapy because of their countertransferences that prey on the "transference manifestation of wanting to be loved, the need to acquiesce, and the patient's passive longings" (p. 248). Even Freud noted that homosexuality cannot be classified as an illness (Freud, 1950). Furthermore, Freud noted that "to undertake to convert a fully developed homosexual into a heterosexual does not offer much more prospect of success than the reverse, except that for good practical reasons the latter is never attempted" (Freud, 1955, p. 151). Despite these admonitions from the founder of psychoanalysis, this minority of practitioners maintain their biases.

An additional faulty assumption of these psychoanalysts is that people with same-sex orientations need help because of their inability to have successful intimate relationships. The assumption that problematic intimate relationships are a marker for the need for reorientation is faulty. These types of problems are no more true for people with same sex-orientations than they are for heterosexuals. Throckmorton uses Nicolosi (1991) as proof of this argument. In his 1991 work, Nicolosi states that "researchers were unable to find a single male couple that was able to maintain sexual fidelity for more than five years" (p. 111). Nicolosi uses this statement to denote the inability for people with same-sex orientations to have fulfilling or lasting relationships due to the regressed and fixated nature of this sexual orientation. Simple logic informs us that heterosexual people are responsible for 100% of all divorces. Heterosexuals have also experienced divorce rates as high as 50% rate across heterosexual relationships (Peck, 1993). One only has to watch something such as TV's Jerry Springer Show to see heterosexuality continually and consistently displayed as a failed experiment. Throckmorton does not mention any inherent problems with heterosexuality in terms of relationship difficulties. It is a specious argument that when people with same-sex orientations have problems it is due to their sexual orientation. On the other hand, reorientationists indicate that when heterosexuals have problems it is due to something else. Weiss reported that many homosexuals "did not reveal unrealistic, immature traits or neurotic symptoms, whereas many heterosexuals did" (Panel, 1960, p. 560). Empirical evidence has existed since Evelyn Hooker's landmark study in 1957 that there are few discernible differences between the mental and physical health of people who are homosexual or heterosexual (see a replication of Hooker, 1957 in Freedman, 1971; also see Hart et al., 1978; Hopkins, 1969; Morin & Rothblum, 1991; Reiss, 1980; Ross, Paulsen, & Salstrom, 1988; Thompson, McCandless, & Strickland, 1971).

A final faulty assumption is that these practitioners continue their work without the idea that their treatment can caused harm—a dangerous ethical precipice for any practitioner to stand on! Throckmorton makes the statement that "Since it has not been shown that such counseling is intrinsically harmful" (p. 297). There is empirically based evidence that reorientation therapies have caused harm. Throckmorton makes his statement with no empirical support and again demonstrates the myopic view inherent in bias. Liddle (1996) surveyed 392 lesbians and gay men who reported on 923 therapy experiences. In an additional analyses, Liddle found that of these 923 therapists, only a small minority ($n = 64$) discounted, argued against, or pushed their clients to renounce their same-sex orientations. When clients reported this behavior, 58% reported that that particular therapist was "destructive" and 22% reported the therapist was "not at all helpful"—a powerful indictment of both the futility and potential harm of reorientation therapies. Isay (1985) noted that reorientation therapy can cause symptomatic depression and social problems later in life by contributing to an already damaged self-esteem. Sleek (1997), quoting Linda Garnets, Ph.D., Chair of APA's Board for the Advancement of Psychology in the Public Interest, states that reorientation therapies "feed upon society's prejudice towards gays and may exacerbate a client's problems with poor self-esteem, shame, and guilt." Haldeman (1994) noted that religious-based programs are "possibly exacerbating the harm to naive, shame-ridden counselees" (p. 224). Throckmorton notes, but then discounts, the ever-burgeoning "Ex-Ex-Gay Movement." This movement strongly demonstrates that people are feeling harmed by the activities of reorientationists.

Furthermore, Throckmorton does not make note in any way of the minority identity development literature (Helms, 1995; Pederson, 1988; Sue, Arredondo, & McDavis, 1992). This literature alerts mental health practitioners to this vital point: the typical period of self-loathing that occurs as individuals try to come to terms emotionally and cognitively with their minority status in a context that does not necessarily value them (Coleman, Butcher, & Carson, 1984). This is a time when social prejudice can easily become internalized (Cass, 1979; Myers et al., 1991). Working with clients to continue the internalization of this injurious and biased process is contrary to the ethical practices of counselors and psychologists (ACA, 1998; APA, 1998). Herr and Cramer (1988) state that counselors must work with client groups to reduce the "stereotypes, discrimination, and environmental barriers that impeded the development of such groups" (p. 154). By ignoring this body of research, reorientation counselors can easily engage in harmful practices with clients. They do so by colluding with them in accepting prejudicially based beliefs and attitudes. To say there is no harm caused by reorientation therapies is dangerous!

Conclusions

The main purpose of this article is to provide a different stance to Throckmorton's article. This stance shows that reorientation therapies are based on bias and logical fallacies stemming from faulty assumptions and lack of awareness of the wide breadth of knowledge available on same-sex orientation. This stance also shows that the problems underlying reorientation therapies are being passed off to the consumer public not as problems, but as good science. ACA has followed suit with other major mental health organizations such as the APA and the American Psychiatric Association by stating that when there is no illness, there is no cure. A minority of practitioners continue, however, to feel propelled to offer a cure. An explanation for this is that certain practitioners possess a cultural and personal bias (Ferguson, 1994). Garnets, Hancock, Cochran, Goodchilds, and Peplau (1991) have documented biased, inappropriate, and inadequate practice when it came to understanding people with same-sex orientations, their identity developments, relationships, and parenting practices.

It is time for the field of mental health to finally come to the conclusion that reorientation counselors act out of bias though they pass their work off as science. An examination of the faulty logic, lack of good empirical support, specious arguments, and ignorance of vast bodies of multicultural theory leads to this conclusion. A review of Throckmorton's article reveals only an extensive literature review, but it does not lead to a convincing conclusion that ACA has taken a position that is anything less than ethical.

References

American Counseling Association, (1998). *ACA code of ethics and standards of practice.* Alexandria, VA: Author.

American Psychiatric Association, (1973). *Diagnostic and statistical manual of mental disorders* (2nd ed.) Washington, DC: Author.

American Psychiatric Association, (1952). *Diagnostic and statistical manual of mental disorders.* Washington, DC: Author.

American Psychological Association, (1998). *Resolution of therapeutic responses to sexual orientation.* Washington, DC: Author.

American Psychological Association, (1994). *Publication Manual* (4th ed.). Washington, DC: Author.

Bayer, R. (1987). *Homosexuality and the practice of psychiatry* (2nd ed.), Princeton, NJ: Princeton University Press.

Bieber, I., Dain, H. J., Dince, P. R., Drellich, M. G., Grand, H. G., Gundlach, R. H., Kremer, M. W., Rifkin, A. H., Wilbur, C. B., & Bieber, T. B. (1962). *Homosexuality.* New York: Basic Books.

Birk, L. (1980). The myth of classical homosexuality: View of a behavioral psychotherapist. In J. Marmor (Ed.), *Homosexual behavior.* New York: Basic Books.

Blair, R. (1982). *Ex-gay.* New York: Homosexual Counseling Center.

Buie, J. (1990, March). 'Heterosexual ethic' mentality is decried. *APA Monitor,* 20.

Cass, V. C. (1979). Homosexual identity formation: A theoretical model. *Journal of Homosexuality, 4,* 219–235.

Cautela, J. R. (1967). Covert sensitization. *Psychological Report, 20,* 459–468.

Coleman, J. C., Butcher, J. N., & Carson, R. C. (1984). *Abnormal psychology and modern life* (7th ed.), Glenview, IL: Scott, Foresman.

Edwards, R. (1996, September). Can sexual orientation change with therapy? *APA Monitor,* 27 49.

Feldman, M. P., & MacCulloch, M. J. (1965). The application of anticipatory avoidance learning to the treatment of homosexuality: Theory, techniques, and preliminary results. *Behavior Research and Therapy, 3,* 165–183.

Ferguson, M. (1994). Fixation and regression in the psychoanalytic theory of homosexuality: A critical evaluation. *Journal of Homosexuality, 27,* 309–327.

Ford, C. S., & Beach, F. A. (1951). *Patterns of sexual behavior.* New York: Harper & Row.

Freedman, M. (1971). *Homosexuality and psychological functioning.* Belmont, CA: Brooks/Cole.

Freud, S. (1950). A letter from Freud. *American Journal of Psychiatry, 107,* 786–787.

Freud, S. (1955). Psychogenesis of a case of homosexuality in a woman. In J. Strachey (Ed. & trans.) *Standard edition of the complete works of Sigmund Freud,* (Vol. 18). London: Hogarth Press.

Garnets, L., Hancock, K. A., Cochran, S. D., Goodchilds, J., & Peplau, L. A. (1991). Issues in psychotherapy with lesbians and gay men. *American Psychologist, 46,* 964–972.

Golden, C. (1987). Diversity and variability in women's sexual identities. In the Boston Lesbian Psychologies Collective (Eds.), *Lesbian psychologies: Exploration and challenges* (pp. 18–34). Urbana, IL: University of Illinois Press.

Gonsiorek, J. (1991). The empirical basis for the demise of the illness model of homosexuality. In J. Gonsiorek & J. Weinrich (Eds.), *Homosexuality: Research implications for public policy* (pp. 115–136). Newbury Park, CA: Sage.

Gonsiorek, J. C., Sell, R. L., & Weinrich, J. D. (1995). Definition and measurement of sexual orientation. *Suicide and Life Threatening Behavior, 25* (Suppl), 40–51.

Hadden, S. B. (19666). Treatment of male homosexuals in group. *International Journal of Group Psychotherapy, 16,* 13–22.

Haldeman, D. C. (1991). Conversion therapy for gay men and lesbians: A scientific examination. In J. Gonsiorek & J. Weinrich (Eds.), *Homosexuality: Research implications for public policy* (pp. 149–160). Newbury Park, CA: Sage.

Haldeman, D. C. (1994). The practice and ethics of sexual orientation conversion therapies. *Journal of Consulting and Clinical Psychology, 62,* 221–227.

Hart, M., Roback, H., Tittler, B., Weitz, L., Walston, B., & McKee, E. (1978). Psychological adjustment of nonpatient homosexuals: Critical review of the research literature. *Journal of Clinical Psychiatry, 39,* 604–608.

Helms, J. E. (1995). An update of Helm's white and people of color racial identity models. In J. G. Ponterotto, J. M. Casas, L. A. Suzuki, & C. M. Alexander (Eds.), *Handbook of multicultural counseling* (pp. 181–198). Thousand Oaks, CA: Sage.

Herek, G. (1998). Stigma and sexual orientation: Understanding prejudice against lesbians, gay men, and bisexuals. *Psychological Perspectives on Lesbian and Gay Issues, 4,* 223–255.

Herr, E., & Cramer, S. (1988). *Career guidance: Counseling through the lifespan* (3rd ed.). Glenview, IL: Scott, Foresman.

Hooker, E. (1957). Male homosexuality in the Rorschach. *Journal of Projective Techniques, 22,* 33–54.

Hopkins, J. (1969). The lesbian personality. *British Journal of Psychiatry, 115,* 1433–1436.

Isay, R. A. (1985). On the analytic treatment of homosexual men. *Psychoanalytic Study of the Child, 40,* 235–254.

Kinsey, A. C., Pomeroy, W. B., & Martin, C. E. (1948). *Sexual behavior in the human male.* Philadelphia: W. B. Saunders.

Lawson, R. (1987, June). *Scandal in the Adventist-funded program to 'heal' homosexuals: Failure, sexual exploitation, official silence, and attempts to rehabilitate the exploiter and his methods.* Paper presented at the annual convention of the American Sociological Association, Chicago, IL.

Leck, G. (1994). Politics of adolescent sexual identity and queer responses. *The High School Journal, 77,* 186–192.

Liddle, B. J. (1996). Therapist sexual orientation, gender, and counseling practices as they relate to ratings of helpfulness by gay and lesbian clients. *Journal of Counseling Psychology, 43,* 394–401.

McConaghy, N. (1976). Is a homosexual orientation irreversible? *British Journal of Psychiatry, 129,* 556–563.

Martin, A. D. (1984). The emperor's new clothes: Modern attempts to change sexual orientation. In T. Stein & E. Hetrick (Eds.), *Innovations in psychotherapy with homosexuals* (pp. 24–57). Washington, DC: American Psychiatric Press.

Mayerson, P., & Lief, H. I. (1965). Psychotherapy of homosexuals: A follow-up study of nineteen cases. In J. Marmor (Ed.), *Sexual inversion* (pp. 302–344). New York: Basic Books.

Mintz, E. E. (1966). Overt male homosexuals in combined group and individual treatment. *Journal of Consulting Psychology, 30,* 193–198.

Morin, S. F. (1977). Heterosexual bias in research on lesbianism and male homosexuality. *American Psychologist, 32,* 629–637.

Morin, S. F., & Rothblum, E. D. (1991). Removing stigma: Fifteen years of progress. *American Psychologist, 46,* 947–949.

Myers, L. J., Speight, S. L., Highlen, P. S., Cox, C. I., Reynolds, A. L., Adams, E. M., & Hanley, C. P. (1991). Identity development and world view: Toward an optimal conceptualization. *Journal of Counseling and Development, 70,* 54–63.

Nicolosi, J. (1991). *Reparative therapy for male homosexuality.* Northvale, NJ: Jason Aronson.

Nicolosi, J. (1993). *Healing homosexuality.* Northvale, NJ: Jason Aronson.

Panel (1960). Theoretical and clinical aspects of male homosexuality. *American Psychoanalytic Association, 8,* 552–566.

Peck, D. L. (1993). The fifty-percent divorce rate: Decontructing a myth. Special issue: Focus on family issues. *Journal of Sociology and Social Welfare, 20*(3), 135–144.

Pederson, P. (1988). *A handbook for development of multicultural awareness.* Alexandria, VA: American Counseling Association.

Reiss, B. F. (1980). Psychological tests in homosexuality. In J. Marmor (Ed.), *Homosexual behavior: A modern reappraisal* (pp. 296–311). New York: Basic Books.

Ross, M. W., Paulsen, J. A., & Salstrom, O. W. (1988). Homosexuality and mental health: A cross-cultural review. *Journal of Homosexuality, 15,* 131–152.

Rothblum, E. (1994). I only read about myself on bathroom walls: The need for research on the mental health of lesbians and gay men. *Journal of Consulting and Clinical Psychology, 62,* 213–220.

Schreier, B. A. (1998). Talking 'bout my generation: Responding to bisexual and transgendered student identities. *Commission VII: Counseling and Psychological Services, 24*(2), 4–5.

Schüklenk, U., & Ristow, M. (1996). The ethics of research into the causes of homosexuality. *The Journal of Homosexuality, 31*(3), 5–30.

Shively, M. G., & DeCecco, J. P. (1977). Components of sexual identity. *Journal of Homosexuality, 2,* 41–48.

Sleek, S. (1997, October). Concerns about conversion therapy. *APA Monitor, 28,* 15.

Socarides, C. (1979). The psychoanalytic theory of homosexuality: With special reference to therapy. In I. Rosen (Ed.), *Sexual deviation* (2nd ed. pp. 243–277). New York: Oxford University Press.

Stein. T. S., & Cohen, C. J. (1986). Introduction. In T. S. Stein & C. J. cohen (Eds.), *Contemporary perspectives on psychotherapy with lesbians and gay men.* New York: Plenum Press.

Sue, D. W., Arredondo, P., & McDavis, R. J. (1992). Multicultural counseling competencies and standards: A call to the profession. *Journal of Counseling and Development, 70,* 477–786.

Suppe, F. (1985). In defense of a multimodal approach to sexual identity. *Journal of Homosexuality, 103*-4), 7–14.

Thompson, N. L., McCandless, B. R., & Strickland, B. R. (1971). Personal adjustment of male and female homosexual. *Journal of Abnormal Psychology, 78,* 237–240.

Troiden, R. R. (1989). The formation of homosexual identities. *Journal of Homosexuality, 17*(1/2), 43–73.

Welch, B. L. (1990, January 26). Statement. Washington, DC: American Psychological Association.

Wolpe, J. (1973). *The practice of behavior therapy* (2nd ed.), New York: Pergamon Press.

CHALLENGE QUESTIONS

Is Treating Homosexuality Ethical and Effective?

1. What message does providing assistance to individuals who are dissatisfied with their homosexual orientation convey to satisfied gay and lesbian individuals? Does the potential threat to a minority's identity outweigh some individuals' right to choose to reject that identity?
2. Why have some people argued that there is no empirical evidence supporting conversion therapy's effectiveness? What do they say are the problems with the research literature? Illustrate the supposed problems with a description of a real study.
3. The values of each author are a major issue in this debate. Is it possible to escape one's values? Can one value be proven to be truer than another?
4. In what ways does the surrounding political and religious dialogue about homosexuality influence the debate over conversion therapy?

ISSUE 14

Does Electroshock Therapy Cure Depression?

YES: Max Fink, from *Electroshock: Restoring the Mind* (Oxford University Press, 1999)

NO: Leonard R. Frank, from "Shock Treatment IV: Resistance in the 1990s," in Robert F. Morgan, ed., *Electroshock: The Case Against* (Morgan Foundation, 1999)

ISSUE SUMMARY

YES: Physician Max Fink argues that electroconvulsive therapy (ECT) is a safe procedure that will reduce the cost of patient care in the long term.

NO: Leonard R. Frank, editor and cofounder of the Network Against Psychiatric Assault, protests that ECT is a dangerous, brainwashing practice no matter what modifications have been made to make it safer.

For over 60 years, the field of psychiatry has used electroconvulsive therapy (ECT) as a treatment for certain mental illnesses. This procedure involves the administration of an electric current through the brain by way of electrodes attached to the temples. The shock sends the patient into a convulsion. The theory behind ECT is that the shock alters the chemistry of the brain, stimulating positive changes in the neurons.

First used to treat patients with severe depression, ECT was subsequently abused by hospital staff who used it to discipline and control unruly patients. With this development came waves of criticism and controversy concerning the effectiveness of and need for electroconvulsive therapy as a therapeutic practice. As a result, the use of ECT waned in the 1970s. However, interest in ECT has increased in recent years due in part to modifications made in the procedure.

In the following selection, Max Fink declares that the recent modifications have made electroconvulsive therapy a safe procedure. He maintains that ECT is an effective intervention not only for people with severe depression but also for those with schizophrenia, mania, and catatonia. Fink asserts that social stigmas and philosophical biases have prevented ECT from becoming a more widely used treatment. He supports ECT as an alternative to drug therapy for many inpatients. Fink also cites reports that show that the costs for a hospital stay during which the patient is treated with ECT are less than a hospital stay involving treatment with drug therapy. He states that ECT will make a comeback because as managed care organizations seek to reduce costs, "the demand for the most efficient treatments will gain support."

In the second selection, Leonard R. Frank argues that electroconvulsive therapy is a dangerous, brainwashing practice, and he objects to its resurgence. He offers vivid descriptions of his own experiences as a patient being treated with ECT as well as its precursor, insulin-shock therapy. Frank supports his objections by citing a comprehensive report in which the author concluded that he was "unable to cite a single study purporting to show the long-term, or even medium-term, benefits from ECT." Modifications in the procedure do not increase the safety of ECT, according to Frank. He also contends that the current drive for increasing the use of ECT is purely economic in nature.

POINT

- ECT is a safe procedure.

- ECT reduces costs for inpatient facilities.

- Current philosophical biases and social stigmas associated with ECT are unwarranted because they are drawn from earlier treatment methods.

- ECT is not used as extensively as it should be, because the pharmaceutical industry, managed care organizations, and political forces have underfunded psychiatric research.

COUNTERPOINT

- ECT results in brain damage, memory loss, and even death.

- 20–50 percent of patients relapse within six months of a "successful" course of ECT.

- The side effects of ECT, such as amnesia, denial, euphoria, apathy, mood swings, helplessness, and submissiveness, are just as common today as they were 60 years ago.

- Psychiatrists who prescribe ECT earn twice the income of psychiatrists who do not.

Max Fink  **YES**

Electroshock in the 1990s

W ithin the past decade, clinical and research interest in ECT [electroconvulsive therapy] has revived. The resurgence has been most marked in the United States, where the greatest efforts are under way to improve its safety and its efficacy. Psychiatrists in other countries have sought to reintroduce ECT, but its use varies widely. ECT is an accepted part of psychiatric practice in the Scandinavian countries, Great Britain, Ireland, Australia, and New Zealand, and usage is similar to that in the United States. A stigma attached to ECT limits its use in Germany, Japan, Italy, and the Netherlands to a few academic medical centers. Low reimbursement rates hamper its use in Canada and Japan, and also affect its availability in the United States. The unavailability of modern equipment and the expense of the medicines for anesthesia prevent its use in Africa, Asia, and Eastern Europe, and many patients in these countries who do receive it are subjected to unmodified ECT, such as was delivered in the 1930s and 1940s.

ECT is mainly a treatment for hospitalized patients, although many institutions are developing programs for outpatient ECT. The equipment and trained personnel are, for the most part, in the academic hospitals. Academic leaders recognize the merits of the treatment; some even encourage research and teaching. ECT is ignored by the research scientists at the National Institute of Mental Health. Few of the state, federal, or Veterans Administration hospitals provide ECT, and where it is available its use is infrequent. While 8 percent to 12 percent of adult inpatients at academic hospitals receive ECT, fewer than 0.2 percent of adults at nonacademic centers do. Such a discrepancy reflects the continuing social stigma and philosophical bias against electroshock. Before the federal Medicare and the Hill-Burton legislative acts of the 1960s opened access for all patients to any hospital facility, such discrepancies may have been common. But now that the nation has adopted an open-admission policy to its psychiatric facilities, the discrepancy is unjustified. It is shameful that many agencies licensed to treat the mentally ill lack the facilities to give the treatment.

Effects of Research on Practice

When ECT was revived in the late 1970s, the principal concern was its effects on cognition and memory. Unilateral ECT won favor with many practitioners after demonstrations that it reduced effects on memory. But other practitioners reported that unilateral ECT required more treatments than, and was not as effective as, bilateral ECT. The seizures in unilateral ECT were often brief, with poorly defined EEG seizure patterns. Studies of the interaction of electrode placement, energy dosing, and current form show that unilateral treatments, even with precise energy dosing, are less efficient than bilateral ECT. As a result, bilateral ECT is now preferred. When unilateral ECT is considered, its use includes precise energy dosing. Sinusoidal currents elicited unnecessarily high degrees of EEG and memory effects, compared with brief pulse square-wave currents, so the former have now been discarded.

We have learned that monitoring the motor seizure is not sufficient to measure the adequacy of an individual treatment, so we now look to EEG measures as more reliable indices. By recording and displaying the seizure EEG, we rely on the seizure characteristics as a guide to an effective treatment. Practitioners depend more on these characteristics than on criteria based on the motor convulsion and the change in heart rate as measures of beneficial treatment.

The interseizure EEG has stimulated research interest. Studies in 1957 had shown that a good clinical response in ECT depended on the slowing of the frequencies in the interseizure EEG. The observation was confirmed in 1972 and again in 1996, and the interseizure EEG is once again used as a guide to an effective course of treatment.

The indications for ECT have been broadened. As we have seen, it has gone from being a last resort for unresponsive depressed and suicidal patients to being a treatment option for patients with delusional depression, mania, schizophrenia, and catatonia. ECT can also be useful in patients with parkinsonism and those suffering from neuroleptic drug toxicity. Treatment can be safely given in the presence of complex systemic disorders and mental retardation.

Yet research on ECT is limited. Most of the research is directed at determining which treatment—medication or continuation ECT—can best maintain the benefits of a course of ECT in patients with severe depression. Some scientists still believe that sophisticated brain-imaging methods will find evidence of persistent brain dysfunction after ECT. So far, such studies have yielded no new information about mental illness or about ECT. Others seek the benefits of ECT without a seizure by the use of rapid magnetic pulses instead of electrical ones. The method, called "rapid transcranial magnetic stimulation" (rTMS), has yet to be proven of benefit.

Future of Electroshock

Psychiatric care in the United States is in such turmoil that the problem of restoring the availability of electroshock seems nearly insignificant. American psychiatry lacks the leaders to stand up to the pharmaceutical industry and the managed care executives who are taking ever larger portions of the financial resources allocated to treating mental illness. State legislatures are cutting funds for mental health care, urging their mental hospital administrators to reduce patient admissions and shorten durations of stay. The state mental hospitals, which served as the ultimate haven for the mentally ill, are being closed and patients are being consigned to a motley collection of inadequate substitutions. The nonthreatening and passive homeless are on the streets; those who are more ill go in and out of the revolving doors of community centers and emergency wards or to hospitals equipped only for short-term care. Those who fall between end up in halfway houses and adult homes.

At one time the states supported research centers that were the jewels of the nation's mental health activities. Few institutes are still supported by the states, and even these are forced to compete for larger portions of their budgets from federal resources and private charity.

Academic researchers depend on industry to support increasing portions of their salaries. Industry sponsorship has taken over major aspects of the training of psychiatric residents by providing funds for lectures and seminars at medical schools and hospitals, and for national and international meetings. Industry employees organize carefully crafted symposia, and the ensuing discussions are published as supplements to freely distributed psychiatric journals. The opportunity for independent assessment and open dialogue about the efficacy and safety of psychoactive drugs, and especially comparisons with other treatments such as electroshock, has been virtually eliminated.

The leaders of the lay agencies that speak for the mentally ill are confused, torn between the promises of an industry hawking its products, state mental health agencies seeking to self-destruct, and managed care companies striving to limit expenditures for the care of the mentally ill. The lay agencies are sensitive to the stigma of electroshock and avoid mention of it for fear of losing members and financial support. For that reason, they do not encourage state and municipal legislatures to provide the treatment.

In this turmoil, few psychiatrists speak up in behalf of electroshock for their patients. The two U.S. manufacturers who make modern ECT devices and support educational efforts are too small to do more than survive. Although their new devices have highly sophisticated EEG-recording capabilities that can monitor electroshock treatments with great precision, these manufacturers can do little to ensure that their instruments are properly used.

In the brouhaha over the revival of ECT in the 1970s, the anti-ECT lobby tried to persuade the FDA to limit the sale and use of ECT devices in the United States. Their claim was that the devices were unsafe. In the early 1980s the FDA ruled that the devices in use were safe and reliable. The devices delivered energies with a fixed maximum under standard conditions, a maximum that had been set arbitrarily. Patients' seizure thresholds, however, rise with age, and many of the elderly need higher energies for effective treatment. The device manufacturers developed such devices, but when they applied to the FDA for modification of the standards, they were turned down and could not sell their equipment. The devices now sold in the United States are inadequate for effective treatment of some patients. Since the higher-energy devices are sold in the rest of the world, we have the awkward situation that patients in Canada, Europe, and Australia are being effectively treated while we in this country fail in treating some patients with similar conditions.

There is one opportunity on the economic horizon for a broader recognition of the merits of electroshock. The duration of inpatient treatment for patients receiving electroshock seems to be longer than for those receiving other treatments. But patients come to ECT after drug trials, often many trials, have failed. If the duration of inpatient care of patients given ECT is estimated from the day of the decision to use ECT, it is shorter and the costs are lower than the costs for psychotropic drugs. In one academic general hospital, of 19 depressed patients treated with ECT alone, the average hospital stay averaged 41 days, and for the 55 patients treated with tricyclic antidepressants (TCA) alone, the average stay was 55 days. The longest stay was for patients first treated with TCA and, when those failed, with ECT—an average length of stay of 71 days. The estimated cost of the stay for ECT treatment was $20,000 and for TCA alone it was $26,500, a savings of $6,500 for ECT over TCA. The same financial advantage is found when outpatient ECT is prescribed.

A study of patients discharged from general hospitals with a principal diagnosis of depressive disorder found that the initiation of ECT within five days of admission leads to shorter and less costly inpatient treatment than for those treated with drugs alone or delayed ECT. Other studies found that the antidepresssant effects of ECT occur earlier and are more robust than those of antidepressant drugs.

For the present, few managed care insurers recognize the merits of ECT, either as a relief for their insured ill patients or as a financial benefit to their shareholders. Payment for ECT is rarely approved for a patient with schizophrenia, so that patient must endure one drug trial after another. The most specious arguments are made about patients seen as catatonic, where neuroleptic drug trials are required, despite the evidence that neuroleptic drugs may precipitate the more acute state of neuroleptic malignant syndrome (NMS).

As managed care organizations assume a greater role in medical care, they reduce costs by limiting the conditions for which payments will be made, cutting professional fees and negotiating cheaper hospital costs. Once these measures have squeezed out of the system all the "excess" costs they can, the demand for the most efficient treatments will gain support. The advantages of ECT over medication should promote its greater use. Such an effect is already apparent in the expanding number of institutions seeking to develop qualified ECT facilities, in the interest of practitioners in obtaining education credits for ECT, and in the overt inclusion of electroshock as a valid treatment in algorithms now recommended for depression.

Many object to the revival of ECT by reminding others of the problems with electroshock when it was first introduced; at the time it was virtually the only effective treatment for the mentally ill. Such criticism is wholly unwarranted today; it is no more reasonable than to speak of the excesses in tonsillectomy, hysterectomy, pallidotomy, insulin coma, and labotomy that marked the enthusiastic reception of those procedures in earlier decades. Our appreciation of electroshock must be based on its present practice. We call on it because it is effective, often more so than alternate treatments, and because modern practice has made it safe.

 **NO**

Shock Treatment: Resistance in the 1990s

Electroshock: Death, Brain Damage, Memory Loss, and Brainwashing

Since its introduction in 1938, electroshock, or electroconvulsive therapy (ECT), has been one of psychiatry's most controversial procedures. Approximately 100,000 people in the United States undergo ECT yearly, and recent media reports indicate a resurgence of its use. Proponents claim that changes in the technology of ECT administration have greatly reduced the fears and risks formerly associated with the procedure. I charge, however, that ECT as routinely used today is at least as harmful overall as it was before these changes were instituted. I recount my own experience with combined insulin coma–electroshock during the early 1960s and the story of the first electroshock "treatment." I report on who is now being electroshocked, at what cost, where, and for what reasons. I discuss ECT technique modifications and describe how ECT is currently administered. I examine assertions and evidence concerning ECT's effectiveness....

In October 1962, at the age of 30, I had a run-in with psychiatry and got the worst of it. According to my hospital records (Frank, 1976), the "medical examiners," in recommending that I be committed, wrote the following: "Reportedly has been showing progressive personality changes over past two or so years. Grew withdrawn and asocial, couldn't or wouldn't work, and spent most of his time reading or doing nothing. Grew a beard, ate only vegetarian food, and lived life of a beatnik—to a certain extent" (p. 63). I was labeled "paranoid schizophrenic, severe and chronic," denied my freedom for nine months, and assaulted with a variety of drugs and fifty insulin-coma and thirty-five electroshock "treatments."

Each shock treatment was for me a Hiroshima. The shocking destroyed large parts of my memory, including the two-year period preceding the last shock. Not a day passes that images from that period of confinement do not float into consciousness. Nor does the night provide escape, for my dreams bear them as well. I am back there again in the "treatment room;" coming out of that last insulin coma (the only one I remember); strapped down, a tube in my nose, a hypodermic needle in my arm; sweating, starving, suffocating, struggling to move; a group of strangers around the bed grabbing at me; thinking—Where am I? What the hell is happening to me?

Well into the shock series, which took place at Twin Pines Hospital in Belmont, California, a few miles south of San Francisco, the treating psychiatrist wrote to my father:

> In evaluating Leonard's progress to date, I think it is important to point out there is some slight improvement, but he still has all the delusional beliefs regarding his beard, dietary regime, and religious observances that he had prior to treatment. We hope that in continuing the treatments we will be able to modify some of these beliefs so that he can make a reasonable adjustment to life. (p. 77)

During the comatose phase of one of my treatments, my beard was removed—as "a therapeutic device to provoke anxiety and make some change in his body image," the consulting psychiatrist had written in his report recommending this procedure. He continued, "Consultation should be obtained from the TP [Twin Pines] attorney as to the civil rights issue—but I doubt that these are crucial. The therapeutic effort is worth it—inasmuch that he can always grow another" (p. 76).

Earlier, several psychiatrists had tried unsuccessfully to persuade me to shave off my beard. "Leonard seems to attach a great deal of religious significance to the beard," the treating psychiatrist had noted at the time. He had even brought in a local rabbi to change my thinking (p. 75), but to no avail. I have no recollection of any of this. It is all from my medical records.

> Genuine religious conversions are also seen after the new modified lobotomy operations. For the mind is freed from its old strait-jacket and new religious beliefs and attitudes can now more easily take the place of the old. (Sargant, 1957, p. 71)
>
> At the "Mental Health Center" [in Albuquerque] where I work, there is a sign on the wall near the inpatient wards that reads: "PATIENTS' RIGHTS: Patients have the right to religious freedom unless clinically contraindicated." (Jones, 1988, p. 2)

One day, about a week after my last treatment, I was sitting in the day room, which was adjacent to the shock-treatment wing of the hospital building. It was just before lunch and near the end of the treatment session (which lasts about five hours) for those being insulin-shocked. The thick metal door separating the two areas had been left slightly ajar. Suddenly, from behind the door, I heard the scream of a young man whom I had recently come to know and who was then starting an insulin course. It was a scream like nothing I had ever heard before, an all-out scream. Hurriedly, one of the nurses closed the door. The screams, now less audible, continued a while longer. I do not remember my own screams; his, I remember.

> [The insulin-coma patient] is prevented from seeing all at once the actions and treatment of those patients further along in their therapy... As much as possible, he is saved the trauma of sudden introduction to the sight of

patients in different stages of coma—a sight which is not very pleasant to an unaccustomed eye. (Gralnick, 1944, p. 184)

During the years since my institutionalization, I have often asked myself how psychiatrists, or anyone else for that matter, could justify shocking a human being. Soon after I began researching my book *The History of Shock Treatment* (1978), I discovered Gordon's (1948) review of the literature, in which he compiled fifty theories purporting to explain the "healing" mechanism of the various forms of shock therapy then in use, including insulin, Metrazol, and electroshock. Here are some excerpts:

Because prefontal lobotomy improves the mentally ill by destruction, the improvement obtained by all the shock therapies must also involve some destructive processes.
They help by way of a circulatory shake up ...
It decreases cerebral function.
The treatments bring the patient and physician in closer contact. Helpless and dependent, the patient sees in the physician a mother.
Threat of death mobilizes all the vital instincts and forces a reestablishment of contacts with reality....
The treatment is considered by patients as punishment for sins and gives feelings of relief.
Victory over death and joy of rebirth produce the results.
The resulting amnesia is healing.
Erotization is the therapeutic factor.
The personality is brought down to a lower level and adjustment is obtained more easily in a primitive vegetative existence than in a highly developed personality. Imbecility replaces insanity. (pp. 399–401)

One of the more interesting explanations I found was proposed by Manfred Sakel, the Austrian psychiatrist who, in 1933, introduced insulin coma as a treatment for schizophrenia. According to Sakel (cited in Ray, 1942, p. 250):

[W]ith chronic schizophrenics, as with confirmed criminals, we can't hope for reform. Here the faulty pattern of functioning is irrevocably entrenched. Hence we must use more drastic measures to silence the dysfunctioning cells and so liberate the activity of the normal cells. This time we must *kill* the too vocal dysfunctioning cells. But can we do this without killing normal cells also? Can we *select* the cells we wish to destroy? I think we can. [italics in original]

Electroshock may be considered one of the most controversial treatments in psychiatry. As I document below, the last decade has witnessed a resurgence of ECT's popularity, accompanied by assertions from proponents concerning its effectiveness and safety—assertions which deny or obscure basic facts about the historical origins of ECT, the economic reasons behind its current popularity, as well as its potential for destroying the memories and lives of those subjected to it....

Electroshock Facts and Figures

Since 1938, between ten and fifteen million people worldwide have undergone electroshock. While no precise figure is available, it is estimated that about 100,000 people in the United States are electroshocked annually (Fink, cited in Rymer, 1989, p. 68). Moreover, the numbers appear to be increasing. Recent media accounts report a resurgence of ECT interest and use. One reason for this is the well-publicized enthusiasm of such proponents as Max Fink, editor-in-chief of *Convulsive Therapy,* the leading journal in the field. Fink was recently cited as saying that "[ECT should be given to] all patients whose condition is severe enough to require hospitalization" (Edelson, 1988. p. 3).

A survey of the American Psychiatric Association (APA) membership focusing on ECT (APA, 1978) showed that 22% fell into the "User" category. Users were defined as psychiatrists who had "personally treated patients with ECT" or "recommended to residents under their supervision that ECT be used on patients" during the last six months (p. 5). If valid today, this figure indicates that approximately 7,700 APA members are electroshock Users.

A survey of all 184 member hospitals of the National Association of Private Psychiatric Hospitals (Levy and Albrecht, 1985) elicited the following information on electroshock practices from the 153 respondents (83%) who answered a nineteen-item questionnaire sent to them in 1982. Fifty-eight percent of the respondents used electroshock (3% did not use electroshock because they considered it to be "inappropriate treatment for any illness").

The hospitals using ECT found it appropriate for a variety of diagnoses:

100% for "major depressive disorder," 58% for "schizophrenia," and 13% for "obsessive-compulsive disorder." Twenty-six percent of the ECT-using hospitals reported no contraindications in the use of the procedure.

Darnton (1989) reported that the number of private free-standing psychiatric hospitals grew from 184 in 1980 to 450 in 1988. In addition, nearly 2,000 general hospitals offer inpatient psychiatric service (p. 67). While the use of ECT in state hospitals has fallen off sharply over the last twenty years, the psychiatric wards of general hospitals have increased their reliance on ECT in the treatment of their adult inpatients (Thompson, 1986).

In cases of depression, an ECT series ranges from six to twelve seizures—in those of schizophrenia, from fifteen to thirty-five seizures—given three times a week, and usually entails four weeks of hospitalization. In 72% of the cases, according to the APA (1978, p. 8) survey cited above, electroshock costs are paid for by insurance companies. This fact led one psychiatrist to comment, "Finding that the patient has insurance seemed like the most common indication for giving electroshock" (Viscott, 1972, p. 356). The overall cost for a series of electroshock in a private hospital ranges from $10,000 to $25,000. With room rates averaging $500 to $600 a day, and bed occupancy generally falling, some hospitals have obtained considerable financial advantage from their use of ECT. A regular ECT User can expect yearly earnings of at least $200,000, about twice the median income of other psychiatrists. *Electroshock is a $2-3 billion-a-year industry.*

More than two-thirds of electroshock subjects are women, and a growing number are elderly. In California, one of the states that requires Users to report quarterly the number and age categories of electroshock subjects, "the percentage 65 and over" being electroshocked increased gradually from 29% to 43% between 1977 and 1983 (Warren, 1986, p. 51). More recently, Drop and Welch (1989) reported that 60% of the ECT subjects in a recent two-year period at the Massachusetts General Hospital in Boston were over 60 years and 10% were in their eighties (p. 88).

There are published reports of persons over 100 years old (Alexopoulos, Young, and Abrams, 1989) and as young as 34½ months (Bender, 1955) who have been electroshocked. In the latter case, the child had been referred in 1947 to the children's ward of New York's Bellevue Hospital "because of distressing anxiety that frequently reached a state of panic.... The child was mute and autistic." The morning after admission he received the first of a series of twenty electroshocks and was discharged one month later. "The discharge note indicated a 'moderate improvement' since he was eating and sleeping better, was more friendly with the other children, and he was toilet trained" (pp. 418–419).

Children continue to be electroshocked. Black, Wilcox, and Stewart (1985) reported on "the successful use of ECT in a prepubertal boy with severe depression." Sandy, 11 years old, received twelve unilateral ECTs at the University of Iowa Hospitals and Clinics in Iowa City. He "improved remarkably" and "was discharged in good condition. Follow-up over the next eight years revealed five more hospitalizations for depression" (p. 98).

Some of the better known people who have undergone shock treatment include: Antonin Artaud, Thomas Eagleton, Claude Eatherly, Frances Farmer, Zelda Fitzgerald, James Forrestal, Janet Frame, Ernest Hemingway, Vladimir Horowitz, Bob Kaufman, Seymour Krim, Vivien Leigh, Oscar Levant, Robert Lowell, Vaslav Nijinsky, Jimmy Pearsall, Robert Pirsig, Sylvia Plath, Paul Robeson, Gene Tierney, and Frank Wisner.

In the early 1970s electroshock survivors—together with other former psychiatric inmates/"patients"—began forming organizations aimed at regulating or abolishing electroshock and other psychiatric practices which they believed were harmful. In 1975, one group, the Network Against Psychiatric Assault (San Francisco/Berkeley), was instrumental in the passage of legislation that regulated the use of electroshock in California. Since then, more than thirty states have passed similar legislation.

In 1982, the Coalition to Stop Electroshock led a successful referendum campaign to outlaw ECT in Berkeley, California. Although the courts overturned the ban six weeks after it went into effect, this was the first time in American history that the use of any established medical procedure had been prohibited by popular vote.

The Committee for Truth in Psychiatry (CTIP), all of whose members are electroshock survivors, was formed in 1984 to support the Food and Drug Administration (FDA) in its original (1979) classification of the ECT device in the high risk category of medical devices, Class III, which earmarks a device of its related procedure for a safety investigation. To prevent an investigation of ECT, the APA had petitioned the FDA in 1982 for reclassification of the ECT device to Class II, which signifies low risk. After many years of indecision, the FDA proposed in 1990 to make this reclassification—but has not yet done so. . . .

Claims of Electroshock Effectiveness

Virtually all the psychiatrists who evaluate, write about, and do research on electroshock are themselves Users. This partially explains why claims regarding ECT's effectiveness abound in the professional literature—while the risks associated with the procedure are consistently understated or overlooked. User estimates of ECT's effectiveness in the treatment of the affective disorders (i.e., depression, mania, and manic-depression) usually range from 75% to 90%. Two important questions, however, need to be addressed: What is meant by effectiveness, and how long does it last?

Breggin (1979, p. 135; 1981, pp. 252–253) has proposed a "brain-disabling hypothesis" to explain the workings of electroshock. The hypothesis suggests that ECT "effectiveness" stems from the brain damage ECT causes. As happens in cases of serious head injury, ECT produces amnesia, denial, euphoria, apathy, wide and unpredictable mood swings, helplessness and submissiveness. Each one of these effects may appear to offset the problems which justified the use of ECT in the first place.

Amnesia victims, having forgotten their problems, tend to complain less. Denial serves a similar purpose. Because of their embarrassment, ECT subjects tend to discount or deny unresolved personal problems, as well as ECT-caused intellectual deficits. With euphoria, the subject's depression seems to lift. With apathy, the subject's "agitation" (if that had been perceived as part of the original problem) seems to diminish. Dependency and submissiveness tend to make what may have been a resistive, hostile subject more cooperative and friendly. In hailing the wonders of electroshock, psychiatrists often simply redefine the symptoms of psychiatrogenic brain damage as signs of improvement and/or recovery.

Electroshock advocates themselves unwittingly provide support for the brain-disabling hypothesis. Fink, Kahn, and Green (1958) offered a good example of this when describing a set of criteria for rating improvement in ECT subjects: "When a depressed patient, who had been withdrawn, crying, and had expressed suicidal thoughts, no longer is seclusive, and is jovial, friendly and euphoric, denies his problems and sees his previous thoughts of suicide as 'silly' a rating of 'much improved' is made" (p. 117). Two additional illustrations are given below; see Cleckley (cited in Thigpen, 1976) and Hoch (1948).

On the question of duration of benefit from ECT, Weiner (1984)—in one of the most important review articles on ECT published during the last decade —was unable to cite a single study purporting to show long-term, or even medium-term, benefits from ECT. Opton (1985) drew this conclusion from the Weiner review: "In this comprehensive review of the literature, after fifty years of research on ECT, no methodologically sound study was found that reported beneficial effects of ECT lasting as long as four weeks" (p. 2). Pinel (1984), in his peer commentary on the Weiner article, accepted Weiner's conclusion that "the risks of ECT-related brain damage are slight" and then added, "it is difficult to justify any risks at all until ECT has been shown unambiguously to produce significant long-term therapeutic benefits" (p. 31).

The following excerpt from an article in *Clinical Psychiatry News* reveals the short-range outlook of many ECT Users:

> The relapse rate after successful treatment for affective disorders is very high, from 20% to 50% within six months after a *successful* course of ECT, according to Dr. Richard Abrams [a well-known ECT proponent]. "I think it is reasonable and appropriate to always initiate maintenance in the form of a tricyclic [an antidepressant drug] or lithium" he said. For patients who relapse despite adequate drug therapy, maintenance ECT [periodic single electroshocks, spaced several weeks or months apart] has been used successfully. (Klug, 1984, p. 16) [italics added]

The underlying assumption of this approach is that affective disorders are for the most part chronic and irreversible. There is a popular saying among psychiatrists, "Once a schizophrenic, always a schizophrenic." While not a maxim, "Once a depressive, always a depressive" is nevertheless a core belief among many ECT Users. It "explains" so much for them. From this perspective, there are hardly any ECT failures, only patients with recurring depressive episodes who require ongoing psychiatric treatment, intensive and maintenance by turns.

Proponents also claim, but cannot demonstrate, that ECT is effective in cases of depression where there is a risk of suicide. They often cite a study by Avery and Winokur (1976) to support their position. But this study makes no such claim, as we can see from the authors' own conclusion: "In the present study, treatment [ECT and antidepressants] was not shown to affect the suicide rate" (p. 1033). Nevertheless, Allen (1978), in the very first paragraph of his article on ECT observed, "Avery and Winokur showed that suicide mortality in patients afflicted with psychotic depression was lower in patients treated with ECT than in those who were not" (p. 47)....

Electroshock Modifications

In recent years, to allay growing public fears concerning the use of electroshock, proponents have launched a media campaign claiming, among other things, that with the introduction of certain modifications in the administration of ECT, the problems once associated with the procedure have been solved, or at least substantially reduced. These techniques center around the use of anesthetics and muscle relaxants, changes in electrode placement, and the use of brief-pulse electrical stimulation.

However, investigation and common sense indicate that while these modifications may offer some advantages—for example, muscle relaxants prevent the subject's thrashing about, thereby greatly reducing the risk of bone and spinal fractures, and making the procedure less frightening to watch—the basic facts underlying the administration of electroshock have not changed at all. The nature of the human brain and that of electricity are the same today as they were more than fifty years ago when ECT was introduced. Whatever may be the ame- liorating factors of the newer delivery techniques, when a convulsogenic dose of electricity is applied to the brain, there is going to be a certain amount of brain damage, some of which will be permanent.

There is even evidence that the drug modifications make ECT more de- structive than ever because the central nervous system depressants, anesthetics and muscle relaxants raise the subject's convulsive threshold which, in turn, makes it necessary to apply a larger dose of electricity to set off the convulsion. And, the more current applied, the more amnesia and brain damage. As Reed (1988) noted, "The amnesia directly relating to ECT depends on the amount of current used to trigger the generalized convulsion" (p. 29).

Other problems are associated with the use of premedications in ECT. In his study of 254 ECT deaths, Impastato (1957) reported that thirteen of sixty-six persons from the "cerebral death" group had received muscle relaxants and that these "appear to play a major role in the death of some of these patients" (p. 42). There were also five other patients who died immediately after receiving muscle relaxants but before being given the electric shock. These figures are from a period when muscle relaxants were not widely used. More recently, Ulett (1972) concurred with Impastato on the danger of muscle relaxants in ECT: "The objection to the use of muscle relaxants is that, although decreasing the rate of fracture complication, they unquestionably increase the chance of fatal accident" (p. 284). Given the paucity of ECT-death studies in recent years, it is difficult to gauge the extent of this problem in current practice.

Another modification, unilateral ECT, has received much attention since its introduction in the late 1950s but has not replaced—and is not likely to re- place—bilateral ECT as the standard technique. According to the APA survey on ECT (1978, p. 6), 75% of the Users reported using bilateral electrode placement exclusively. In bilateral ECT, the electrodes are placed on the subject's temples so that the current passes through the brain's frontal lobe area. In unilateral ECT, one electrode is placed on a temple and the other just above the back of the neck on the same (usually the nondominant) side of the head. Unilateral placement, proponents claim, results in less memory loss. But proponents of bilateral ECT assert that unilateral ECT is less effective and therefore requires more treatments (Gregory, Shawcross, and Gill, 1985).

Cleckley (cited in Thigpen, 1976) offered this explanation for the ineffec- tiveness of unilateral ECT: "My thought about unilateral stimulation is that it fails to cure. I think this failure to cure is in direct proportion to the avoidance of memory loss" (p. 40). During his interview with Abrams (1988b), Kalinowsky made this comment about unilateral ECT: "My experience is completely nega- tive and if patients improve at all, it's probably due to the repeated anesthesia induction with methohexital" (p. 38).

Given the need for "somewhat more current to produce a seizure" in each treatment session (Fink, 1978, p. 79) and for more treatment sessions per series, unilateral ECT may be more brain damaging in some cases than bilateral ECT.

The problems associated with brief-pulse stimulation, another innova- tion in ECT adminstration, are similar to those associated with unilateral ECT. While brief-pulse stimulation may cause less amnesia than the routinely used sine-wave stimulation, the newer technique "may be insufficient to induce an adequate generalized seizure" (Reed, 1988, p. 29).

What Ulett (1972) wrote about unidirectional current stimulation—a supposed advance in ECT technology introduced by Liberson (1948)—may also apply to brief-pulse stimulation, and to unilateral ECT as well: "[I]t is often necessary to give a greater number of these milder treatments to achieve the desired therapeutic result" (p. 287)....

Conclusion

Mystification and conditioning have undoubtedly played an important role in shaping the public's tolerant attitude toward electroshock. But it is not only the uniformed and misinformed public that has stood by silently during the electroshock era. There has hardly been a voice of protest from the informed elite—even when one of its own has been victimized.

While undergoing a series of involuntary electroshocks at the famed Mayo Clinic in 1961, Ernest Hemingway told visitor A. E. Hotchner, "Well, what is the sense of ruining my head and erasing my memory, which is my capital, and putting me out of business? It was a brilliant cure but we lost the patient. It's a bum turn, Hotch, terrible." (cited in Hotchner, 1967, p. 308).

A few days after his release from the Mayo Clinic following a second course of ECT, Hemingway killed himself with a shotgun. With all that has been written about him since his death, no recognized figure from the world of literature, academia, law religion or science has spoken out against those responsible for this tragedy. As might have been expected, the psychiatric professional has also been silent. Not only did the psychiatrist who electroshocked Hemingway escape the censure of his colleagues, but a few years later they elected him president of the American Psychiatric Association.

Since ancient times, physicians have been trying to cure epilepsy. One might therefore think that they would object to the use of artificially-induced seizures as a method of treatment. But no such objection has been forthcoming. On the contrary, the medical profession's passive acquiescence to the use of electroshock has recently turned to active support:

The AMA [American Medical Association] has endorsed the use of electroconvulsive therapy (ECT) as an effective treatment modality in selected patients, as outlined by the American Psychiatric Association.... [The AMA] recognized ECT as a safe procedure in proper hands. (ECT, Animal Rights, 1989, p. 9)

ECT User Robert Peck titled his book *The Miracle of Shock Treatment* (1974). Antonin Artaud (cited in Sontag, 1976), the French actor and playwright, who was electroshocked in the early 1940s, wrote afterwards: "Anyone who has gone through the electric shock never again rises out of its darkness and his life has been lowered a notch" (p. 530). In which perspective—or at what point between these two perspectives—is the truth to be found? This is no trivia question. For some, it will be the gravest question they will ever have to answer.

References

Abrams, R. (1988b). Interview with Lothar Kalinowsky, M.D. *Convulsive Therapy*, 4, 25–39.

Alexopoulos, C. S., Young, R. C., and Abrams, R. C. (1989). ECT in the high-risk geriatric patient. *Convulsive Therapy*, 5, 75–87.

Allen, M. R. (1978). Electroconvulsive therapy: An old question, new answers, *Psychiatric Annals*, 8, 47–65.

American Psychiatric Association. (1978). *Electroconvulsive Therapy*. Task Force Report 14. Washington, D.C.: American Psychiatric Association.

Avery, D., and Winokur, O. (1976). Mortality in depressed patients treated with electroconvulsive therapy and antidepressants. *Archives of General Psychiatry* 33, 1029–1037.

Bender, L. (1955). The development of a schizophrenic child treated with electric convulsions at three years of age. In C. Caplan (Ed.), *Emotional Problems of Early Childhood* (pp. 407–425). New York: Basic Books.

Black, D. W., Wilcox, J. A., and Stewart, M. (1985). The use of ECT in children: Case report. *Journal of Clinical Psychiatry* 46, 98–99.

Breggin, P. R. (1979). *Electroshock: Its Brain-Disabling Effects*. New York: Springer.

Darnton, N. (1989, July 31). Committed youth. *Newsweek*, pp. 66–72.

Drop, L. J., and Welch, C. A. (1989). Anesthesia for electroconvulsive therapy in patients with major cardiovascular risk factors. *Convulsive Therapy*, 5, 88–101.

ECT, animal rights among topics discussed at AMA's Dallas meeting. (1989, January 20). *Psychiatric News*, p. 9;23.

Edelson, E. (1988, December 28). ECT elicits controversy—and results. *Houston Chronicle*, p. 3.

Fink, M. (1978). Electroshock therapy: Myths and realities. *Hospital Practice*, 13, 77–82.

Fink, M., Kahn, R. L., and Green, M. (1958). Experimental studies of electroshock process. *Diseases of the Nervous System*, 19, 113–118.

Frank, L. R. (1976). The Frank papers. In J. Friedberg, *Shock Treatment is not Good for Your Brain* (pp. 62–81). San Francisco: Glide Publications.

Frank, L. R. (1978). *The History of Shock Treatment*. San Francisco: Frank.

Gordon, H. L. (1948). Fifty shock therapy theories. *Military Surgeon*, 103, 397–401.

Gralnick, A. (1944). Psychotherapeutic and interpersonal aspects of insulin treatment. *Psychiatric Quarterly*, 18, 177–196.

Gregory, S., Shawcross, C. R., and Gill, D. (1985). The Nottingham ECT study: A double-blind comparison of bilateral, unilateral and simulated ECT in depressive illness. *British Journal of Psychiatry*, 146, 520–524.

Hoch, P. H. (1948). Discussion and concluding remarks. *Journal of Personality*, 17, 48–51.

Hotchner, A. E. (1967). *Papa Hemingway*. New York: Bantam.

Impastato, D. (1957). Prevention of fatalities in electroshock therapy. *Diseases of the Nervous System*, 18 (supplement), 34–75.

Jones, T. (1988, June). Letter. *Dendron* (Eugene, Oregon), p. 2.

Klug, J. (1984, June). Benefits of ECT outweigh risks in most patients. *Clinical Psychiatry News*, p. 16.

Levy, S. D., and Albrecht, E. (1985). Electroconvulsive therapy: A survey of use in the private psychiatric hospital. *Journal of Clinical Psychiatry*, 46, 125–127.

Liberson, W. T. (1948). Brief stimuli therapy: Physiological and clinical observations. *American Journal of Psychiatry*, 105, 28–39.

Opton, E. M., Jr. (1985, June 4). Letter to the members of the panel. National Institute of Health Consensus Development Conference on Electroconvulsive Therapy.

Peck, R. E. (1974). *The Miracle of Shock Treatment*. Jericho, New York: Exposition Press. Philadelphia Psychiatric Society. (1943). Symposium: Complications of and contraindications to electric shock therapy. *Archives of Neurology and Psychiatry*, 49, 786–791.

Pinel, J. PJ. (1984). After forty-five years ECT is still controversial. *Behavioral and Brain Sciences, 7,* 30–31.

Ray, M. B. (1942). *Doctors of the Mind: The Story of Psychiatry.* Indianapolis and New York: Bobbs-Merrill.

Reed, K. (1988). Electroconvulsive therapy: A clinical discussion. *Psychiatric Medicine,* 6, 23–33.

Rymer, R. (1989, March-April). Electroshock. *Hippocrates,* pp. 65–72.

Sargant, W. (1957). *Battle for the Mind: A Physiology of Conversion and Brainwashing.* Baltimore: Penguin.

Thigpen, C. H. (1976). Letter. *Convulsive Therapy Bulletin,* 1, 40.

Thompson, J. W. (1986). Utilization of ECT in U.S. psychiatric facilities, 1975 to 1980. *Psychopharmacology Bulletin, 22,* 463–465.

Ulett, G. A. (1972). *A Synopsis of Contemporary Psychiatry.* St. Louis: C. V. Mosby.

Viscott, D. (1972). *The Making of a Psychiatrist.* Greenwich, Connecticut: Faucett.

Warren, C. A. B. (1986). Electroconvulsive therapy: "new" treatment of the 1980s. *Research in Law, Deviance and Social Control, 8,* 41–55.

Weiner, R. D. (1984). Does electroconvulsive therapy cause brain damage? *Behavioral and Brain Sciences, 7,* 1–22 (peer commentary section, pp. 22–54).

CHALLENGE QUESTIONS

Does Electroshock Therapy Cure Depression?

1. Fink argues that the use of ECT has been hampered because of social stigmas and philosophical biases. What should those who support the use of ECT do to shake off these stigmas?
2. Frank asserts that changes in the field of ECT are economically driven. Is the continued use of ECT warranted just because insurance companies and hospitals will save money in the long term?
3. ECT has been a controversial issue since its inception. Should such a controversial procedure continue to be researched? What recent research can you find?
4. Imagine that a close relative of yours has been committed to an institution and diagnosed as having major depressive disorder. During a visit your relative tells you that the staff has decided to start ECT sessions next week. Do you allow the sessions to take place?

ISSUE 15

Are Medications for Treating Depression Harmful?

YES: Peter R. Breggin, from "Psychotherapy in Emotional Crises Without Resort to Psychiatric Medications," *The Humanist Psychologist* (Spring 1997)

NO: Peter D. Kramer, from *Listening to Prozac: A Psychiatrist Explores Antidepressant Drugs and the Remaking of the Self* (Viking Penguin, 1993)

ISSUE SUMMARY

YES: Psychiatrist Peter R. Breggin argues that psychotherapeutic interventions are preferred over medications for treating depression because psychotropic medications damage the brain and hurt the morale of both clients and therapists.

NO: Psychiatrist Peter D. Kramer contends that antidepressant drugs such as Prozac can alleviate depression and transform clients' personalities from withdrawn and timid to outgoing and fun loving, with almost no side effects.

T he antidepressant drug Prozac seemed to take the world by storm in 1988. The media and many medical practitioners hailed it and similar antidepressants as miracle drugs, promising not only the alleviation of depression but also the transformation of personality. Two years later, Prozac became the world's most popular antidepressant; nearly 28 million Americans have now taken Prozac or similar antidepressants

Why is Prozac so popular? Until the advent of this class of antidepressants, people who used psychotropic medications experienced many bothersome and even life-threatening side effects, such as heart abnormalities, tremors, and irregular blood pressure. Prozac and other antidepressants, such as Paxil and Zoloft, which are part of a more recent class of antidepressants called selective serotonin re-uptake inhibitors, have comparatively few side effects. Why not take advantage of this medical technology if it will make us happier, better people without the troubling side effects?

Not everybody, however, is excited about the popularity of antidepressants. In the following selection, Peter R. Breggin argues strongly against psychology openly adopting the medical model. He fears that too many therapists and counselors automatically recommend drugs like Prozac to clients who experience emotional crises. Breggin calls for a return to psychotherapeutic principles such as empathy in times of emotional crisis. Breggin further asserts that psychiatric medications disable the brain, disempower both client and therapist, and diminish the public's faith in the therapeutic relationship.

In the second selection, Peter D. Kramer shares in the excitement of the new Prozac era. In an excerpt from his best-selling book *Listening to Prozac,* Kramer describes the experience of one of his clients to whom he prescribed Prozac. Not only did her depression diminish, but her personality was reshaped in more positive ways. This timid and withdrawn client began to be likable, sociable, and outgoing. It seemed as if her identity was being transformed before his very eyes! Through this and other similar experiences, Kramer has become convinced of the almost magical power of modern antidepressants.

POINT

- Antidepressant medications narrow the range of emotions and produce sedation and emotional indifference.
- Whether old or new, antidepressants impair brain function and do not improve brain functioning or correct chemical imbalances.
- Turning to antidepressants to change personality disempowers both client and therapist and places false hope in medication.
- Many psychiatric drugs, including antidepressants, can cause or exacerbate depression, agitation, suicide, and violence.
- Antidepressants create an artificial sense of well-being.

COUNTERPOINT

- Antidepressant medications are amazingly effective.

- The newer antidepressants, such as Prozac, are more effective than the older antidepressants.

- Some patients who take antidepressant drugs report improvement both in their depression and in their personalities.

- Research and experience have overwhelmingly indicated the effectiveness and safety of antidepressants.

- Many patients do not feel as well when they are off the medication as when they are on it.

Peter R. Breggin    YES

Psychotherapy in Emotional Crises Without Resort to Psychiatric Medications

ABSTRACT: Mental health professionals are being pressured to rely upon the medical model, including psychiatric diagnosis and medication. But there are many reasons not to turn to psychiatric drugs in emotional crises, including their impact on the brain and mind, and their disempowering effect on the morale of clients and therapists alike. Meanwhile, there are sound, empathic psychotherapy principles for helping clients in severe, acute distress. This article presents the case for therapists relying upon these psychotherapeutic interventions instead of drugs in dealing with emotional crises and emergencies.

There are innumerable kinds of crises and emergencies that psychotherapists and counselors deal with in community service agencies and private practices, including threats of suicide and homicide, potentially violent behavior, trauma from rape or battery, newly discovered cancer or HIV, separation and divorce, death of a loved one, sexual or physical abuse in a family, illness in a loved one, bankruptcy, unemployment and homelessness.

Sometimes these emergencies seem situationally determined by recent life events: a family with few resources abruptly becomes unemployed, loses its social service support, or becomes homeless; a young man or woman is diagnosed with a fatal disease; a chronically ill patient loses his or her insurance coverage; or a child is killed in an accident. Sometimes the cause of the emotional crisis seems more rooted in longstanding psychological distress or interpersonal conflicts: a middle-aged woman gradually lapses into depression and becomes suicidal, a young college student unexpectedly goes on a rampage, a child steals money for drugs and runs away from home.

Within psychiatry, psychotherapeutically oriented practitioners increasingly feel pressured to offer medication. This pressure comes from biologically oriented colleagues, from some patients, and from managed care providers. Psychologists, counselors and other non-medical therapists are also feeling coerced to adopt the medical model, especially in dealing with crises or extremes of misconduct and emotional turmoil. The American Psychiatric Association's (1994) *Diagnostic and Statistical Manual of Mental Disorders* has become a significant part of counseling and psychology school curricula and professional certification examinations. Students are routinely taught that they should refer their more difficult clients or situations for psychiatric evaluation and possible medication.

The use of psychiatric diagnosis and medication as a "last resort" too often goes unquestioned. As an unintended result, the psychotherapist's self-confidence in handling difficult situations and crises is bound to be undermined and to deteriorate. The care of clients also deteriorates when their options become limited to medication (see below). The vitality of humanistic psychology is threatened by these trends.

Psychotherapy and to some extent humanistic psychology has sometimes defined itself as the profession that deals with "normal" rather than "abnormal" psychological development. Thus Nugent (1994) observed:

> Counselors are trained to work with a person's normal developmental conflicts, while other mental-health workers generally are trained to diagnose and treat pathology and work with dysfunctional behavior or chronic mental illness of clients and their families. (p. 7)

This definition of counseling (or humanistic psychotherapy) encourages a reliance on psychiatric interventions for more difficult clients and situations. It also increasingly fails to describe the actual activities of non-medical therapists who, as Nugent himself acknowledges, are frequently being called upon to take more comprehensive roles in health maintenance organizations (HMOs), community agencies, and other settings.

Nor have humanistic psychologists historically limited themselves to "normal" clients. They have applied psychotherapy techniques to the paradigm of extreme mental disorder, patients labelled schizophrenic (Stevens, 1967; Rogers, 1967). This author's mental health career began as a college student volunteer case aide using empathic psychotherapy techniques with profoundly impaired inmates of a state mental hospital during the mid-1950's (Umbarger, Dalsimer, Morrison & Breggin, 1962; also described in Breggin, 1991). The volunteer program succeeded in getting the majority of our patients discharged from the hospital.

The distinction between normal and abnormal psychology may itself lack validity. Szasz (1961) reasoned that all psychiatric diagnoses ultimately turn out to be "problems in living." That is, they are better understood from a humanistic psychology paradigm than a psychiatric or pathological model. Criticism of the medical model continues to this day (Breggin, 1997b; Mosher & Burti, 1994; Sanua, 1996). Psychologists are being urged not to support or join the psychiatric establishment in its reliance on medication (Sanua, 1995).

In an in-depth analysis of patients labelled schizophrenic and their families, Laing (1967) and Laing and Esterson (1970) found that seemingly "crazy" responses instead reflect understandable family communications and processes. They took so-called schizophrenia out of the world of pathology and grounded it in the developmental history of the family. Psychosocial approaches to patients labeled schizophrenic continue to gain clinical and empirical support (Breggin & Stern, 1996; Karon & Vanden-Bos, 1981; Mosher & Burti, 1994). Psychotherapists should not consider their approaches to be less profound or efficacious than medical interventions. The empathic, humanistic psychology model may be the most powerful one of all for healing human distress. Later in his life, Rogers (1995) wrote:

> Over the years, however, the research evidence has kept piling up, and it points strongly to the conclusion that a high degree of empathy in a relationship is possibly *the* most potent factor in bringing about change and learning. And so I believe it is time for me to forget the caricatures and misrepresentations of the past and take a fresh look at empathy.

Notice that Rogers states that empathy may be "*the* most potent factor in bringing about change and learning." Can we have two most potent methods, drugs on the one hand, and empathic psychotherapy on the other? It is time for psychotherapists to confront that question directly.

Reasons Not to Use Medications in Emotional Crises

There are many reasons not to turn to psychiatric medications in difficult situations, emotional crises, or emergencies. The following analysis of the limits and hazards of psychiatric medication is documented in detail elsewhere (Breggin 1991, 1997a; Breggin & Breggin, 1994).

The Disempowering Impact of Reliance on Medication

When we rely on medications during difficult times we disempower the client and the therapist alike by confirming that technological interventions into the brain constitute the final resort during critical situations. Where we turn for our last therapeutic resort defines our underlying philosophy and psychology. If we rely on medication in the toughest situations—when we feel stretched to the limits of our abilities—we confirm the medical model and technological interventions as the ultimate "power" in human healing. We communicate to our clients and to ourselves that human support and understanding and personal self-determination and empowerment is not enough.

Even if medication turns out not to work, the act of referring the client for a drug evaluation communicates to the client, "You do not have the personal resources to handle the crisis, and neither do I. In fact, neither does anyone else, so let's hope that drugs can help."

If, instead, we try harder to build rapport and trust, to create empathy, to develop what can be called healing presence and healing aura (Breggin, 1997b), and to utilize other human resources in the family or support network, then we have defined human relationship and human services as our ultimate resort. We have confirmed that human distress can best be handled by empathic human interventions. This is not merely a lesson for the moment but for the lifetime of the client.

Faith in Ourselves Versus Faith in Medication

Professionals sometimes find it very distressing that a psychiatrist like myself does not advocate *starting* the use of psychiatric drugs under *any* circumstances. (When individuals come to me on medication, I will sometimes continue to prescribe for them if drug withdrawal proves too difficult or too hazardous, or if they don't wish to stop.) Often I will be questioned intensively by professionals who want to unearth one exception, one extreme circumstance, in which I would start someone on a psychiatric drug. Why do many professionals seem disturbed about the idea of never starting a client on drugs? Why is it so disconcerting to offer psychotherapy without the alternative of drugs? The answer in part has to do with faith and confidence—or lack of faith and confidence—in ourselves and in human resources. If there are no exceptions that justify the use of drugs, then we have nothing to rely on except ourselves—our own personal resources—including our capacity, in collaboration with our clients, to bring other human resources to bear on the situation. The therapist's refusal to make exceptions that allow for starting clients on drugs in effect declares, "Human caring and human services are the ultimate resort." This is frightening to many professionals who hope for a greater power to rely on beyond themselves, their clients, and other mere mortals. The resort to drugs in this light becomes reliance on a "higher power" than psychotherapy itself. Faith in this materialistic, technological authority has grave limitations and implications.

If, by contrast, we refuse to turn to medical interventions, we define ourselves, and other human beings, as the ultimate resource. We communicate to the client, "You and I together, with the help of other people, and perhaps with reliance on a genuine Higher Power, possess the necessary resources to solve or transform your crisis for the better."

The Brain-Disabling Effect of Psychiatric Drugs

There is another major reason not to turn to psychiatric drugs in emotional crises or emergencies: All psychiatric drugs exert their principle or therapeutic impact by impairing the function of the brain and mind. Conversely, none of these agents improve brain function.

There are two basic effects produced in the brain by toxic agents, including psychoactive drugs: They can narrow the range of emotions, producing varying degrees of sedation or emotional indifference, or they can create an artificial sense of well-being or euphoria (Breggin, 1997a). If clinically effective, they will also take the edge off mental processes in general, reducing to some degree intellectual functions such as abstract reasoning, judgment and insight. Individuals taking psychiatric drugs, much as persons intoxicated on alcohol, are often rendered unable to accurately judge the drug effects or their overall mental condition.

Individuals frequently choose to diminish their mental function in order to ease suffering. They do this with non-prescription agents such as alcohol and marijuana or with illicitly obtained sedatives or uppers. There is no doubt that these individuals, like many people who received psychiatric drugs, feel grateful for a respite from painful emotions. But should psychotherapists support these methods? Is it consistent with the empathic, humanistic or existential principles of therapy to promote mind-dulling or artificially stimulating agents?

During crises individuals need their full mental function in order to transform these emergencies into opportunities for growth. They need unimpaired mental faculties and a full range of emotions. A therapist should welcome a client's painful feelings as signs of life and as signals pointing to the source of the problem. When a client does welcome a client's most painful feelings, the client is likely to view these emotions in a far more positive light, one that transforms helpless suffering into a positive energy.

Confirming Genetic and Biological Myths

There is yet another reason not to turn to drugs at a critical time in a person's life. The use of psychiatric diagnoses and drugs gives the false impression that emotional crises are caused by genetic or biochemical factors that are amenable to pharmacological interventions into the brain. There is no evidence that any emotional crises routinely treated by professionals are caused by genetic or biological defects. Even the classic psychiatric diagnoses, such as schizophrenia and bipolar disorder, have never been proven to be genetic or biological in origin (Breggin, 1991).

There are many mutually contradictory speculations about physical causes for psychological suffering and none of them are supported by a convincing body of evidence. In regard to the acute or emergency situations treated by psychotherapists, the genetic and biological speculations are even more flimsy.

Even if some emotional crises are in part caused by a defect in the brain, all currently available psychiatric drugs further impair brain function. None of them improve brain function or correct a specific biochemical imbalance and psychiatric disorder (Breggin, 1991, 1994, 1997a). None of them can do anything to ameliorate the effects of a presumed abnormal genetic endowment.

Finally, it is worth noting that the efficacy of pharmacological interventions has been vastly exaggerated by the psychiatric establishment (see critiques in Bleuler, 1978; Breggin, 1991, 1997a; Breggin & Breggin, 1994; Fisher & Greenberg, 1989; Greenberg, Bornstein, Greenberg & Fisher, 1992; Mosher & Burti, 1994). In contrast, the efficacy of psychotherapeutic interventions, even for severely disturbed persons, has been more documented than is generally appreciated (Antonuccio, Ward & Tearnan, 1989; Beck, Rush, Shaw & Emery, 1979; Breggin, 1991; Breggin & Stern, 1996; Fisher & Greenberg, 1989; Greenberg, Bornstein, Greenberg & Fisher, 1992; Karon & VandenBos, 1981; Mosher & Burti, 1994; Wexler & Cicchetti, 1992).

In regard to emergencies or crises, there is even less evidence for the usefulness of psychiatric medications. The efficacy of psychiatric drugs in this regard seems limited to the capacity of neuroleptics to physically subdue or pharmacologically straitjacket extremely excited (manic) inmates in confinement. The testing protocols used for the approval of psychiatric drugs by the Food and Drug Administration (FDA) usually eliminate any clinical subjects who are in an emergency state (Breggin, 1997a; Breggin & Breggin, 1994). The

FDA has never approved a drug specifically for the prevention or control of suicide or violence. There is no significant body of research demonstrating that any psychiatric medication can reduce the suicide rate or prevent violence. Instead, there is substantial evidence that many classes of psychiatric drugs —including neuroleptics or antipsychotics, antidepressants, and minor tranquilizers—can cause or exacerbate depression, agitation, suicide, and violence (Breggin, 1997a; Breggin & Breggin, 1994). Overall, there's no compelling evidence of the efficacy of psychiatric medications in emotional crises, let alone in situational emergencies created by real-life stressors, such as divorce, bereavement, life-threatening illness, or loss of a job.

An Empathic Psychotherapy Approach to Emotional Crises

At the root of almost every emotional crisis lies a feeling of personal helplessness combined with alienation from other people. The individual feels both personally overwhelmed and incapable of getting adequate support from anyone else. Empathic psychotherapy aims at overcoming the client's sense of helplessness and alienation. This section draws on the principles of empathic psychotherapy described in *The Heart of Being Helpful* (Breggin, 1997b).

Whether or not help is actually available, the individual who experiences an emotional crisis has usually lost faith in his or her capacity to benefit from it. Once confidence is restored, "solutions" or improved approaches can almost always be found.

Emotional crises offer potential for escalating growth as the individual learns to handle the worst imaginable stresses. As confidence is regained, crises can be transformed into periods of exceptional growth. The individual learns that even his or her worst fears can be handled, overcome, and turned into opportunities.

Focus first on the person, not the crisis.

Every human being wants to be recognized as an individual with unique attributes and special value. This, of course, is an axiom of psychotherapy, but it's easily forgotten when a client presents for help amid great fear, turmoil and hopelessness. When clients arrive in crisis, don't focus on the details of their "emergency" ahead of offering a warm greeting and welcome. Don't put "fixing them" ahead of appreciating them as human beings.

If you as a counselor or therapist can feel and demonstrate that you're happy that your distressed client is alive, that you're glad to make his or her acquaintance, and eager to learn more about the person and then the problem —you may find that the acute emergency begins to abate before your eyes. If your client does not immediately feel more secure and confident, you have at the least laid the initial groundwork for your work together in an empathic relationship.

At the heart of every emotional crisis can be found a resurgence of child-like feelings of fear and helplessness.

From the start, the therapist must be careful not to get dragged emotionally into the client's helpless and fearful state of mind. Instead, the therapist should address these feelings of helplessness and fear in himself or herself and in the client. Often it is useful to openly discuss the underlying feelings of helplessness and fear, and how they relate to our heritage as children.

Most emotional crises involve a sense of alienation or abandonment.

The individual undergoing an emotional crisis no longer has faith in the healing capacities of other human beings or in his or her own ability to connect to other people. The psychotherapist's task is to become a person with whom the client can relate with a feeling of safety, confidence, and human caring.

If the psychotherapist feels the need to involve others, he or she can begin by asking the client if it would be useful to involve family and friends—even through a brief phone call. Involving extended family and friends can be life-saving. They can provide support, encouragement, companionship, good ideas, or direct help in the form of money or shelter. Also, the therapist's desire to help by involving other people sends a message of caring and confirms that people are the ultimate resource.

An empathic relationship in itself can often quickly ease a client's feelings of fear and helplessness, and alienation.

Emotional crises often require what can be called empathic self-transformation (Breggin, 1997b)—finding the resources within ourselves to feel empathic with the other human being. As we learn to find the strength and understanding in ourselves to remain calm, caring, and in touch during severely stressful situations, we communicate confidence, safety, and hope to the client.

The psychotherapist should focus on a *rational, loving,* and *confident* (but realistic) center in himself or herself that does not get caught up in the "emergency." This requires working on one's sense of healing presence (Breggin, 1997b)—the capacity to find an empathic attitude within oneself regardless of the fear and helplessness, anguish and alienation, generated in oneself during the apparent emergency.

Beware defining emotional crises as emergencies requiring desperate interventions.

When faced with a client who feels hopeless and doomed with nowhere to turn, it is tempting for the therapist to gear up for emergency mode. This only confirms the client's worst fears. A psychotherapist should avoid joining the client in feeling desperate.

It can be easy for a therapist to lose perspective and to identify with the client in a way that promotes the client's feelings of fear and helplessness. The

antidote for ourselves as psychotherapists is to understand out own vulnerabilities so that we do not overreact. If we are terrified of cancer or AIDS, then we
must remain especially alert not to encourage our clients' terror in the face of
these health crises. Similarly, if we are uncomfortable with our own suicidal or
violent impulses, we may push our client into greater fear of his or her own
anger and aggression.

*Resist doing something to the client; instead, calm yourself and find your
healing presence.*

The therapist should put more emphasis on his or her own feelings of
comfort rather than power or potence. Some emergencies may call for quick
action, but this is relatively rare. Almost always, if we can maintain our sense
of calm and connectedness, the client will begin to feel more safe and secure,
more rational, and more able to find positive new approaches.

*Overcome one's own judgmental attitudes by finding a personal experience
that resonates with what the client is undergoing.*

Conducting psychotherapy can test our capacity to feel sympathy and
caring for the client. We can become unsympathetic toward their fear and
helplessness, intolerant toward their negative or destructive behavior, impatient
with their failure to take more responsibility for themselves. In these instances,
it can be helpful to find within ourselves our own experience of emotional distress that most closely resonates with our client's. Very probably our judgmental
attitude toward the client reflects an intolerance toward our own similar vulnerabilities. We need to recognize and then to *welcome* this aspect of ourselves and
our client.

*Most emotional crises build on a chain of earlier events, often reaching back
to childhood stresses and trauma.*

Although the current event seems like the sole or primary "cause" of the
client's distress, it's more likely the proverbial straw that broke the camel's back.
If possible, help the client understand this chain of prior events in order to
provide more perspective on the present crisis.

People vary enormously concerning their responses to even the most devastating threats and losses. Even when there are very real objective threats, the
individual's subjective response to it remains the key to healing. One person
may be demoralized by learning they have cancer; another may mobilize to improve his or her life. One person is devastated by a separation while another
feels liberated. It can help a client to realize that human beings are capable of
persevering and even growing in the face of seemingly overwhelming threats.

*Advice and direction may be useful, but too often they disempower the indi-
vidual.*

It is tempting to come up with advice, directions, plans or strategies in handling an emergency. Too often this involves turning to experts, in the extreme, a psychiatrist for possible medication. Sometimes people do need guidance, but it will fall on deaf ears as long as the client feels terrorized by his or her situation or emotional condition. The crisis as such is likely to abate when a safe, caring relationship is established. Only then is advice likely to be useful and then it may no longer be necessary to the client who has become empowered to think for himself or herself. Instead of your own power and authority, enhance your client's sense of self-determination by providing moral courage and human connection.

Avoid all forms of coercion.

It can be tempting to use emotional threats or even direct force, such as commitment to a mental hospital, in order to handle a crisis. These interventions may stave off an immediate suicide, for example, but in the long run, by disempowering and humiliating the individual, they can do more harm than good. It may be necessary to point out to a client that there are alternatives, such as crisis centers and psychiatric hospitals, but bringing up these alternatives can indicate to the client that the psychotherapist is afraid the situation cannot be handled through their mutual personal resources.

There are no studies that confirm the usefulness of emotional bullying or more formal measures such as involuntary psychiatric treatment. Intuition and empathic self-insight are likely to convince us that people don't benefit from being forced into conformity with the therapist's expectations. The development of an empathic relationship requires mutual respect rather than coercion.

Emotional crises are opportunities for accelerated personal growth for the client and sometimes for the therapist.

Crises provide a window into an individual's greatest vulnerabilities. They allow the opportunity to explore the client's worst fears. They bring out into the open the individual's worst feelings of personal helplessness. It introduces the person to raw material of human existence. The self-understanding gained from this can be applied throughout life, enabling an individual to have a deeper psychological awareness of self and others. They not only gain a new understanding of themselves, they gain new insights into the human condition itself.

When individuals face and understand their own worst fears, and then overcome them, they feel greatly empowered. Having faced and overcome their most self-defeating emotional reactions, they can gain in confidence and faith in themselves. They learn that they can triumph over seemingly impossible threats to reach new heights of psychological or spiritual transformation. This also increases their confidence in everyday living.

Hanna, Giordano, Dupuy, and Puhakka (1995) recently studied "Agency and transcendence: The experience of therapeutic change." They describe "major change moments" involving "distinct psychological or metacognitive acts such as intending, deciding, willing, detaching, and confronting as well as directing awareness, thought and affect." They go on to point out, "Many of these changes also had to do with such acts as deliberately tolerating anxiety or ambiguity and recognizing the limits of one's own decisional and thinking abilities" (p. 150). These critical moments often occur during emotional crises in which the modern therapist will be tempted to refer the client for medication. It is important to keep in mind the power of "deliberately tolerating anxiety or ambiguity" in the process of taking charge of one's life in new and creative ways.

Conclusion

In one of his later publications, Rogers (1995, p. 140) wrote of a growing "willingness on the part of many [professionals] to take another look at ways of being with people that locate the power in the person, not the expert." Medication and the medical model place power in the doctor. For Rogers, the time was ripe for another alternative that would truly empower the client—empathy as the center of the healing process.

Nowadays, if the emotional crisis or emergency is severe enough, the non-medical therapist is likely to feel compelled to refer the client to a psychiatrist for medication. The myth of medication efficacy grips the mental health profession and undermines the human service interventions that are far more likely to handle the emergency to the ultimate empowerment of the client. It is time for the psychotherapy profession to return to its basic roots in empathic human services. Human beings, not medications, must remain our ultimate resort. Psychotherapists should not shrink from this truth. The well-being of our patients and clients, and the vitality of psychotherapy and humanistic psychology, depend upon taking a principled stand on these issues.

References

American Psychiatric Association. (1994). *Diagnostic and statistical manual of mental disorders,* 4th edition. Washington, DC: Author.

Antonuccio, D., Ward, C. & Tearnan, B. (1989). The behavioral treatment of unipolar depression in adult outpatients. In Hersen, M., Eisler, R. M., & Miller, P. M. (Eds.), *Progress in behavior modification.* Orlando, FL: Academic Press.

Beck, A.T., Rush, A.J., Shaw, B.F. & Emery, G. (1979). *Cognitive therapy of depression.* New York: Guilford Press.

Bleuler, M. (1978). *The schizophrenic disorders.* New Haven: Yale University.

Breggin, P. (1991). *Toxic psychiatry: How therapy, empathy and love must replace the drugs, electroshock, and biochemical theories of the 'new psychiatry.'* New York: St. Martin's.

Breggin, P. (1997a). *Brain-disabling treatments in psychiatry: Drugs, electroshock and the role of the FDA.* New York: Springer.

Breggin, P. (1997b). *The heart of being helpful: Empathy and the creation of a healing presence.* New York: Springer.

Breggin, P. & Breggin, G. (1994). *Talking back to Prozac: What doctors aren't telling you about today's most controversial drug.* New York: St. Martin's.

Breggin, P. & Stern, E.M. (Eds.). (1996). *Psychosocial approaches to deeply disturbed patients.* New York: Haworth Press.

Fisher, S. & Greenberg, R. (1989). *The limits of biological treatments for psychological distress: Comparisons of psychotherapy and placebo.* Hillsdale, NJ: Lawrence Erlbaum.

Greenberg, R., Bornstein, R., Greenberg, M. & Fisher, S. (1992). A meta-analysis of antidepressant outcome under 'blinder' conditions. *Journal of Consulting and Clinical Psychology 60,* 664–669.

Hanna, F., Giordano, F., Dupuy, P., & Puhakka, K. (1995). Agency and transcendence: The experience of therapeutic change. *Humanistic Psychologist, 23,* 139–160.

Karon, B. & vandenBos, G. (1981). *Psychotherapy of schizophrenia: The treatment of choice.* New York: Aronson.

Laing, R. D. (1967). *The politics of experience.* New York: Ballantine.

Laing, R. D. & Esterson, A. (1970). *Sanity, madness and the family.* New York: Penguin.

Mosher, L. & Burti, L. (1994). *Community mental health: A practical guide.* New York: Norton.

Nugent, F. A. (1994). *An introduction to the profession of counseling* (2nd ed.). New York: Merrill.

Rogers, C. (1961). Some learnings from a study of psychotherapy with schizophrenics. In Rogers, C. & Stevens, B. (Eds.), *On becoming a person: A therapist's view of psychotherapy* (pp. 183–196). New York: Houghton Mifflin.

Rogers, C. (1995). *A way of being.* New York: Houghton Mifflin.

Sanua, V. (1995). "Prescription privileges" vs. psychologists' authority. *Humanistic Psychologist, 23,* 187–212.

Sanua, V. (1996). The myth of organicity of mental disorders. *Humanistic Psychology, 24,* 55–88.

Shlien, J. (1961). A client-centered approach to schizophrenia: First approximation. In Rogers, C. & Stevens, B. (Eds.), *On becoming a person: A therapist's view of psychotherapy* (pp. 149–165). New York: Houghton Mifflin.

Szasz, T. (1961). *The myth of mental illness: Foundations of a theory of personal conduct.* New York: Hoeber-Harper.

Umbarger, C., Dalsimer, J., Morrison, A., & Breggin, P. (1962). *College students in a mental hospital.* New York: Grune & Stratton.

Wexler, B. & Cicchetti, D. (1992). The outpatient treatment of depression. *Journal of Nervous and Mental Disease, 180,* 277–286.

Peter D. Kramer

Makeover

My first experience with Prozac involved a woman I worked with only around issues of medication....

Tess was the eldest of ten children born to a passive mother and an alcoholic father in the poorest public-housing project in our city. She was abused in childhood in the concrete physical and sexual senses which everyone understands as abuse. When Tess was twelve, her father died, and her mother entered a clinical depression from which she had never recovered. Tess—one of those inexplicably resilient children who flourish without any apparent source of sustenance—took over the family. She managed to remain in school herself and in time to steer all nine siblings into stable jobs and marriages....

Meanwhile, Tess had made a business career out of her skills at driving, inspiring, and nurturing others....

That her personal life was unhappy should not have been surprising. Tess stumbled from one prolonged affair with an abusive married man to another. As these degrading relationships ended, she would suffer severe demoralization. The current episode had lasted months, and, despite a psychotherapy in which Tess willingly faced the difficult aspects of her life, she was now becoming progressively less energetic and more unhappy. It was this condition I hoped to treat, in order to spare Tess the chronic and unremitting depression that had taken hold in her mother when she was Tess's age....

⁕

What I found unusual on meeting Tess was that the scars were so well hidden. Patients who have struggled, even successfully, through neglect and abuse can have an angry edge or a tone of aggressive sweetness. They may be seductive or provocative, rigid or overly compliant. A veneer of independence may belie a swamp of neediness. Not so with Tess.

She was a pleasure to be with, even depressed. I ran down the list of signs and symptoms, and she had them all: tears and sadness, absence of hope, inability to experience pleasure, feelings of worthlessness, loss of sleep and appetite, guilty ruminations, poor memory and concentration. Were it not for her many obligations, she would have preferred to end her life. And yet I felt comfortable in her presence....

Tess had... done poorly in her personal life. She considered herself unattractive to men and perhaps not even as interesting to women as she would have liked. For the past four years, her principal social contact had been with a married man—Jim—who came and went as he pleased and finally rejected Tess in favor of his wife. Tess had stuck with Jim in part, she told me, because no other men approached her. She believed she lacked whatever spark excited men; worse, she gave off signals that kept men at a distance.

Had I been working with Tess in psychotherapy, we might have begun to explore hypotheses regarding the source of her social failure: masochism grounded in low self-worth, the compulsion of those abused early in life to seek out further abuse.... For the moment, my function was to treat my patient's depression with medication.

◈

I began with imipramine, the oldest of the available antidepressants and still the standard by which others are judged. Imipramine takes about a month to work, and at the end of a month Tess said she was substantially more comfortable. She was sleeping and eating normally—in fact, she was gaining weight, probably as a side effect of the drug. "I am better," she told me. "I am myself again."

She did look less weary. And as we continued to meet, generally for fifteen minutes every month or two, all her overt symptoms remitted. Her memory and concentration improved. She regained the vital force and the willpower to go on with life. In short, Tess no longer met a doctor's criteria for depression. She even spread the good word to one of her brothers, also depressed, and the brother began taking imipramine.

But I was not satisfied.

◈

It was the mother's illness that drove me forward. Tess had struggled too long for me to allow her, through any laxness of my own, to slide into the chronic depression that had engulfed her mother.

Depression is a relapsing and recurring illness. The key to treatment is thoroughness. If a patient can put together a substantial period of doing perfectly well—five months, some experts say; six or even twelve, say others—the odds are good for sustained remission. But to limp along just somewhat improved, "better but not well," is dangerous. The partly recovered patient will likely relapse as soon as you stop the therapy, as soon as you taper the drug. And the longer someone remains depressed, the more likely it is that depression will continue or return.

Tess said she was well, and she was free of the signs and symptoms of depression. But doctors are trained to doubt the report of the too-stoical patient, the patient so willing to bear pain she may unwittingly conceal illness. And, beyond signs and symptoms, the recognized abnormalities associated with a given syndrome, doctors occasionally consider what the neurologists call "soft signs," normal findings that, in the right context, make the clinical nose twitch.

I thought Tess might have a soft sign or two of depression.

She had begun to experience trouble at work—not major trouble, but something to pay attention to. The conglomerate she worked for had asked Tess to take over a company beset with labor problems. Tess always had some difficulty in situations that required meeting firmness with firmness, but she reported being more upset by negotiations with this union than by any in the past. She felt the union leaders were unreasonable, and she had begun to take their attacks on her personally. She understood conflict was inevitable; past mistakes had left labor-management relations too strained for either side to trust the other, and the coaxing and cajoling that characterized Tess's management style would need some time to work their magic. But, despite her understanding, Tess was rattled.

As a psychotherapist, I might have wondered whether Tess's difficulties had a symbolic meaning. Perhaps the hectoring union chief and his foot-dragging members resembled parents—the aggressive father, the passive mother —too much for Tess to be effective with them. In simpler terms, a new job, and this sort especially, constitutes a stressor. These viewpoints may be correct. But what level of stress was it appropriate for Tess to experience? To be rattled even by tough negotiations was unlike her.

And I found Tess vulnerable on another front. Toward the end of one of our fifteen-minute reviews of Tess's sleep, appetite, and energy level, I asked about Jim, and she burst into uncontrollable sobs. Thereafter, our meetings took on a predictable form. Tess would report that she was substantially better. Then I would ask her about Jim, and her eyes would brim over with tears, her shoulders shake. People do cry about failed romances, but sobbing seemed out of character for Tess.

These are weak reeds on which to support a therapy. Here was a highly competent, fully functional woman who no longer considered herself depressed and who had none of the standard overt indicators of depression. Had I found her less remarkable, considered her less capable as a businesswoman, been less surprised by her fragility in the face of romantic disappointment, I might have declared Tess cured. My conclusion that we should try for a better medication response may seem to be based on highly subjective data—and I think this perception is correct. Pharmacotherapy, when looked at closely, will appear to be as arbitrary—as much an art, not least in the derogatory sense of being impressionistic where ideally it should be objective—as psychotherapy. Like any other serious assessment of human emotional life, pharmacotherapy properly rests on fallible attempts at intimate understanding of another person.

〜◎〜

When I laid out my reasoning, Tess agreed to press ahead. I tried raising the dose of imipramine; but Tess began to experience side effects—dry mouth, daytime tiredness, further weight gain—so we switched to similar medications in hopes of finding one that would allow her to tolerate a higher dose. Tess changed little.

And then Prozac was released by the Food and Drug Administration. I prescribed it for Tess, for entirely conventional reasons—to terminate her depression more thoroughly, to return her to her "premorbid self." My goal was not to transform Tess but to restore her.

✦

But medications do not always behave as we expect them to.

Two weeks after starting Prozac, Tess appeared at the office to say she was no longer feeling weary. In retrospect, she said, she had been depleted of energy for as long as she could remember, had almost not known what it was to feel rested and hopeful. She had been depressed, it now seemed to her, her whole life. She was astonished at the sensation of being free of depression.

She looked different, at once more relaxed and energetic—more available —than I had seen her, as if the person hinted at in her eyes had taken over. She laughed more frequently, and the quality of her laughter was different, no longer measured but lively, even teasing.

With this new demeanor came a new social life, one that did not unfold slowly, as a result of a struggle to integrate disparate parts of the self, but seemed, rather, to appear instantly and full-blown.

"Three dates a weekend," Tess told me. "I must be wearing a sign on my forehead!"

Within weeks of starting Prozac, Tess settled into a satisfying dating routine with men. She had missed out on dating in her teens and twenties. Now she reveled in the attention she received. She seemed even to enjoy the trial-and-error process of learning contemporary courtship rituals, gauging norms for sexual involvement, weighing the import of men's professed infatuation with her.

I had never seen a patient's social life reshaped so rapidly and dramatically. Low self-worth, competitiveness, jealousy, poor interpersonal skills, shyness, fear of intimacy—the usual causes of social awkwardness—are so deeply ingrained and so difficult to influence that ordinarily change comes gradually if at all. But Tess blossomed all at once.

"People on the sidewalk ask me for directions!" she said. They never had before.

The circle of Tess's women friends changed. Some friends left, she said, because they had been able to relate to her only through her depression. Besides, she now had less tolerance for them. "Have you ever been to a party where other people are drunk or high and you are stone-sober? Their behavior annoys you, you can't understand it. It seems juvenile and self-centered. That's how I feel around some of my old friends. It is as if they are under the influence of a harmful chemical and I am all right—as if I had been in a drugged state all those years and now I am clearheaded."

The change went further: "I can no longer understand how they tolerate the men they are with." She could scarcely acknowledge that she had once thrown herself into the same sorts of self-destructive relationships. "I never think about Jim," she said. And in the consulting room his name no longer had the power to elicit tears.

This last change struck me as most remarkable of all. When a patient displays any sign of masochism, and I think it is fair to call Tess's relationship with Jim masochistic, psychiatrists anticipate a protracted psychotherapy. It is rarely easy to help a socially self-destructive patient abandon humiliating relationships and take on new ones that accord with a healthy sense of self-worth. But once Tess felt better, once the weariness lifted and optimism became possible, the masochism just withered away, and she seemed to have every social skill she needed. . . .

❧

There is no unhappy ending to this story. It is like one of those Elizabethan dramas—Marlowe's *Tamburlaine*—so foreign to modern audiences because the Wheel of Fortune takes only half a turn: the patient recovers and pays no price for the recovery. Tess did go off medication, after about nine months, and she continued to do well. She was, she reported, not quite so sharp of thought, so energetic, so free of care as she had been on the medication, but neither was she driven by guilt and obligation. She was altogether cooler, better controlled, less sensible of the weight of the world than she had been.

After about eight months off medication, Tess told me she was slipping. "I'm not myself," she said. New union negotiations were under way, and she felt she could use the sense of stability, the invulnerability to attack, that Prozac gave her. Here was a dilemma for me. Ought I to provide medication to someone who was not depressed? I could give myself reason enough—construe it that Tess was sliding into relapse, which perhaps she was. In truth, I assumed I would be medicating Tess's chronic condition, call it what you will: heightened awareness of the needs of others, sensitivity to conflict, residual damage to self-esteem— all odd indications for medication. I discussed the dilemma with her, but then I did not hesitate to write the prescription. Who was I to withhold from her the bounties of science? Tess responded again as she had hoped she would, with renewed confidence, self-assurance, and social comfort.

❧

I believe Tess's story contains an unchronicled reason for Prozac's enormous popularity: its ability to alter personality. Here was a patient whose usual method of functioning changed dramatically. She became socially capable, no longer a wallflower but a social butterfly. Where once she had focused on obligations to others, now she was vivacious and fun-loving. Before, she had pined after men; now she dated them, enjoyed them, weighed their faults and virtues. Newly confident, Tess had no need to romanticize or indulge men's shortcomings.

Not all patients on Prozac respond this way. Some are unaffected by the medicine; some merely recover from depression, as they might on any antidepressant. But a few, a substantial minority, are transformed. Like Garrison Keillor's marvelous Powdermilk biscuits, Prozac gives these patients the courage to do what needs to be done.

What I saw in Tess—a quick alteration in ordinarily intractable problems of personality and social functioning—other psychiatrists saw in their patients as well. Moreover, Prozac had few immediate side effects. Patients on Prozac do not feel drugged up or medicated. Here is one place where the favorable side-effect profile of Prozac makes a difference: if a doctor thinks there is even a modest chance of quickly liberating a chronically stymied patient, and if the risk to the patient is slight, then the doctor will take the gamble repeatedly.

And of course Prozac had phenomenal word of mouth, as "good responders" like Tess told their friends about it. I saw this effect in the second patient I put on Prozac. She was a habitually withdrawn, reticent woman whose cautious behavior had handicapped her at work and in courtship. After a long interval between sessions, I ran into her at a local bookstore. I tend to hang back when I see a patient in a public place, out of uncertainty as to how the patient may want to be greeted, and I believe that, while her chronic depression persisted, this woman would have chosen to avoid me. Now she strode forward and gave me a bold "Hello." I responded, and she said, "I've changed my name, you know."

I did not know. Had she switched from depression to mania and then married impulsively? I wondered whether I should have met with her more frequently. She had, I saw, the bright and open manner that had brought Tess so much social success.

"Yes," she continued, "I call myself Ms. Prozac."

There is no Ms. Asendin, no Ms. Pamelor. Those medicines are quite wonderful—they free patients from the bondage of depression. But they have not inspired the sort of enthusiasm and loyalty patients have shown for Prozac.

❧

No doubt doctors should be unreservedly pleased when their patients get better quickly. But I confess I was unsettled by Ms. Prozac's enthusiasm, and by Tess's as well. I was suspicious of Prozac, as if I had just taken on a cotherapist whose charismatic style left me wondering whether her magic was wholly trustworthy.

The more rational component to my discomfort had to do with Tess. It makes a psychiatrist uneasy to watch a medicated patient change her circle of friends, her demeanor at work, her relationship to her family. All psychiatrists have seen depressed patients turn manic and make decisions they later regret. But Tess never showed signs of mania. She did not manifest rapid speech or thought, her judgment remained sound, and, though she enjoyed life more than she had before, she was never euphoric or Pollyannaish. In mood and level of energy, she was "normal," but her place on the normal spectrum had changed, and that change, from "serious," as she put it, to vivacious, had profound consequences for her relationships to those around her.

As the stability of Tess's improvement became clear, my concern diminished, but it did not disappear. Just what did not sit right was hard to say. Might a severe critic find the new Tess a bit blander than the old? Perhaps her tortured intensity implied a complexity of personality that was now harder to locate. I wondered whether the medication had not ironed out too many character-giving wrinkles, like overly aggressive plastic surgery. I even asked myself whether Tess would now give up her work in the projects, as if I had administered her a pill to cure warmheartedness and progressive social beliefs. But in entertaining this thought I wondered whether I was clinging to an arbitrary valuation of temperament, as if the melancholy or saturnine humor were in some way morally superior to the sanguine. In the event, Tess did not forsake the projects, though she did make more time for herself.

Tess, too, found her transformation, marvelous though it was, somewhat unsettling. What was she to make of herself? Her past devotion to Jim, for instance—had it been a matter of biology, an addiction to which she was prone as her father had been to alcoholism? Was she, who defined herself in contrast to her father's fecklessness, in some uncomfortable way like him? What responsibility had she for those years of thralldom to degrading love? After a prolonged struggle to understand the self, to find the Gordian knot dissolved by medication is a mixed pleasure: we want some internal responsibility for our lives, want to find meaning in our errors. Tess was happy, but she talked of a mild, persistent sense of wonder and dislocation. . . .

◦◀◉▶◦

I wondered what I would have made of Tess had she been referred to me just before Jim broke up with her, before she had experienced acute depression. I might have recognized her as a woman with skills in many areas, one who had managed to make friends and sustain a career, and who had never suffered a mental illness; I might have seen her as a person who had examined her life with some thoroughness and made progress on many fronts but who remained frustrated socially. She and I might suspect the trouble stemmed from "who she is"—temperamentally serious or timid or cautious or pessimistic or emotionally unexpressive. If only she were a little livelier, a bit more carefree, we might conclude, everything else would fall into place.

Tess's family history—the depressed mother and alcoholic father—constitutes what psychiatrists call "affective loading." (Alcoholism in men seems genetically related to depression in women; or, put more cautiously, a family history of alcoholism is moderately predictive of depression in near relatives.) I might suspect that, in a socially stymied woman with a familial predisposition to depression, Prozac could prove peculiarly liberating. There I would sit, knowing I had in hand a drug that might give Tess just the disposition she needed to break out of her social paralysis.

Confronted with a patient who had never met criteria for any illness, what would I be free to do? If I did prescribe medication, how would we characterize this act?

For years, psychoanalysts were criticized for treating the "worried well," or for "enhancing growth" rather than curing illness. Who is not neurotic? Who is not a fit candidate for psychotherapy? This issue has been answered through an uneasy social consensus. We tolerate breadth in the scope of psychoanalysis, and of psychotherapy in general; few people today would remark on a patient's consulting a therapist over persistent problems with personality or social interactions, though some might object to seeing such treatments covered by insurance under the rubric of illness.

But I wondered whether we were ready for "cosmetic psycho-pharmacology." It was my musings about whether it would be kosher to medicate a patient like Tess in the absence of depression that led me to coin the phrase. Some people might prefer pharmacologic to psychologic self-actualization. Psychic steroids for mental gymnastics, medicinal attacks on the humors, anti-wallflower compound—these might be hard to resist. Since you only live once, why not do it as a blonde? Why not as a peppy blonde? Now that questions of personality and social stance have entered the arena of medication, we as a society will have to decide how comfortable we are with using chemicals to modify personality in useful, attractive ways. We may mask the issue by defining less and less severe mood states as pathology, in effect saying, "If it responds to an antidepressant, it's depression." Already, it seems to me, psychiatric diagnosis had been subject to a sort of "diagnostic bracket creep"—the expansion of categories to match the scope of relevant medications.

How large a sphere of human problems we choose to define as medical is an important social decision. But words like "choose" and "decision" perhaps misstate the process. It is easy to imagine that our role will be passive, that as a society we will in effect permit the material technology, medications, to define what is health and what is illness. . . .

⋅᠁⟨⊙⟩᠁⋅

An indication of the power of medication to reshape a person's identity is contained in the sentence Tess used when, eight months after first stopping Prozac, she telephoned me to ask whether she might resume the medication. She said, "I am not myself."

I found this statement remarkable. After all, Tess had existed in one mental state for twenty or thirty years; she then briefly felt different on medication. Now that the old mental state was threatening to re-emerge—the one she had experienced almost all her adult life—her response was "I am not myself." But who had she been all those years if not herself? Had medication somehow removed a false self and replaced it with a true one? Might Tess, absent the invention of the modern antidepressant, have lived her whole life—a successful life, perhaps, by external standards—and never been herself?

When I asked her to expand on what she meant, Tess said she no longer felt like herself when certain aspects of her ailment—lack of confidence, feelings of vulnerability—returned, even to a small degree. Ordinarily, if we ask a person why she holds back socially, she may say, "That's just who I am," meaning shy or hesitant or melancholy or overly cautious. These characteristics often persist throughout life, and they have a strong influence on career, friendships, marriage, self-image.

Suddenly those intimate and consistent traits are not-me, they are alien, they are defect, they are illness—so that a certain habit of mind and body that links a person to his relatives and ancestors from generation to generation is now "other." Tess had come to understand herself—the person she had been for so many years—to be mildly ill. She understood this newfound illness, as it were, in her marrow. She did not feel herself when the medicine wore off and she was rechallenged by an external stress.

On imipramine, no longer depressed but still inhibited and subdued, Tess felt "myself again." But while on Prozac, she underwent a redefinition of self. Off Prozac, when she again became inhibited and subdued—perhaps the identical sensations she had experienced while on imipramine—she now felt "not myself." Prozac redefined Tess's understanding of what was essential to her and what was intrusive and pathological.

This recasting of self left Tess in an unusual relationship to medication. Off medication, she was aware that, if she returned to the old inhibited state, she might need Prozac in order to "feel herself." In this sense, she might have a lifelong relationship to medication, whether or not she was currently taking it. Patients who undergo the sort of deep change Tess experienced generally say they never want to feel the old way again and would take quite substantial risks —in terms, for instance, of medication side effects—in order not to regress. This is not a question of addiction or hedonism, at least not in the ordinary sense of those words, but of having located a self that feels true, normal, and whole, and of understanding medication to be an occasionally necessary adjunct to the maintenance of that self.

Beyond the effect on individual patients, Tess's redefinition of self led me to fantasize about a culture in which this biologically driven sort of self-understanding becomes widespread. Certain dispositions now considered awkward or endearing, depending on taste, might be seen as ailments to be pitied and, where possible, corrected. Tastes and judgments regarding personality styles do change. The romantic, decadent stance of Goethe's young Werther and Chateaubriand's René we now see as merely immature, overly depressive, perhaps in need of treatment. Might we not, in a culture where overseriousness is a medically correctable flaw, lose our taste for the melancholic or brooding artists—Schubert, or even Mozart in many of his moods?

These were my concerns on witnessing Tess's recovery. I was torn simultaneously by a sense that the medication was too far-reaching in its effects and a sense that my discomfort was arbitrary and aesthetic rather than doctorly. I wondered how the drug might influence my profession's definition of illness and its understanding of ordinary suffering. I wondered how Prozac's success would interact with certain unfortunate tendencies of the broader culture. And I asked just how far we—doctors, patients, the society at large—were likely to go in the direction of permitting drug responses to shape our understanding of the authentic self.

My concerns were imprecisely formulated. But it was not only the concerns that were vague: I had as yet only a sketchy impression of the drug whose effects were so troubling. To whom were my patients and I listening? On that question depended the answers to the list of social and ethical concerns; and the exploration of that question would entail attending to accounts of other patients who responded to Prozac.

༺✿༻

My first meeting with Prozac had been heightened for me by the uncommon qualities of the patient who responded to the drug. I found it astonishing that a pill could do in a matter of days what psychiatrists hope, and often fail, to accomplish by other means over a course of years: to restore to a person robbed of it in childhood the capacity to play. Yes, there remained a disquieting element to this restoration. Were I scripting the story, I might have made Tess's metamorphosis more gradual, more humanly comprehensible, more in sync with the ordinary rhythm of growth. I might even have preferred if her play as an adult had been, for continuity's sake, more suffused with the memory of melancholy. But medicines do not work just as we wish. The way neurochemicals tell stories is not the way psychotherapy tells them. If Tess's fairy tale does not have the plot we expect, its ending is nonetheless happy.

By the time Tess's story had played itself out, I had seen perhaps a dozen people respond with comparable success to Prozac. Hers was not an isolated case, and the issues it raised would not go away. Charisma, courage, character, social competency—Prozac seemed to say that these and other concepts would need to be re-examined, that our sense of what is constant in the self and what is mutable, what is necessary and what contingent, would need, like our sense of the fable of transformation, to be revised.

CHALLENGE QUESTIONS

Are Medications for Treating Depression Harmful?

1. The newer classes of antidepressants have fewer side effects than the older classes, but they still have them. What are the side effects of the newer classes? List and discuss them and their probabilities.
2. Breggin talks about psychology adopting the "medical model." What is this model? What effect does it have on psychological treatment? Are there alternative models? What would be their advantages and disadvantages?
3. How do antidepressants, such as selective serotonin re-uptake inhibitors, work? Investigate this through a professorial interview or a neuroscience text.
4. How do you feel about the prospects of a "transformation of personality"? Kramer discusses this positively, but could this also have negative implications? Could even the promise of being "sociable" and "outgoing" have negative ramifications?

On the Internet . . .

Journal of Personality and Social Psychology

This site contains a description of the *Journal of Personality and Social Psychology,* the current issue's table of contents (with abstracts), past tables of contents, and selected online articles from the journal. Looking over the tables of contents should provide you with an overview of current topics of interest to social psychologists.

http://www.apa.org/journals/psp.html

Society for the Psychological Study of Social Issues (SPSSI)

This home page of the Society for the Psychological Study of Social Issues (SPSSI) provides information about current research in social psychology as well as abstracts of issues of the *Journal of Social Issues.*

http://www.spssi.org

Feminists for Free Expression

This page features the position statement on pornography of Feminists for Free Expression (FFE), as well as other position statements, further reading, and related links.

http://www.well.com/user/freedom/pornography.html

PART 7

Social Psychology

*S*ocial *psychology is the study of humans in their social environment. A central concern of social psychologists is how society affects the individual. For example, does religiosity improve mental health and well-being? Another particularly controversial example is the question of whether or not pornography negatively influences men's treatment of women. Of more recent concern is the effect that the Internet has on psychological health. These concerns are addressed in this section.*

- Does the Internet Have Psychological Benefits?

- Does Religious Commitment Improve Mental Health?

- Is Pornography Harmful?

ISSUE 16

Does the Internet Have Psychological Benefits?

YES: James E. Katz and Philip Aspden, from "A Nation of Strangers?" *Communications of the ACM* (December 1997)

NO: Robert Kraut et al., from "Internet Paradox: A Social Technology That Reduces Social Involvement and Psychological Well-Being?" *American Psychologist* (September 1998)

ISSUE SUMMARY

YES: Research scientist James E. Katz and Philip Aspden, executive director of the Center for Research on the Information Society, contend that the Internet has positive effects on the lives of its users. They also maintain that the Internet creates more opportunities for people to foster relationships with people, regardless of their location.

NO: Robert Kraut, a professor of social psychology and human computer interaction, and his colleagues at Carnegie Mellon University question how beneficial Internet use really is. They argue that Internet use reduces the number and quality of interpersonal relationships that one has.

Not long ago, phrases like "surfing the Web" were understood by only the most technologically advanced. Now the Internet is accessible by almost anyone from almost anywhere, including classrooms, homes, and businesses. People can even check their e-mail in some malls. People spend increasing amounts of time on the Internet and use it for an increasing number of things. With the touch of a button, people can gain access to oceans of information and all sorts of new activities. What effects does the explosion of Internet access have on the psychological well-being of Internet users? Is it beneficial or harmful?

Many people feel that the Internet gives them greater opportunities to meet new friends in chat rooms and through other forms of Internet communication. The Internet offers the potential for thousands of new relationships and the protection of relative anonymity. No one knows if a user is attractive, has a particular ethnicity, or has a good job. All that an individual's chat room companions know is what she or he tells them. The problem is that Internet relationships require people to spend time in relative isolation—time in front of a machine. This has spurred some to predict that the Internet will decrease community and family involvement. They feel that the time spent in front of a computer monitor, communicating with people who cannot be seen, greatly detracts from more healthy relationships. Instead of talking to immediate family members or friends, the Internet user spends hours talking to people who require little from the user. Critics maintain that Internet relationships are largely superficial and that some are even deceptive.

In the following selection, James E. Katz and Philip Aspden contend that the Internet is anything but harmful. They indicate that the Internet is, in fact, beneficial to the psychological health of its users. Internet use merely adds to traditional forms of social ties, they argue, and users of the Internet are just as active in social organizations as nonusers. Rather than shrinking a person's social contacts, the Internet expands social opportunities. Katz and Aspden also argue that Internet use does not negatively influence the quantity or quality of time spent with family and friends.

In the second selection, Robert Kraut et al. hold that Internet use not only decreases family communication but also increases depression and loneliness. Although they acknowledge that the Internet does allow for a greater number of friendships, they argue that the kinds of friendships gained on the Internet are of a poorer quality than more traditional friendships. They suggest that "people are substituting poorer quality social relationships for better relationships, that is, substituting weak ties for strong ones." Kraut et al. maintain that Internet use should be carefully balanced with real-life social involvement in order to curtail the negative psychological effects of reliance on Web friends.

POINT

- Internet use leads to more relationships, regardless of geography or convenience.

- Internet use does not have a significant effect on time spent with friends and family.

- The number one use of the Internet is interpersonal communication.

- Sixty percent of the people who have met friends on the Internet also went on to meet them face-to-face.

COUNTERPOINT

- Relationships gained on the Internet block people from "real," more satisfying relationships and reduces social involvement.

- Greater use of the Internet causes declines in family communication as well as increased rates of depression and loneliness.

- Internet use is associated with physical inactivity and less face-to-face contact.

- Only 22 percent of people who have used the Internet for at least two years have ever made a new friend on the Internet.

James E. Katz and Philip Aspden

 **YES**

A Nation of Strangers?

Readers of New York tabloid newspapers may have been shocked [in 1997] by a front-page photograph showing a local computer expert being led away in handcuffs, having been arrested on charges of raping a woman he had met via the Internet. But troubles with Internet acquaintances are by no means unique. Stories appear in the news media with disturbing frequency about young boys or girls running away from their homes with adults they met through computer bulletin boards or chat groups.... As similar stories arise about Internet friendships going awry, or even of these "friendships" being malicious cons in the first place, concerns over the Internet's social impact will increase. Of course the concern is by no means limited to the one-on-one level of interpersonal friendships. National and international bodies are grappling with questions about what to do about various extremist political or religious groups who are aiming to suborn or recruit large groups of people. The mass suicide of the Heaven's Gate cult, which had a presence on the Internet, was a ready target for those who fear the way the Internet is changing society.

But the Internet situation is not unique. Every new technology finds dour critics (as well as ebullient proponents). Communication technologies in particular can be seen as opening the doors to all varieties of social ills. When the telegraph, telephone and the automobile were in their infancy, each of these three earlier "communication" technologies found vitriolic critics who said these "instruments of the devil" would drastically alter society (which they did) with disastrous consequences for the quality of life and the moral order (readers may judge for themselves about this point). The Internet is no exception to this rule. Indeed, it has stimulated so many commentators that not even the most indefatigable reader can stay abreast of the flood of speculation and opinion. Yet, as might be expected in light of the conflicts, difficulties, and tragedies associated with the Internet mentioned previously, one area in particular has been singled out for comment: the way the Internet affects social relationships generally and participation in community life in particular. Among those who have criticized the Internet are MIT's Sherry Turkle, who claims that it leads to the destruction of meaningful community and social integration, and Berkeley's Cliff Stoll, who says it reduces people's commitment to and enjoyment of real friendships....

From James E. Katz and Philip Aspden, "A Nation of Strangers?" *Communications of the ACM*, vol. 40, no. 12 (December 1997). Copyright © 1997 by The Association for Computing Machinery. Reprinted by permission. References omitted.

By contrast, optimists argue that genuinely meaningful communities can be established in cyberspace, and indeed even fostered via online communications. Rheingold holds that since virtual interfacing obscures social categories we ordinarily use to sift our relationships (race, sex, age, location), the possibility of new relationships and hence new communities is multiplied. An even more utopian argument is that new, powerful communities will arise in cyberspace, supplanting physical ones of the past, and becoming to an unprecedented extent cohesive, democratic, and meaningful for its members. Indeed, Internet pioneer and Lotus Corporation cofounder Mitch Kapor sees virtual communities ringing in at last the Jeffersonian ideal of community. "Life in cyberspace seems to be shaping up exactly like Thomas Jefferson would have wanted: founded on the primacy of individual liberty and a commitment to pluralism, diversity, and community."

But all these theories have been based on personal impressions, anecdotal evidence or case studies rather than systematic investigation. We wanted to get a broader, more objective picture of what is going on in terms of friendship formation and community involvement for the denizens of the Internet. (We use the term Internet to encompass such aspects of cyberspace as networked computers, computer bulletin boards, and email). Hence in late 1995 we carried out a national random telephone survey which had among its objectives to: compare "real-world" participation for Internet users and non-users, and to examine friendship creation via the Internet.

Our approach was to consider the perspectives of five different Internet awareness/usage groups:

- Those not aware of the Internet,
- Non-users who were aware of the Internet,
- Former users,
- Recent users—those who started using the Internet in 1995,
- Longtime users—those who started using the Internet prior to 1995.

By comparing those who were on the Internet versus those who were not, and controlling statistically for demonstrable demographic differences among user categories, we would be in a position to see if, on average, Internet users were less likely to belong to various voluntary organizations, thus strengthening the hand of those who see the Internet as socially pernicious. Of course if they belonged to more organizations than their non-Internet-using counterparts, the celebrationists would be supported. Likewise, by getting a representative sample of Internet users to speak about their experiences with friendship formation, we would also have some more reliable views of what the typical or majority experiences have been in this regard, without having our understanding biased by a few extraordinary reports.

Our October 1995 survey yielded 2,500 respondents—8% reported being Internet users, 8% reported being former Internet users, 68% reported being aware of the Internet but not being users, and 16% reported not being aware of the Internet. The sample of Internet users was augmented by a national random telephone sample of 400 Internet users. Of the total of 600 Internet users, 49%

reported being longtime Internet users. As a whole, our survey of 2,500 respondents closely matches socioeconomic patterns of the U.S. population on key variables: compared to 1990/91 U.S. Census data, our sample reflects national averages in gender, ethnic mix, and age, and is slightly wealthier and better educated.

No Evidence of Internet Users Dropping Out of Real Life

We explored respondents' community involvement in the real world by asking them how many religious, leisure, and community organizations they belonged to.

Religious organizations.   Our survey showed no statistically significant differences across the five awareness/usage categories in membership rates of religious organizations. Fifty-six percent of respondents reported belonging to one religious organization, while a further 8% reported belonging to two or more religious organizations....

Leisure organizations.   Here we found that non-users reported belonging to fewer organizations than users, both former and current. Non-users who were not aware of the Internet reported being members of fewest leisure organizations—11% reported belonging to one leisure organization and a further 13% belonged to two or more leisure organizations. Non-users who were aware of the Internet reported belonging to significantly more leisure organizations— 21% reported belonging to one leisure organization and a further 19% belonged to two or more leisure organizations.

Reported membership rates for former and current users were much higher—21% of former users reported belonging to one leisure organization and 28% to two or more; 24% of recent users reported belonging to one leisure organization and 25% to two or more; and 24% of longtime users reported belonging to one leisure organization and 29% to two or more. However when we statistically controlled for demographic variables, these differences disappeared.

Community organizations.   The aggregate responses to the question about membership of community organizations did not appear to display a pattern relating to the awareness/usage categories. Those who were not aware of the Internet and recent users appeared to belong to the fewest community organizations....

Non-users who were aware of the Internet and former users belonged to more community organizations....

Longtime Internet users reported belonging to most community organizations—27% reported belonging to one organization and a further 22% to two or more. Overall, the survey results provide no evidence that Internet users belong to fewer community organizations....

The Internet Is Augmenting Involvement in Existing Communities

... Contact with family members.   An area where the Internet appeared to have a significant impact on social involvement was communications with family members where just under half the users reported contacting family members at least once or twice. Longtime users reported contacting family members more often than recent members. Thirty-five percent of longtime users reported contacting family members at least several times a month, twice the proportion of recent users.

Participation in Internet communities.   We also asked users the extent they participated in Internet communities. Again we found a significant degree of participation—31% of longtime users and 17% of recent users reported doing so. The distribution of the number of communities belonged to for both longtime and recent users was not statistically different (Chi square = 3.6, sig. = 0.6, with 5 degrees of freedom). Of those who reported participating in various Internet communities, 58% participated in one or two communities, 28% participated in three or four communities, and 14% participated in five or more communities.

Change in face-to-face/phone communications.   For the vast majority of both longtime and recent users, use of the Internet did not appear to have much impact on the time spent with friends and family. The two groups' views were not statistically different. Eighty-eight percent of users reported that the time spent with friends and family face-to-face or by phone since they started using Internet had not changed. The same proportions (6%) of users reported they spent more time with friends and family face-to-face or by phone, as those who spent less time.

The Internet Is Emerging as a Medium for Friendship Creation

Friendship formation.   As part of our survey, we asked Internet users whether they knew people only through the Internet whom they considered their friends. Of our 601 Internet users, a significant minority (82 respondents, 14% of our sample of Internet users) reported knowing people in this way.

Propensity to form friendships through the Internet appeared to relate more strongly to general measures of Internet usage and experience, rather than demographic variables. For example, those with self-identified higher Internet skill levels appeared more likely to make Internet friends. Nine percent of novices, 13% of those with average skill levels, 22% of those with above average skill levels, and 27% of those with excellent skill levels reported making Internet friendships.

Somewhat surprisingly, we found no statistical relationships between propensity to make friends and a wide range of measures of traditional forms of social connectedness and measures of personality attributes.... This perhaps points to the Internet deemphasizing the importance of sociability and personality differences.

Number of friendships formed.   For the 81 users who reported establishing friendships via the Internet, a substantial proportion said they had made numerous friendships. Thirty percent of the group (24 respondents) reported having established friendships with 1 to 3 people, 40% (32 respondents) with 4 to 10 people, 22% (18 respondents) with 11 to 30 people, and 9% (7 respondents) with 31 or more people. The best predictor of the number of friends made was again a general measure of Internet usage. Longtime users reported making more friends....

Internet friendships leading to meetings.   A majority of people who reported making friends through the Internet met one or more of them. Of the 81 respondents who reported making friends via the Internet, 60% reported meeting one or more of these friends. Those reporting higher numbers of Internet friends were more likely to have met at least one of them....

Number of friends met.   For the 49 users who reported meeting Internet friends, a substantial number of meetings were reported. Thirty-seven percent of the group (18 respondents) reported meeting with 1 to 3 Internet friends, 29% (14 respondents) with 4 to 10 Internet friends, 22% (11 respondents) with 11 to 30 Internet friends, and 12% (6 respondents) met with 31 or more Internet friends....

Although it is always dangerous to extrapolate, we will do so nonetheless. Based on the data, it would be our guess that perhaps two million new face-to-face meetings have taken place due to participation on the Internet. We do not know, since we did not ask, what the purpose of these meetings might have been (dating services, support groups, hobbyists, political activism?). We hope to explore questions along these lines in our future work.

Pessimism for Pessimistic Theories

Based on our national snapshot, we found no support for the pessimistic theories of the effects of cyberspace on community involvement. When controlling for demographic differences between users and non-users, we found no statistical differences in participation rates in religious, leisure, and community organizations.

Moreover, the Internet appeared to augment existing traditional social connectivity. Just under half of Internet users reported contacting family members at least once or twice via the Internet. A significant minority of users also reported participating in Internet communities. In addition, the vast majority of both longtime and recent users reported that time spent with friends and family in face-to-face contact or by phone had not changed since they started using the Internet.

Further, our survey suggests that the Internet is emerging as a medium for cultivating friendships which, in a majority of cases, lead to meetings in the real world. The Internet is currently a medium where Internet skills appear to be the most important determinant of friendship formation, eclipsing personality characteristics such as sociability, extroversion, and willingness to take risks.

... We also found—due to people's Internet activities, the formation of many new friendships, the creation of senses of community, and reports of voluminous contact with family members. In sum, although the "Jeffersonian ideal" may not be realized, a high proportion of Internet users are engaging in lots of social contact and communication with friends and family. Many family members are keeping in touch and new friendships are being formed. Far from creating a nation of strangers, the Internet is creating a nation richer in friendships and social relationships.

Robert Kraut et al.  **NO**

Internet Paradox

Fifteen years ago, computers were mainly the province of science, engineering, and business. By 1998, approximately 40% of all U.S. households owned a personal computer; roughly one third of these homes had access to the Internet. Many scholars, technologists, and social critics believe that these changes and the Internet, in particular, are transforming economic and social life (e.g., Anderson, Bikson, Law, & Mitchell, 1995; Attewell & Rule, 1984; King & Kraemer, 1995). However, analysts disagree as to the nature of these changes and whether the changes are for the better or worse. Some scholars argue that the Internet is causing people to become socially isolated and cut off from genuine social relationships, as they hunker alone over their terminals or communicate with anonymous strangers through a socially impoverished medium (e.g., Stoll, 1995; Turkle, 1996). Others argue that the Internet leads to more and better social relationships by freeing people from the constraints of geography or isolation brought on by stigma, illness, or schedule. According to them, the Internet allows people to join groups on the basis of common interests rather than convenience (e.g., Katz & Aspden, 1997; Rheingold, 1993)....

Whether the Internet is increasing or decreasing social involvement could have enormous consequences for society and for people's personal well-being. In an influential article, Putnam (1995) documented a broad decline in civic engagement and social participation in the United States over the past 35 years. Citizens vote less, go to church less, discuss government with their neighbors less, are members of fewer voluntary organizations, have fewer dinner parties, and generally get together less for civic and social purposes. Putnam argued that this social disengagement is having major consequences for the social fabric and for individual lives. At the societal level, social disengagement is associated with more corrupt, less efficient government and more crime. When citizens are involved in civic life, their schools run better, their politicians are more responsive, and their streets are safer. At the individual level, social disengagement is associated with poor quality of life and diminished physical and psychological health. When people have more social contact, they are happier and healthier, both physically and mentally (e.g., S. Cohen & Wills, 1985; Gove & Geerken, 1977).

From Robert Kraut, Michael Patterson, Vicki Lundmark, Sara Kiesler, Tridas Mukopadhyay, and William Scherlis, "Internet Paradox: A Social Technology That Reduces Social Involvement and Psychological Well-Being?" *American Psychologist*, vol. 53, no. 9 (September 1998). Copyright © 1998 by The American Psychological Association. Reprinted by permission. References omitted.

Although changes in the labor force participation of women and marital breakup may account for some of the declines in social participation and increase in depression since the 1960s, technological change may also play a role. Television, an earlier technology similar to the Internet in some respects, may have reduced social participation as it kept people home watching the set. By contrast, other household technologies, in particular, the telephone, are used to enhance social participation, not discourage it (Fischer, 1992). The home computer and the Internet are too new and, until recently, were too thinly diffused into American households to explain social trends that originated over 35 years, but, now, they could either exacerbate or ameliorate these trends, depending on how they are used....

Internet for Entertainment, Information, and Commerce

If people use the Internet primarily for entertainment and information, the Internet's social effects might resemble those of television. Most research on the social impact of television has focused on its content; this research has investigated the effects of TV violence, educational content, gender stereotypes, racial stereotypes, advertising, and portrayals of family life, among other topics (Huston et al., 1992). Some social critics have argued that television reinforces sociability and social bonds (Beniger, 1987, pp. 356–362; McLuhan, 1964, p. 304). One study comparing Australian towns before and after television became available suggests that the arrival of television led to increases in social activity (Murray & Kippax, 1978). However most empirical work has indicated that television watching reduces social involvement (Brody, 1990; Jackson-Beeck & Robinson, 1981; Neuman, 1991; Maccoby, 1951). Recent epidemiological research has linked television watching with reduced physical activity and diminished physical and mental health (Anderson, Crespo, Bartlett, Cheskin, & Pratt, 1998; Sidney et al., 1998)....

Like watching television, using a home computer and the Internet generally imply physical inactivity and limited face-to-face social interaction. Some studies, including our own, have indicated that using a home computer and the Internet can lead to increased skills and confidence with computers (Lundmark, Kiesler, Kraut, Scherlis, & Mukopadhyay, 1998). However, when people use these technologies intensively for learning new software, playing computer games, or retrieving electronic information, they consume time and may spend more time alone (Vitalari, Venkatesh, & Gronhaug, 1985). Some cross-sectional research suggests that home computing may be displacing television watching itself (Danko & McLachlan, 1983; Kohut, 1994) as well as reducing leisure time with the family (Vitalari et al., 1985).

Internet for Interpersonal Communication

The Internet, like its network predecessors (Sproull & Kiesler, 1991), has turned out to be far more social than television, and in this respect, the impact of the Internet may be more like that of the telephone than of TV. Our research has shown that interpersonal communication is the dominant use of the Internet at home (Kraut, Mukhopadhyay, Szczypula, Kiesler, & Scherlis, 1998). That people use the Internet mainly for interpersonal communication, however, does not imply that their social interactions and relationships on the Internet are the same as their traditional social interactions and relationships (Sproull & Kiesler, 1991), or that their social uses of the Internet will have effects comparable to traditional social activity.

... Strong ties are relationships associated with frequent contact, deep feelings of affection and obligation, and application to a broad content domain, whereas weak ties are relationships with superficial and easily broken bonds, infrequent contact, and narrow focus. Strong and weak ties alike provide people with social support. Weak ties (Granovetter, 1973), including weak on-line ties (Constant, Sproull, & Kiesler, 1996), are especially useful for linking people to information and social resources unavailable in people's closest, local groups. Nonetheless, strong social ties are the relationships that generally buffer people from life's stresses and that lead to better social and psychological outcomes (S. Cohen & Wills, 1985; Krackhardt, 1994). People receive most of their social support from people with whom they are in most frequent contact, and bigger favors come from those with stronger ties (Wellman & Wortley, 1990).

Generally, strong personal ties are supported by physical proximity. The Internet potentially reduces the importance of physical proximity in creating and maintaining networks of strong social ties. Unlike face-to-face interaction or even the telephone, the Internet offers opportunities for social interaction that do not depend on the distance between parties. People often use the Internet to keep up with those whom they have preexisting relationships (Kraut et al., 1998). But they also develop new relationships on-line. Most of these new relationships are weak. . . .

Whether a typical relationship developed on-line becomes as strong as a typical traditional relationship and whether having on-line relationships changes the number or quality of a person's total social involvements are open questions. . . .

Current Data

Katz and Aspden's national survey (1997) is one of the few empirical studies that has compared the social participation of Internet users with nonusers. Controlling statistically for education, race, and other demographic variables, these researchers found no differences between Internet users' and nonusers' memberships in religious, leisure, and community organizations or in the amount of time users and nonusers reported spending communicating with family and friends. From these data, Katz and Aspden concluded that "[f]ar from creating a nation of strangers, the Internet is creating a nation richer in friendships and social relationships" (p. 86).

Katz and Aspden's (1997) conclusions may be premature because they used potentially inaccurate, self-report measures of Internet usage and social participation that are probably too insensitive to detect gradual changes over time. Furthermore, their observation that people have friendships on-line does not necessarily lead to the inference that using the Internet increases the people's social participation or psychological well-being; to draw such a conclusion, one needs to know more about the quality of their on-line relationships and the impact on their off-line relationships. Many studies show unequivocally that people can and do form on-line social relationships (e.g., Parks & Floyd, 1995). However, these data do not speak to the frequency, depth, and impact of on-line relationships compared with traditional ones or whether the existence of on-line relationships changes traditional relationships or the balance of people's strong and weak ties.

Even if a cross-sectional survey were to convincingly demonstrate that Internet use is associated with greater social involvement, it would not establish the causal direction of this relationship. In many cases, it is as plausible to assume that social involvement causes Internet use as the reverse. For example, many people buy a home computer to keep in touch with children in college or with retired parents. People who use the Internet differ substantially from those who do not in their demographics, skills, values, and attitudes. Statistical tests often under-control for the influence of these factors, which in turn can be associated with social involvement (Anderson et al., 1995; Kraut, Scherlis, Mukhopadhyay, Manning, & Kiesler, 1996; Kohut, 1994).

A Longitudinal Study of Internet Use

The research described here uses longitudinal data to examine the causal relationship between people's use of the Internet, their social involvement, and certain likely psychological consequences of social involvement. The data come from a field trial of Internet use, in which we tracked the behavior of 169 participants over their first one or two years of Internet use. It improves on earlier research by using accurate measures of Internet use and a panel research design. Measures of Internet use were recorded automatically, and measures of social involvement and psychological well-being were collected twice, using reliable self-report scales. Because we tracked people over time, we can observe change and control statistically for social involvement, psychological states, and demographic attributes of the trial participants that existed prior to their use of the Internet. With these statistical controls and measures of change, we can draw stronger causal conclusions than is possible in research in which the data are collected once.

Method

Sample

The HomeNet study consists of a sample of 93 families from eight diverse neighborhoods in Pittsburgh, Pennsylvania.... Children younger than 10 and uninterested members of the households are not included in the sample....

Families received a computer and software, a free telephone line, and free access to the Internet in exchange for permitting the researchers to automatically track their Internet usage and services, for answering periodic questionnaires, and for agreeing to an in-home interview....

Data Collection

We measured demographic characteristics, social involvement, and psychological well-being of participants in the HomeNet trial on a pretest questionnaire, before the participants were given access to the Internet. After 12 to 24 months, participants completed a follow-up questionnaire containing the measures of social involvement and psychological well-being. During this interval, we automatically recorded their Internet usage using custom-designed logging programs. The data reported here encompass the first 104 weeks of use after a HomeNet family's Internet account was first operational for the 1995 subsample and 52 weeks of use for the 1996 subsample....

Internet usage   Software recorded the total hours in a week in which a participant connected to the Internet. Electronic mail and the World Wide Web were the major applications that participants used on the Internet and account for most of their time on-line. Internet hours also included time that participants read distribution lists such as listservs or Usenet newsgroups and participated in real-time communication using the Web chat lines, MUDs, and Internet Relay Chat. For the analyses we report here, we averaged weekly Internet hours over the period in which each participant had access to the Internet, from the pretest up to the time he or she completed the follow-up questionnaire. Our analyses use the log of the variable to normalize the distribution.

Personal electronic mail use   We recorded the number of e-mail messages participants sent and received. To better distinguish the use of the Internet for interpersonal communication rather than for information and entertainment, we excluded e-mail messages in which the participant was not explicitly named as a recipient in our count of received mail. These messages typically had been broadcast to a distribution list to which the participant had subscribed. We believe these messages reflect a mix of interpersonal communication and information distribution....

Social Involvement

Family communication   ... The analysis of family communication showed that teenagers used the Internet more hours than did adults, but Whites did not differ from minorities, and female participants did not differ from male participants in their average hours of use. Different families varied in their use of the Internet... but the amount of communication that an individual family member had with other members of the family did not predict subsequent Internet use.... For our purposes, the most important finding is that greater use of the Internet was associated with subsequent declines in family communication.

Size of participants' social networks   ... Greater social extroversion and having a larger local social circle predicted less use of the Internet during the next 12 to 24 months. Whites reported increasing their distant social circles more than minorities did, and teens reported increasing their distant circles more than adults did; these groups did not differ in changes to their local circles.

Holding constant these control variables and the initial sizes of participants' social circles, greater use of the Internet was associated with subsequent declines in the size of both the local social circles ($p < .05$) and, marginally, the size of the distant social circle ($p < .07$)....

Psychological Well-Being

Loneliness   ... Note that initial loneliness did not predict subsequent Internet use. Loneliness was stable over time. People from richer households increased loneliness more than did those from poorer households, men increased loneliness more than did women, and minorities increased loneliness more than did Whites. Controlling for these personal characteristics and initial loneliness, people who used the Internet more subsequently reported larger increases in loneliness. The association of Internet use with subsequent loneliness was comparable to the associations of income, gender, and race with subsequent loneliness....

Depression   ... Initial depression did not predict subsequent Internet use. Minorities reported more increases in depression than did Whites, and those with higher initial stress also reported greater increases in depression. For the purposes of this analysis, the important finding is that greater use of the Internet was associated with increased depression at a subsequent period, even holding constant initial depression and demographic, stress, and support variables that are often associated with depression. This negative association between Internet use and depression is consistent with the interpretation that use of the Internet caused an increase in depression. Again, it is noteworthy that depression... did not predict using the Internet subsequently.

Discussion

Evaluating the Causal Claim

The findings of this research provide a surprisingly consistent picture of the consequences of using the Internet. Greater use of the Internet was associated with small, but statistically significant declines in social involvement as measured by communication within the family and the size of people's local social networks, and with increases in loneliness, a psychological state associated with social involvement. Greater use of the Internet was also associated with increases in depression. Other effects on the size of the distant social circle, social support, and stress did not reach standard significance levels but were consistently negative.

Our analyses are consistent with the hypothesis that using the Internet adversely affects social involvement and psychological well-being. The panel research design gives us substantial leverage in inferring causation, leading us to believe that in this case, correlation does indeed imply causation. Initial Internet use and initial social involvement and psychological well-being were included in all of the models assessing the effects of Internet use on subsequent social and psychological outcomes. Therefore, our analysis is equivalent to an analysis of change scores, controlling for regression toward the mean, unreliability, contemporaneous covariation between the outcome and the predictor variables, and other statistical artifacts (J. Cohen & Cohen, 1983). Because initial social involvement and psychological well-being were generally not associated with subsequent use of the Internet, these findings imply that the direction of causation is more likely to run from use of the Internet to declines in social involvement and psychological well-being, rather than the reverse. The only exception to this generalization was a marginal finding that people who initially had larger local social circles were lighter users of the Internet.

The major threat to the causal claim would arise if some unmeasured factor varying over time within individuals were to simultaneously cause increases in their use of the Internet and declines in their normal levels of social involvement and psychological well-being. One such factor might be developmental changes in adolescence, which could cause teenagers to withdraw from social contact (at least from members of their families) and to use the Internet as an escape. Our data are mixed regarding this interpretation. In analyses not reported . . . , statistical interactions of Internet use with age showed that increases in Internet use were associated with larger increases in loneliness ($\beta = -.16$, $p < .02$) and larger declines in social support ($\beta = -.13$, $p < .05$) for teenagers than for adults. On the other hand, increases in Internet use were associated with smaller increases in daily stress for teenagers than adults ($\beta = -.16$, $p < .02$). There were no statistical interactions between Internet use and age for family communication, depression, or size of social circle. . . .

Finally, we can generalize our results only to outcomes related to social behavior. In particular, we are not reporting effects of the Internet on educational outcomes or on self-esteem related to computer skill learning. Participants gained computer skills with more Internet usage. Several parents of teenagers who had spent many hours on-line judged that their children's positive educational outcomes from using the Internet outweighed possible declines in their children's social interaction. Future research will be needed to evaluate whether such trade-offs exist. . . .

Displacing social activity   The time that people devote to using the Internet might substitute for time that they had previously spent engaged in social activities. According to this explanation, the Internet is similar to other passive, nonsocial entertainment activities, such as watching TV, reading, or listening to music. Use of the Internet, like watching TV, may represent a privatization of entertainment, which could lead to social withdrawal and to declines in psychological well-being. Putnam (1995) made a similar claim about television viewing.

The problem with this explanation is that a major use of the Internet is explicitly social. People use the Internet to keep up with family and friends through electronic mail and on-line chats and to make new acquaintances through MUDs, chats, Usenet newsgroups, and listservs. Our previous analyses showed that interpersonal communication was the dominant use of the Internet among the sample studied in this research (Kraut et al., 1998). They used the Internet more frequently for exchanging electronic mail than for surfing the World Wide Web and, within a session, typically checked their mail before looking at the Web; their use of electronic mail was more stable over time than their use of the World Wide Web; and greater use of e-mail relative to the Web led them to use the Internet more intensively and over a longer period (Kraut et al., 1998). Other analyses, not reported here, show that even social uses of the Internet were associated with negative outcomes. For example, greater use of electronic mail was associated with increases in depression.

Displacing strong ties   The paradox we observe, then, is that the Internet is a social technology used for communication with individuals and groups, but it is associated with declines in social involvement and the psychological well-being that goes with social involvement. Perhaps, by using the Internet, people are substituting poorer quality social relationships for better relationships, that is, substituting weak ties for strong ones (e.g., Granovetter, 1973; Krackhardt, 1994). People can support strong ties electronically. Indeed, interviews with this sample revealed numerous instances in which participants kept up with physically distant parents or siblings, corresponded with children when they went off to college, rediscovered roommates from the past, consoled distant friends who had suffered tragedy, or exchanged messages with high school classmates after school.

However, many of the on-line relationships in our sample, and especially the new ones, represented weak ties rather than strong ones. Examples include a woman who exchanged mittens with a stranger she met on a knitting listserv, a man who exchanged jokes and Scottish trivia with a colleague he met through an on-line tourist website, and an adolescent who exchanged (fictional) stories about his underwater exploits to other members of a scuba diving chat service. A few participants met new people on-line and had friendships with them. For instance, one teenager met his prom date on-line, and another woman met a couple in Canada whom she subsequently visited during her summer vacation. However, interviews with participants in this trial suggest that making new friends on-line was rare. Even though it was welcomed when it occurred, it did not counteract overall declines in real-world communication with family and friends. Our conclusions resonate with Katz and Aspden's (1997) national survey data showing that only 22% of the respondents who had been using the Internet for two or more years had ever made a new friend on the Internet. Although neither we nor Katz and Aspden provide comparison data, we wonder whether, in the real world, only a fifth of the population make a friend over a two-year period.

On-line friendships are likely to be more limited than friendships supported by physical proximity. On-line friends are less likely than friends developed at school, work, church, or in the neighborhood to be available for help with tangible favors, such as offering small loans, rides, or baby-sitting. Because on-line friends are not embedded in the same day-to-day environment, they will be less likely to understand the context for conversation, making discussion more difficult (Clark, 1996) and rendering support less applicable. Even strong ties maintained at a distance through electronic communication are likely to be different in kind and perhaps diminished in strength compared with strong ties supported by physical proximity (Wellman & Wortley, 1990). Both frequently of contact and the nature of the medium may contribute to this difference. For example, one of our participants who said that she appreciated the e-mail correspondence she had with her college-aged daughter also noted that when her daughter was homesick or depressed, she reverted to telephone calls to provide support. Although a clergyman in the sample used e-mail to exchange sermon ideas with other clergy, he phoned them when he needed advice about negotiating his contract. Like that mother and clergyman, many participants in our sample loved the convenience of the Internet. However, this convenience may induce people to substitute less involving electronic interactions for more involving real-world ones. The clergyman in the sample reported that his involvement with his listserv came at the expense of time with his wife. . . .

Both as a nation and as individual consumers, we must balance the value of the Internet for information, communication, and commerce with its costs. Use of the Internet can be both highly entertaining and useful, but if it causes too much disengagement from real life, it can also be harmful. Until the technology evolves to be more beneficial, people should moderate how much they use the Internet and monitor the uses to which they put it.

CHALLENGE QUESTIONS

Does the Internet Have Psychological Benefits?

1. Do you use the Internet? Discuss how it has increased or decreased your ability to create and sustain relationships. Integrate your experiences with current research.
2. One of the issues embedded in this controversy is the importance of face-to-face contact. How significant are a body, nonverbal communication, and the environment of communication in such contact?
3. Are there benefits of the Internet other than social? Review the research on this, and discuss it in light of the social relationship issue.
4. Take a survey of at least 20 people who use the Internet. Ask them questions about how and why they use the Internet. Use your results to support or disprove a hypothesis that you might have regarding social relationships.

ISSUE 17

Does Religious Commitment Improve Mental Health?

YES: David B. Larson, from "Have Faith: Religion Can Heal Mental Ills," *Insight* (March 6, 1995)

NO: Albert Ellis, from "Dogmatic Devotion Doesn't Help, It Hurts," *Insight* (March 6, 1995)

ISSUE SUMMARY

YES: David B. Larson, president of the National Institute for Healthcare, maintains that religious commitment improves mental health and that spirituality can be a medical treatment.

NO: Albert Ellis, president of the Institute for Rational-Emotive Therapy, challenges Larson's studies and questions particularly whether a religious commitment of "fanatic" proportions is truly mentally healthy.

Before the modern forms of medicine and psychotherapy were ever formulated, many religious people were considered healers. The Judeo-Christian tradition and its literature are filled with claims about healing powers and reports of healing even psychological disorders. Part of the reason that these healing claims have been discounted is that some periods of history equated religious sin with psychological disorder. The people of these periods assumed that what we would now call "schizophrenia" and "depression" were really the results of sin or the indwelling of an evil spirit.

Recently, however, the healing claims of some religious people have gained a new hearing. Few of these people would contend that all psychological and emotional problems are simply sin or an evil spirit. But they caution us that although medical and living problems play an important role in psychological disorders, religious factors may also be influential. And although biological and psychological treatments have enjoyed some success, religious variables, such as spirituality, can also be important factors in alleviating mental or emotional problems. At the very least, they argue, this is an empirical rather than a religious question. Do religious factors, such as spirituality and religious commitment, improve one's mental health?

David B. Larson believes that this type of improvement has been demonstrated in numerous empirical studies. In the following selection, he presents research findings showing that spirituality is an effective treatment for drug and alcohol abuse and depression as well as an effective reducer of teen suicide and divorce. Larson explains how spirituality and religious commitment accomplish these results. Unfortunately, Larson says, psychologists' bias against religion has resulted in a continuing neglect of research on religious factors. Such bias has prevented therapists and policymakers from fully understanding the role of religion in health care. This, in turn, has deprived patients of a vital tool in coping with psychological disorders.

In the second selection, Albert Ellis questions how vital this "tool" really is. Ellis distrusts the objectivity of the studies that Larson cites. Nearly all the studies, he contends, were conducted by religious believers and published in religious journals. These people, according to Ellis, can hardly be considered to be dispassionate observers of "reality." Ellis also asserts that the more seriously people take their religious beliefs, the more fanatical they can become. Fanaticism, he suggests, is mentally and emotionally unhealthy. Therefore, the seriously religious—those who are committed and convinced—cannot be the psychologically healthy.

POINT

- The religiously committed report a higher rate of marital satisfaction than the nonreligious.
- Many mental health professionals resist positive findings on religious people because of antireligious views.
- Religious people have a greater sense of overall life satisfaction than nonreligious people.
- Mental health status improves for those who attend religious services on a regular basis.
- Studies show that religious commitment is the best predictor of a lack of substance abuse.

COUNTERPOINT

- Religious people are more likely than nonreligious people to respond in a socially desirable fashion.
- Many studies of religious people do not present a true picture of the mental health benefits of being religious.
- Many religious people have a tendency to claim happier and less stressful lives than they actually have.
- There is a high degree of correlation between dogmatic religiosity and mental disorder.
- Most of these studies are conducted by religious believers who are motivated to prove that religionists are healthier than nonreligionists.

David B. Larson

 **YES**

Have Faith: Religion Can Heal Mental Ills

If a new health treatment were discovered that helped to reduce the rate of teenage suicide, prevent drug and alcohol abuse, improve treatment for depression, reduce recovery time from surgery, lower divorce rates and enhance a sense of well-being, one would think that every physician in the country would be scrambling to try it. Yet, what if critics denounced this treatment as harmful, despite research findings that showed it to be effective more than 80 percent of the time? Which would you be more ready to believe—the assertions of the critics based on their opinions or the results of the clinical trials based upon research?

As a research epidemiologist and board-certified psychiatrist, I have encountered this situation time and again during the last 15 years of my practice. The hypothetical medical treatment really does exist, but it is not a new drug: It is spirituality. While medical professionals have been privately assuming and publicly stating for years that religion is detrimental to mental health, when I actually looked at the available empirical research on the relationship between religion and health, the findings were overwhelmingly positive.

Just what are the correlations that exist between religion and mental health? First, religion has been found to be associated with a decrease in destructive behavior such as suicide. A 1991 review of the published research on the relationship between religious commitment and suicide rates conducted by my colleagues and I found that religious commitment produced lower rates of suicide in nearly every published study located. In fact, Stephen Stack, now of Wayne State University, showed that non-church attenders were four times more likely to kill themselves than were frequent attenders and that church attendance predicted suicide rates more effectively than any other factor including unemployment.

What scientific findings could explain these lower rates of suicide? First, several researchers have noted that the religiously committed report experiencing fewer suicidal impulses and have a more negative attitude toward suicidal behavior than do the nonreligious. In addition, suicide is a less-acceptable alternative for the religiously committed because of their belief in a moral accountability to God, thus making them less susceptible than the nonreligious to this life-ending alternative. Finally, the foundational religious beliefs in an afterlife, divine justice and the possibility of eternal condemnation all help to reduce the appeal of potentially self-destructive behavior.

If religion can reduce the appeal of potentially self-destructive behavior such as suicide, could it also play a role in decreasing other self-destructive behavior such as drug abuse? When this question has been examined empirically, the overwhelming response is yes. When Richard Gorsuch conducted a review of the relationship between religious commitment and drug abuse nearly 20 years ago, he noted that religious commitment "predicts those who have not used an illicit drug regardless of whether the religious variable is defined in terms of membership, active participation, religious upbringing or the meaningfulness of religion as viewed by the person himself."

More recent reviews have substantiated the earlier findings of Gorsuch, demonstrating that even when employing varying measures of religion, religious commitment predicted curtailed drug abuse. Interestingly, a national survey of 14,000 adolescents found the lowest rates of adolescent drug abuse in the most "politically incorrect" religious group—theologically conservative teens. The drug-abuse rates of teens from more liberal religious groups rose a little higher but still sank below rates of drug abuse among nonreligious teens. The correlations between the six measures of religion employed in the survey and the eight measures of substance abuse all were consistently negative. These findings lead the authors of the study to conclude that the amount of importance individuals place on religion in their lives is the best predictor of a lack of substance abuse, implying that "the (internal) controls operating here are a result of deeply internalized norms and values rather than fear... or peer pressure." For teens living in a society in which drug rates continue to spiral, religion may not be so bad after all.

Just as religious commitment seems to be negatively correlated with drug abuse, similar results are found when examining the relationship between religious commitment and alcohol abuse. When I investigated this area myself, I found that those who abuse alcohol rarely have a strong religious commitment. Indeed, when my colleagues and I surveyed a group of alcoholics, we found that almost 90 percent had lost interest in religion during their teenage years, whereas among the general population, nearly that same percentage reported no change or even a slight increase in their religious practices during adolescence. Furthermore, a relationship between religious commitment and the nonuse or moderate use of alcohol has been extensively documented in the research literature. Some of the most intriguing results have been obtained by Acheampong Amoateng and Stephen Bahr of Brigham Young University, who found that whether or not a religion specifically proscribed alcohol use, those who were active in a religious group consumed substantially less than those who were not active.

Not only does religion protect against clinical problems such as suicide and drug and alcohol abuse, but religious commitment also has been shown to enhance positive life experiences such as marital satisfaction and personal well-being. When I reviewed the published studies on divorce and religious commitment, I found a negative relationship between church attendance and divorce in nearly every study that I located.

To what can these lower rates of divorce be attributed? Some critics argue that the religiously committed stay in unsatisfactory marriages due to religious prohibitions against divorce. However, research has found little if any support for this view. In my review I found that, as a group, the religiously committed report a higher rate of marital satisfaction than the nonreligious. In fact, people from long-lasting marriages rank religion as one of the most important components of a happy marriage, with church attendance being strongly associated with the hypothetical willingness to remarry a spouse—a very strong indicator of marital satisfaction. Could these findings be skewed because, as is believed by some in the mental-health field, religious people falsify their response to such questions to make themselves look better? When the studies were controlled for such a factor the researchers found that the religiously committed were not falsifying their responses or answering in a socially acceptable manner and truly were more satisfied in their marriages.

Although the religiously committed are satisfied with their marriages, is this level of satisfaction also found in the sexual fulfillment of married couples? Though the prevailing public opinion is that religious individuals are prudish or even sexually repressed, empirical evidence has shown otherwise. Using data from *Redbook* magazine's survey of 100,000 women in 1975, Carole Tavris and Susan Sadd contradicted the longstanding assumption that religious commitment fosters sexual dysfunction. Tavris and Sadd found that it is the most religious women who report the greatest happiness and satisfaction with marital sex—more so than either moderately religious or nonreligious women. Religious women also report reaching orgasm more frequently than nonreligious women and are more satisfied with the frequency of their sexual activity than the less pious. Thus, while surprising to many, research suggests that religious commitment may play a role in improving rather than hindering sexual expression and satisfaction in marriage.

Not only has religious commitment been found to enhance sexual satisfaction, but overall life satisfaction as well. For example, David Myers of Hope College reviewed well-being literature and found that the religiously committed have a greater sense of overall life satisfaction than the nonreligious. Religion not only seems to foster a sense of well-being and life satisfaction but also may play a role in protecting against stress, with religiously committed respondents reporting much lower stress levels than the less committed. Even when the religiously committed have stress levels that are similar to the nonreligious, the more committed report experiencing fewer mental-illness problems than do the less committed.

Mental-health status has been found to improve for those attending religious services on a regular basis. Indeed, several studies have found a significant reduction in diverse psychiatric symptomatology following increased religious involvement. Chung-Chou Chu and colleagues at the Nebraska Psychiatric Institute in Omaha found lower rates of rehospitalization among schizophrenics who attended church or were given supportive aftercare by religious homemakers and ministers. One of my own studies confirmed that religious commitment can improve recovery rates as well. When my colleagues and I examined elderly women recovering from hip fractures, we found that those women with stronger religious beliefs suffered less from depression and thus were more likely to walk sooner and farther than their nonreligious counterparts.

❦

Yet, despite the abundance of studies demonstrating the beneficial effects of religious commitment on physical and mental health, many members of the medical community seem immune to this evidence. This resistance to empirical findings on the mental-health benefits of religious commitment may stem from the anti-religious views espoused by significant mental-health theorists. For example, Sigmund Freud called religion a "universal obsessional neurosis" and regarded mystical experience as "infantile helplessness" and a "regression to primary narcissism." More recently, Albert Ellis, the originator of rational-emotive therapy, has argued that "unbelief, humanism, skepticism and even thoroughgoing atheism not only abet but are practically synonymous with mental health; and that devout belief, dogmatism and religiosity distinctly contribute to, and in some ways are equal to, mental or emotional disturbance." Other clinicians have continued to perpetuate the misconception that religion is associated with psychopathology by labeling spiritual experiences as, among other things, borderline psychosis, a psychotic episode or the result of temporal-lobe dysfunction. Even the consensus report, "Mysticism: Spiritual Quest or Psychological Disturbance," by the Group for the Advancement of Psychiatry supported the long-standing view of religion as psychopathology; calling religious and mystical experiences "a regression, an escape, a projection upon the world of a primitive infantile state."

What is perhaps most surprising about these negative opinions of religion's effect on mental health is the startling absence of empirical evidence to support these views. Indeed, the same scientists who were trained to accept or reject a hypothesis based on hard data seem to rely solely on their own opinions and biases when assessing the effect of religion on health. When I conducted a systematic review of all articles published in the two leading journals of psychiatry, the *American Journal of Psychiatry* and the *Archives of General Psychiatry,* which assessed the association between religious commitment and mental health, I found that more than 80 percent of the religious-mental health associations located were clinically beneficial while only 15 percent of the associations were harmful—findings that run counter to the heavily publicized opinion of mental-health professionals. Thus, even though the vast majority of published research studies show religion as having a positive influence on mental health, religious commitment remains at best ignored or at worst, maligned by the professional community.

The question then begs to be asked: Why do medical professionals seem to ignore such positive evidence about religion's beneficial effect on mental health? One possible source of this tension could lie in clinicians' unfamiliarity with or rejection of traditional religious expression. For example, not only do mental-health professionals generally hold levels of religious commitment that diverge significantly from the general population, but they have much higher rates of atheism and agnosticism as well. The most recent survey of the belief systems of mental-health professionals found that less than 45 percent of the members of the American Psychiatric Association and the American Psychological Association believed in God—a percentage less than half that of the general population. When asked whether they agreed with the statement, "My whole approach to life is based on my religion," only one-third of clinical psychologists and two-fifths of psychiatrists agreed with that statement—again, a percentage that is nearly half that of the U.S. population. Indeed, more than 25 percent of psychiatrists and clinical psychologists and more than 40 percent of psychoanalysts claimed that they had abandoned a theistic belief system, compared with just less than 5 percent of the general population reporting the same feelings.

Science is assumed to be a domain that progresses through the gradual accumulation of new data or study findings, yet the mental-health community seems to be stalled in its understanding of the interface between religion and mental health. If a field is to progress in its knowledge and understanding of a controversial issue such as religion, empirical data and research must be relied upon more than personal opinions and biases. At a time when the rising cost of health care is causing so much discussion in our country, no factor that may be so beneficial to health can be ignored. The continuing neglect of published research on religion prevents clinicians and policymakers from fully understanding the important role of religion in health care and deprives patients as well as themselves of improved skills and methods in clinical prevention, coping with illness and quality of care. The mental health establishment needs to begin to recognize that it is treating a whole person—mind, body and, yes, even spirit.

NO

Albert Ellis

Dogmatic Devotion Doesn't Help, It Hurts

According to the psychological studies cited by David Larson, religious believers have more satisfying marriages, more enjoyable sex lives, less psychological stress, less depression and less drug and alcohol abuse than nonreligious people. Do these studies present a "true" picture of the mental health benefits of being religious? Probably not, for several reasons. First, the scientific method itself has been shown by many postmodernists to be far from "objective" and unassailable because it is created and used by highly subjective, often biased individuals. Scientists are never purely dispassionate observers of "reality" but frequently bring their own biases to their experiments and conclusions.

Second, practically all the studies that Larson cites were conducted by religious believers; some were published in religious journals. Many of the researchers were motivated to structure studies to "prove" that religionists are "healthier" than nonreligionists and only to publish studies that "proved" this.

None of the studies cited—as I noted when I read many of them myself —eliminated the almost inevitable bias of the subjects they used. I showed, in two comprehensive reviews of personality questionnaires that were published in the *Psychological Bulletin* in 1946 and 1948 and in several other psychological papers, that people often can figure out the "right" and "wrong" answers to these questionnaires and consequently "show" that they are "healthy" when they actually are not. I also showed, in an article in the *American Sociological Review* in 1948, that conservative and religious subjects probably more often were claiming falsely to have "happier" marriages on the Burgess-Locke Marriage Prediction Test than were liberal and nonreligious subjects.

This tendency of conservative, religious, job-seeking and otherwise motivated individuals to overemphasize their "good" and deemphasize their "poor" behavior on questionnaires has been pointed out by a number of other reviewers of psychological studies. Because all these studies included a number of strongly religious subjects, I would guess that many of these religionists had a distinct tendency to claim to be happier, less stressful and less addictive personalities than a good clinician would find them to be. I believe that this is a common finding of psychologists and was confirmed by my reviews mentioned previously.

Although Larson has spent a number of years locating studies that demonstrated that religious believers are healthier than nonreligious subjects, a large number of researchers have demonstrated the opposite. Several other studies have found that people who rigidly and dogmatically maintain religious views are more disturbed than less-rigid religious followers. But all these studies, once again, are suspect because none of them seem to have eliminated the problem of the biased answers of some of their subjects who consciously or unconsciously want to show how healthy they are.

Larson points out that many psychologists are sure that religionists are more disturbed than nonreligionists in spite of their having no real scientific evidence to substantiate their opinions. He is largely right about this, in view of what I have already said. Nonetheless, some reasonably good data back up the views of these psychologists that devout religionists often are disturbed.

Antiabortion killers such as Paul Hill have demonstrated that fanatical beliefs can have deadly consequences. But lesser-known fanatical religious believers have used ruthless tactics to oppose such "enlightened" views as birth control, women's liberation and even separation of church and state. Some religious zealots have jailed, maimed or even killed liberal proponents of their own religions. Nobel laureate Naguib Mahfouz is still recovering from stab wounds inflicted by Muslim extremists last October near his home in Cairo. (Mahfouz, considered by many to be a devout Muslim, frequently has ridiculed religious hypocrisy in his work.) Indian-born author Salman Rushdie has lived for seven years under a death sentence pronounced by the late Ayatollah Khomeini. Rushdie explained to the *New York Times* that dissidents within the Muslim world become "persons whose blood is unclean and therefore deserves to be spilled."

Religious persecution and wars against members of other religions have involved millions of casualties throughout human history. Islamic fundamentalists from North Africa to Pakistan have established, or done their best to establish, state religions that force all the citizens of a country or other political group to strictly obey the rules of a specific religious group.

People diagnosed as being psychotic and of having severe personality disorders frequently have been obsessed with religious ideas and practices and compulsively and scrupulously follow religious teachings.

The tragic, multiple suicides of members of the Switzerland-based Order of the Solar Temple last October is only the most recent illustration of an extremist religious cult which manipulated its adherents and induced some of them to harm and kill themselves.

Do these manifestations of religious-oriented fanaticism, despotism, cultism and psychosis prove that religious-minded people generally are more disturbed than nonreligious individuals? Of course not. Many—probably most—religionists oppose the extreme views and practices I have just listed, and some actually make efforts to counteract them. One should not conclude, then, that pious religiosity in and of itself equals emotional disturbance.

However, as a psychotherapist and the founder of a school of psychotherapy called rational emotive behavior therapy, I have for many years distinguished between people who hold moderate religious views and those who espouse devout, dogmatic, rigid religious attitudes. In my judgment, most intelligent and educated people are in the former group and temperately believe God (such as Jehovah) exists, that He or She created the universe and the creatures in it, and that we preferably should follow religious, ethical laws but that a Supreme Being forgives us fallible humans when we do not follow His or Her rules. These "moderate" religionists prefer to be "religious" but do not insist that the rest of us absolutely and completely always must obey God's and the church's precepts. Therefore, they still mainly run their own lives and rarely damn themselves (and others) for religious nonobservance. In regard to God and His or Her Commandments, they live and let live.

The second kind of religious adherents—those who are devout, absolutistic and dogmatic—are decidedly different. They differ among themselves but most of them tend to believe that there absolutely has to be a Supreme Being, that He or She specifically runs the universe, must be completely obeyed and will eternally damn all believers and nonbelievers who deviate from His or Her sacred commands.

Another devout and absolutistic group of people do not believe in anything supernatural, but do rigidly subscribe to a dogmatic, secular belief system —such as Nazism, Fascism or Communism—which vests complete authority in the state or in some other organization and which insists that nonallegiance or opposition to this Great Power must be ruthlessly fought, overthrown, punished and annihilated.

As an advocate of mental and emotional health, I have always seen "moderate" religious believers as reasonably sound individuals who usually are no more neurotic (or otherwise disturbed) than are skeptical, nonreligious people. Like nonbelievers, they are relatively open-minded, democratic and unbigoted. They allow themselves to follow and experience "religious" and "secular" values, enjoyment and commitments. Therefore, they infrequently get into serious emotional trouble with themselves or with others because of their religious beliefs and actions.

This is not the case with fanatical, pietistic religionists. Whether they are righteously devoted to God and the church or to secular organizations and cults (some of which may be atheistic) these extreme religionists are not open-minded, tolerant and undamning. Like nonreligious neurotics and individuals with severe personality disorders, they do not merely wish that other religionists and nonbelievers agree with them and worship their own Supreme Being and their churchly values. They insist, demand and command that their God's and their church's will be done.

Since the age of 12, I have been skeptical of anything supernatural or god-like. But I always have believed that undogmatic religionists can get along well in the world and be helpful to others, and I relate nicely to them. Many, if not most, of the mental-health professionals with whom I have worked in the field of rational emotive behavior therapy are religious. A surprisingly large number of them have been ordained as Protestant ministers, Catholic priests or nuns or Jewish rabbis. A few have even been fundamentalists! So some forms of psychotherapy and moderate religious belief hardly are incompatible.

The important question remains: Is there a high degree of correlation between devout, one-sided, dogmatic religiosity and neurosis (and other personality disorders)? My experience as a clinical psychologist leads me to conclude that there well may be. Some of the disturbed traits and behaviors that pietistic religionists tend to have (but, of course, not always have) include these:

A dearth of enlightened self-interest and self-direction. Pietistic religionists tend to be overdevoted, instead, to unduly sacrificing themselves for God, the church (or the state) and to ritualistic self-deprivation that they feel "bound" to follow for "sacred" reasons. They often give masochistic and self-abasing allegiance to ecclesiastical (and/or secular) lords and leaders. Instead of largely planning and directing their own lives, they often are mindlessly overdependent on religious-directed (or state-directed) creeds, rules and commandments.

Reduced social and human interest. Dogmatic religionists are overly focused on godly, spiritual and monastic interests. They often give greater service to God than to humanity and frequently start holy wars against dissidents to their deity and their church. Witness the recent murders by allegedly devout antiabortionists!

Refusal to accept ambiguity and uncertainty. In an obsessive-compulsive fashion, they hold to absolute necessity and complete certainty, even though our universe only seems to include probability and chance. They deny pliancy, alternative-seeking and pluralism in their own and other people's lives. They negate the scientific view that no hypothesis is proved indisputably "true" under all conditions at all times.

Allergy to unconditional self-acceptance. Emotionally healthy people accept themselves (and other humans) unconditionally—that is, whether they achieve success and whether all significant others approve of them. Dogmatic religionists unhealthily and conditionally accept themselves (and others) only when their God, their church (or state) and similar religionists approve of their thoughts, feelings and behaviors. Therefore, they steadily remain prone to, and often are in the throes of, severe anxiety, guilt and self-condemnation.

In rational-emotive therapy we show people that they "get" emotionally disturbed not only by early or later traumas in their lives but mainly by choosing goals and values that they strongly prefer and by unrealistically, illogically and defeatingly making them into one, two or three grandiose demands: (1) "I absolutely must succeed at important projects or I am an utterly worthless person"; (2) "Other people must treat me nicely or they are totally damnable"; (3) "Life conditions are utterly obligated to give me everything that I think I need or my existence is valueless."

When people clearly see that they are largely upsetting themselves with these godlike commandments, and when they convert them to reasonable—but often still compulsive—desires, they are able to reconstruct their disturbed thoughts, feelings and actions and make themselves much less anxious, depressed, enraged and self-hating and much more self-actualizing and happy.

Being a philosophical system of psychotherapy, rational emotive behavior therapy has much to learn from theological and secular religions. But individuals who choose to be religious also may learn something important from it, namely: Believe whatever you wish about God, the church, people and the universe. But see if you can choose a moderate instead of a fanatical form of religion. Try to avoid a doctrinal system through which you are dogmatically convinced that you absolutely must devote yourself to the one, only, right and unerring deity and to the one, true and infallible church. And try to avoid the certitude that you are God. Otherwise, in my view as a psychotherapist, you most probably are headed for emotional trouble.

CHALLENGE QUESTIONS

Does Religious Commitment Improve Mental Health?

1. Explain why Ellis feels that the data concerning the benefits of religion are not objective. Could his explanation be applied to other types of psychological research?
2. Ellis is the founder of a major school of psychotherapy—rational-emotive therapy. Find a description of this therapy, and discuss how Ellis's own nonreligious values might influence his formulation of this therapy.
3. If it were generally agreed that religious factors were beneficial for mental health, how might psychotherapists use these factors? What problems might a person encounter in employing these factors?
4. How does Ellis distinguish between those who adopt moderate forms of religion and those who adopt fanatical forms of religion? How is this distinction different from the distinction between those who consider their religion relatively superficially and those who take their religious beliefs seriously?
5. For the last few centuries, religion and science have been considered completely separate endeavors. How might this historical separation play into the controversy between Larson and Ellis?

ISSUE 18

Is Pornography Harmful?

YES: Diana E. H. Russell, from *Dangerous Relationships: Pornography, Misogyny, and Rape* (Sage Publications, 1998)

NO: Michael C. Seto, Alexandra Maric, and Howard E. Barbaree, from "The Role of Pornography in the Etiology of Sexual Aggression," *Aggression and Violent Behavior* (vol. 6, 2001)

ISSUE SUMMARY

YES: Sociology professor Diana E. H. Russell argues that pornography is profoundly harmful because it predisposes men to want to rape women and undermines social inhibitions against acting out rape fantasies.

NO: Michael C. Seto, Alexandra Maric, and Howard E. Barbaree, of the Centre for Addiction and Mental Health, contend that evidence for a causal link between pornography use and sexual offense remains equivocal.

The United States has some of the highest rates of violence in the world, particularly among advanced societies. Of special concern are the high rates of violence against women. What causes this? Finding the answer to this question has led numerous psychological researchers to investigate the relationship between pornography, especially violent pornography, and actual violence.

Results from these investigations have led to two basic conclusions. Those who view pornography as a prime cause of violence against women contend that pornography depicts women as objects to be degraded and abused. As they see it, continual exposure to such degradation and abuse eventually leads viewers to engage in the same kind of behavior. Researchers who hold this opinion look to *social learning theory,* a prominent psychological explanation of behavior, as a rationale for their arguments: What people see is eventually what people do. Other psychologists contend that pornography does not negatively affect viewers' attitudes and actions toward women. They consider pornography to be a scapegoat for society's ills, and they maintain that the research does not bear out the direct effect that many people believe exists.

In the following selection, Diana E. H. Russell minces no words in indicting pornography for much of the violence that men perpetrate against women. She contends that pornography predisposes some males to want to rape women and undermines some males' internal and social inhibitions against acting out their desire to rape. According to Russell, pornography objectifies and dehumanizes women, perpetuates the myth that women enjoy rape, and desensitizes males to rape.

Michael C. Seto, Alexandra Maric, and Howard E. Barbaree disagree with Russell's interpretation of pornography research. In the second selection, they point to difficulties in defining pornography and in measuring aggression, and they contend that an individual's predisposition to sexual aggression plays a larger role than many suspect. Indeed, Seto et al. argue that individuals who are not predisposed to violence are unlikely to show an effect of pornography exposure. That is, perpetrators of sexual violence are not predisposed *by* the pornography but predisposed *before* the pornography, which merely accentuates this predisposition.

POINT

- Pornography exposure predisposes individuals to rape in many different ways.
- By demonstrating and reinforcing violence, pornography nurtures a violent tendency where none existed before.

- Research shows that pornography undermines internal inhibitions by objectifying women, teaching rape myths, and trivializing the act of rape.

- Although many things ultimately "cause" sexual violence, there exists abundant evidence to implicate pornography as a major factor.

COUNTERPOINT

- People who rape are predisposed to violence before they are exposed to pornography.
- Although pornography may accentuate a tendency to aggress in those who are already prone to violence, pornography is unlikely to elicit sexual aggression in those who are not prone to violence.
- Pornography research has been seriously limited by subjective definitions of pornography, disputed measures of sexual offending, and experimenter demand effects.
- More research needs to be conducted to understand the extent of pornography's role in sexual violence.

Diana E. H. Russell

 **YES**

Pornography as a Cause of Rape

Sociologist David Finkelhor has developed a very useful multicausal theory to explain the occurrence of child sexual abuse. According to Finkelhor's (1984) model, in order for child sexual abuse to occur, four conditions have to be met. First, someone has to *want* to abuse a child sexually. Second, this person's internal inhibitions against acting out this desire have to be undermined. Third, this person's social inhibitions against acting out this desire (e.g., fear of being caught and punished) have to be undermined. Fourth, the would-be perpetrator has to undermine or overcome his or her chosen victim's capacity to avoid or resist the sexual abuse.

According to my theory, these four conditions also have to be met in order for rape, battery, and other forms of sexual assault on adult women to occur (Russell, 1984). Although my theory can be applied to other forms of sexual abuse and violence against women besides rape, this formulation of it will focus on rape because most of the research relevant to my theory has been limited to this form of sexual assault.

In *Sexual Exploitation* (1984), I suggest many factors that may predispose a large number of males in the United States to want to rape or assault women sexually. Some examples discussed in that book are (a) biological factors, (b) childhood experiences of sexual abuse, (c) male sex-role socialization, (d) exposure to mass media that encourage rape, and (e) exposure to pornography. Here I will discuss only the role of pornography.

Although women have been known to rape both males and females, males are by far the predominant perpetrators of sexual assault as well as the biggest consumers of pornography. Hence, my theory will focus on male perpetrators.

... As previously noted, in order for rape to occur, a man must not only be predisposed to rape, but his internal and social inhibitions against acting out his rape desires must be undermined. My theory, in a nutshell, is that pornography (a) predisposes some males to want to rape women and intensifies the predisposition in other males already so predisposed; (b) undermines some males' internal inhibitions against acting out their desire to rape; and (c) undermines some males' social inhibitions against acting out their desire to rape.

The Meaning of "Cause"

Given the intense debate about whether or not pornography plays a causal role in rape, it is surprising that so few of those engaged in it ever state what they mean by "cause." ...

[P]ornography clearly does not cause rape, as it seems safe to assume that some pornography consumers do not rape women and that many rapes are unrelated to pornography. However, the concept of *multiple causation* (defined below) *is* applicable to the relationship between pornography and rape.

> With the conception of MULTIPLE CAUSATION, various possible causes may be seen for a given event, any one of which may be a sufficient but not necessary condition for the occurrence of the effect, or a necessary but not sufficient condition....

This section will provide the evidence for the ... different ways in which pornography can induce this predisposition.

1. Predisposes by pairing of sexually arousing stimuli with portrayals of rape.   The laws of social learning (e.g., classical conditioning, instrumental conditioning, and social modeling), about which there is now considerable consensus among psychologists, apply to all the mass media, including pornography. As Donnerstein (1983) testified at the hearings in Minneapolis: "If you assume that your child can learn from Sesame Street how to count one, two, three, four, five, believe me, they can learn how to pick up a gun" (p. 11). Presumably, males can learn equally well how to rape, beat, sexually abuse, and degrade females.

A simple application of the laws of social learning suggests that viewers of pornography can develop arousal responses to depictions of rape, murder, child sexual abuse, or other assaultive behavior. Researcher S. Rachman of the Institute of Psychiatry, Maudsley Hospital, London, has demonstrated that male subjects can learn to become sexually aroused by seeing a picture of a woman's boot after repeatedly seeing women's boots in association with sexually arousing slides of nude females (Rachman & Hodgson, 1968). The laws of learning that operated in the acquisition of the boot fetish can also teach males who were not previously aroused by depictions of rape to become so....

2. Predisposes by generating rape fantasies.   Further evidence that exposure to pornography can create in males a predisposition to rape where none existed before is provided by an experiment conducted by Malamuth. Malamuth (1981a) classified 29 male students as sexually force-oriented or non-force-oriented on the basis of their responses to a questionnaire. These students were then randomly assigned to view either a rape version of a slide-audio presentation or a mutually consenting version. The account of rape and the pictures illustrating it were based on a story in a popular pornographic magazine, which Malamuth describes as follows:

> The man in this story finds an attractive woman on a deserted road. When he approaches her, she faints with fear. In the rape version, the man ties her up and forcibly undresses her. The accompanying narrative is as follows:

"You take her into the car. Though this experience is new to you, there is a temptation too powerful to resist. When she awakens, you tell her she had better do exactly as you say or she'll be sorry. With terrified eyes she agrees. She is undressed and she is willing to succumb to whatever you want. You kiss her and she returns the kiss." Portrayal of the man and woman in sexual acts follows; intercourse is implied rather than explicit. (p. 38)

In the mutually consenting version of the story the victim was not tied up or threatened. Instead, on her awakening in the car, the man told her that she was safe and "that no one will do her any harm. She seems to like you and you begin to kiss." The rest of the story is identical to the rape version (Malamuth, 1981a, p. 38).

All subjects were then exposed to the same audio description of a rape read by a female. This rape involved threats with a knife, beatings, and physical restraint. The victim was portrayed as pleading, crying, screaming, and fighting against the rapist (Abel, Barlow, Blanchard, & Guild, 1977, p. 898). Malamuth (1981a) reports that measures of penile tumescence as well as self-reported arousal "indicated that relatively high levels of sexual arousal were generated by all the experimental stimuli" (p. 33).

After the 29 male students had been exposed to the rape audio tape, they were asked to try to reach as high a level of sexual arousal as possible by fantasizing about whatever they wanted but without any direct stimulation of the penis (Malamuth, 1981a, p. 40). Self-reported sexual arousal during the fantasy period indicated that those students who had been exposed to the rape version of the first slide-audio presentation created more violent sexual fantasies than those exposed to the mutually consenting version *irrespective of whether they had been [previously] classified as force-oriented or non-force oriented* (p. 33).

As the rape version of the slide-audio presentation is typical of what is seen in pornography, the results of this experiment suggest that similar pornographic depictions are likely to generate rape fantasies even in previously non-force-oriented male consumers. As Edna Einsiedel (1986) points out,

Current evidence suggests a high correlation between deviant fantasies and deviant behaviors.... Some treatment methods are also predicated on the link between fantasies and behavior by attempting to alter fantasy patterns in order to change the deviant behaviors. (1986, p. 60)

Because so many people resist the idea that a desire to rape may develop as a result of viewing pornography, let us focus for a moment on behavior other than rape. There is abundant testimonial evidence that at least some males decide they would like to perform certain sex acts on women after seeing pornography portraying such sex acts. For example, one of the men who answered Shere Hite's (1981) question on pornography wrote: "It's great for me. *It gives me new ideas to try and see,* and it's always sexually exciting" (p. 780; emphasis added). Of course, there's nothing wrong with getting new ideas from pornography or anywhere else, nor with trying them out, as long as they are not actions that subordinate or violate others. Unfortunately, many of the behaviors modeled in pornography *do* subordinate and violate women, sometimes viciously.

The following statements about men imitating abusive sexual acts that they had seen in pornography were made by women testifying at the pornography hearings in Minneapolis, Minnesota, in 1983 (Russell, Part 1, 1993b). Ms. M testified that

> I agreed to act out in private a lot of the scenarios that my husband read to me. These depicted bondage and different sexual acts that I found very humiliating to do.... He read the pornography like a textbook, like a journal. When he finally convinced me to be bound, he read in the magazine how to tie the knots and bind me in a way that I couldn't escape. Most of the scenes where I had to dress up or go through different fantasies were the exact same scenes that he had read in the magazines.

Ms. O described a case in which a man

> brought pornographic magazines, books, and paraphernalia into the bedroom with him and told her that if she did not perform the sexual acts in the "dirty" books and magazines, he would beat her and kill her.

Ms. S testified about the experiences of a group of women prostitutes who, she said,

> were forced constantly to enact specific scenes that men had witnessed in pornography.... These men... would set up scenarios, usually with more than one woman, to copy scenes that they had seen portrayed in magazines and books.

For example, Ms. S quoted a woman in her group as saying,

> He held up a porn magazine with a picture of a beaten woman and said, "I want you to look like that. I want you to hurt." He then began beating me. When I did not cry fast enough, he lit a cigarette and held it right above my breast for a long time before he burned me.

Ms. S also described what three men did to a nude woman prostitute. They first tied her up while she was seated on a chair, then,

> They burned her with cigarettes and attached nipple clips to her breasts. They had many S and M magazines with them and showed her many pictures of women appearing to consent, enjoy, and encourage this abuse. She was held for twelve hours while she was continuously raped and beaten.

Ms. S also cited the following example of men imitating pornography:

> They [several johns] forced the women to act simultaneously with the movie. In the movie at this point, a group of men were urinating on a naked woman. All the men in the room were able to perform this task, so they all started urinating on the woman who was now naked....

3. Predisposes by creating an appetite for increasingly stronger material. ... Zillmann and Bryant (1984) report that as a result of massive exposure to pornography, "consumers graduate from common to less common forms" (p. 127), including pornography portraying "some degree of pseudoviolence or violence" (p. 154). These researchers suggest that this change may be "because familiar material becomes unexciting as a result of habituation" (p. 127).

According to Zillmann and Bryant's research, then, pornography can transform a male who was not previously interested in the more abusive types of pornography into one who *is* turned on by such material. This is consistent with Malamuth's findings . . . that males who did not previously find rape sexually arousing generate such fantasies after being exposed to a typical example of violent pornography.

The Role of Pornography in Undermining Some Males' *Internal* Inhibitions Against Acting Out Their Desire to Rape

. . . Evidence has [shown] that 25% to 30% of males admit that there is some likelihood that they would rape a woman if they could be assured that they would get away with it. It is reasonable to assume that a substantially higher percentage of males would *like* to rape a woman but would refrain from doing so because of their internal inhibitions against these coercive acts. Presumably, the strength of these males' motivation to rape as well as their internal inhibitions against raping range from very weak to very strong, and also fluctuate in the same individual over time.

[There are] seven ways in which pornography can undermine some males' internal inhibitions against acting out rape desires. . . .

1. Objectifying women.   Feminists have been emphasizing the role of objectification (treating females as sex objects) in the occurrence of rape for many years (e.g., Medea & Thompson, 1974; Russell, 1975). Males' tendency to objectify females makes it easier for them to rape girls and women. Check and Guloien (1989) note that other psychologists (e.g., Philip Zimbardo, H. C. Kelman) have observed that "dehumanization of victims is an important disinhibitor of cruelty toward others" (p. 161). The rapists quoted in the following passages demonstrate the link between objectification and rape behavior.

> It was difficult for me to admit that I was dealing with a human being when I was talking to a woman, because, if you read men's magazines, you hear about your stereo, your car, your chick. (Russell, 1975, pp. 249–250)

After this rapist had hit his victim several times in the face, she stopped resisting and begged him not to hurt her.

> When she said that, all of a sudden it came into my head, "My God, this is a human being!" I came to my senses and saw that I was hurting this person. (p. 249)

Another rapist said of his victim, "I wanted this beautiful fine *thing* and I got it" (Russell, 1975, p. 245; emphasis added). . . .

2. Rape myths.   If males believe that women enjoy rape and find it sexually exciting, this belief is likely to undermine the inhibitions of some of those who would like to rape women. Sociologists Diana Scully (1985) and Martha Burt (1980) have reported that rapists are particularly apt to believe rape myths.

Scully, for example, found that 65% of the rapists in her study believed that "women cause their own rape by the way they act and the clothes they wear"; and 69% agreed that "most men accused of rape are really innocent." However, as Scully points out, it is not possible to know if their beliefs preceded their behavior or constitute an attempt to rationalize it. Hence, findings from the experimental data are more telling for our purposes than these interviews with rapists.

Since the myth that women enjoy rape is widely held, the argument that consumers of pornography realize that such portrayals are false is totally unconvincing (Brownmiller, 1975; Burt, 1980; Russell, 1975). Indeed, several studies have shown that portrayals of women enjoying rape and other kinds of sexual violence can lead to increased acceptance of rape myths in both males and females. In an experiment conducted by Neil Malamuth and James Check (1985), for example, one group of college students saw a pornographic depiction in which a woman was portrayed as sexually aroused by sexual violence, and a second group was exposed to control materials. Subsequently, all subjects were shown a second rape portrayal. The students who had been exposed to the pornographic depiction of rape were significantly more likely than the students in the control group:

1. to perceive the second rape victim as suffering less trauma;
2. to believe that she actually enjoyed being raped; and
3. to believe that women in general enjoy rape and forced sexual acts. (Check & Malamuth, 1985, p. 419)

Other examples of the rape myths that male subjects in these studies are more apt to believe after viewing pornography are as follows:

- A woman who goes to the home or the apartment of a man on their first date implies that she is willing to have sex;
- Any healthy woman can successfully resist a rapist if she really wants to;
- Many women have an unconscious wish to be raped, and may then unconsciously set up a situation in which they are likely to be attacked;
- If a girl engages in necking or petting and she lets things get out of hand, it is her own fault if her partner forces sex on her. (Briere, Malamuth, & Check, 1985, p. 400)

In Maxwell and Check's 1992 study of 247 high school students (described above), they found very high rates of what they called "rape supportive beliefs," that is, acceptance of rape myths and violence against women....

A quarter of girls and 57% of boys expressed the belief that it was at least "maybe okay" for a boy to hold a girl down and force her to have intercourse in one or more of the situations described by the researchers. In addition, only 21% of the boys and 57% of the girls believed that forced intercourse was "definitely not okay" in any of the situations. The situation in which forced intercourse was most accepted was when the girl had sexually excited her date.

In this case, 43% of the boys and 16% of the girls stated that it was at least "maybe okay" for the boy to force intercourse on her (Maxwell & Check, 1992).

According to Donnerstein (1983), "After only 10 minutes of exposure to aggressive pornography, particularly material in which women are shown being aggressed against, you find male subjects are much more willing to accept these particular [rape] myths" (p. 6). These males are also more inclined to believe that 25% of the women they know would enjoy being raped (p. 6).

3. Acceptance of interpersonal violence.   Males' internal inhibitions against acting out their desire to rape can also be undermined if they consider male violence against women to be acceptable behavior. Studies have shown that when male subjects view portrayals of sexual violence that have positive consequences —as they often do in pornography—it increases their acceptance of violence against women. Examples of some of the beliefs used to measure acceptance of interpersonal violence include the following:

- Being roughed up is sexually stimulating to many women;
- Sometimes the only way a man can get a cold woman turned on is to use force;
- Many times a woman will pretend she doesn't want to have intercourse because she doesn't want to seem loose, but she's really hoping the man will force her. (Briere et al., 1985, p. 401) ...

4. Trivializing rape.   According to Donnerstein (1985), in most studies on the effects of pornography, "subjects have been exposed to only a few minutes of pornographic material" (p. 341). In contrast, Zillmann and Bryant (1984) examined the impact on male subjects of what they refer to as "massive exposure" to nonviolent pornography (4 hours and 48 minutes per week over a period of 6 weeks ...). After 3 weeks the subjects were told that they were participating in an American Bar Association study that required them to evaluate a trial in which a man was prosecuted for the rape of a female hitchhiker. At the end of this mock trial, various measures were taken of the subjects' opinions about the trial and about rape in general. For example, they were asked to recommend the prison term they thought most fair.

Zillmann and Bryant (1984) found that the male subjects who had been exposed to the massive amounts of pornography considered rape a less serious crime than they had before they were exposed to it; they thought that prison sentences for rape should be shorter; and they perceived sexual aggression and abuse as causing less suffering for the victims, even in the case of an adult male having sexual intercourse with a 12-year-old girl (p. 132). The researchers concluded that "heavy exposure to common nonviolent pornography trivialized rape as a criminal offense" (p. 117). ...

5. Sex callousness toward females.   In the same experiment on massive exposure, Zillmann and Bryant (1984) found that "males' sex callousness toward women was significantly enhanced" by prolonged exposure to pornography (p. 117). These male subjects, for example, became increasingly accepting of statements such as, "A woman doesn't mean 'no' until she slaps you"; "A man should find them, fool them, fuck them, and forget them"; and "If they are old enough to bleed, they are old enough to butcher." However, judging by these statements, it is difficult to distinguish sex callousness from a general hostility toward women. . . .

6. Acceptance of male dominance in intimate relationships.   A marked increase in males' acceptance of male dominance in intimate relationships was yet another result of the massive exposure to pornography (Zillmann & Bryant, 1984, p. 121). The notion that women are, or ought to be, equal in intimate relationships was more likely to be abandoned by these male subjects (p. 122). Finally, their support of the women's liberation movement also declined sharply (p. 134).

These findings demonstrate that pornography increases the acceptability of sexism. As Van White (1984) points out, "by using pornography, by looking at other human beings as a lower form of life, they [the pornographers] are perpetuating the same kind of hatred that brings racism to society" (p. 186).

For example, Ms. O testified about the ex-husband of a woman friend and next-door neighbor: "When he looked at the magazines, he made hateful, obscene, violent remarks about women in general and about me. He told me that because I am female I am here to be used and abused by him, and that because he is a male he is the master and I am his slave" (Russell, 1993b, p. 51). . . .

7. Desensitizing males to rape.   In an experiment specifically designed to study desensitization, Donnerstein and Linz showed 10 hours of R-rated or X-rated movies over a period of 5 days to male subjects (Donnerstein & Linz, 1985, p. 34A). Some students saw X-rated movies depicting sexual assault; others saw X-rated movies depicting only consenting sex; and a third group saw R-rated sexually violent movies. . . .

By the fifth day, the subjects rated the movies as less graphic and less gory and estimated fewer violent or offensive scenes than after the first day of viewing. They also rated the films as significantly less debasing and degrading to women, more humorous, and more enjoyable, and reported a greater willingness to see this type of film again (Donnerstein & Linz, 1985, p. 34F). Their sexual arousal to this material, however, did not decrease over this 5-day period (Donnerstein, 1983, p. 10).

On the last day, the subjects went to a law school, where they saw a documentary reenactment of a real rape trial. A control group of subjects who had never seen the films also participated in this part of the experiment. Subjects who had seen the R-rated movies: (a) rated the rape victim as significantly more worthless, (b) rated her injury as significantly less severe, and (c) assigned greater blame to her for being raped than did the subjects who had not seen the films. In contrast, these effects were not observed for the X-rated nonviolent films. However, the results were much the same for the violent X-rated films, despite the fact that the R-rated material was "much more graphically violent" (Donnerstein, 1985, pp. 12–13).

Donnerstein and Linz (1985) point out that critics of media violence research believe "that only those who are *already* predisposed toward violence are influenced by exposure to media violence" (p. 34F). This view is contradicted by the fact that Donnerstein and Linz actually preselected their subjects to ensure that they were not psychotic, hostile, or anxious; that is, they were not predisposed toward violence prior to the research. . . .

In summary: I have presented only a small portion of the research evidence for seven different effects of pornography, all of which probably contribute to the undermining of some males' internal inhibitions against acting out their rape desires. This list is not intended to be comprehensive.

Michael C. Seto, Alexandra Maric,
and Howard E. Barbaree

The Role of Pornography in the Etiology of Sexual Aggression

Abstract. Despite the public and scientific attention the topic has received, the evidence for a causal link between pornography use and
sexual offending remains equivocal. This article critically examines the
research literature on the association of pornography and sexual offending, focusing on relevant experimental work. The difficulty of this
research is highlighted in a discussion of operational definitions of
the term *pornography*, the choice of proxy measures for sexual offending in experimental research, and the emphasis given sexual assault
of adult females over other kinds of criminal sexual behavior such as
child molestation, exhibitionism, and voyeurism. We also review the
major theoretical perspectives—conditioning, excitation transfer, feminist, and social learning—and some of the hypotheses that can be
derived from them. From the existing evidence, we argue that individuals who are already predisposed to sexually offend are the most
likely to show an effect of pornography exposure and are the most
likely to show the strongest effects. Men who are not predisposed
are unlikely to show an effect; if there actually is an effect, it is likely
to be transient because these men would not normally seek violent
pornography. . . .

Introduction

Extent of the Problem

Since the first large-scale public inquiry into pornography by the U.S. Commission on Obscenity and Pornography (1970), there has been vociferous debate
about the potentially harmful effects of pornography. Over a quarter of a century later, after at least five other major government inquiries,[1] as well as many
scientific studies, the evidence for a causal link between pornography and sexually aggressive behavior remains equivocal.

The debate is profound because of public and professional concern about
sexual assaults committed against women or children.[2] Sexual victimization is
a major social problem: over 160,000 rapes and 152,000 attempted rapes were

Abridged from Michael C. Seto, Alexandra Maric, and Howard E. Barbaree, "The Role of Pornography in the Etiology of Sexual Aggression," *Aggression and Violent Behavior*, vol. 6 (2001). Copyright
© 2001 by Elsevier Science Ltd. Reprinted by permission of Elsevier Science Ltd. and Michael C.
Seto.

reported to police in the United States in 1993, resulting in a combined incidence rate for rape and attempted rape of approximately 750 per 100,000 American women (Bastian, 1995).[3] It is widely acknowledged that sexual assaults are underreported to police. Estimates of the lifetime prevalence of sexual coercion experienced by females range from 14 to 25% in the majority of studies (see review by Koss, 1993). A large-scale survey in the United States suggests that approximately 27% of females and 16% of males have experienced some form of sexual abuse as children (Finkelhor et al., 1990). The correlates of sexual victimization can be very serious, resembling the symptoms of posttraumatic stress disorder (see reviews by Beitchman et al., 1992; Hanson, 1990; but see also Rind, Tromovitch, & Bauserman, 1998).

At the same time, the pornography industry has been growing rapidly. *Adult Video News*, one of the major trade publications, found in their 1997 survey of retailers that sales and rentals of adult videos doubled in the previous 5 years, with a current annual review of approximately $4.2 billion (Adult Video News, 1998). This estimate obviously does not include other forms of pornography, such as magazines, telephone sex services, CD-ROMs, and Internet services. A finding that pornography use causes sexually aggressive behavior would have important implications for public policy.

Overview

This article will critically evaluate the research literature on the association between pornography and sexual aggression, focusing on relevant experimental work.... [T]he difficulty of this research is highlighted in a discussion of operational definitions of the term *pornography*, the choice of proxy measures for sexual offending, and the emphasis given sexual assault of adult females over other kinds of criminal sexual behavior (child molestation, paraphilic behaviors such as exhibitionism and voyeurism)....

Operational Definitions

In the eighth edition of the *Concise Oxford Dictionary of Current English*, pornography is defined as "the explicit description or exhibition of sexual activity in literature, films, etc., intended to stimulate erotic rather than aesthetic or emotional feelings" (R.E. Allen, 1990). The word pornography derives from the Greek word *pornographos*, typically translated as "the writing of harlots." According to the annotated *Criminal Code of Canada*, Section 163(8), "For the purposes of this definition, the court referred to three categories of pornography: (1) explicit sex with violence; (2) explicit sex without violence but which subjects people to treatment that is degrading or dehumanizing; and (3) explicit sex without violence that is neither degrading nor dehumanizing" (Martin's Annual Criminal Code, 1996). The definition depends on a judgment of the degree of harm and degradation, and requires a test of community standards of acceptability. The obvious difficulty with these definitions is the subjective and relative nature of community standards of aesthetic value, morality, and acceptability.

A distinction has sometimes been made between erotica and pornography. Erotica can be described as sexually explicit material that depicts adult men and women consensually involved in pleasurable, nonviolent, nondegrading, sexual interactions (Fisher & Barak, 1989; Marshall & Barrett, 1990). In contrast, pornography can be described as depictions of sexual activity where one of the participants is objectified or portrayed as powerless or nonconsenting (Marshall & Barrett, 1990). Pornography can be further divided into two broad categories, based on the presence or absence of physical violence or threat of violence against an actor. Violent pornography refers to sexually explicit material portraying sexual aggression, typically enacted by men against women (see also Donnerstein & Berkowitz, 1981; Fisher & Barak, 1989, 1991; Malamuth, 1984; Marshall & Barrett, 1990; Zillmann & Bryant, 1986). Degrading pornography can refer to sexually explicit material that depicts people (usually women) as submissive or hypersexual beings who experience sexual pleasure despite being in degrading or humiliating circumstances (see Fisher & Barak, 1991; Linz et al., 1987). Both violent and degrading pornography depict sexual interactions that are impersonal, without affection or consideration of the actors as individuals (see Marshall & Barrett, 1990).

The identification of degrading pornography is difficult because of the central role of subjective judgment in the definition. Although cues of violence, threat, or nonconsent can be reliably identified in violent pornography because they can be defined in terms of overt behavior, judgments of degradation, depersonalization, and affection are likely to depend on the context of interactions between actors (e.g., affectionate partners engaging in bondage role-play), observer characteristics, and observer inferences about the mental states of the actors. Observer characteristics that may be relevant include gender, age, previous exposure to sexually explicit materials, and attitudes regarding sexuality and depictions of sexuality. However, we believe it is possible to make a valid distinction between violent and nonviolent pornography, where pornography is simply defined as any material depicting sexually explicit activities....

Causal Models

Each of the theories [linking pornography and aggression] can be subsumed under one of the following causal statements: (a) use of pornography causes sexual offending, through such mediating variables as antisocial personality, physical aggressiveness, offense-supportive attitudes and beliefs, or conditioned sexual responding to cues of nonconsent; (b) use of pornography and sexual offending are both caused by third factors such as antisocial personality, hypermasculinity, offense-supportive attitudes and beliefs, or paraphilic interests; or (c) sexual offending is caused by a third factor in conjunction with the use of pornography (e.g., the effect of sexual deviance is potentiated by exposure to arousing pornography).

These causal models are not mutually exclusive, as noted by Seto and Barbaree (1995) in their discussion of the role of alcohol in sexual aggression. Pornography may have both direct and indirect effects on sexual offending, require the presence of an additional "catalyst" factor to have these effects, and may be at least partly related because of common predispositional or situational factors. Regardless of its role, it is also important to recognize that pornography use can be neither a necessary nor sufficient cause of sexual offending, because sexual offenses have been committed by individuals with little or no exposure to pornography, and many users of pornography have not committed sexual offenses.

Review of the Literature

Correlational Studies

Population Level
This method of investigation relies on correlational analyses between changes in pornography consumption and fluctuations in official reports of rape or sexual assault. If pornography consumption increases the likelihood that its consumer will be sexually aggressive, then the incidence of sex crimes as measured by arrest or conviction rates should increase during periods of greater availability of pornography (e.g., liberalized censorship laws). Kutchinsky's (1991) work is a good example of this type of investigation. He examined the prevalence of sex crimes in Denmark, West Germany, Sweden, and the United States during periods when censorship of pornography decreased. Kutchinsky demonstrated that during the 20-year period between 1964 and 1984, as pornography laws became less and less restrictive, the number of reported incidents of rape did not increase more than the number of reported incidents of nonsexually violent crimes in any of these countries. In contrast, Court (1976) found a positive association between availability of pornography and sex crime rate in a study using data from seven countries, and Jaffee and Strauss (1987) found a positive association between sex magazine readership and rates of reported rape across the American states.

A strength of this kind of approach is that structural factors are considered, permitting a test of feminist and other sociocultural hypotheses regarding the effects of pornography. A serious limitation is the imprecision of the level of analysis. A positive association with aggregate data does not actually demonstrate that sexually aggressive men consume more pornography, usually differentiate between types of pornography, distinguish between effects at the individual level (men exposed to pornography are more likely to sexually offend) and at the social level (the prevalence of pornography reflects or promotes a climate that tolerates sexual offending), or provide control over factors such as changes in the pattern of criminal prosecution for sexual offenses.

Individual Level
Another approach is to look at the association of pornography use with the likelihood of sex aggression within individuals. For example, many studies have examined the use of pornography by detected sex offenders. These studies use retrospective self-report and typically find no difference between sex offenders and relevant comparison groups (e.g., Condron & Nutter, 1988; Goldstein et al.,

1971; Langevin et al., 1988; Marshall, 1988). Cook et al. (1971) found that sex offenders reported less frequent exposure to pornography and exposure to less sexually explicit content than a comparison group of non-sex offenders. Interestingly, Carter and colleagues found that, as adults, their sample of 26 child molesters used more pornography than their sample of 38 rapists, and were more likely to incorporate pornography in their sexual offending, for example, viewing photographs before having contact with the victims (Carter et al., 1987). Finally, 160 adolescent sex offenders surveyed by J. V. Becker and Stein (1991) reported that sexually explicit materials played no role in their crimes.

A strength of the individual level approach is its ecological validity, because actual pornography use is assessed and related to the dependent measures of interest. Problems include the possibility of self-report biases (e.g., denying use of pornography so as to appear less sexually deviant) and the generalizability from identified sex offenders (usually incarcerated or involved in the criminal justice system in some way) to the population of sexually aggressive men. Finally, as with other correlation studies, these types of studies do not directly address the question of causality. Pornography use may cause sexual offending, or men who are already predisposed to sexual offending may seek out pornography. One plausible explanation is that men who are sexually deviant, such as pedophiles, may preferentially seek out pornography that depicts content that is highly arousing for them (e.g., materials depicting nude children or children engaged in sexual activities). The analogous argument is that heterosexual men interested in viewing pornography seek out materials that are highly arousing to them, and are therefore unlikely to seek out depictions of homosexual male activity.

Experimental Studies

Laboratory studies are the main mode of empirical investigation into the potential causal role of pornography. Experimental research has focused mostly on either attitudes, beliefs, and cognitions of the participants, or on laboratory analogs of physical aggression against female targets. Studies that examine the effects of pornography exposure on attitudes, beliefs, and cognitions typically use paper-and-pencil measures (e.g., Check, 1985; Linz et al., 1988; Malamuth et al., 1980; Padgett et al., 1989). In contrast, studies that examine the effects of pornography exposure on laboratory analogs of aggression typically use a version of the Buss shock paradigm (e.g., Donnerstein & Berkowitz, 1981; Goldstein, 1973; Langevin et al., 1988; Malamuth & Ceniti, 1986; Marshall, 1988).

A conventional laboratory paradigm entails exposing male university students to violent, coercive, or degrading pornography. A common manipulation in these types of experiments is to have the female confederate anger or treat the male participant unfairly before he is exposed to pornography and given the opportunity to electrically shock the female when she ostensibly makes mistakes on a learning task. Strengths of the experimental approach include high internal validity (because of control over extraneous factors) and the ability to directly test the possibility of a causal relationship. Weaknesses include limits to external validity because of the contrived situations and settings and the possibility of experimental demand. . . .

Effects on Attitudes, Beliefs, and Cognitions

In their meta-analysis of 24 studies with a total of 4,268 participants, M. Allen et al. (1995) concluded that nonexperimental studies (i.e., studies in which participants are questioned about their previous exposure to sexually explicit material and their endorsement of rape myths) showed almost no relationship, while experimental studies (i.e., participants exposed to sexually explicit materials and then asked about their endorsement of rape myths) showed a small positive effect. Specifically, the meta-analysis showed that exposure to pornography, with or without depictions of violence, increased acceptance of rape myths.

However, these findings need to be qualified by the critical issue of whether attitudes, beliefs, or cognitions are good proxy measures of sexual aggression. Although some models suggest antisocial and anti-women attitudes, beliefs, and cognitions play an important role in sexual aggression, they also recognize that other factors are required (Malamuth et al., 1993). For example, Demaré et al. (1993) surveyed 383 males using measures of anti-women attitudes, pornography use, likelihood of sexual aggression, and actual sexual aggression. The measure of sexual aggression included items regarding verbal coercion (lying, persistent arguments) and a potentially ambiguous item about "getting carried away" during sexual activity. In this sample, 86% of the participants had previously used nonviolent pornography, 36% had viewed pornography that depicted forced sexual acts on women, and 25% had viewed pornography depicting rape. Moreover, 16% of the men had been coercive and 12% had previously used force to obtain sex (including the ambiguous item). Demaré et al. found that self-reported likelihood of raping was not related to actual behavior. An obvious potential problem with using self-reported likelihood of using force of committing rape is report bias. Other studies find that negative attitudes toward women do not distinguish rapists from non-sex offenders (Marolla & Scully, 1986; Scott & Tetreault, 1987). . . .

Effects on Sexual Arousal to Rape

Marshall et al. (1991) found that pre-exposure to videotaped depictions of rape increased sexual arousal to rape in a subsequent experimental session, while pre-exposure to videotaped depictions of consenting sex did not. Malamuth and colleagues have found that prior exposure to violent pornography increased subsequent sexual arousal; in a subset of nonoffender controls, prior exposure to depictions of rape increased sexual arousal to rape, while prior exposure to consenting sex did not (Malamuth & Check, 1980; Malamuth et al., 1980). . . . A particularly noteworthy finding is that showing stimuli that depict the female victim as aroused during the forced sexual interaction appears to potentiate the effect of pornography on sexual arousal to rape. Malamuth and Check (1985) found that depicting the victim as aroused by the forced sexual interaction increased men's beliefs in rape myths, particularly those men who were more inclined to be aggressive toward women, while an earlier study of theirs found an increase in both acceptance of interpersonal violence and rape myths (Malamuth & Check, 1981).

Methodological Issues

The Laboratory Analog for Aggression

It is not clear that the Buss shock paradigm provides a good laboratory analog for sexual aggression (see Tedeschi & Quigley, 1996). For example, to support the assumption that delivering an electric shock is a specific analog for sexual aggression, it would be necessary to demonstrate that the effects of pornography increases aggression against female, but not male, targets in heterosexual subjects. However, M. Allen et al. (1995a) found no difference between aggression against female targets versus aggression against male targets, and no difference in effect size for male compared to female participants. This finding suggests that the effect of pornography on aggression is not gender-specific. . . . It also suggests that there is no direct causal link between pornography use and sexual aggression.

A common criticism of the Buss shock paradigm is that aggressive behavior can occur in the absence of negative consequences or a nonaggressive alternative. The findings from these experiments do not necessarily indicate how men may respond to being angered in a "real world" setting where there are potentially serious consequences for their actions, and nonaggressive responses are available (e.g., leaving the potentially aggressive situation). Fisher and Grenier (1994) examined how male participants would choose to handle a situation in which they were angered by a female confederate, exposed to violent pornography, and then given the choice of nonaggressive and aggressive options. The participants were given the following options: (a) speak with the confederate through an intercom, (b) shock her, or (c) proceed directly to the debriefing phase of the experiment (akin to removing themselves from the potentially aggressive situation). Of the 14 participants in the study, Fisher and Grenier found that nine of the participants chose to proceed to the debriefing phase of the experiment, three chose to speak with the confederate via the intercom, and only two chose to be aggressive and sent an electric shock to the confederate. The authors noted that these last two participants had expressed considerable interest and eagerness to use the Buss apparatus when they were shown it, well before viewing the sexually violent stimulus; one of these two subjects tried to use the Buss apparatus prior to the commencement of the experiment. Fisher and Grenier concluded that, when given a nonaggressive option, provocation and exposure to violent pornography did not result in physical aggression by most male subjects against the female confederate. Although the sample size was small, this finding is important to consider in interpreting findings from the shock paradigm.

Finally, participants are often angered or treated unfairly by a female confederate before being exposed to pornography and participating in the shock paradigm (e.g., Donnerstein, 1984; Donnerstein & Berkowitz, 1981). The effect of the experimental manipulation may represent an interaction between provocation (situational factor) and individual differences (person factor). It is possible that only participants who are high in hostility, irritability, or aggressiveness will exhibit aggressive behavior when provoked. Given this possibility, it is not clear how often pornography use is associated with provocation in natural settings. The influence of moderators, such as hostility and aggressive disposition have been explored in the literature on the effects of alcohol on aggression (Bushman & Cooper, 1990; Seto & Barbaree, 1995).

Sample Composition

In a study examining individual differences in sexual arousal to rape depictions, Malamuth and Check (1983) found that university students who chose to volunteer for studies involving sexually explicit stimuli differed significantly from their peers who chose not to volunteer. Volunteers were more oriented toward unconventional sexual activities (e.g., more likely than their nonvolunteer counterparts to engage in anal intercourse or group sex) and less restricted, a priori, in their willingness to use force.

Fisher and Grenier (1994) drew attention to selective attrition in pornography research. They described a study by Check and Guloien (1989) in which participants were repeatedly exposed to violent pornography and compared to a no-exposure group in terms of changes in self-reported likelihood of raping. Check and Guloien found that repeated exposure to violent pornography increased the subject's self-reported likelihood of raping a female when compared to a no-exposure condition. However, Fisher and Grenier (1994) noted that, while the control condition did not lose any subjects, the repeated exposure to violent pornography condition suffered from a 14% attrition rate. Subjects who did not endorse violence against women may have prematurely removed themselves from the experimental condition, providing an alternative explanation for the difference that was found.

Experimental Design

Linz et al. (1987) observed that laboratory studies are limited in that they may be susceptible to an "experimenter demand effect," in which the subjects may try to guess the experimental hypothesis and attempt to confirm it. This indicates a need for manipulation checks and open-ended questions at the end of the study session to see if participants have guessed the researchers' hypotheses.

Length of exposure to the stimulus material in pornography research is also an important methodological issue. Pornography research can be divided into studies that have provided "short-term" exposure to the stimulus material versus studies that have provided "long-term" exposure. In a review of the literature on pornography's effects on attitudes toward rape, Linz (1989) suggested that short-term exposure consisted of less than an hour, while long-term exposure was an hour or more. But pornography use in the real world may continue for weeks, months, even years. The fact that some studies find effects of short-term exposure to pornography in the laboratory suggests that the effects of prolonged exposure in the real world should be very large if additional exposure has an incremental effect.... If so, it is surprising that the experimental findings are not more consistent. It is also interesting to note that another meta-analysis by Allen and his colleagues finds that a short debriefing after participation in pornography research is sufficient to defuse any negative effects of short-term exposure to pornography (M. Allen et al., 1996)....

A lot of the existing pornography research assumes that pornography can have a large effect on attitudes or behavior toward women. This research, therefore, does not control for predisposing factors or the role of other determinants. Candidates include personality factors, such as hypermasculinity (Malamuth et al., 1993), authoritarianism (Walker et al., 1993), and erotophilia (M.A. Becker & Byrne, 1985); attitudes about sex roles (Check & Malamuth, 1983); and the acceptability of interpersonal violence (Malamuth et al., 1986). For example, Lopez and George (1995) found that erotophilic male subjects liked deviant-explicit stimuli better and viewed these stimuli longer than erotophobic subjects. However, males viewed the deviant-explicit stimuli for a shorter period of time if a female confederate was present; this confederate effect was attenuated if the female was portrayed as "curious" about pornography rather than "uncomfortable" with it. This finding suggests that there is a role for normative cues, that is, whether the material is condoned or censured (Sinclair et al., 1995). One way in which experimenter demand could have an effect is the implicit suggestion that the pornographic material chosen by the research is "acceptable" for consumption.

Finally, almost all the reviewed studies have examined the effects of pornography, with or without violent content, on proxy measures of rape (i.e., offense-supportive attitudes on beliefs, aggression). This article, reflecting the research literature, has also focused on the potential effects of pornography on proxy measures of rape. The role of pornography in other kinds of sexually inappropriate behavior, such as child molestation, exhibitionism, and voyeurism, is much less studied. Research is needed to examine whether there are crossover effects in terms of pornography content; for example, does watching violent or degrading pornography involving adults increase an individual's likelihood of offending against children? If so, how can this kind of effect be explained?

Discussion

Overall, there is little support for a direct causal link between pornography use and sexual aggression. The recent meta-analytic reviews by M. Allen and colleagues concluded that exposure to pornography has a reliable effect on proxy measures of sexual aggression, such as rape myth acceptance and physical aggression (Allen et al., 1995a,b). However, many of these studies did not consider the possibility of interactions between individual characteristics and pornography exposure. We argue that individuals who are already predisposed to sexually offend are the most likely to show an effect of pornography exposure and are the most likely to show the strongest effects. Men who are not predisposed are unlikely to show an effect; if there actually is an effect, it is likely to be transient because these men would not normally expose themselves to violent pornography. This question can be addressed only by looking at historical consumption of pornography in participants volunteering for this kind of research, and comparing naive participants with participants reporting a great deal of previous exposure.

Consistent with this view, Mould (1988) has argued that "Donnerstein and Berkowitz's research has relevance only in circumstances in which an already angry individual views a sexually violent depiction and subsequently has access to, and circumstances that permit, aggression against the anger-instigating individual [italics in original]." (p. 339). Similarly, Mosher (1988) has suggested that subjective response to pornography depends on how well the depicted content matches the individual's existing, preferred sexual scripts. Individuals who do not like pornography in general, or who do not like particular kinds of content, are unlikely to seek it out in the real world.

Notes

1. U.S. Attorney General's Committee on Pornography (U.S. Department of Justice, 1986); Surgeon General's Workshop on Pornography and Public Health (Mulvey & Haugaard, 1986); Canada's Special Committee on Pornography and Prostitution (1988); the Australian Joint Select Committee on Video Material (1988); and New Zealand's Ministerial Committee of Inquiry into Pornography (1989).

2. Some sexual assaults are committed against adult males, but they represent a small proportion of sexual assault victims and less is known about them. Also, we focus on male perpetrators because much more empirical research is available.

3. The terms *rape, sexual aggression, sexual assault,* and *sexual coercion* will be used interchangeably here. Rape and sexual assault represent extreme forms of sexual coercion. Sexual coercion can range from psychological pressure or the administration of alcohol or drugs to violent physical assault.

References

Adult Video News. (1998). The 1998 annual entertainment guide. Van Nuys, CA: Author.

Allen, M., D'Alessio, D., & Brezgel, K. (1995a). A meta-analysis summarizing the effects of pornography. II: Aggression after exposure. *Human Communications Research, 22,* 258–283.

Allen, M., Emmers, T., Gebhardt, L., & Giery, M. A. (1995b). Exposure to pornography and acceptance of rape myths. *Journal of Communication, 45,* 5–26.

Allen, M., D'Alessio, D., Emmers, T. M., & Gebhardt, L. (1996). The role of educational briefings in mitigating effects of experimental exposure to violent sexually explicit material: A meta-analysis. *Journal of Sex Research, 33,* 135–141.

Allen, R. E. (Ed.). (1990). *Concise Oxford Dictionary of Current English* (8th edn). Oxford: Clarendon Press.

Australian Joint Selection Committee on Video Material. (1988). *Report of the Joint Select Committee on Video Material.* Canberra: Australian Government Publishing Service.

Bastian, L. (1995). National crime victimization survey: Criminal victimization 1993. *Bureau of Justice Statistics Bulletin.* Rockville, MD: Bureau of Justice Statistics Clearinghouse.

Becker, J. V., & Stein, R. M. (1991). Is sexual erotica associated with sexual deviance in adolescent males? *International Journal of Law and Psychiatry, 14,* 85–95.

Becker, M. A., & Byrne, D. (1985). Self-regulated exposure to erotica, recall errors, and subjective reactions as a function of erotophobia and type A coronary-prone behavior. *Journal of Personality and Social Psychology, 48,* 760–767.

Beitchman, J. H., Zucker, K. J., Hood, J. E., DaCosta, G. A., Akman, D., & Cassavia, E. (1992). A review of the long-term effects of child sexual abuse. *Child Abuse and Neglect, 16,* 101–118.

Bushman, B. J., & Cooper, H. M. (1990). Effects of alcohol on human aggression: An integrative research review. *Psychological Bulletin, 107,* 341–354.

Canada's Special Committee on Pornography and Prostitution. (1988). *Pornography in Canada: Report of the Special Committee: Response to the Victimization of Women and Children, 9,* 16–20.

Carter, D. L., Prentky, R. A., Knight, R. A., Vanderveer, P. L., & Boucher, R. J. (1987). Use of pornography in the criminal and developmental histories of sexual offenders. *Journal of Interpersonal Violence, 2,* 196–211.

Check, J. V. P. (1985). The effects of violent and nonviolent pornography. Report to the Department of Justice. Department of Justice, Department of Supply and Services Contract 05SV. (1920) 0-3-0899.

Check, J. V. P., & Guloien, T. H. (1989). Reported proclivity for coercive sex following repeated exposure to sexually violent pornography, nonviolent dehumanizing pornography, and erotica. In D. Zillmann & J. Bryant (Eds.), *Pornography: Research advances and policy considerations* (pp. 159–184). Hillsdale, NJ: Lawrence Erlbaum Associates.

Check, J. V. P., & Malamuth, N. M. (1983). Sex role stereotyping and reactions to depictions of stranger versus acquaintance rape. *Journal of Personality and Social Psychology, 45,* 344–356.

Condron, M. K., & Nutter, D. E. (1988). A preliminary examination of the pornography experience of sex offenders, paraphiliacs, sexual dysfunction patients, and controls based on Meese Commission recommendations. *Journal of Sex and Marital Therapy, 14,* 285–298.

Cook, R. E., Fosen, R. H., & Pacht, A. (1971). Pornography and the sex offender: Patterns of previous exposure and arousal effects of pornographic stimuli. *Journal of Applied Psychology, 55,* 503–511.

Court, J. H. (1976). Pornography and sex-crimes: A re-evaluation in the light of recent trends around the world. *International Journal of Criminology and Penology, 5,* 129–157.

Demaré, D., Lips, H. M., & Briere, J. (1993). Sexually violent pornography, anti-women attitudes, and sexual aggression: A structural equation model. *Journal of Research in Personality, 27,* 285–300.

Donnerstein, E. (1984). Pornography: Its effect on violence against women. In N. M. Malamuth & E. Donnerstein (Eds.), *Pornography and Sexual Aggression* (pp. 53–84). Orlando, FL: Academic Press.

Donnerstein, E., & Berkowitz, L. (1981). Victim reactions in aggressive erotic films as a factor in violence against women. *Journal of Personality and Social Psychology, 41,* 710–724.

Finkelhor, D., Hotaling, G., Lewis, I. A., & Smith, C. (1990). Sexual abuse in a national sample of adult men and women: Prevalence, characteristics, and risk factors. *Child Abuse and Neglect, 14,* 19–28.

Fisher, W. A., & Barak, A. (1989). Sex education as a corrective: Immunizing against possible effects of pornography. In D. Zillmann & J. Bryant (Eds.), *Pornography: Recent Research, Interpretations, and Policy Considerations* (pp. 289–320). Hillsdale, NJ: Erlbaum.

Fisher, W. A., & Barak, A. (1991). Pornography, erotica, and behavior: More questions than answers. *International Journal of Law and Psychiatry, 14,* 65–83.

Fisher, W. A., & Grenier, G. (1994). Violent pornography, antiwoman thoughts, and antiwoman acts: In search of reliable effects. *Journal of Sex Research, 31,* 23–38.

Goldstein, M. J. (1973). Exposure to erotic stimuli and sexual deviance. *Journal of Social Issues, 29,* 197–219.

Goldstein, M. J., Kant, H., Judd, L., & Green, R. (1971). Experience with pornography: Rapists, pedophiles, homosexuals, transsexuals, and controls. *Archives of Sexual Behavior, 1,* 1–15.

Hanson, R. K. (1990). The psychological impact of sexual assault on women and children: A review. *Annals of Sex Research, 3,* 187–232.

Jaffee, D., & Straus, M. A. (1987). Sexual climate and reported rape: A state-level analysis. *Archives of Sexual Behavior, 16,* 107–123.

Koss, M. P. (1993). Detecting the scope of rape: A review of prevalence research methods. *Journal of Interpersonal Violence, 8,* 198–222.

Kutchinsky, B. (1991). Pornography and rape: Theory and practice? *International Journal of Law and Psychiatry, 14,* 47–64.

Langevin, R., Lang, R. A., Wright, P., Handy, L., Frenzel, R. R., & Black, E. L. (1988). Pornography and sexual offences. *Annals of Sex Research, 1,* 335–362.

Linz, D., Donnerstein, E., & Penrod, S. (1987). The findings and recommendations of the Attorney General's Commission on Pornography: Do the psychological "facts" fit the political fury? *American Psychologist, 42,* 946–953.

Linz, D., Donnerstein, E., & Penrod, S. (1988). The effects of long-term exposure to violent and sexually degrading depictions of women. *Journal of Personality and Social Psychology, 55,* 758–768.

Lopez, P. A., & George, W. H. (1995). Attitudes and gender-specific attitudes and gender-specific norms. *Journal of Sex Research, 32,* 275–288.

Malamuth, N. M. (1984). Aggression against women: Cultural and individual causes. In N. M. Malamuth & E. Donnerstein (Eds.), *Pornography and Sexual Aggression* (pp. 19–52). Orlando, FL: Academic Press.

Malamuth, N. M., & Ceniti, J. (1986). Repeated exposure to violent and nonviolent pornography: Likelihood of raping ratings and laboratory aggression against women. *Aggressive Behavior, 12,* 129–137.

Malamuth, N. M., & Check, J. V. P. (1980). Penile tumescence and perceptual responses to rape as a function of victim's perceived reactions. *Journal of Applied Social Psychology, 10,* 528–547.

Malamuth, N. M., & Check, J. V. P. (1981). The effects of mass media exposure on acceptance of violence against women: A field experiment. *Journal of Research in Personality, 15,* 436–446.

Malamuth, N. M., & Check, J. V. P. (1983). Sexual arousal to rape depictions: Individual differences. *Journal of Abnormal Psychology, 92,* 55–67.

Malamuth, N. M., & Check, J. V. P. (1985). The effects of aggressive pornography on beliefs in rape myths: Individual differences. *Journal of Research in Personality, 19,* 299–320.

Malamuth, N. M., Check, J. V. P., & Briere, J. (1986). Sexual arousal in response to aggression: Ideological, aggressive, and sexual correlates. *Journal of Personality and Social Psychology, 50,* 330–340.

Malamuth, N. M., Haber, S., & Feshbach, S. (1980). Testing hypotheses regarding rape: Exposure to sexual violence, sex differences, and the "normality" of rapists. *Journal of Research in Personality, 14,* 121–137.

Malamuth, N. M., Heavey, C. L., & Linz, D. (1993). Predicting men's antisocial behavior against women: The interaction model of sexual aggression. In G. C. N. Hall, R. Hirschman, J. R. Graham, & M. S. Zaragoza (Eds.), *Sexual aggression: Issues in etiology, assessment, and treatment* (pp. 63–97). Washington, DC: Taylor and Francis.

Marolla, J., & Scully, D. (1986). Attitudes toward women, violence, and rape: A comparison of convicted rapists and other felons. *Deviant Behavior, 7,* 337–355.

Marshall, W. L. (1988). The use of sexually explicit stimuli by rapists, child molesters, and nonoffenders. *Journal of Sex Research, 25,* 267–288.

Marshall, W. L., & Barrett, S. (1990). *Criminal neglect: Why sex offenders go free.* Toronto: Doubleday.

Marshall, W. L., Seidman, B. T., & Barbaree, H. E. (1991). The effects of prior exposure to erotic and nonerotic stimuli on the rape index. *Annals of Sex Research, 4,* 209–220.

Martin's Annual Criminal Code. (1996). Aurora, ON: Canada Law Book.

Mosher, D. L. (1988). Pornography defined: Sexual involvement theory, narrative context, and goodness-of-fit. *Journal of Psychology and Human Sexuality, 1,* 67–85.

Mould, D. E., (1988). A critical analysis of recent research on violent erotica. *Journal of Sex Research, 24,* 326–340.

Mulvey, E. P., & Haugaard, J. L. (1986). *Report of the Surgeon General's Workshop on Pornography and Public Health.* Washington, DC: U.S. Department of Health and Human Services, Office of the Surgeon General.

New Zealand's Ministerial Committee of Inquiry into Pornography. (1989). Report of the Ministerial Committee of Inquiry into Pornography. Wellington, New Zealand: Crown Copyright.

Padgett, V. R., Brislin-Slutz, J. A., & Neal, J. A. (1989). Pornography, erotica, and attitudes toward women: The effects of repeated exposure. *Journal of Sex Research, 26,* 479–491.

Rind, B., Tromovitch, P., & Bauserman, R. (1998). A meta-analytic examination of assumed properties of child sexual abuse using college samples. *Psychological Bulletin, 124,* 22–53.

Scott, R. L., & Tetreault, L. A. (1987). Attitudes of rapists and other violent offenders toward women. *Journal of Social Psychology, 127,* 375–380.

Seto, M. C., & Barbaree, H. E. (1995). The role of alcohol in sexual aggression. *Clinical Psychology Review, 15,* 545–566.

Sinclair, R. C., Lee, T., & Johnson, T. E. (1995). The effect of social-comparison feedback on aggressive responses to erotic and aggressive films. *Journal of Applied Social Psychology, 25,* 818–837.

Tedeschi, J. T., & Quigley, B. M. (1996). Limitations of laboratory paradigms for studying aggression. *Aggression and Violent Behavior, 1,* 163–177.

U.S. Commission on Obscenity and Pornography. (1970). *Report of the Commission on Obscenity and Pornography.* Washington, DC: Government Printing Office.

U.S. Department of Justice. (1986). *Attorney General's Commission on Pornography: Final report.* Washington, DC: Author.

Walker, W. D., Rowe, R. C., & Quinsey, V. L. (1993). Authoritarianism and sexual aggression. *Journal of Personality and Social Psychology, 65,* 1036–1045.

Zillmann, D., & Bryant, J. (1986). Shifting preferences in pornography consumption. *Communication Research, 13,* 560–578.

CHALLENGE QUESTIONS

Is Pornography Harmful?

1. Why do both authors shy away from the notion of a "direct cause"? What is the difference between pornography predisposing individuals to rape and pornography being a direct and sufficient cause of an individual's rape? How might this distinction affect this issue?
2. If pornography does cause men to be violent toward women, what might this imply about other types of media and other types of behavior?
3. Do the methodological problems that Seto and his colleagues note invalidate the research that Russell reviews? How serious are these research limitations in drawing conclusions about pornography's effects?
4. If an aggressive nature, rather than pornography, is to blame for sexual violence, will avoiding pornography help to reduce rape? If so, why? If pornography avoidance will *not* help, what will?

Contributors to This Volume

EDITOR

BRENT SLIFE is a clinical psychologist and a professor of psychology at Brigham Young University in Provo, Utah. A fellow of the American Psychological Association, he has published over 80 articles and books, including *What's Behind the Research? Discovering Hidden Assumptions in the Behavioral Sciences,* coauthored with Richard N. Williams (Sage Publications, 1995), which attempts to make accessible to students the many conceptual issues of psychology. Recently voted Teacher of the Year at Brigham Young, he is also editor of the *Journal of Theoretical and Philosophical Psychology* and serves in editorial capacities on the *Journal of Mind and Behavior* and *Theory and Psychology.* He received his Ph.D. from Purdue University, where he and Joseph Rubinstein, coeditor of the first seven editions of *Taking Sides: Clashing Views on Controversial Psychological Issues,* began the dialogue approach to psychology that is the basis of this volume.

STAFF

Theodore Knight   List Manager
David Brackley   Senior Developmental Editor
Juliana Gribbins   Developmental Editor
Rose Gleich   Administrative Assistant
Brenda S. Filley   Director of Production/Design
Juliana Arbo   Typesetting Supervisor
Diane Barker   Proofreader
Richard Tietjen   Publishing Systems Manager
Larry Killian   Copier Coordinator

AUTHORS

PHILIP ASPDEN is executive director of the Center for Research on the Information Society (CRIS) in Pennington, New Jersey. He has consulted in telecommunications and technology-based economic development for a wide range of high-tech firms, public bodies, and foundations in both the United States and Europe. He has also been a scientific civil servant in the British Civil Service and a research scholar at the International Institute for Applied Systems Analysis.

ELIZABETH BALDWIN is a research ethics officer for the American Psychological Association's Science Directorate. Her work involves a broad range of research ethics issues, including those relating to the use of animals in research. She has also worked at the Congressional Research Service in the Division of Science Policy. She holds a B.A. in biology, an M.S. in entomology, and an M.A. in science, technology, and public policy.

HOWARD E. BARBAREE is clinical director of the Law and Mental Health Program at the Centre for Addiction and Mental Health and a professor in the Department of Psychiatry at the University of Toronto. He has devoted most of his professional career to research, teaching, and clinical practice related to sexual aggression and sexual deviance. He is also founding director of the Warkworth Sexual Behaviour Clinic, a Canadian Federal Penitentiary treatment program for sex offenders. Dr. Barbaree has published numerous journal articles and book chapters on the topic, and he is coeditor, with William L. Marshall and Stephen M. Hudson, of *The Juvenile Sex Offender* (Guilford, 1993).

DIANA BAUMRIND is a research psychologist and the principal investigator for the Family Socialization and Developmental Competence Project of the University of California's Institute for Human Development in Berkeley, California. She has contributed numerous articles to professional journals and books, and she is on the editorial board of *Developmental Psychology.* She is also the author of *Child Maltreatment and Optimal Caregiving in Social Contexts* (Garland, 1995).

MAY BENATAR is a clinical social worker in private practice in Montclair, New Jersey. She currently teaches and lectures to professional groups on sexual abuse and the treatment of dissociative disorders.

MARISSA S. BEYERS is a freelance writer with an M.A. in theoretical psychology.

JOSEPH BIEDERMAN is chief of the Joint Program in Pediatric Psychopharmacology at the Massachusetts General and McLean Hospitals in Boston, Massachusetts, and a professor of psychiatry at Harvard Medical School. He is board certified in general and child psychiatry. His clinical program treats more than 2,000 children, adolescents, and adults, and evaluates more than 300 new patients every year. Dr. Biederman's research focus is on attention deficit hyperactivity disorder, juvenile mood and anxiety disorders, and studies of children at risk.

ALAN D. BOWD is a professor of educational psychology and director of the School of Education at Lakehead University in Thunder Bay, Ontario, Canada. He received an M.A. in psychology from the University of Sydney and a Ph.D. in educational psychology from the University of Calgary. His main interest is in the ethical treatment of animals, and his published research has focused on the development of beliefs and attitudes about animals during childhood.

PETER R. BREGGIN is a psychiatrist in private practice in Bethesda, Maryland. He is also national director of the Center for the Study of Psychiatry and Psychology and a faculty associate in the Johns Hopkins University Department of Counseling. Dr. Breggin is the author of many books, including *The Antidepressant Fact Book: What Your Doctor Won't Tell You About Prozac, Zoloft, Paxil, Celexa, and Luvox* (Perseus, 2001) and *Reclaiming Our Children: A Healing Plan for a Nation in Crisis* (Perseus Books Group, 1999).

BRANDON S. CENTERWALL is an assistant professor of epidemiology in the School of Public Health and Community Medicine at the University of Washington in Seattle, Washington. He is coauthor, with Terry Rakolta and William S. Abbott, of *Monster in a Box: Television Violence, the First Amendment, and the Case for Government Regulation* (Aletheia Press, 1996).

PAUL CHANCE is a psychologist, writer, and teacher. He teaches at the James H. Groves Adult High School in Georgetown, Delaware, and he is the author of *Thinking in the Classroom* (Teachers College Press, 1986).

ANDREW CHRISTENSEN is a professor of psychology at the University of California, Los Angeles. He is coauthor, with Neil S. Jacobson, of *Integrative Couple Therapy: Promoting Acceptance and Change* (W. W. Norton, 1996).

ALBERT ELLIS, founder of rational-emotive therapy, is president of the Institute for Rational-Emotive Therapy, located in New York City. He received his Ph.D. in clinical psychology from Columbia University, and he has authored or coauthored more than 600 articles and over 50 books on psychotherapy, marital and family therapy, and sex therapy, including *Why Some Therapies Don't Work: The Dangers of Transpersonal Psychology,* coauthored with Raymond Yaeger (Prometheus Books, 1989).

STEPHEN V. FARAONE, a clinical psychologist, is an associate professor in the Department of Psychiatry at Harvard Medical School at the Massachusetts Mental Health Center and director of Pediatric Psychopharmacology Research at Massachusetts General Hospital. He is coeditor of the journal *Neuropsychiatric Genetics* and statistical section editor of the *Journal of Child and Adolescent Psychopharmacology.* He is also a member of the Panel of Biostatistical and Methodology Consultants for the *Journal of the American Academy of Child and Adolescent Psychiatry.* The author or coauthor of over 300 journal articles, editorials, chapters, and books, he was the eighth highest producer of high-impact papers in psychiatry from 1990 to 1999, as determined by the Institute for Scientific Information.

MAX FINK is a professor of psychiatry and neurology at the State University of New York at Stony Brook. He has been studying electroconvulsive therapy (ECT) since 1954, he has published over 200 articles on ECT, and he is the founding editor of the scientific journal *Convulsive Therapy*. He is director of the ECT Service at University Hospital at Stony Brook and executive director of the International Association for Psychiatric Research. His publications include *Electroshock: Restoring the Mind* (Oxford University Press, 1999).

HELEN FISHER is a member of the Center for Human Evolutionary Studies and a research associate in the Department of Anthropology at Rutgers University. She received her Ph.D. from the University of Colorado in 1975, and she is a fellow of the American Anthropological Association and of the American Association of Physical Anthropologists. Her research interests include human evolution, primatology, human sexual behavior, reproductive strategies, and the neurological and biological basis of behavior. She is the author of *The First Sex: The Natural Talents of Women and How They Are Changing the World* (Random House, 1999).

LEONARD R. FRANK, a former editor of *Madness Network News* and cofounder of the Network Against Psychiatric Assault (NAPA), is an outspoken critic of electroshock and all forms of psychiatric "treatment" applied forcibly or without genuine informed consent. He is the editor and publisher of *The History of Shock Treatment* (1978) and of *Influencing Minds: A Reader in Quotations* (1994).

HOWARD GARDNER is the John H. and Elisabeth A. Hobbs Professor in Cognition and Education at the Harvard Graduate School of Education. He also holds positions as adjunct professor of psychology at Harvard, adjunct professor of neurology at the Boston University School of Medicine, and codirector of Harvard Project Zero. He has received numerous honors, including a MacArthur Prize Fellowship in 1981. He is the author of several hundred articles and 18 books, including *Extraordinary Minds* (Basic Books, 1997) and *The Disciplined Mind: What All Students Should Understand* (Simon & Schuster, 1999).

LINDA S. GOTTFREDSON is a professor of educational studies at the University of Delaware, where she has been teaching since 1986, and codirector of the Delaware–Johns Hopkins Project for the Study of Intelligence and Society. She earned her Ph.D. in sociology from the Johns Hopkins University in 1977 and won the Mensa Research Foundation Award for Excellence in Research, 1999–2000. Her research interests include intelligence and social inequality, employment testing and job aptitude demands, and affirmative action and multicultural diversity.

NEIL S. JACOBSON is a professor of psychology at the University of Washington in Seattle, Washington. His research interests include behavior, marital therapy, depression, and family therapy. He is coauthor, with John M. Gottman, of *When Men Batter Women: New Insights Into Ending Abusive Relationships* (Simon & Schuster, 1998).

JAY JOSEPH is associated with La Familia Counseling Service in Hayward, California.

JAMES E. KATZ is a professor of communication at Rutgers University and a senior scientist at Bellcore (Bell Communications Research) in New Jersey. He has examined a variety of issues concerning the Internet and its societal consequences, and he is an expert in privacy policy. He has also been involved in the World Wide Web Consortium and U.S. National Science Foundation planning exercises for research on knowledge networks.

ALFIE KOHN writes and lectures widely on education and human behavior. His books include *Punished by Rewards* (Houghton Mifflin, 1993) and *Beyond Discipline: From Compliance to Community* (Association for Supervision and Curriculum Development, 1996).

PETER D. KRAMER is a psychiatrist and the author of *Moments of Engagement: Intimate Psychotherapy in a Technological Age* (W. W. Norton, 1989).

ROBERT KRAUT is a professor of social psychology and human computer interaction at Carnegie Mellon University, with joint appointments in the Department of Social and Decision Sciences, the Human Computer Interaction Institute, and the Graduate School of Industrial Administration. His current research focuses on the design and social impacts of information technologies in small groups, in the home, and between organizations. He is coauthor of *Research Recommendations to Facilitate Distributed Work* (National Academy Press, 1994).

DAVID B. LARSON is an assistant secretary of planning at the Department of Health and Human Services in Washington, D.C.

ALEXANDRA MARIC is affiliated with the Forensic Division of the Clarke Institute of Psychiatry, which is part of the University of Toronto's Centre for Addiction and Mental Health.

PAUL R. McHUGH is the Henry Phipps Professor of Psychiatry and chair of the Department of Psychiatry and Behavioral Sciences in the Johns Hopkins University School of Medicine. He has also taught at the Oregon Health Sciences Center and in the School of Medicine at Cornell University, where he founded and acted as first director for the Bourne Behavioral Research Laboratory of New York Hospital. He earned his M.D. at Harvard Medical School, and he is coauthor, with Phillip R. Slavney, of *The Perspectives of Psychiatry,* 2d ed. (John Hopkins University Press, 1998).

STANLEY MILGRAM (1933–1984) was an experimental social psychologist and a professor of psychology at the Graduate School and University Center of the City University of New York. He is especially well known for his series of controversial investigations regarding obedience to authority, which were performed at Yale University from 1960 to 1963. His publications include *Obedience to Authority: An Experimental View* (Harper & Row, 1975).

FRANK W. PUTNAM is a child and adolescent psychiatrist with 20 years' experience directing National Institute of Mental Health (NIMH) intramural research programs. He is also director of the Mayerson Center for Safe and Healthy Children. He is the author of *Dissociation in Children and Adolescents: A Developmental Perspective* (Guilford, 1997).

S. DuBOSE RAVENEL is a board-certified pediatrician in private practice in High Point, North Carolina. He served for 11 years on the pediatric faculty of the University of North Carolina School of Medicine prior to entering private practice.

JEFFREY S. REBER is a freelance writer with an M.A. in social psychology.

SUSAN P. ROBBINS is an associate professor in the Graduate School of Social Work at the University of Houston in Texas. She is the author of *River and Jungle* (Random House, 1993).

D. L. ROSENHAN is a professor of law and psychology at Stanford University and a social psychologist whose focal concern has been clinical and personality matters. He has also been a faculty member at Princeton University, the University of Pennsylvania, and Swarthmore College.

DIANA E. H. RUSSELL is a professor emeritus of sociology at Mills College in Oakland, California. A leading authority on sexual violence against women and girls, she has performed research and written articles and books on rape, incest, the misogynist murder of women, and pornography for 25 years. Her publications include *Against Pornography: The Evidence of Harm* (Russell, 1994) and *Making Violence Sexy: Feminist Views on Pornography* (Teachers College Press, 1993).

BARRY A. SCHREIER is coordinator of training for Counseling and Psychological Services at Purdue University in West Lafayette, Indiana. His areas of interest include gay, lesbian, bisexual, and transgendered issues; interpersonal supervision and training; and clinical ethics. He earned his Ph.D. in counseling psychology from the University of Missouri at Kansas City.

MARTIN E. P. SELIGMAN is a professor in the Department of Psychology at the University of Pennsylvania and is well known for his formulation of the learned helplessness model. A member of the APA's Public Education Campaign Advisory Task Force, Seligman has published over 15 books, including *What You Can Change and What You Can't: The Complete Guide to Successful Self-Improvement* (Alfred A. Knopf, 1994) and *Helplessness: On Depression, Development, and Death* (W. H. Freeman, 1992).

MICHAEL C. SETO is a research psychologist in the Law and Mental Health Program at the Centre for Addiction and Mental Health in Toronto, Ontario, Canada. He earned his Ph.D. from Queen's University in 1997.

KENNETH J. SHAPIRO is executive director of Psychologists for the Ethical Treatment of Animals and editor of the academic biannual *Society and Animals*. His background is in clinical psychology, phenomenological psychology, and intellectual history. He has published scholarly work in phenomenological psychology, developing and applying methods for the study of both human and nonhuman animals.

BRIAN SIANO is a writer and researcher based in Philadelphia, Pennsylvania. His column "The Skeptical Eye" appears regularly in *The Humanist*.

ROBERT L. SPITZER is affiliated with the New York State Psychiatric Institute in New York City. He is a former chairman of the American Psychiatric Association and its Task Force on Nomenclature and Statistics.

MURRAY A. STRAUS is a professor of sociology and codirector of the Family Research Laboratory at the University of New Hampshire in Durham, New Hampshire. He has held academic appointments at Cornell University, the University of Minnesota, the University of Wisconsin, and Washington State University, as well as at universities in England, India, and Sri Lanka. He has published over 150 articles and 15 books, including *Physical Violence in American Families,* coauthored with Richard J. Gelles (Transaction, 1995).

WARREN THROCKMORTON is director of College Counseling and an associate professor of psychology at Grove City College in Grove City, Pennsylvania. He holds an M.A. from Central Michigan University and a Ph.D. from Ohio University.

DEN A. TRUMBULL is a board-certified pediatrician in private practice in Montgomery, Alabama. He is a member of the Section on Developmental and Behavioral Pediatrics of the American Academy of Pediatrics.

Index